POWER AND IDEOLOGY IN
AMERICAN SPORT

A Critical Perspective

Second Edition

George H. Sage, EdD
University of Northern Colorado

Human Kinetics

Library of Congress Cataloging-in-Publication Data

Sage, George Harvey.
    Power and ideology in American sport : a critical perspective /
George H. Sage. -- 2nd ed.
        p.   cm.
    Includes bibliographical references and index.
    ISBN 0-88011-660-9 (pbk.)
    1. Sports--Social aspects--United States.   I. Title.
GV706.5.S228   1998
306.4'83'0973--dc21   98-17002
                                                                CIP

ISBN: 0-88011-660-9

Acquisitions Editor: Becky Lane; **Developmental Editor:** Marni Basic; **Assistant
Editor:** Henry Woolsey; **Copyeditor:** Allen Gooch; **Proofreader:** Myla Smith; **Indexer:**
Joan K. Griffitts; **Graphic Designer:** Nancy Rasmus; **Graphic Artist:** Denise Lowry;
Photo Editor: Boyd LaFoon; **Cover Designer:** Stuart Cartwright; **Illustrator:** Chuck
Nivens; **Printer:** United Graphics

Printed in the United States of America   10   9   8   7   6   5   4   3   2   1

Human Kinetics
Web site: http://www. humankinetics.com/

United States: Human Kinetics, P.O. Box 5076, Champaign, IL 61825-5076
1-800-747-4457
e-mail: humank@hkusa.com

Canada: Human Kinetics, Box 24040, Windsor, ON N8Y 4Y9
1-800-465-7301 (in Canada only)
e-mail: humank@hkcanada.com

Europe: Human Kinetics, P.O. Box IW14, Leeds LS16 6TR, United Kingdom
(44) 1132 781708
e-mail: humank@hkeurope.com

Australia: Human Kinetics, 57A Price Avenue, Lower Mitcham, South Australia 5062
(088) 277 1555
e-mail: humank@hkaustralia.com

New Zealand: Human Kinetics, P.O. Box 105-231, Auckland 1
(09) 523 3462
e-mail: humank@hknewz.com

*Dedicated
to my extended family,
Liz, Michael, Larry, Kathy, Tyler,
Garrett, Lucas, Elise —
for their support and love*

Contents

Chapter 5   Structures of Social Inequality: Racial Inequality in Sport   81

Chapter 6   Sport and the State: The Political Economy of American Sport   101

Chapter 7   Commercialization of Sport: From Informal to Corporate Organization   129

Chapter 8 Mass Media and Sport: Managing Images, Impressions, and Ideology 159

Chapter 9 The Professional Team Sports Industry 189

Chapter 10 Power and Ideology in Intercollegiate Sport 225

Preface to the Second Edition

The motivating force behind my writing this second edition is the same force that was behind the first edition; namely, I want to introduce readers to thinking more carefully and more critically about both American society and American sport. Sport is a vital part of America's popular culture. Developments there have an impact on American society, and conditions and trends in American society affect and influence sporting practices.

My hope is that readers will gain a heightened awareness of the problems, issues, and controversies facing American sport—especially highly organized and commercialized sport—and arrive at some conclusions and solutions of what might be done collectively to address them. This will require an open mind and a willingness to consider views that may challenge conventional ideas about both American society and American sport to achieve this end.

In the first two chapters, I provide the theoretical framework for this book. In chapter 1, I emphasize the characteristics of both a sociological perspective and a critical perspective. Chapter 2 identifies two social images of how American society works. The remaining chapters employ the critical social framework to examine sport and social class, gender, and race; the commercialization of sport, media sport, professional sport, intercollegiate sport, and youth and school sport; in the last chapter I examine agency, resistance, and transformation in sport.

This book constitutes a small beginning aimed at cultivating a critical theoretical perspective toward American sport and at encouraging a humanistic stance toward American society and those involved in sport.

Preface to the First Edition

Sport is one of the most popular cultural practices in American society. Indeed, involvement in sport, as either a participant or a spectator, is considered almost a public duty. Furthermore, sport is woven into the patterns of all the major social institutions—politics, economics, education, mass media. James Reston, a columnist for the *New York Times,* has claimed that sport in America plays a role in our lives that is probably more important than even the social scientists believe.

Reston may be right, but social scientists do believe that sport is an important and pervasive social practice that deserves serious study. The 1970s and 1980s have produced a substantial body of scholarly literature on the social aspects of sport, and several journals regularly publish theoretical and empirical research about the subject. Two professional societies serve as outlets for scholars to share their work—the North American Society for the Sociology of Sport (NASSS) and the International Committee for the Sociology of Sport (ICSS).

I intend this book to be an introduction to the sociology of sport, presented in a particular theoretical framework. I have also chosen to pursue a critical theme (thus the subtitle *A Critical Perspective).* I discuss in chapter 1 what this means, along with the role of critique and criticism. I see critical analysis as the first step in improving existing conditions in sport. When social reality is defined by one group and alternative interpretations are suppressed, distortion may be the result. It is the role of the critic to flesh out inconsistencies and inaccuracies promulgated by a one-sided view of social reality, exposing them for what they are, communicating alternative perspectives, and hoping that truth will prevail and the human condition will be improved.

To gain an accurate understanding of sport, I believe it must be situated historically and culturally within the larger social entity. The traditional tendency to separate sport from the rest of society, treating it and its participants as isolated from the rest of the social world and as existing in a value-free and ideologically pristine environment is erroneous—it presumes that there are no links between sport and our other social institutions and cultural practices. Such a view disguises the real connections between sport and society and opens the door to serious social dangers, for sport can be used to conceal material and cultural exploitation and oppression.

I want with this book to provoke you into thinking more critically and carefully about both American society and American sport. You will need an open mind and a willingness to consider views that may challenge your ideas about both to achieve this end. I hope that you will become more aware of the problems, issues, and controversies facing the world of contemporary sport—especially highly organized and commercialized sport—and that you will arrive at some conclusions and potential collective solutions. My vision for what American sport can be entails egalitarian cooperation, solidarity of people with one another, respect for individual and group differences, and guarantees of individual rights. It involves an ongoing process of change in social and cultural consciousness that may generate a revolution in social relations among people in sport. Perhaps together we can effect that change.

Acknowledgments

A book such as this represents the work of not one but a community of scholars. What is valuable here I have learned from others. Many colleagues throughout the world have contributed to this book. I give thanks to all of them for the ideas and insights I have gained in hearing them speak at conventions of the NASSS and from reading their works. It is impossible for me to acknowledge my indebtedness to them individually. I have attempted through the Notes section to indicate the sources of original information and ideas, and I hope I have met the demands of that task.

To my students, I owe a special debt of gratitude for their continuing challenges to my lectures and comments in class discussions. I wish especially to thank my many colleagues in sport sociology throughout the world for their compliments about the first edition of this book and their encouragement to write a second edition. I want to extend special thanks to Becky Lane for prodding me to get started on this edition and to Mary McDonald and Marni Basic whose reviews and critiques of an earlier draft of this work were invaluable in my final revision.

Finally, I express my heartfelt gratitude to my wife, Liz. She has, in a way, been a volunteer research assistant for me, keeping a sharp eye out for newspaper and magazine articles, as well as book titles, that might be useful to me. Beyond that, she has been an incredibly patient and supportive companion. Without her constant encouragement, the lonely and arduous task of writing this book would have been impossible. She made it all worthwhile.

Chapter 1

A Sociological Perspective of Sport

The study of sport can take us to the very heart of critical issues in the study of culture and society.

Elliott J. Gorn, professor of history and American studies, and Michael Oriard, professor of English

Much evidence affirms that Americans are devoted to sport. Today, the average person is inundated by sports. This deluge is due, in part, to the enormous increase in youth, high school, and intercollegiate athletics, enlarged physical recreation programs, and the massive growth of professional sports during the past 30 years; it is also the result of expanded mass media coverage of sports events, especially on television. As its meanings and practices have changed in the transformation from casual, informal play forms to commodity-governed spectacles shaped by marketplace rationality, sport has aroused increasing interest as a social phenomenon.

In the 1970s and 1980s, sport emerged as an active domain of study and research in the social sciences. Sociology, the perspective of this book, is one of those social sciences, and the sociology of sport promises to be a dynamic field of study in the century ahead.

A number of good books describe the current social conditions and demographics of sport involvement, but most make no attempt to pursue relationships between sport, political economy, ideological power, and domination. Because the words *ideology* (*ideological*) and *power* are used frequently throughout this volume, now is an appropriate time to describe what I mean by these two words. There are numerous variations of the definition of *ideology*, but the concept generally implies a system of interdependent ideas that explain and justify particular political, economic, moral, and social conditions and interests, making them seem right or natural. If something is *ideological*, then, it relates to or is concerned with this system of ideas. By *power*, I subscribe to social theorist Michael Parenti's description, which is that power means "the ability to get what one wants, either by having one's interests prevail in conflict with others or by preventing others from raising their demands."[1]

My approach to studying sport from a sociological perspective assumes that an analysis of sport must be based on an understanding of its societal moorings. To do this, sport is seen as more than merely a place of personal achievement and entertainment; it is viewed as a social, cultural, and structural phenomenon. Sociology provides the appropriate intellectual framework for this type of analysis of sport.

The Sociological Perspective

Sociology is dedicated to the study of human society, to observing and analyzing human social activities wherever and whenever they occur. Such study can take both global and personal forms; at one extreme, you can find sociologists investigating international relations among governments and at the other, sociologists studying divorce patterns of couples belonging to different churches. Fertile ground exists for sociological analysis wherever you find social organizations and people interacting with each other. Moreover, there is no precise dividing line between sociology and the other social sciences (economics, political science, anthropology, etc.); indeed, there is a great deal of interdependence among all of them.

Sociology, then, is first and foremost a study of social organization and behavior, based on social theory and empirical research, as opposed to hunch, tradition, and blind faith. A sociological perspective requires taking a particular orientation, which has been expressed in various metaphors, toward human social organization and actions. One suggests a "recalibration" of one's way of thinking about social life, another proposes "using a different lens for viewing," another advises that one must assume a "social consciousness," and finally there is the notion that one must take on what one sociologist called a "sociological imagination." The assumption in all these is that a sociological perspective requires a unique framework, or special mind-set, for trying to understand society. Several of the most important foundations of this perspective are described in the remainder of this section.

The Social Construction of Reality

One of the core insights of sociology is that society is socially constructed. It follows, then, that all meanings about human social life are *socially constructed*. Meanings are interpretations about situations, ideas, objects, or events with reference to how one should respond. Thus, meanings are rooted in the collective responses—in behaviors—that become mobilized around situations, ideas, objects, or events, and this fundamentally shapes the world in which we live.

Social reality, then, is socially constructed; that is, humans actively contribute to the creation of meaning. As Max Weber, one of the founders of sociology, said, "Human beings live in webs of meaning they themselves have spun." So, we cannot approach the study of human society as we do the study of objects or events in the natural world. Natural laws can be defined precisely, and they hold true with no variation throughout the world; they do not change with time or by human negotiation. But such is not the case for human social behavior, which varies from group to group (e.g., poor and wealthy), from culture to culture (e.g., language, customs, attitudes, values), and across time (e.g., colonial and contemporary lifestyles). Societies only exist insofar as they are created and re-created in human actions. This being the case, definitions, explanations, and meanings are open to reinterpretation and change.

To use an example of how meanings are socially constructed, we can take a sport slogan familiar to most: "Winning isn't everything, it's the only thing." Is this a universal truth, a law of nature? Of course not. It is a socially constructed piece of lore around which some very specific meanings about the quest for victory in sport have been formed. But take another example: "It's not whether you win or lose, but how you play the game." This, too, is a socially constructed description of sports competition that implies particular social attitudes and behaviors toward sports activities.

These two slogans convey two very different views about the meaning of winning in sport. At different times and in different places, each has been the leading view of one group or another. Yet which is the "correct" view? Before an answer to this question is attempted, a closer look at the consequences of meanings is needed.

The principal significance of meanings is that they shape how people behave. That is, they are real in their consequences. If someone walked by you holding a pole with a sheet of white cloth attached, you probably would not react, but if the cloth were red, white, and blue

© Unicorn/Aneal Vohra

Baseball has been known as "the national pastime" for over 100 years. This is a cultural practice deeply embedded in American cultural life. Indeed, it is often contended that many American cultural values are manifested in and through baseball.

with the stars and stripes, you would probably stand up. Why the different behavior? Because of the *meaning* of the American flag to many Americans.

The meanings in the two sports slogans I cited suggest a number of social attitudes, perceptions, and behaviors toward winning in sports. In the context of this discussion, the "correctness" of one or the other is moot. What the slogans demonstrate is that meanings (in this case winning in sports) are socially constructed, and certain norms, values, and behaviors will become mobilized around the meaning that an idea, object, or event has come to have.

Another sport example of the social construction of meaning is the word *excellence*. For the ancient Greeks—the people who gave us the original Olympic Games—sporting excellence meant to be an all-round athlete, to be good in a variety of sports. The truly excellent athlete was the pantathlete. From the time organized sports became a part of popular culture in the United States in the latter 19th century until about 40 years ago, the athlete who was considered the epitome of "excellence" was the three-sport athlete, the all-round athlete. It is only in the past quarter of a century or so that specialization has become the basis for excellence. Only quite recently has the specialist, with a single-minded devotion to being good at one sport, been viewed as the athlete truly pursuing excellence. The changed meaning of the word *excellence* has resulted in an increased number of young athletes specializing in one sport. Thus is demonstrated again the social construction of meaning in sport, how it can change over time, and how it can shape attitudes and behaviors.

The Influence of Social Structure

Another core insight of the sociological perspective is the notion that *social structural forces* beyond an individual's conscious control have a profound effect on human behavior. The term *social structure* refers to the patterned relationships that connect different parts of society to one another, including individuals, groups, communities, and even entire societies. For example, the social structure of sport includes not only the relationships among athletes and coaches but also the relationships that connect sports teams, leagues, organizations (such as the National Collegiate Athletic Association and U.S. Olympic Committee), sporting goods firms, sports media, and so forth.

Social structure also refers to the ways in which people are distributed among various social positions, as well as to the distribution of various rewards, such as power, wealth, and prestige. For example, social class status is related to variations in occupation, educational achievement, criminal behavior, and the presence of mental disorders. Sport in the United States is structured so that women and African Americans rarely occupy the prestigious coaching and administration positions and are, therefore, denied the high income and status that accompany those positions.

The term *social structure* is useful in sociology because it focuses attention on various patterns of social relationships and distributions of power, wealth, and prestige that are fundamental to social life. It thus helps us to understand that social structural arrangements shape conduct, independent of the characteristics of individuals. This contrasts sharply with conventional American beliefs about the responsibility for human actions, namely that individual behaviors are merely the product of individual internal motivations.

The tradition of attributing human actions solely to the individual derives from several sources central to American culture. First, the rugged individualism of the colonial and frontier periods in American history has been glorified through folklore and legend. Second, capitalism, the economic foundation of American society, has as its basic constituents private initiative and private enterprise, both obsessively individualistic. Third, the mass popularity of psychological explanations for human behavior, which tend to focus on individual needs and satisfactions, is a compelling influence in American society. The multiple influences of the individualistic tradition are so potent that it is difficult to displace in the American mind. Indeed, because of powerful societal forces nurturing and promoting this tradition, there tends to be little realization of an alternative vision—a sociological perspective—of human social action.

Sociologist C. Wright Mills provided a good description of the differences between the individual, or psychological, perspective and sociological perspectives. According to Mills, problems that at first glance seem to require solutions at the personal level are actually the consequence of broader political, economic, or social forces. Divorce, for instance, is a very personal matter. Yet the fact that divorce rates vary with social class, ethnic and religious affiliation, and other demographic variables suggests that divorce, despite its personal nature, is greatly affected by social structure.[2] Mills supplied us with another example with unemployment: "When in a city of 100,000 only one man is unemployed, that is his personal trouble, and for its relief we properly look to the character of the man, his skills, and his immediate opportunities. But when in a nation of 100 million employees, 12 million are unemployed, that is a public issue, and we may not hope to find its solution within the range of opportunities open to any one individual. The very structure of opportunities has collapsed. Both the correct statement of the problem and the range of possible solutions require us to consider the economic and political institutions of the society, and not merely the personal situation and character of a scatter of individuals."[3]

Certainly, the psychological perspective makes important contributions to our understanding of humans and their patterns of organization and behavior. But the sociological perspective moves the focus beyond the individual, examining the ways the individual is shaped by the social environment.

The Sociological Imagination

A sociological perspective necessitates what Mills called a "sociological imagination." Having a sociological imagination means standing apart mentally from our place in society and seeing (imagining) the linkage between personal and social events—tracing the connections between patterns and events in our own lives and those in our society. A sociological imagination involves three kinds of sensitivity: historical, comparative, and critical.

Historical Sensitivity

Mills claimed that "all sociology worthy of the name is 'historical sociology.'" In support of Mills's assertion, sociologist Irving Zeitlin contended that "the social scientist who studies a social structure without studying its history will never truly understand any given state of that structure or the forces operating to change it."[4] I could readily apply that statement to the present discussion: "The person who studies sport without studying its history will never truly understand any given state of sport or the forces operating to change it."

E.G. Boring, the eminent historian of psychology, provided additional sanction to Mills's notion about the importance of developing a historical sensitivity. According to Boring, attention to history is valuable not to predict the future but to understand the present better.[5] The shared insight in each of these statements is that a historical sensitivity is essential in sociological analysis because it helps us gain a more informed understanding of present conditions.

Comparative Sensitivity

Mills's call for comparative sensitivity refers to the necessity for learning about and understanding other cultures and societies. Only by doing so do we come to appreciate the diversity of human societies and of the social constructions of the meanings of social organization and behavior. Comparative sensitivity also allows us to break free of ethnocentrism, or our tendency to believe that the modes of social organization and behavior in our society are somehow superior to those of all other cultures. And there is no doubt that such an attitude is firmly entrenched in American society. We have a strong tendency to universalize our own cultural norms and practices.

A comparative sensitivity in the study of sport can help us understand that the popularity and meanings of different sports vary across cultures. For example, the game we know as football is rarely played in other countries, while soccer is immensely popular throughout the world.

Critical Sensitivity

Mills noted that the sociological imagination combines with the task of sociology in contributing to the critique of existing societal formations. In other words, sociology necessarily has a critical quality; it cannot be a disinterested and remote scholarly pursuit. The sociological imagination looks beyond commonly accepted descriptions of social structures and social processes to demystify and to demythologize. Thus, a critical sensitivity empowers us with a willingness to think and act critically, to problematize conventional definitions of reality, thus ferreting out falsehoods and contradictions when they exist.

Sociology and the Legacy of Karl Marx

Study in sociology, even the sociology of sport, invariably brings references to Karl Marx and Marxism because Marx is one of history's most noted social theorists. His name will occasionally appear in this book, and it seems appropriate to say something about Marx and his ideas because there are several dimensions of his work: his own social theoretical writing, numerous interpreters and revisers of his ideas, and nation-states that purport to follow his ideas.

Unfortunately, it is only the last dimension that most people are familiar with, and discourse about so-called Marxist states tends to be highly politicized. Many Americans have come to think of Marx and Marxism as synonymous with evil because of the link to former and present communist nations that have been portrayed as enemies of the United States. But it is essential to distinguish between Marxism as a body of knowledge providing insights into society, politics, and economics and Marxism as ideology guiding so-called Marxist countries.

Karl Marx died in 1883, long before the Russian Revolution in 1917. So he had nothing to do with the creation of the Soviet Union or any of the other communist countries. Moreover, Marx would never have expected that Russia might experiment with his political-economic ideas because he wrote about industrial, capitalist countries, and Russia during his lifetime was feudalistic and industrially underdeveloped. All great thinkers attract legends and misinterpretations, and often what they said or wrote is distorted by those who impose their own subjective preconceptions on the original ideas. The most prominent figure—after Friedrich Engels—in the enlargement and elaboration of Marx's ideas was V.I. Lenin, the first leader of the Soviet Union, and he greatly distorted much of Marx's work and ideas by creating the foundations of Soviet Union totalitarianism.

Marx cannot be held responsible for contemporary socialist ideas; much of what has transpired in "Marxist" countries in his name would have horrified him. Marx was a critic of oppression, discrimination, and domination. He was the leading social scientist to place power and class relations at the center of an interpretation of the social structure of capitalist societies; he was a critic of the corrupting quality of power and class society, not the quality of human beings. Fundamentally, he supported the promotion of human liberty, dignity, and equality. Perhaps the most distinctive heritage of Marx's ideas is their ecumenical character of internationalism and the insistence that all people throughout the world are dependent on one another. His vision was a profoundly moral and ethical one, and perhaps this is one reason for its enduring strength.

The best-known former and current communist countries—the Soviet Union, East Germany, and the People's Republic of China—have not been good representatives of Marx's ideas. Indeed, many Marxists have been as critical of these countries as they are of capitalist countries because the governmental policies of these countries have been antithetical to the socialist ideals of a democratic and equalitarian society. Workers in these countries were not freed from oppressive conditions. In fact, wage labor was not abolished, strikes and industrial conflict prevailed, gender and racial domination was not eliminated, and little advancement to the free and full development of all individuals occurred.

Although there have been political organizations in the United States sympathetic to Marx's political-economic writings for more than a century, Marxist ideas have never posed a revolutionary threat to the established social order in America. Marxist ideas have, however, taken root as the major social theoretical critique of capitalist society.

In his book *Sociology: A Brief but Critical Introduction,* British sociologist Anthony Giddens writes: "To declare sympathy with certain of Marx's conceptions does not imply accepting his views, or those of his self-professed followers, in their entirety. . . . But neither do I reject Marx. Marx's writings are of continuing significance to sociology. . . . At the same time, there are conspicuous weaknesses in Marx's work."[6] This insight informs and guides the references to Karl Marx and his social theories in this book.

The Sociological Perspective of This Book

The subtitle of this book proclaims that it employs a critical perspective. I take a specific social theoretical orientation toward social institutions and cultural practices in American society. This orientation centers on what is called *hegemony* (pronounced \'hej-ə-'mō-nē\ or \hi-'jem-ə-nē\), which refers to dominance and influence. This approach attempts to provide insights into the historical construction of societal dominance and the roles of the political, economic, and cultural patterns in capitalist societies. Although there are varying interpretations and unresolved issues in hegemony theory, they all force us to think more critically about the operative and underlying roots of modern society, a perspective not generally fostered by mainstream analyses of American culture.

I will use selected aspects of hegemony theory to sensitize you to the role dominant groups play in American government, economic system, mass media, education, and sport in maintaining and promoting their interests. By dominant groups, I mean the powerful and wealthy who own most of the land, capital, and technology and who employ most of the nation's labor. They also translate their enormous economic resources into social and political power by occupying the top elective and appointed governmental positions, regardless of the political party to which they belong. The social structure of dominance in American society also privileges men over women, rich over poor, and whites over people of color. I will emphasize relationships between power, domination, and ideology and social class, gender, and race as they relate to sport.

In doing this, sport is stripped of its presumed innocence and linked to the political, economic, and cultural milieu of which it is a part. I expect this process to challenge the views you hold, perhaps even unknowingly, about sport vis-à-vis American society and culture. I hope that it also provokes you to be more reflective and critical of contemporary sport forms and practices. Being reflective means evaluating your own current knowledge, values, and beliefs on the basis of new information and asking whether they are justified in light of the new information.

Having said that this book employs a theoretical framework, I want to hasten to make two points: First, please do not fear this book as one of those tomes devoted to the dreary weighing of pros and cons about ideas promulgated by social theorists long since dead. My description of social theory is targeted to readers with little background in the subject. I do not go into great detail, nor do I try to explain the protracted debates over various interpretations of hegemony theory. Although this may be unsatisfactory for the professional scholars of sport studies, there are numerous other sources to which they may turn for more in-depth theoretical analyses.

Second, through the perspective of this book, I hope to provide you with a better understanding of the role of sport in American society. But it is not meant to provide justifications for existing sport, exercise, fitness, or any physical activity programs. This does not mean that it is antisport or opposed to exercise and fitness for health and well-being. A major purpose of the book is to make you think about and reflect on the relationship of sport to the larger society in the hopes that you will form a social consciousness (meaning cognitively make sense of our world, the knowledge we have of how it works, and our place in it) about sport and physical activities that goes beyond the blind transmission of slogans and clichés traditionally advanced about sport.

Value judgments necessarily permeate all aspects of all the sciences, both natural and social, and I make no claim to value neutrality here, nor can any scholar or scientist. I do, however, attempt to portray conditions and situations as accurately as I can based on my study and research. One of the strengths of a social science perspective lies in the richness of its diversity and in the vigor of the debate between different analysts trying to make sense of the social world.

This volume is "critical" in two ways. First, it is critical of the ideas that form the conventional wisdom about sport in American society. In the realm of sport, as in many others, privileged groups use political, economic, and cultural resources to define societal norms and values and to reinforce and sustain their influence. Their interests are legitimated by compatible ideologies disseminated by schools, mass media, and various agencies of social control, and the processes they use tend to suppress or marginalize alternative versions.

The second way this book is critical is through my use of hegemony theory, which is directly linked to social criticism of modern capitalist society. One consequence of employing this perspective is that many myths and distortions that have crept into the social discourse about sports are unmasked.

Benefits of a Critical Social Analysis of Sport

A critical social perspective invites us to step back from thinking about sport as merely a place of personal achievement and entertainment and study sport as a cultural practice embedded in political, economic, and ideological formations. Relevant issues involve how sport is related to social class, race, gender, and the control, production, and distribution of economic and cultural power in the commodified sport industry.

By and large, Americans are not encouraged to critically examine the prevalent attitudes, values, myths, and folklore about sport. This is unfortunate in any social arena because if we do not critically examine cultural practices, such as sport, we cannot see the extent to which they are socially constructed. We will have difficulties not just in separating facts from values but also in recognizing how our viewpoints are influenced by the surrounding political, economic, and cultural context.

Although it is difficult to read and listen to points of view that problematize or criticize our own cherished attitudes, values, and beliefs, as long as we unquestioningly hold our own points of view absolute while interpreting other views as merely misguided, the most important step has not been taken. That step is having the courage to subject all points of view, including our own, to a critical analysis.

There may be times when you think I am overly critical. This is an understandable reaction, one that has been conditioned, to some extent, by what you have heard about sport and by your own sport experiences: "We've got to pull together to win"; "Be obedient, don't ask questions"; "Do as you are told"; "Be a team player." These sport slogans, and the hierarchical arrangements pervading sport organizations, condition people against critical thought. Moreover, a powerful cheerleader/boosterism mentality is promoted by all sport organizations. Their message to fans and players is to give uncritical support; if you don't, you're not being loyal or you're not a team player. That most of us fail to consider alternatives to contemporary sport organizations and practices is testimony to the effectiveness of our socialization.

I want to assure you that I am sensitive to and supportive of the many features of American society and its sports forms. My critical perspective is not an attack on sports activities themselves nor on those who participate in sport. To expose the abuses, discrimination, and injustices of contemporary sport is not to denigrate sport itself. Indeed, since my childhood I have experienced the joy and excitement of sports. But the inspirations that sport gives us, through our own accomplishments and through the achievements of outstanding athletes, should not deter us from taking a critical stance toward sport. Criticism is actually a form of commitment, a way of saying: "If there are problems here and unwarranted breaches of social justice and human equality, let's identify them and work to transform things to make sport better."

Is a critical perspective toward contemporary sport being antisport, even un-American, as some might claim? I would reply by substituting "sport" for "country" in the following quotes. The first is from J. William Fulbright, who was a distinguished U.S. senator from Arkansas: "To criticize one's country is to do it a service and pay it a compliment. It is a service because it may spur the country to do better than it is doing, it is a compliment because it evidences a belief that a country can do better than it is doing. Criticism, in short, is an act of patriotism, a higher form of patriotism, I believe, than the familiar rituals of national adulation."[7] In a similar vein, one of America's most articulate social analysts, Michael Parenti, has argued: "There is no better way to love one's country, no better way to strive for the fulfillment of its greatness, than to entertain critical ideas and engage in the pursuit of social justice."[8]

Obstacles to a Critical Analysis of Sport

Critical social analysts of sport are confronted by several obstacles. First, they are often confronted with the question, "You're good at criticizing, but what is your plan for change or reform?" The clear implication is that unless the critic has a strategy for social change, merely identifying existing injustices, corruption, and exploitation is worthless. But critical analysis implies a concern for identifying, scrutinizing, and clarifying, and in this way it helps overcome the obstacles barring the way to the attainment of an overall understanding of the phenomena under study. The purpose, then, is to facilitate understanding what is and not present a detailed plan for what ought to be. It is the task of *everyone* who is moved or persuaded by the validity of critical analysis to attempt to do something to change the situation. As sport philosopher William Morgan eloquently put it, "While theory can inform the work of enlightenment, it cannot prescribe the risky decisions of strategic action at the political level. These can only be justified by the participants themselves, who in their practical discourse with one another decide what strategies to follow and what risks to take with what expectations."[9]

A second obstacle to critical analysis of sport is that throughout American society there tends to be a blissful unawareness about the social relations that control sport and other forms of physical activity, a frightening naiveté about the social context and material conditions underlying physical culture. Although sport practices embody specific and identifiable purposes, values, and meanings, they are typically viewed by both participants and spectators as ahistorical and apolitical in nature. This is true largely because most of our written and broadcast information does not confront people with questions about the larger social issues and political and economic consequences of modern sport and physical activity. Instead, we are fed a diet of traditional slogans, clichés, and ritualized trivia about sport. These may all be very comforting, but they do not come to grips with the realities of sport organizations nor the sport culture.

A third obstacle to a critical analysis of sport in American society is that people typically receive little encouragement to become aware of the sociocultural forces and institutions that shape the world of sport. Moreover, sport leaders tend to view themselves as impartial facilitators operating in a value-free and ideological neutral setting. Few of them have seriously thought through their own basic premises, but instead proceed on unexamined assertions, mottoes, and slogans. The assumed unproblematic nature of current sport forms is reflected in a statement extolling a school "sport education" program, whose purpose was said to be to socialize students "to participate in sport . . . and behave toward sport in ways that serve to preserve, protect, and enhance the sport culture."[10] Contemporary sport culture is not presented as even potentially problematic; instead, it is presented as something to be blindly learned and followed.

A fourth obstacle to a critical social analysis of American sport is that sport and society have traditionally been seen as discrete social institutions, with sport being a realm in which character is built and virtue pursued. Americans tend to cherish the illusion that coaches and athletes are paragons of nobility. The sports world itself encourages the belief that sports are "just fun and games" and has vigorously fought any attempt to change this image.

This separating out of sport from all that is serious in American life has been one of the most persistent barriers to meaningful analysis of the relationship of sport to society. But sport cannot be examined as isolated from the social, economic, political, and cultural context in which it is situated. Sport is a set of social practices and relations that are structured by the culture in which they exist, and any adequate account of sport must be rooted in an understanding of its location within society. The essence of sport is to be found within the nature of its relationship to the broader stream of societal forces of which it is a part. Thus, a real necessity for everyone trying to understand the sociocultural role of sport in American society is to approach sport *relationally,* always asking, "What are the interconnections of sport to other aspects of American society?"

Summary and Preview

Sport and physical recreations are extremely popular in American life, and there is a growing interest among social scientists in the organization and behavior of people involved in sport and in sport's larger social meanings. Connections between sport and political, economic, and cultural systems are of particular interest. One of my purposes in this book is to apply a critical sociological perspective to sport so as to help you better understand its important sociocultural role. In this chapter, I have discussed the characteristics of a critical sociological perspective and have described some of the ramifications for studying sport with a "sociological imagination."

In chapter 2, I identify two social images that have been constructed for examining questions about who governs the social and cultural life of society and what role those who govern play. Linkages are made between these social images and their relationship to sport.

Suggested Readings

Eitzen, D. Stanley, and George H. Sage. *Sociology of North American Sport.* 6th ed. Madison, WI: Brown & Benchmark, 1997.

Fay, Brian. *Critical Social Science.* Ithaca, NY: Cornell University Press, 1987.

Giddens, Anthony. *Introduction to Sociology.* 2nd ed. New York: Norton, 1996.

Ingham, Alan G., and John W. Loy, eds. *Sport in Social Development: Traditions, Transitions, and Transformations.* Champaign, IL: Human Kinetics, 1993.

Lapchick, Richard, ed. *Sport in Society: Equal Opportunity or Business as Usual?* Thousand Oaks, CA: Sage, 1996.

Mills, C. Wright. *The Sociological Imagination.* New York: Oxford University Press, 1959.

Morgan, William J. *Leftist Theories of Sport: A Critique and Reconstruction.* Urbana, IL: University of Illinois Press, 1994.

Parenti, Michael. *Democracy for the Few.* 6th ed. New York: St. Martin's Press, 1995.

Rader, Benjamin. *American Sports: From the Age of Folk Games to the Age of Spectators.* 2nd ed. Englewood Cliffs, NJ: Prentice Hall, 1990.

Ray, Larry J. *Rethinking Critical Theory.* Newbury Park, CA: Sage, 1993.

Chapter 2
Social Images and Sport

We cannot approach society . . . as we do objects or events in the natural world, because societies only exist insofar as they are created and re-created in our own actions as human beings.

Anthony Giddens, sociologist

M ost people begin the sociological study of sport with little knowledge about social theories, which are descriptions and interpretations about how societies work. They also typically understand little about the nature of social institutions, corporate organizations, and cultural practices and their compelling roles in the making of social and cultural life. Finally, there is often no awareness of the links between social theory, social life, and cultural practices like sport and other physical activities. In this chapter, I will begin to articulate these relationships by describing two social theories—which I call images—and applying their insights and interpretations to American social institutions (e.g., business, government, schools, religion, family) and cultural life.

Two Images of American Society

Trying to understand the social organization and cultural processes of a society begins with a mental picture—an image—of its structure and dynamics. Social theories help construct mental images of a society. Thus, they are general perspectives for understanding various features of the social world.[1] They influence what one sees and how one explains the phenomena that occur within a society. This is how the theories, or images, discussed in this chapter should be understood. No attempt is made to fully articulate their subtleties and complexities. Instead, only the basic outlines of two prominent social images, or theories, are described in an effort to acquaint you with different ways of perceiving the social realities of American society.

The average person has usually internalized a particular view of American social life as though it were the one legitimate image of social reality, not realizing that there are several social theories that attempt to portray the salient features of social organization and culture in American society. This chapter introduces two contrasting social models of American society and their relationships to sport.

We begin with two general questions:

1. Who are the dominant sources of power and influence over the attitudes, values, beliefs, norms, and worldviews within American society?
2. What role do they play in American social and cultural life?

The importance of trying to understand the locus of power, control, and influence is that those who have these resources can mold and shape societal attitudes, values, and beliefs and thus influence all the social institutions and cultural practices, including sport.

Understanding how any society works is a complex and demanding task that is rife with differences of opinion. The two social-political images of society that I describe are the *pluralistic image* and the *hegemonic image.* Let us examine how each addresses the two questions posed earlier.

The Pluralistic Image

The orthodox view fostered by major American social institutions and cultural groups is called *pluralism.* A pluralistic image contends that a broad and diverse set of social institutions, organizations, and interest groups embodies the beliefs, values, and worldviews of citizens. This model asserts that power and influence are exerted by a multitude of interests whose countervailing centers of power check one another to prevent abusive power and agenda setting by any one group. Thus, according to the pluralistic version of American society, although groups are not necessarily equal in terms of power and influence, America is "a government of the people, by the people, and for the people"; we have "equality of opportunity," and we have "liberty and justice for all." These are the underpinnings of pluralism, and they suggest that no particular groups are able to dominate, control, or influence attitudes, values, or beliefs in this society.

According to this image, the major business, governmental, and cultural organizations are unable to achieve a collective dominance because the unorganized mass of people exercises some power over interest groups; thus, no one private or public sector is capable of acting with unity and power on the range of public issues. With respect to the corporate business community, it is argued that because of its heterogeneity, business has no collective interests at all. Business owners reflect a constantly shifting set of coalitions and thus find it difficult to form themselves into a solidified group.

Social and cultural influence within society is seen as broadly distributed among a variety of groups and organizations. Through public policy, cultural tendencies are seen to be set by a rough equilibrium of group influences, and there is therefore a reasonable approximation of society's preferences—a sort of equality of cultural production. According to this view of society, although most citizens

© Terry Wild Studio/Chris Stutz

Intercollegiate sport has become a major commercial entertainment industry. College football games are played in stadiums packed with thousands of loyal fans while millions of radio listeners and television viewers follow their favorite university team.

may not participate directly in social-cultural decision making, norm setting, and value creation, they can make their influence felt through participation in organized groups; thus an underlying ideology of equality sets the social agenda.

It may be seen, then, that the pluralistic model of American society as an amalgam of the general population's ideals, values, and worldviews includes implicit assumptions about power and influence and their distribution. The most obvious of these is that commercial, governmental, and cultural organizations are personifications of everyone's collective attitudes, interests, and values because no group or class is significantly powerful and influential over others. All citizens have roughly the same interests in society, and all have basically equal shares of power and influence; thus, social order is based on a consensus of their cultural values. A pluralistic image represents society as though there are few serious economic or cultural problems, and minimal pressing conflicts of interest between social classes and various groups.

That the interests of the people form the policies of business and government is a pervasive theme perpetuated by many public forums that advance the notion of pluralism in the United States. These forums suggest that business and governmental goals correspond with and are indistinguishable from those of average citizens. Moreover, this mutual compatibility is seen as harmonizing and accommodating conflicting interests and values, thereby preserving the consensus and social accord.

The Hegemonic Image

A second and very different image of the nature of capitalist societies is called the hegemonic (\,hej-ə-'män-ik\) image. Hegemonic social thought was constructed to apply to all modern capitalist societies, not just one nation like the United States. But because this book's focus is American society, I shall refer to the United States in describing the hegemonic image.

Hegemony literally means dominance, but when it is used to refer to the social relations that tend to exist in modern capitalist societies (e.g., United States), it has a less direct, autocratic meaning. In this case, it refers to a society in which dominant groups that control the critically important economic and political institutions of a society also have principal access to the other social institutions—education and mass media, for example—as well as many cultural norms and practices. They use their power and influence to promote and shape attitudes, values, beliefs, and worldviews in ways that ultimately secure a willing consent of the mass of citizens; this process forms a social cement that tends to promote and preserve a sense of unity for the entire society.

This image of society is quite different from pluralism because it suggests that major societal power, control, and influence emanate from economically, politically, and culturally dominant groups, even though they are muted and filtered through the popular consent of "the people."

The writings of Italian social theorist Antonio Gramsci, completed while he was in a fascist prison (where he had been put by Mussolini) from 1926 until 1935, have popularized the hegemonic image of advanced capitalist societies, and it is almost always associated with him. But the concept is not unique to Gramsci, and it has been used by a number of social scientists both before him and after his death. However, the strains of hegemonic social thought vary considerably, but the theme of socially dominant actors who establish their own moral, political, and cultural values as the conventional norms is common throughout. What is especially important from the standpoint of this book is that hegemonic social theory is considered to be applicable to all democratic capitalistic societies; thus its insights and interpretations may appropriately be applied to American society.[2]

Gramsci's writings contain no precise definition of hegemony. One social analyst described Gramsci's meaning of hegemony in this way: Hegemony refers "broadly to the organization of the cultural, moral, and ideological consent of the population to the prevailing political and economic system through the institutions of civil society, such as schools, churches, and [political] parties, etc."[3] This consent exists because of the prestige (and consequent confidence) that such groups enjoy because of their position in the productive sector (meaning the economy) and their cultural power.[4]

A hegemonic image of advanced capitalist societies provides a powerful framework for analyzing social organization and social processes within these societies. It complements Marx's emphasis on the economic institution but goes beyond Marx to analyze the ways that political, cultural, and ideological institutions and practices are integrated with the economy to form the whole. Gramsci's work unravels the complex web of political, economic, cultural, and ideological practices that bind a society into a relative unity.

Gramsci, as well as others writing in this tradition, makes the underlying assumption that capitalist societies are first and foremost *class societies*. He saw the character of capitalist societies in terms of class relations and disharmony among classes, so the pertinent social institutions, organizations, and processes are exactly those through which the various classes are constituted and through which they are associated with one another. Gramsci noted that "though hegemony is ethico-political, it must also be economic, must necessarily be based on the decisive function exercised by the leading group in the decisive nucleus of economic activity."[5]

Societal Power

In the hegemonic image of society, sociocultural values and beliefs are viewed as embodying the values, ideals, and interests of dominant groups more than any sort of pluralistic, generalized interests. To be specific, the hegemonic image sees political-economic domination and intellectual and moral leadership carried out *not* by a single, unified "ruling class" but by a complex coalition of powerful and wealthy groups that own most of the capital, land, and technology and that employ most of the country's labor force. But beyond the political-economic characteristics is also cultural dominance, which has been historically manifested in male white-skin privilege. It is through dominant groups that the "commonsense" and everyday practices of the masses of people are managed. The ways of life and versions of culture and civilization of the dominant actors are fashioned in a direction that, while perhaps not yielding unquestioned advantage for narrow dominant interests, persuades the masses to embrace a consensus that supports the existing social arrangements.

In describing power relations, Gramsci identified two ways in which dominant actors exercise power and preserve social control: force (coercion) and consent. Gramsci said that the dominant social alliance "dominates antagonistic groups, which it tends to 'liquidate,' or to subjugate perhaps even by armed force; it leads kindred and allied groups."[6] Concerning antagonists, Gramsci meant that powerful groups use their control over the resources of government, the legal system, the police, the military, and other services to establish their view of the society as legitimate, all-inclusive, and universal. By kindred and allied groups he meant those that are compatriots of hegemonic groups; they exercise influence on behalf of dominant interests through a moral and intellectual guidance whereby their interpretations and meanings become widely understood, shared, and supported. One analyst refers to this as a leadership based on the consent of the led, but a consent that has been established through a diffusion and popularization of the worldview of the dominant groups.

To a large extent, then, hegemony is a silent domination; that is, it is not consciously experienced because there is an orchestration of consent in conjunction with, and coercion (force, if necessary) of, subordinate groups into harmony with the established social order.

Hard-and-fast lines cannot be drawn between the mechanisms of consent and the mechanisms of coercion, but in any society they are interwoven. According to Gramsci, consent is normally in the lead but operating behind "the armour of coercion."[7]

Means of Domination

The specific actions pursued by dominant social alliances to main-tain their power and status vary according to the prevailing condi-tions and the historical moment. They may range from various forms of persuasion, negotiation, concession, and compromise to manipu-lation and repressive action. Regardless of the tactics, the preferable means of domination is to subdue opposition, absorbing it into patterns of thought that are congruent with the ideological prefer-ences of the dominant actors. Thus, domination is contoured prima-rily through an "active consent" of subordinate groups, but a consent that has been molded through intellectual, political, and moral leadership that ultimately rests on the officious apparatus of the state (i.e., government, the military, the legal system).

Reliance upon force in the long run will render hegemony unstable. Thus, hegemony cannot succeed by simply forcing beliefs and thought patterns of the dominant groups into the heads of subordinate groups. Instead, an important way in which it is produced and disseminated is through shaping "popular beliefs" because they help to organize human actions and are a way in which social consciousness itself is formed. How popular beliefs become part of the dominant group milieu is a complex process, involving the school system, mass media, religion, patriotic rituals and ceremonies, and a political system that enjoys a facade of popular consensus. But the specific means through which various ideas and assumptions become domi-nant material forces in society is through ideology.

Ideological Domination

As I previously noted, ideology refers to a set of explanations, justifications, and legitimations for the current social relations in a society. It is the driving force for dominant groups, according to hegemony theory. Ideology legitimates current social beliefs and practices in a way that makes them seem right and natural—just common sense, or just human nature. Gramsci stressed what he called *rule by consent* or *ideological domination.* He argued that the masses of people who enable a society to function smoothly tend to internal-ize and endorse dominant groups' explanations and definitions, and thus, through their consent, ideological domination succeeds. In this way, hegemonic groups can penetrate all levels of the society with their version of social reality.[8]

Hegemonic ideologies are produced and disseminated through social institutions—political and economic systems, the family, schools—and through popular cultural practices—art, music, sport. Intellectuals and other cultural workers (e.g., scientists, teachers, writers) are especially valuable for fostering ideologies that prescribe conformist acceptance of existing social arrangements because they have the know-how and creativity to organize and mold cultural organizations.

Ideologies of dominant groups, according to the hegemonic model, legitimate the existing society and its institutions and ways of life by persuading the general public to consider society and its norms and values to be natural, good, and just, thus concealing the inherent system of domination. In this way, hegemonic ideologies are inscribed into everyday consciousness and become a means of "indirect rule" and thus a powerful force for social cohesion and stability.[9]

The fundamental consequence of hegemonic ideologies is to consolidate the present social conditions with rationalizations stemming from the status quo, thus protecting and shielding particularized interests—mainly those of dominant groups—and the existing society against alternatives. Opposition or struggles against dominant ideologies are made to seem disruptive and counterproductive to the social order. Labor union strikes and environmental protests would be two contemporary examples of unwanted disruptions.

Maintaining Hegemony

Although dominant coalitions certainly wield power and influence, it is a continual and formidable task for them to sustain their hegemony. As one social scientist points out, hegemony "does not just passively exist as a form of dominance. It has continually to be renewed, recreated, defended, and modified. It is also continually resisted, limited, altered, challenged by pressures not at all its own."[10] Other writers make the point more emphatically: "Hegemonic ideologies are not monolithic apparatuses that a group of omniscient conspirators impose on a mass of cultural dopes. Instead, they are articulated by superordinates in ways that resonate with people's common sense, thereby winning popular consent."[11] Hegemony, then, is never guaranteed to a dominant group; indeed, a dominant group can only sustain moral, cultural, and intellectual leadership if it remains responsive to some of the demands of social and cultural opposition.

Thus, successful hegemony is an ongoing process of accommodation and compromise. Because there is never a single, unified ruling class, but instead there are coalitions of powerful groups engaged in an enduring ideological struggle for legitimate authority, patterns of hegemony vary according to their history, structure, and current circumstances. Indeed, one scholar argued that "ideological domination . . . requires an *alliance* between powerful economic and political groups on the one hand, and cultural elites on the other. . . . It is best understood as a collaborative process rather than an imposed, definitively structured order; in general, hegemony is a condition of the social system as a whole rather than a cunning project of the ruling group. Indeed, the effectiveness of hegemony depends to a great extent on the inability or unwillingness of those subjected to it to organize together to oppose it."[12]

Although there has been a tendency to think of the hegemonic image of the distribution of social power and dominance as applying only to economic and social class considerations, the notion of hegemony has become much broader. The emergence of new social movements around issues such as gender and race has emphasized that hegemony cannot be subsumed within the logic of economic and class issues. Feminist and racial theorists have incorporated hegemonic themes into their work. They examine gender and racial domination as relatively autonomous yet related systems of power, inequality, and domination. They see a close link between economic inequality and other forms of social inequality involving race and gender. In this way, they have broadened the concept of hegemony, thus articulating a more complex hegemony with intersecting relationships of power. Those perspectives are particularly useful in the study of sport and are illustrated in various places in this book—especially chapters 4 and 5.

Dominant Groups

In any discussion of hegemony theory, the question arises, Who are the dominant groups? From a hegemonic perspective, there is no single dominant group but rather an alliance of factions of the most powerful, wealthy, and influential persons and groups in business, commerce, government, education, and mass media (and in some societies, religion). In every society, these individuals and groups have the most opportunities for intervening in and shaping cultural values, beliefs, and practices in their own interests, thus allowing it to become the social authority expressing "society's view."

Consider the following facts in reflecting on whether such a concentration of power, wealth, and influence could be said to exist that might constitute a dominant social alliance—and thus represent the societal view—in the United States.

- A small percentage of America's population owns a large percentage of the nation's personal wealth. The *wealthiest 10 percent* of America's families and individuals now own 71 percent of the nation's wealth; the superrich families and individuals, the *top 1 percent,* now own 40 percent, a greater share than at any time since the 1920s. Meanwhile, the *bottom 90 percent* owns just 29 percent of the wealth, a drop of 22 percent in less than 20 years (see figure 2.1).

- A great deal of wealth among the wealthiest individuals in the United States is inherited. According to information

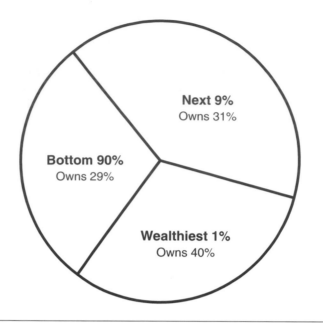

Figure 2.1   Ownership of private wealth in the United States—1998.

published in 1996 and 1997 in *Forbes* magazine, *56* percent of individuals and families in the United States inherited wealth of more than $1 million, and 43.5 percent inherited sufficient wealth to rank among the *Forbes* 400 wealthiest.

- The corporation has been instrumental in influencing key economic and political activities. The top echelons of American corporate life are occupied primarily by people of upper-middle-class and upper-class social origin.
- Of the 500 largest industrial corporations, 150 are controlled by one or more members of a single family.
- About half of all top corporate and governmental leaders are alumni of just 12 well-known private universities, most notably Ivy League colleges.
- Most politicians in America are white, male, and affluent; a preponderance of them are lawyers. Many past and present top politicians (such as the Roosevelts, Rockefellers, Kennedys, and Bushes) were born into wealthy families and inherited great wealth. Twenty-nine percent of current U.S. senators are millionaires. Of the 100 senators, only nine are female and only one is African American.

- According to the authors of *The Buying of the President* (1996), "The wealthiest interests bankroll and, in effect, help to preselect the specific major candidates months and months before a single vote is cast. . . . We are thus allowing our government of the people, by the people, and for the people to be led by someone initially chosen by only some of the people—narrow, vested interests with a direct financial stake in specific government policies and decisions."[13]

- It is estimated that about 6,000 Americans—*less than .003 percent!*—exercise formal authority over institutions that control roughly half the nation's resources in industry, finance, utilities, insurance, mass media, foundations, education, law, and civic and cultural affairs.

- About 32 percent of some 7,000 top corporate positions are interlocked with other top positions, resulting in linkages among corporations in which some individuals serve on the boards of directors of two or more companies.

- The people who control the flow of information in America are among the most powerful. American television is dominated by four private corporations—ABC, CBS, NBC, and Turner Broadcasting Company. These networks are only subsidiaries of even larger corporations. ABC is owned by Walt Disney/Capital Cities Communications, NBC by General Electric, CBS by Westinghouse, and Turner by Time Warner.

- Leadership positions in American corporations are over-whelmingly occupied by white males. Very few top corporate leaders are female or members of a minority. Only 57 women out of 2,430 people (2.4 percent) held positions in the highest ranks of corporate America, according to *The 1996 Catalyst Census of Women Corporate Officers and Top Earners.* In the annual lists of top chief executive officers, 90 percent to 95 percent are white males.

These facts about American society, of course, are not themselves sufficient evidence that the rich and powerful exercise dominance directly or uniformly over social discourses, values, or cultural norms or that they set the national social agenda. But they do indicate the existence of an extensive network of economic, political, and social alliances and mutual interests in a complex system of institutional, organizational, and cultural alliances. Although no social grouping does hegemonic work only, those who are a part of this network certainly have the resources of material wealth, status, and power to specialize in producing, relaying, and sustaining hegemonic ideologies. However, their primary hegemonic influence is exercised through the organizations they control, the social networks to which they belong, and the cultural resources they command.[14]

A Conspiracy of Power?

The actual degree of coordination and implementation of ideology by dominant interests in America is hotly debated by social analysts. Pluralists typically argue against any significant accord among powerful private and public organizations. But their argument is belied by considerable evidence that wealthy capitalists and the top managerial class have sufficiently mutual interests to evolve a collective strategy and, furthermore, that there is a symbiosis between top governmental officials and the capitalist class. So the hegemonic analytical framework sees much more unity within the dominant group community than does the pluralistic one, as shared material interests as well as cultural traditions, such as those that oppress women and minorities, engineer consent and, if necessary, coerce behavior in the interests of the system of power and privilege.[15]

Which Social Image Is Accurate?

What we have, then, are two visions—the pluralistic image and the hegemonic image—about the dominant sources of power and influence over the attitudes, values, beliefs, norms, and worldviews in American society and the role they play in social and cultural life. The first image assumes the existence of equality of opportunity, that everyone plays a somewhat equal role in affecting society. The pluralistic perspective maintains that where power and influence do exist, they are the collective result of all citizens' attitudes, interests, and values.

By and large, the pluralistic view is the "official" model of social reality conveyed by the dominant groups through private and public organizations and social groups that they control or at least exert a great deal of influence over. The image of pluralism so thoroughly permeates the major organizations that shape American attitudes and beliefs that it is considered to be "common sense" and is taken for granted by the average person—which is not surprising, because alternative visions of social reality are marginalized or discredited as inaccurate, even un-American.

The second vision, the hegemonic image, argues that dominant groups exercise power, control, and influence in the creation and maintenance of the national social agenda. In this view of American society, dominant groups do not normally exert their power and influence by force, intimidation, or violence; they do it more subtly, by controlling the major social institutions and agencies. Thus, they are able to orchestrate social life through an alliance of factions. Publicly, they promote a pluralistic version of American life because it is in their interests; after all, they are the major beneficiaries of the present system.

Sufficient empirical evidence demonstrates that the hegemonic model is more consonant with American historical experience and corresponds more closely to the realities of contemporary American life than the pluralistic one, which has a very restrictive and inadequate conception of power and influence.

Still, the question of whether the pluralistic or hegemonic image more accurately represents American society cannot be settled with ease or with certainty. Each image should be seen as a sensitizing perspective, each providing a different interpretation of social reality, each having plausible elements.

The most important result of understanding the pluralistic and hegemonic images is realizing that there is more than one view of the social reality in the United States and other modern capitalist societies. And likewise there is more than one way of understanding the relationship of sport and leisure activities to the larger society.

Applying the Social Images to Sport

Having examined how the pluralistic and hegemonic images view society at large, we are now in a position to turn to an analysis of how they relate to sport and physical recreation. Their perspectives of how society is structured and controlled have necessary implications for the structure and control of sport as a cultural practice.

Pluralism and Sport

In the pluralistic model, sport is seen as an arena in which society's collective interests are promoted and sustained through the sociocultural attitudes, values, and beliefs promulgated in sporting activities. Accompanying that assumption is the notion that sports' main organizational structures, systems of rules, and collective meanings have been constructed by and are shared by most of society. Baseball, for example, is said to be the "national pastime"; the Dallas Cowboys are called "America's Team."

Beyond that, though, sport and society are seen as discrete, separate social domains, with sport a realm of social life set off from the "realities" of the political and economic world, an escape from the pressure and problems of everyday life, a place that allows people to release tensions and enjoy themselves. Therefore, sport is viewed as apolitical, and political intervention into sporting activities is resented. Indeed, many sport leaders publicly condemn the increasing expansion of government involvement into sport and the "politicization" of sport that seems to have accompanied this expansion.

Hegemony and Sport

Applying the insights of hegemony to sport activities produces a number of implications that are quite different from pluralist notions about sport. One of the most foundational is that, in order to grasp the social significance of sporting practices, we must see them as part of larger political-economic and ideological configurations. Although there is an essential internal logic in sporting practices, contemporary institutional sport is not a separate and distinct social entity. It is fully integrated with the broader social organization and processes of society. It actually plays a role in advancing hegemonic interests.

Hegemonic ideologies require social institutions and cultural practices to reinforce and reproduce them. Dominant groups use their power and influence over social institutions (e.g., economic, political) and cultural industries (e.g., mass media, sports) to subtly mold and shape a willing consent of the masses to the legitimacy of their ideologies. From a hegemonic theoretical standpoint, modern sport, rather than being merely a diversionary entertainment, is considered to be an important popular cultural practice upon which dominant ideologies are constructed, maintained, and reproduced; sport thus plays a broad social reproductive role in American society.

This is the case because sport's institutional and ideological features have evolved in a way that corresponds with, and helps to strengthen and reproduce, the norms, values, and worldviews upon which dominant ideologies are based. In other words, the norms, practices, and ideas surrounding sport continually create a setting in which the interests of the dominant groups are served. Indeed, one of the most compelling roles of sport is to serve as a symbolic expression of the values and beliefs of the broader society, thus strengthening the structure of the economic, political, and cultural hegemony of dominant groups. Sport's importance, then, is rooted in its power to promote and structure relations in accordance with the proclivities of the dominant interests.

The popularity of spectator sports make it easy for them to penetrate everyday life and to represent and reproduce the dominant ideologies. Contemporary sports' popularity among the masses may be seen as one manifestation of their incorporation into the reigning ideological system. From this perspective, sport serves as one means of winning the hearts and minds of subordinate classes and of instilling their respect for and conformity to society's power holders. This acquiescence by the public actually inhibits the development of a critical social consciousness about the consequences of modern sport for human development, much less the characteristics of the broader society. This does not mean, however, that there is only passive compliance to hegemonic domination; resistance to, evasion of, and challenges to the autocratic, bureaucratic, and oppressive characteristics of contemporary sport and the broader social hegemony are constantly taking place.

Analysts of societywide hegemony contend that contemporary sport reflects and promotes capitalist ideology through its emphasis on competitiveness, individualism, obedience to authority, work discipline, and glorification of commercialism. One sport-studies scholar has made a point that deserves to be quoted at length: "One cannot help but be struck by the degree to which so much of the organization and culture of modern sport seems to have been influenced by capitalist productive forces and relations. For example, 'amateur' sports at their highest levels have almost become monuments to such new sciences as biomechanics, exercise physiology, and sport psychology where a market rationality is expressed in a mechanical quest for efficiency in human performance that is indentured to state and commercial sponsorship. Professional sports, meanwhile, have gone a great distance toward reducing the meaning of athletic contests to a simple dramatization of commodity relations."[16]

To illustrate, elite athletes now train year-round in special Olympic training centers where resident sport scientists use the latest technology to enhance performance for the sole purpose of producing medal winners. In addition, professional athletes are bought (drafted) and traded in much the same way as Wall Street tycoons buy, sell, and trade securities.

The whole domain of popular culture is a crucial area for constructing forms of consent and conformity. Cultural practices like language, informal education, the media, art, the theater, and habits and customs help to fashion hegemony. One form of popular culture is sport culture, and it functions through symbols and rituals embedded in various aspects of it—sports literature, sports customs, media sport presentations, and "official" sport mythology—that closely reflect the culture of the dominant social actors. Dominant groups use sport effectively to reproduce their views and interests through its myths, rituals, and ceremonies and through its communal celebrations that provide opportunities for large masses of people to be "part of the action," such as the Super Bowl, World Series, Stanley Cup play-offs, and so forth.

In many ways sporting practices—indeed, all leisure activity — help to continually reinforce the hegemonic structure of power and privilege in capitalist society. Spectator sports in particular, because they are commercialized, are mediated by the press and broadcasting, and are subject to government intervention. Thus they provide many opportunities for dominant groups to associate themselves with them in various ways and to intervene in and use them to advance their own interests.

By understanding sport through a perspective of hegemony theory, one becomes more aware of its societal role for producing and reproducing the present power and dominance relationships. One will also likely become more skeptical of suggestions about the "naturalness" of contemporary practices and events and more willing to seriously consider alternative ways and means for the promotion of personal development and social justice through sports activities.

Summary and Preview

The reality of American society is not perceived by everyone in the same way. As a consequence, there are various social images about how our society works—how power, control, and influence are distributed in the major social institutions and cultural practices—and who the major beneficiaries of this system are. Whoever has power, control, and influence can set the social agenda; the powerful are the dominant forces over societal attitudes, values, beliefs, norms, and worldviews.

I have identified and described two social images—the pluralist and the hegemonic—in terms of two foundational questions: (1) Who are the sources of power and influence over the attitudes, values, beliefs, norms, and worldviews within American society? and (2) What role do they play in American social and cultural life? I believe that the hegemonic image more accurately reflects the realities of contemporary American society.

One of the consequences of social organization in America is that people with certain characteristics are treated unequally. Despite popular beliefs that in America there is equality of opportunity and we are all treated equally, the fact is that widespread social inequality exists. Sociologists call this structured inequality *social stratification;* it exists when entire categories of people have unequal access to various societal rewards. As a cultural practice that supports and helps sustain hegemony, sport in America has historically promoted and supported various forms of class, gender, and racial social inequalities. These issues will be taken up in the next three chapters.

Suggested Readings

Allen, Michael P. *The Founding Fortunes: A New Anatomy of the Super-Rich Families.* New York: Dutton, 1987.

Domhoff, G. William. *The Power Elite and the State: How Policy Is Made in America.* New York: Aldine de Gruyter, 1990.

Fontana, Benedetto. *Hegemony and Power.* Minneapolis: University of Minnesota Press, 1993.

Germino, Dante. *Antonio Gramsci: Architect of a New Politics.* Baton Rouge: Louisiana State University, 1990.

Gibson, John. *Performance v. Results: A Critique of Values in Contemporary Sports.* Albany, NY: SUNY Press, 1993.

Gramsci, Antonio. *Selections From the Prison Notebooks.* Edited by Q. Hoare and G.N. Smith. New York: International Publishing Co., 1971.

Hargreaves, John. *Sport, Power and Culture.* New York: St. Martin's Press, 1986.

Lewis, Charles, and the Center for Public Integrity. *The Buying of the President.* New York: Avon Books, 1996.

McDermott, John. *Corporate Society: Class, Property, and Contemporary Capitalism.* Boulder, CO: Westview Press, 1991.

Simon, Roger. *Gramsci's Political Thought: An Introduction.* London: Lawrence & Wishart, 1991.

Chapter 3

Structures of Social Inequality: Social Class and Sport

American sport became stratified as a result of several influences: the way wealth sorts people, the different lifestyles of different groups, the desire for class exclusivity and status (snobbery), and the internalization of class norms and values.

Timothy J. Curry and Robert M. Jiobu, sociologists

H aving a sociological perspective requires coming to grips with the concepts of social inequality and social injustice. Structures of social inequality among groups of people is called social stratification by social scientists. Social stratification is an institutionalized system of power arrangements—of domination and subordination—because those who possess social power and resources can control and shape the lives of those who lack them. Social stratification is said to be institutionalized because its patterns are sustained and reproduced by the main institutions of society—the family, economy, polity, education, and religion.

Stratification is a pervasive source of injustice, oppression, exploitation, and often even conflict and violence in the lives of those subject to it. Moreover, the nature of social inequality creates not only a set of oppressive social relations but also a form of social consciousness favorable to reinforcing and reproducing this inequality.

A fundamental feature of all modern societies—and most premodern societies as well—is that they are stratified along a variety of categorical lines. Because it is so ubiquitous throughout the world, stratification is one of the central topics in the social sciences. Documenting, interpreting, and explaining structured inequality has been a central focus for sociologists since sociology became a recognized field of study.

Because structures of social inequality cut across all the topics in this book, I will describe three of the most prominent and pervasive forms of American stratification—class, gender, and race—in this and the following two chapters. In the chapters that follow these three, systems of social inequality will be a continuing background theme.

Class, gender, and race are simultaneous and interlocking structures of inequality, frequently operating with and through one another to produce discrimination and social injustice. In each, and collectively, inequalities exist that shape the patterns of social life of many people, severely limiting the extent of social justice, social health, and opportunities for self-development.[1]

Sports forms can only be understood in light of the class, gender, and racial stratification systems that underlie social institutional and cultural life in the United States. Integrating and analyzing the complex intersections and crosscurrents of these stratification systems is a formidable task; it is my hope that I accomplish this in a meaningful way in this and the following two chapters.

The first part of this chapter is devoted to describing the main features of class stratification in the United States, which will provide a background for examining the theme of social class in American sport in the following sections of the chapter.

Class Stratification

One common form of stratification is an unequal distribution of material rewards, such as wealth and income. Social scientists refer to this system of patterned social inequality as the *social class structure*. Although the term "social class" is commonly used, a continuing debate is waged over its meaning. For our purposes, a social class can be thought of as a group of people whose members are characterized by relative similarities of wealth, income, prestige, lifestyle, education, and culture.

Social class is one of the most pervasive variables determining life chances (health, illness, marital decisions, longevity, probabilities of suffering societal disadvantages or benefiting from societal opportunities) and patterns of social interaction (family life, friendships, lifestyle, patterns of sport involvement, political attitudes, and even religious involvement); all are structured and heavily influenced by one's individual class position and the class position of one's parents. It is also essential to recognize that class is a system of power and not just difference. Power is unequally distributed among social classes.[2]

Despite heated debates among social scientists about what constitutes social class characteristics, there is no lack of class designations. Class as an economic concept was first articulated by Karl Marx, who analyzed the structure of industrial capitalist societies in terms of two great classes: capitalist (made up of those who own the means of production) and proletariat (the workers, who do not own the means of production). Marx considered such social factors as prestige, lifestyle, and social interaction patterns as being derived solely from economic class conditions. So class was not just a demographic characteristic for Marx but a dynamic interrelationship of wealth and power and the formation of an entire social and cultural order.

Today, stratification theorists agree that the capitalist-proletariat distinction is inadequate. They have broadened the concept of class to apply to categories of people who share economic resources, prestige, and political power. Thus, social class divisions have come to have anywhere from three to 20 categories, with the labels upper, middle, and lower—with subcategories within each (e.g., upper-middle, lower-middle, etc.)—being the most popular.

My preference when referring to American class structure is to use the terms *capitalist class, middle class,* and *working class.* The capitalist class is elite in terms of wealth, income, ownership, privilege, and power; members of this class hold extensive control over the economic system because they own most of the nation's capital and land, and they employ most of the labor force. Capital refers to goods or other forms of wealth that are not needed for immediate consumption but can be used to produce further capital or other goods or services.

Although numerically the capitalist class is very small—most estimates are about 2 percent of the population—it wields great influence. Indeed, it is extremely influential in defining the essential character of society as a whole because it has the wherewithal to control important societal resources. Consequently, the capitalist class plays a crucial role in shaping the beliefs and thought patterns that legitimate and perpetuate the existing social class system.[3] The capitalist class is a major component of the dominant group complex of intersecting relationships of power that was described in chapter 2.

At the other end of the spectrum is the working class, the many people who own no productive property, who do not supervise others, and who do not help plan the work or private lives of others.

Examples here are skilled, semiskilled, and unskilled workers, including farm laborers and service workers. Millions of working-class Americans live in conditions of poverty. The proportion of the population classified as working class varies from 55 percent to 70 percent, depending on the criteria used for class assignment.[4]

The middle class, as its name suggests, is a bridge between the other two classes. Examples of middle-class occupations are professionals, administrators, managerial and nonmanagerial white-collar workers, and nonretail sales workers. Members of this class are income earners who do not own sufficient means of production to otherwise support themselves; they share this characteristic with the working class. On the other hand, the middle class does share some of the power that capital exercises over workers by owning small productive property, exercising supervisory authority over workers, or designing and planning the work of others. The middle class dominates working-class labor but is itself subordinate to capital; this simultaneous dominance and subordination is what puts it in the middle. Still, the middle class typically aligns itself with the capitalist elite and constitutes "a genuine class with interests *in opposition to the working class.*"[5]

Capitalism and Class Stratification

American society is driven by a particular form of economic enterprise—capitalism—that is inextricably related to its other social institutions as well as its cultural practices. However, many Americans avoid using the word capitalism or referring to the United States's economy as capitalistic. For example, many business leaders, politicians, journalists, and even some social scientists use euphemisms such as "free enterprise" or "free market system" or "market economy" in place of capitalism. But capitalism is the more precise term to use when referring to the American economic system.

In its basic meaning, capitalism is nothing more than an economic system based on the accumulation and investment of capital by private individuals who then become the owners of the means of production and distributors of goods and services—an accurate characterization of the American economy. Capitalism is merely one means of producing and distributing goods and services—there is nothing inherently American about it.

Capitalist organization presupposes a system stratified into social classes based on the relations between capital and wage labor, especially power relations whereby those who own and control the means of production—capitalists—hold power over those who produce the goods and services—workers. Furthermore, in its control of the means of production, the capitalist class has much greater resources and power than do workers who lack productive ownership. Thus, although capitalists (and their agents, such as managers and supervisors) and the working class depend on one another, the dependence is fundamentally unbalanced. This imbalance means that the capitalist view of the world becomes the dominant view.

Because the United States has a capitalist economy, it is inherently a class-divided society, and class relationships directly link the economic organization of capitalism to the social relations and institutions making up the rest of the society. Capitalism, then, is not only an economic system, it is also a complete social system. It functions not only to produce cars and television sets that make a profit for industry owners, "it also produces a whole communication universe, a symbolic field, a culture, a control over various social institutions."[6]

There is deep-seated American folklore that the United States is an equalitarian society—a classless society. But despite a societal mythology touting the absence of class, even a cursory analysis convincingly shows that American society is indeed a class society. To make any headway toward understanding our society—its social institutions, organizations, and the behaviors of its people—it is essential to come to terms with this fact about American life. A social analysis of any aspect of American culture that ignores the importance of social class differences is simply incomplete and unsatisfactory.

Social Consciousness and Class Stratification

For many Americans, the notion that we live in a society of social classes is quite foreign; more than that, it is so objectionable that one can encounter strong resentment by even suggesting there are classes in America. When the topic of class is raised, it is often dismissed as a dead Marxist dogma or as insignificant in the United States. When he was president, George Bush asserted that class is "for European democracies or something else—it isn't for the United States of America. We are not going to be divided by class." One social analyst noted that "coming from the lips of a . . . tennis-playing, fly-fishing, quail-hunting, Skull and Bones Yalie [who] is by all accounts . . . a millionaire many times over on his own but also the son of a U.S. Senator and married into money . . . is proof that an American class system does exist."[7]

The source of the attitude expressed by Bush is rooted in the everyday dominant discourse that conceals the class nature of American society. Americans are exposed to, and come to firmly believe, pluralistic ideas about equality and opportunity. These ideas are derived from our most important national documents, including the

Declaration of Independence and the U.S. Constitution: America is the land of opportunity. All men [sic] are created equal. We all enjoy equality of opportunity. These slogans, and others like them, are embedded in the dominant ideologies to such an extent that, as the author of a book on American social class noted, "Although most Americans sense that they live within an extremely complicated system of social classes and suspect that much of what is thought and done here is prompted by considerations of [class], the subject has remained murky. And always touchy. You can outrage people today simply by mentioning social class.[8] One sociologist has called class "America's forbidden thought"; another claims that "classlessness [has] become part of America's official ideology."[9]

Despite the rhetoric and denials about class in American society, compelling evidence shows that there are layers of social classes that are unequal with regard to wealth, income, power, and prestige. The box on this page details some of that evidence.

Do We Have Social Classes In America? Myth And Reality

Consider these social-economic conditions for the poor:

1. The official poverty rate for all citizens in 1998 was 14.1%, nearly 35 million Americans. Between 35% and 40% of African Americans and Hispanics live below the poverty line. Two-thirds (66%) of poor Americans are white.

2. Nearly 20% of full-time workers are impoverished. They are what is called "the working poor." Their wages are so low that their earnings do not raise them above the poverty line (In 1998 that line was $15,835 for a family of four).

3. In 1998 the income for the average poor family was $4,000 *below* the poverty line. More Americans live in poverty now than did in any year since 1962. The average poor family now falls further below the poverty line than at any time since 1963.

4. Fifty-two percent of children living in a family headed by a woman live below the poverty line.

5. In 1998 household income for the lowest one-fifth of families was 60% below that of middle-income families, and household income of middle-income families was 70% below that of the top one-fifth of families.

6. In 1998 average household income of the lowest one-fifth of families was $13,226, $32,688 for middle-income families, and $108,824 for the top one-fifth of families.

On the other hand, consider these socioeconomic conditions for the rich:

1. The top 1% of wealth holders control 40% of total household wealth. They own 20% of all real estate and 80% of family-owned trusts. The top 10% of American households control approximately 71% of individual and family wealth.

2. Close to 50% of publicly held stock, as well as about 80% of bonds, are concentrated in the hands of the richest 1% of the population. The bottom 80% of households own less than 2% of the total value of these assets.

3. The major economic fact of the 1980s and '90s is that the gap between the rich and the poor *widened dramatically.* The percentage of U.S. family *income* in the hands of the top 5% was 16% in 1977; in 1998, it was 22%! The U.S. leads all other major industrial countries in the gap dividing the upper fifth of the population from the lower fifth.

4. In 1998 the average net worth of members of the *Forbes* magazine's 400 wealthiest Americans exceeded $1 billion.

Reasons for the muted class consciousness by Americans have been the subject of much speculation and research.[10] A persisting question for social scientists has been who benefits from the existing silenced class consciousness. Some of the responses that have been generated to this question are as follows: it conceals the privileges and dominance that the dominant social alliance enjoys; it prevents the working and middle classes from forming an accurate understanding about existing unequal and unjust social conditions; it prevents the working class and middle class from realizing that the dominant class has a class interest and behaves mostly on behalf of those class interests to the detriment of the other classes; it makes it difficult for working classes to organize on behalf of their interests; and, finally, it conceals the blatant discrimination that sustains it (e.g., exploitation in the workplace, unequal taxation, unequal health care, unequal education). These responses illustrate quite clearly that it is the capitalist class, the dominant alliance, that is the beneficiary of silencing class consciousness.

Studies of social class in the United States convincingly demonstrate that during the past 150 years, class struggle by workers has consistently been crushed by the power of the capitalist class and the enormous resources it commands. In the face of this overwhelming power, and even though working Americans know deep down that classes exist, they have been unable to construct a public discourse that foregrounds class as a key concept in understanding American social life.[11]

The awesome power of capital has also been accompanied by a systematic and consistent ideological discourse designed to advance pluralistic imagery and convince Americans that considerations of class are irrelevant. Corporate advertising continually suggests that owners, managers, and workers are all part of one big team with no social distinctions; witness the Ford Motor Company commercials showing assembly-line workers, engineers, and managers seemingly working together and its slogan: "Quality is job 1."

The effectiveness of this combination of power and persuasion in stifling class consciousness in the general population is seen in the absence of a viable political party that stands for working-class interests, the absence of any major newspapers and magazines representing working-class interests, a general hostility toward union organization, and a relatively small, disunited union movement (in 1998 only 11 percent of private-sector workers, and 15 percent of workers overall, were union members).[12]

Consequences of Class Stratification

Wherever class stratification exists, institutional barriers are created by those in power to ensure that unequal access to resources and rewards is maintained. For example, not only do members of the capitalist class have more property, income, and wealth than do other class groups, but they also are able to reproduce this inequality from one generation to the next through such means as inheritance and education.

Class stratification is also perpetuated through a widespread ideology that makes class inequality seem appropriate and reasonable. One of the basic tenets of capitalism is that individuals receive economic and social benefits commensurate with their talents and efforts. The fundamental precept of this ideology is grounded in the pluralistic notion of equality of opportunity. The logic of this ideology and its sequence of consequences is shown in the box on page 43.

As the box illustrates, persons who possess wealth and power are considered to deserve their privileged status because they have a wide range of talents and positive characteristics, and they have worked hard, have sacrificed, and were dedicated, whereas those of

Ideology of Equality of Opportunity in the United States

Major Premise:

Opportunity for economic advancement based on hard work is equally available for all citizens (popularized in the "equal opportunity for all" slogan). Two deductions follow from this.

1. Individuals are personally responsible for their own economic fate: where one winds up in the distribution of economic rewards depends on the effort one puts into acquiring and applying the necessary skills and attitudes and on the natural talent with which one begins.

2. Because individual outcomes are proportional to individual talent and effort, the resulting rewards are fair and equitable.

Therefore:

— Those who are rich *deserve their wealth and status.*

— Those who are not rich have *only themselves to blame.*

Result:

Social class inequality is viewed as natural, not a product of ideology. The poor are blamed for their economic condition. And the poor tend to blame themselves because they have been socialized to the dominant ideology.

lower status deserve to be there because they possess inferior traits and habits. Thus, those who possess a disproportionate amount of the nation's wealth, income, and power are believed to deserve it because they earned what they have, while the poor deserve their condition because they do not have the requisite talents and/or they are lazy and do not work hard.

A 1994 *New York Times*/CBS News poll found that more Americans think the poor are poor because of a lack of effort than because of circumstances beyond their control. In other words, "It is the moral fabric of individuals, not the social and economic structure of society, that is taken to be the root of the problem."[13] The consequence is that an ideology that justifies economic inequality has come to be widely accepted by those who are the major beneficiaries of the class system, but it has even come to be believed by the poor who are oppressed by it, thus illustrating that the effectiveness of hegemonic ideology depends on the consent of the oppressed to submit to their own domination.

Of course the very idea of equality of opportunity is meaningless unless there is a corresponding "equality of conditions." Unfortunately, equality of conditions does not exist in American society. There are enormous variations in social conditions. For example, family socioeconomic conditions and overall social milieu among social classes contours the opportunities that one will actually have. By the nature of their respective location within the socioeconomic order, people in the different social classes have quite different opportunities.

Class Stratification and Sport

Sport and physical recreation in the United States are shaped by structures of social inequality. Class stratification in sport is particularly manifested in terms of patronage, access, control, and social mobility. Employing the historical sensitivity embodied in Mills's sociological imagination is helpful for examining these manifestations of class stratification in sport.

Social Class Patronage

The socioeconomic elite have always been prominent figures in sport. Patronage in sport, as in fashion, has generally trickled down from the upper to the lower classes. Indeed, patronage of the upper class was responsible for the creation and promotion of a number of American sports. For example, America's national pastime, baseball, when its rules were first codified around the mid-19th century, was played primarily in "gentlemen's clubs" made up of men of wealth or professional standing. According to one sport historian, the first of these baseball clubs, the Knickerbockers of New York, was "primarily a social club with a distinctly exclusive flavor—somewhat similar to what country clubs represented in the 1920s and 1930s, before they became popular with the middle class in general. . . . To the Knickerbockers a ball game was a vehicle for genteel amateur recreation and polite social intercourse rather than a hard-fought contest for victory."[14]

American football got its early start and achieved its initial popularity in the elite private colleges of the Northeast (e.g., Princeton, Harvard, Yale). Students of these colleges were overwhelmingly from wealthy families. Basketball originated at the YMCA Training School, a private college (now Springfield College), and initially became popular at exclusive women's colleges in New England (e.g., Smith, Vassar, Wellesley).

Exceptions to this pattern of patronage do exist, of course, but many modern sports have a social-class linkage with the upper classes of the past.

Social Class and Access to Sport

Historically and at the present time, access to sport is evident in the time and material resources needed to engage in many sports and in various formal and informal restrictions to participation. Persons in the upper class have tended to play sports more often because they have the leisure time and the money to engage in such "nonproductive" activities. Thorstein Veblen, a social theorist influential at the beginning of the 20th century, advanced the idea that those in what he referred to as the "leisure class" engaged in sport as a means of conspicuously displaying their wealth and status; in other words, social elites could flaunt themselves by lavishing time and money on sport.[15]

At the other extreme, historically, members of the working class devoted so much time to their labor that little time or energy was left for leisure activities. And lack of money limited their sport involvement as well. This situation has improved somewhat over time—today's working class has more "nonwork" time and more discretionary money than did workers in previous generations—but these developments for the working class have certainly not eliminated the inequities in access to sport. As a matter of fact, a new trend has emerged that makes access of sport and physical recreation more restricted. Leisure time has actually been declining over the past 25 years. According to one estimate, workers are now on the job 163 hours per year longer than they were in 1970; that is the equivalent of an extra month a year.[16]

Although sport is no longer an exclusive privilege of the affluent, it is far from being a democratized, universal activity. Involvement in various sports is not distributed evenly among the social classes. Research has consistently found a strong relationship between socioeconomic status and sport and physical recreation involvement—the higher the socioeconomic status, the greater the sport involvement.[17] Moreover, in 1998 about 36.5 million Americans (about 14 percent of the population) were living below the poverty line. For both the poor and the homeless—growing segments of the population—lack of resources and the unavailability of teams, equipment, or facilities make access to organized sport almost nonexistent.

Barriers to Sport Participation

Wealthy and powerful groups have traditionally restricted access to "their" sports. The majority of urban sporting clubs and country clubs during the latter 19th century were upper-middle-class institutions operated by and for members of the urban socially elite class. A common mechanism of control at sports and country clubs has been steep membership fees and rules requiring that new members be approved by election, thus creating both economic and social barriers to access. One sport historian noted that this pattern was set in place more than 100 years ago: "The first American country club, Brookline, opened in 1882 as a center for Boston's elite in polo, [horse] racing, and the hunt. Soon it added golf links, making available to its

© Terry Wild Studio

Basketball is called the "city game" because the cement and asphalt city playgrounds provide inexpensive sport for millions of poor American youth. It is also the sport that many inner-city youth believe can raise them from proverty to wealth.

© Terry Wild Studio

A mainstay of social class exclusivity, golf requires several hours to play, expensive equipment, and costly green fees. Until rather recently golf has been associated with socially elite country clubs, who tightly restrict membership to only the " right people."

aristocratic membership yet another sport whose expense barred it from the common citizen."[18]

Restricted access and class inequalities are widespread in many current professional and elite amateur sports because of the enormous amounts of money needed for quality competitive experiences and coaching. To use polo as an example, the expense of outfitting a player with a string of trained horses and equipment costs $70,000 or more, plus additional thousands of dollars for daily care in and out of the polo season. As one writer observed, "That polo's reputation as snobby is a given. After all, Ralph Lauren never considered naming his pricey line *Bowling* or *Softball.*"[19]

It is almost impossible to become a professional athlete in golf or tennis without years of private instruction and access to country clubs and national tournaments. Working-class families simply cannot provide the financial support for their children to excel in such sports.

Elite national- and international-level gymnasts, swimmers, figure skaters, and skiers (to name a few sports) must have years of private instruction—in fact, many athletes move far from home to get the best coaching—to acquire the skills and experience necessary to achieve elite standing. In her book about elite gymnasts and figure skaters, investigative reporter Joan Ryan said that the training expenses for a top figure skater can run $75,000 per year and $30,000 per year for a top gymnast.[20] With expenses like these, it is quite obvious that social-class status excludes all but the reasonably affluent.

Even public high school athletics are becoming more difficult to participate in for students from low-income families. Two trends are responsible. The first is the "pay-for-play" system that is growing rapidly throughout the nation. In this system, high schools assess fees that must be paid by all athletes. Although most school districts make exceptions for athletes from poor families, the embarrassment of having to request this exemption discourages many students from going out for the sports teams.

The second trend is the growing practice of high school coaches demanding that their athletes enroll in several sport camps each year to improve their caliber of play. A weeklong camp can cost as much as $200. Again, many high school students from low-income homes simply cannot afford the camps. Even when waivers of payment are available, students are often too embarrassed to seek them.

Untold numbers of students from low-income homes opt out of high school sports because of their socioeconomic circumstances. Meanwhile, high school students from middle- and upper-class families are overrepresented in interscholastic athletics.[21]

Barriers to sport involvement are weaker for some sports. Sports like boxing, wrestling, and stock car racing have traditional working-class cultural linkages and have maintained their ties to that social class. Basketball, though it originated in an American college and received its early promotion in higher education, has become a "city game." The inner city has become a training ground, especially for poor African American youth, for the upper reaches of basketball competition—colleges and the National Basketball Association. So some opportunities and resources do exist for working-class achievement at the highest levels in a few popular sports.

Social Class and Sport Consumers

Contemporary sport is highly commercialized, and, like all commercial enterprises, it depends on consumers to purchase its product. In sport, consumers are called spectators, and they fall into two categories: those who attend a contest and those who see or hear it broadcast. Seeing a professional or collegiate sports event in person can be expensive, given the cost of tickets and related expenses (as much as $200 for a family of four); consequently, there is a strong relationship between sport attendance and social class, and those with higher incomes are much more likely to attend. Corporate-owned tickets, which in some professional sports venues constitute more than 50 percent of the season tickets, are typically used by upper management and executives for their entertainment. Surveys of attendance at the annual Super Bowl indicate that about 80 percent of the fans are executives, managers, sales representatives, or professionals.[22]

Commercial network television is ostensibly free, but advertising costs are passed on to consumers in higher prices for products that are advertised. Such costs will have a greater proportional impact on the household expenditures of working-class people than affluent television viewers. Cable television broadcasts the majority of sports events, and cable fees are often too expensive for many low-income viewers. Furthermore, with the increase in pay-for-view sporting events, lower-income viewers are able to see fewer and fewer of the premier sporting events.

Social Class and Control of Sport

Control of sport is unequally distributed among the social classes, and it in fact almost totally resides in the wealthy and powerful social groups. Owners of professional sport teams are among the wealthiest people in the United States. Each year the richest 400 people in America are identified and profiled in *Forbes* magazine; invariably, 20 to 30 of them are professional team sport owners. (The topic of professional sports is examined in detail in chapter 9.)

The Amateur Athletic Union (AAU) controlled and dominated amateur athletics from the latter 19th century until the 1960s, when the U.S. Olympic Committee and its sport federations seized the control of amateur sports. Both organizations have been and continue to be overwhelmingly associated with American wealth and power. The linkages between the AAU, the U.S. Olympic movement, and social elitism is illustrated through two men who played prominent roles in both organizations—Casper Whitney and Avery Brundage. Whitney was a wealthy editor of one of the most popular sporting magazines in the latter 19th and early 20th centuries. Through his magazine and through his upper-class social standing, he was a powerful influence in the promotion of amateur sport and an advocate of both the AAU and the U.S. Olympic movement. Brundage, although born into a working-class family, participated in the 1912 Olympic Games and became a millionaire rather early in his business career. He parlayed his Olympic experience and his upper-class social status into two important positions in American amateur sport: president of the AAU and president of the U.S. Olympic committee (he was also president of the International Olympic Committee from 1952 to 1972).

The system of amateur athletics has also been a means of controlling working-class participation in sport, for amateurism (participation without financial remuneration and for social, emotional, or personal satisfaction) is a product of the 19th-century aristocratic class that established rules and social arrangements that were exclusionary and based on social class; in effect it created sport segregation, with white, upper-class males firmly in control. Although contemporary sport appears to be more democratized than in previous generations, several studies have demonstrated a continued relationship between high socioeconomic status and authority and control of amateur sport organizations.

Despite some apparent improvements, there has been no significant reduction of control over sport organizations and policies on the part of the upper echelon; class inequities remain large. Furthermore, when the level of class stratification is narrowed to an analysis within sport itself, inequalities of control are glaring. Professional athletes, the equivalent of the working class in sport—although they earn huge salaries—have very little significant control over any aspects of the sport they play. (This point will be discussed in detail in chapter 9.) The same is true for intercollegiate athletes; they are powerless. All the power in intercollegiate athletics is vested in the separate colleges and in the National Collegiate Athletic Association (NCAA) and the National Association of Intercollegiate Athletics (NAIA). I shall discuss this more fully in chapter 10.

Social Mobility Through Sport

An important issue in class stratification is the extent to which, and how, social mobility—meaning movement from one social class to another—occurs in the United States. One of the most deep-seated beliefs among Americans is that this country is dedicated to the ideal of a pluralistic, egalitarian, and socially mobile society in which everyone can reach the top. As previously noted, one of America's basic cultural creeds is equality of opportunity, which is reinforced by rags-to-riches stories about Americans born into poverty who worked hard, saved their money, and rose through sheer initiative and effort to positions of social, economic, and occupational importance.

The actual empirical evidence about social mobility shows that upward mobility is much more limited than American slogans and folklore suggest. Moreover, most of the upward mobility that does occur is short range in nature (rarely from lower class to upper class). There is also downward mobility; indeed, nearly 20 percent of Americans are downwardly mobile each generation. Finally, throughout the 1990s, the United States has had the largest gap between rich and poor of any major industrialized nation.[23]

The dominant American ideology, functioning through slogans, symbols, and notions about equality of opportunity and rags to riches, has been incorporated into a work-ethic orientation toward social mobility. The essence of this orientation is that individuals are responsible for their own fates and that each person who wants to get ahead can do so. All that is necessary is hard work, sacrifice, and dedication to one's job. Accordingly, those who do not apply themselves diligently, do not work hard, so the message goes, and are not successful in material terms have only themselves to blame.

It has often been claimed that sport serves as an avenue of upward social mobility in American society. But does it? The substantial body of literature on the topic is of two types. The first is largely polemical and impressionistic and claims that sport pulls many young people upward in socioeconomic standing. One form of evidence for this claim consists of testimonials from former athletes that sport taught them skills and values that also brought success in the occupational world, resulting in achievements that would not otherwise have occurred. A variation of this consists of accounts of present or former athletes from lower-class social backgrounds who are now successful and wealthy, the implication being that their sport experiences are responsible for their social mobility.

The second type of argument about sport's ability to bring about upward social mobility takes a more skeptical, empirical view. The focus is on the extent to which sport career opportunities are actually available and on an individual's likelihood of securing one of these positions. In reality, there are extremely few professional sport career opportunities. Fewer than 4,000 jobs exist for male athletes in professional sports, and there are some 66,500,000 males who are employed in the U.S. workforce. Thus, professional male athletes make up about one per 16,625 workers in the American workforce! Sport sociologist Wilbert Leonard has calculated the odds and probabilities of males advancing from high school to college to professional sports in the major U.S. team sports. Overall, only about 5 percent of high school athletes in these sports play at the collegiate level, 3 percent of the collegiate athletes play these sports at the professional level, and *two-tenths of 1 percent* of high school athletes make it to the professional sport level (see table 3.1).[24] The chances of becoming a professional athlete are even smaller for female athletes because there are so few women's professional sports. So the potential for sport to directly provide social mobility for significant numbers of Americans is largely imaginary.

It is true that participation in high school sports may facilitate social mobility for some athletes. High school athletes from poor socioeconomic backgrounds sometimes are awarded athletic scholarships, enabling them to acquire a college education that would have been unlikely without the scholarship. A college degree can open up high-paying careers that would otherwise be out of the reach of the young man or woman from a poor family.

Table 3.1

Approximate Numbers and Probabilities of Males Advancing From One Level of Sport to Another, C. 1995

	# players in high school	Players advancing from HS to college (%)	# players in college	Players advancing from college to profess-ional (%)	# players in professional sport	Players advancing from HS to professional (%)	Avg. pro career * (years)
Football	928,134	.06	51,162	.03	1,400	.002	4-5
Basketball	530,068	.03	13,365	.03	405	.001	4-6
Baseball	438,846	.05	22,575	.03	700	.002	4-7
Ice Hockey	22,032	.16	3,527	.18	650	.03	4-7
Total	1,919,080	.05	90,629	.03	3,155	.002	4-7

Sources: National Collegiate Athletic Association data; National Federation of State High School Associations data, 1994.

* Average career figures can be deceptive because short careers (those of only a few years) are much more common than long careers (those of eight years or more).

Adapted with permission from W. M. Leonard II, 1996, "The Odds of Transiting From One Level of Sports Participation to Another," *Sociology of Sport Journal*, 13 (3): 292.

Two points need to be remembered: First, many high school athletes come from reasonably affluent socioeconomic backgrounds and would have attended college even without an athletic scholarship. Second, only about 5 percent of high school athletes are talented enough to play intercollegiate athletics, so while the claim that high school sport participation is a means of upward social mobility contains a grain of truth, the small truth tends to obscure the greater reality of how few athletes this is in relation to the total number of high school students.[25] Social mobility through sports, in terms of a significant, measurable rise in social class status of large numbers of athletes, is more illusionary than real.

The overall effect of the few athletes who do become professional athletes reproduces the belief system among the general public that the American social class system is more open to social mobility than it really is. Because the few rags-to-riches athletes are made so visible, the social mobility theme is maintained. This reflects the opportunity structure of American society in general—the success of a few reproduces the belief in widespread social mobility among the many.

Social Mobility Through Sport and Dominant Ideology

Dominant cultural ideology is the social cement that tends to bind and preserve ideological unity within an entire society. And it needs to be confirmed, or at least apparently confirmed, by a range of real experiences. Despite the limited extent of actual social mobility through sport, sport, more than almost any other American cultural practice, is one of the most powerful contributors to the hegemonic ideology of the openness of American society and its meritocratic social order based on hard work.

Natural ability, self-discipline, hard work, dedication, and sacrifice are all used to explain variations in material success in the American occupational structure. These same attributes are used as explanations for sporting achievements. The so-called work ethic, especially, is viewed as accounting for variations in income in the marketplace. In sport, too, the work ethic is seen as legitimating achievements and outcomes in sports (popular locker-room slogans: "Winners Are Workers," "Success Is 99 Percent Perspiration and 1 Percent Inspiration"). Coaches often refer to their best performing athletes as "hard workers."

Because organized sport in the United States is meritocratic—that is, superior performance and winning brings status and rewards—it provides convincing symbolic support for the hegemonic ideology that ambitious, dedicated, hardworking individuals, regardless of social origins, can achieve success and ascend in the social hierarchy, obtaining high status and material rewards. On the other hand, those athletes and teams who do not strive in the accepted ways, and do not achieve sporting success, are considered losers and are ridiculed ("Lose Is a Four-Letter Word," "Losing Is for Losers"). They are considered to have not worked hard enough and therefore are not dedicated, or are simply inadequate, and get what they deserve. The ideological content, then, of sport closely parallels the hegemonic ideology in American society toward economic inequality.

Sport has many virtues, but one of its consequences is to legitimize and reproduce the ideology about social class inequality in American society and social mobility based on effort. There is a correspondence between the ideologies of the economic and sport worlds. This is derived from sports' existence as a "dramatic life world," where the values of American society are highlighted, reaffirmed, and reproduced in a different human context.

Summary and Preview

A persisting feature of all modern societies is that they are stratified along a variety of categorical lines. One of the most prominent and pervasive forms of American stratification is social class. The system of patterned social inequality in the distribution of material rewards is referred to as the social class structure.

Despite American folklore's premise that the United States is a classless society, even a cursory analysis of American society shows clearly that it is not. American sport is shaped by social class stratification in terms of patronage, access, control, and social mobility.

The next chapter will focus on another structured form of social inequality—gender. Gender ideology and its consequences will be examined. The connections between gender inequality in the larger American society and in American sport will then be analyzed.

Suggested Readings

Allen, Michael P. *The Founding Fortunes: A New Anatomy of the Super-Rich Families.* New York: Dutton, 1987.

Bina, Cyrus, Laurie M. Clements, and Chuck Davis, eds. *Beyond Survival: Wage Labor in the Late Twentieth Century.* Armonk, NY: M.E. Sharpe, 1996.

Burke, Martin J. *The Conundrum of Class: Public Discourse on the Social Order in America.* Chicago: University of Chicago Press, 1995.

Chow, Esther Ngan-Ling, Doris Wilkerson, and Maxine Baca Zinn, eds. *Race, Class, and Gender: Common Bonds, Different Voices.* Thousand Oaks, CA: Sage, 1996.

Danziger, Sheldon, and Peter Gottschalk. *America Unequal.* Cambridge: Harvard University Press, 1996.

DeMott, Benjamin. *The Imperial Middle: Why Americans Can't Think Straight About Class.* New York: Morrow, 1990.

Domhoff, G. William. *The Power Elite and the State: How Policy Is Made in America.* New York: Aldine de Gruyter, 1990.

Ehrenreich, Barbara. *Fear of Falling: The Inner Life of the Middle Class.* New York: Pantheon Books, 1989.

Grimes, Michael D. *Class in Twentieth-Century American Sociology.* New York: Praeger, 1991.

Kalra, Paul. *The American Class System: Divide and Rule.* Pleasant Hill, CA: Antenna Publishing, 1995.

Leonard, Wilbert M, II. "The Odds of Transiting From One Level of Sports Participation to Another." *Sociology of Sport Journal* 13, no. 3 (1996): 288-99.

Nelson, Joel I. *Post-Industrial Capitalism: Exploring Economic Inequality in America.* Thousand Oaks, CA: Sage, 1995.

Schwarz, John E., and Thomas J. Volgy. *The Forgotten Americans: Thirty Million Working Poor in the Land of Opportunity.* New York: Norton, 1992.

Vanneman, Reeve, and Lynn W. Cannon. *The American Perception of Class.* Philadelphia: Temple University Press, 1987.

Wolff, Edward. *Top Heavy: A Study of Increasing Inequality of Wealth in America.* New York: The Twentieth Century Fund, 1995.

Chapter 4

Structures of Social Inequality: Gender Inequality in Sport

Women's presence in weight rooms and gyms, like women's presence in boardrooms and bars, is subtly and insistently challenging men to see women as peers, and to adapt their playing style to what women want and need. . . . Sports participation has given millions of women new self-confidence and has taken them to where they never were before—onto what used to be male turf.

Mariah Burton Nelson, lecturer and writer on American sports

Some social scientists have attempted to explain gender stratification in the United States primarily in terms of social class, but gender stratification cannot be understood simply in terms of social class divisions because gender inequalities are historically more deeply rooted than are social class structures. Furthermore, although women's work—in the home and in the workplace—does play a pivotal role in the social class system, class divisions clearly interlock and overlap with other forms of gender oppression and injustice. This latter perspective offers a more fruitful framework for analyzing gender inequality. So in this chapter—and throughout this book—gender inequality is approached from a multifaceted analytical framework.

A variety of theoretical frameworks for analyzing social inequality are found in the social science literature because the study of social inequality has been of central interest in the social sciences. In this and the following chapter, ideas are borrowed from several of these positions, but the main focus is on distributive and relational analysis. In the former, the focus is on material and symbolic social structural factors as they relate to opportunities and rewards (such as income, property, status, opportunities to participate in sport, for example) available or unavailable to entire categories of people (females, in this chapter); this approach is concerned with who gets what, and why.

Relational analysis is concerned with the social relations among and between people and their social contexts, and the focus centers on issues of dominance and control over the social agenda. A fundamental assumption of relational analysis is that social relations are historically produced, socially constructed, and culturally defined to serve the interests and needs of dominant groups in society. When relational analysis is applied to gender inequalities, the focus centers on historically produced, socially constructed, and culturally defined social relations and social contexts that promote, reinforce, and reproduce gender oppression and injustice.[1]

A great deal of controversy exists in the biological and social sciences about the appropriate use of *sex* and *gender*. It has been customary to restrict the use of the word *sex* to individual biological maleness or femaleness and the word *gender* to social characteristics that are associated with each sex. In recent years, however, there has been a trend to use sex and gender interchangeably because the biological aspects of sex may interact with the social aspects of gender, and it is difficult to distinguish between the two. In this chapter, I use the word gender mostly without any assumption that gender results from socialization and sex implies only biological features.

Patriarchy and Gender Relations

Social relations are largely based on and sustained by shared ideological principles. As with ideology that legitimates social class inequality, gender inequality is sustained and perpetuated by a stable ideology known as patriarchy. Patriarchy is a structured and ideological system of personal relationships that legitimate male power over women and the services they provide. Figure 4.1 illustrates the social dynamics of the system of gender inequality. The following sections will clarify the various components of this figure.

The history of western civilization is a long, persistent patriarchal story, and one of its pillars is that gender relations are determined by "human nature." Aristotle, considered by many as one of western civilization's most enlightened philosophers, wrote: "The male is by nature superior, and the female inferior; and one rules and the other

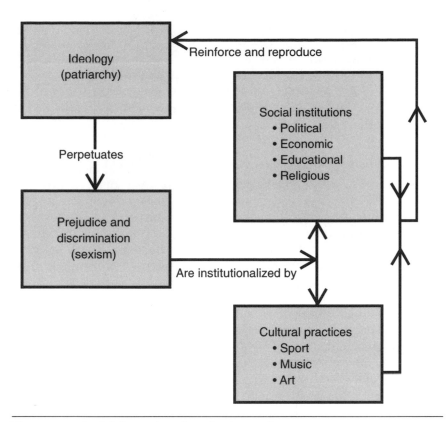

Figure 4.1   Social dynamics of gender inequality.

is ruled." Even Christian theologians advanced a patriarchal ideology. St. Thomas Aquinas wrote: "The woman is subject to the man on account of the weakness of her nature, both of mind and body. . . . Woman is in subjection according to the law of nature."[2] The framers of the American Declaration of Independence wrote that "all men are created equal." There is no reference to women anywhere in the document.

Patriarchy is also a social and economic arrangement whose material basis is men's control over the major social institutions and over women's labor power, fertility, and sexuality. As such, it has been the ideological nucleus of women's oppression. A patriarchal society is driven by a male-centered ideology rooted in a male worldview; mainstream thought is male-stream thought.

Although the history of human societies is a patriarchal story, there has been considerable variation in the degree and nature of male superiority and dominance. Men everywhere have some authority over women, and they have a culturally sanctioned right to women's servitude and compliance. Private patriarchy is found in male domination and female oppression in interpersonal relations, especially within the family but also in informal interpersonal relations (e.g., dating, sex). Public patriarchy exists in male domination and exploitation of females in social institutions and cultural practices of the larger society, such as the economy, education, politics, mass media, the arts, and entertainment.

Sectors of Gender Inequality in American Society

Every American is immersed in a complex network of gender relations that are socially constructed under historically specific conditions, and they structure social relations between males and females. As expectations about gender relationships are communicated by various means, they continue to produce people who tend to conform to their socialized concepts of masculinity and femininity, which in turn has historically reinforced the patriarchal culture.

Traditional American gender relationships for females have emphasized passive, nurturing, and dependent behaviors, whereas traditional expectations for males have accentuated individual achievement, aggressiveness, and independence. Women as mothers, nurses, and teachers, and men as soldiers, physicians, and politicians, are social manifestations of these gender images.

Our images of "appropriate" gender relations have far-reaching consequences for both males and females as well as society at large; the differentiation values males and females in a way that has historically made females unequal in wealth, power, prestige, and presumed worth in relation to males. Furthermore, males have more dominant positions in the control of both their personal lives and their social activities. A recent Gallup Poll found that 73 percent of men and women believe that American society generally favors men over women.[3]

Gender Inequality in the Workplace

Occupations are one of the major locations within which the gender order is actively and repeatedly reinforced and reproduced. Gender inequality is obvious in the U.S. labor market. It is not that women are excluded from the workplace; indeed, about 59 percent of women 18 years and older hold paid jobs outside the home, up from 39 percent in 1965 (see figure 4.2).

The combination of patriarchy and capitalism makes gender inequality pervasive. With some exceptions, women fill the lower ranks while men occupy the prestigious and decision-making positions in

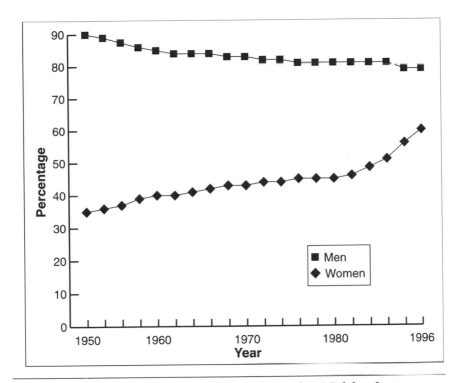

Figure 4.2   Women and men (age 18 and older) in the U.S. labor force.

the labor force. Indeed, more than one-third of all employed women work in clerical jobs. Of the 400 to 500 job categories in the United States, men are distributed throughout most of the occupational hierarchy, whereas 72 percent of female workers are ghettoized in about 30 female-dominated and poorly paid occupations.[4] White men make up only 29 percent of the labor force, but they hold 97 percent of senior management (vice president and above) positions. Women hold only 2 percent of the powerful positions in *Fortune* 500 companies, and they hold only 10 percent of the seats on boards of directors in the country's top 1,000 companies.[5]

The average wage of employed women is still below that of men, although the gap has been narrowing in the past decade. In 1998 the average earnings for white women working full time, year-round were 75 percent of white men's earnings; African American women's earnings were 64 percent of white men's earnings and 88 percent of African American men's earnings; and Hispanic women's earnings were 53 percent of white men's earnings and 89 percent of Hispanic men's earnings. Even within the same occupational categories, women earn less than men for comparable jobs and find fewer opportunities for advancement than do men. Female college graduates working full time have earnings approximately equal to those of male high school dropouts.[6]

The consequence of these various occupational conditions is male control over the production and distribution of goods and services, assuring men of control over economic wealth and power, whereas females' career and occupational outlets typically rank low in income, power, and prestige. The interaction and overlapping between class stratification and gender inequality are clear, especially when one realizes that more than 8 million women with children under 18 years of age are heads of household and thus the main source of household income.

Gender Inequality in Politics and Religion

Women are greatly underrepresented at all levels of government and religion. In 1997, women held just 11.7 percent of the seats in the U.S. House of Representatives and 9 percent of the seats in the Senate, ranking the United States 24th of 54 western democracies in terms of women's representation in national legislatures. Women occupy only 21.5 percent of the nation's state legislative seats, and less than 10 percent of the state governors and city mayors are women.

Most religious organizations reflect male supremacy in their hierarchical structures. Indeed, many have policies denying women access to esteemed and powerful positions in the clergy.[7]

Gender Inequality in Education

From 70 percent to 74 percent of the nation's classroom teachers are women, but less than 3 percent of the school superintendents are women; 85 percent of elementary schoolteachers are women, yet only 39 percent of the elementary and secondary school administrators are women.[8] Clearly, children learn the differential status of men and women, and the patriarchal social order, simply by observing who the leaders are while they are attending school.

During the past 10 years, a substantial body of literature has documented the systematic bias that females face in education from preschool through college. For example, boys receive more of the teachers' attention and recognition than do girls, and analyses of school textbooks demonstrate that traditionally "masculine" activities are emphasized more than "feminine" activities.[9]

Gender Relations in the Home

Gender relations in the public sector are tied to gender roles in the private sector, especially in the family. As wives and mothers, women earn no money for their domestic labor of caring for the needs of their children, husbands, or homes. These roles also carry low societal power and prestige because domestic labor does not produce exchangeable commodities, which are the foundation of wealth, power, and prestige in capitalist societies.

Furthermore, women in the workforce still bear most of the responsibility for housework. The shift to paid employment has not meant a corresponding decline in the number of hours most married women spend in the household economy. Patriarchy's material base is in men's control over women's labor; both in the household and in the labor market, the division of labor benefits men.[10]

Violence as a Form of Gender Inequality

Oppression and injustice that accompany every structure of social inequality are often manifested in violence toward the oppressed group. This has certainly been true in the case of females. Patriarchal culture is a culture of violence against women; domestic violence, sexual harassment, and rape are three of the most common forms. Men have used their superior physical strength and social power against women in the home, and domestic violence is widespread and a common experience of many wives. An estimated 10 million to 12 million women are beaten by their male partners each year, and domestic violence is the leading cause of injury for women age 15 to 44.[11]

Sexual harassment is a second form of violence against women, and it is common in the workplace and in public settings. One study found that seven out of 10 women report sexual harassment during the course of their working lives. In social settings of all kinds, women are frequently the targets of sexually explicit comments, gestures, and unwanted touching by men.[12]

A third type of male violence against women is rape. More than 100,000 forcible rapes were reported in the United States in 1997. It is estimated that as many as five times that many rapes are committed because only a small portion of rapes are actually reported to law enforcement agencies.[13]

Struggles Against Gender Inequality

The consequences of gender relations that privilege men over women are structured social practices that systematically foster the development of men while constraining the development of women. These social practices encompass norms and values that reinforce social relations and attitudes toward women and that legitimize their relative subordinate status. In effect, these practices are an important means by which males control the social relations from which they benefit.

The struggle to redress the injustices of patriarchy in America and expand the rights of women has a long history. Throughout the 19th and early 20th centuries in the United States, women's suffragists gave speeches and organized marches and street demonstrations on behalf of equality and social justice for women. In the late 1960s, a massive women's liberation movement began that remains a significant force in American society. Feminists have pressed for political, economic, and social equality, choice in reproductive decisions, and reform in laws. Focusing on the social and cultural construction of gender differences, and on how the social constructions serve as a constitutive element for all social and political relationships, feminist intellectuals have forced a rethinking and revision of traditional norms, practices, and behaviors with respect to conditions for women.

But feminism is not just about women. It is a fundamental way of approaching issues of power—Who has it? Why? Who benefits and who is harmed?—in society. Feminism has also changed men's lives in profound ways by giving men more possibilities to be nurturing and to reject masculine stereotypes that have restricted their social behavior.

Gender Stratification and Sport

Historically, societies have expected males and females to learn and conform to specific gender roles that were considered appropriate for each sex. Gender, then, is socially constructed; it is not inherited. Various means are used for socializing each generation about gender-role expectations, but the various social institutions (e.g., family, economy, polity) and cultural practices (e.g., media, art, music, literature) are potent sources for teaching and enforcing gender ideology.

Gender differentiation in the United States has been powerfully constructed through sport and the culture of sport. Moreover, organized sport has been a powerful cultural arena for reinforcing the ideology and actuality of male superiority and dominance; its traditions, symbols, and values have tended to preserve patriarchy and women's subordinate position in society.

Although patriarchal ideology is an ancient belief system, its links with the rise of modern sport in the latter 19th century can be seen through two major social movements in the United States that coincided with the rise of organized sport: the American industrial revolution and the cult of masculinity. Conditions for industrialized labor were typically physically harsh and psychologically unpleasant, alienating workers from their work and creating a yearning in workers for recreational outlets. At the same time, modernization in industrial society and lifestyles outside the workplace were transforming traditional means of male expression and identity through tasks that were less independent, assertive, and physically demanding. Many of those occupational tasks could be performed by women. Thus, women's increasing encroachment into the workforce and public life weakened the traditional basis of male dominance in the family and public sector. One consequence of these trends was a growing concern about male identity, a concern that these trends were leading to male effeminacy.

In the face of this concern, the "cult of manliness" arose and had widespread social appeal in the latter 19th and early 20th centuries. As two historians report, "Male dominance owes much to the ideal of manliness . . . [that] became a widely pervasive and inescapable feature of middle class existence in Britain and America. . . . [I]t captured that excessive commitment to physical activity which was an unquestionable feature of . . . male society in Britain and the United States in the second half of the nineteenth century."[14]

Sport was an activity that served two purposes for men during this era: it met their recreational needs, and it was a perfect antidote for their anxieties about effeminacy. Sport's demands for strength, aggressiveness, and displays of courage were congruent with perceptions of masculinity and incongruent with those of femininity. It was through sport activities that manliness, as then defined, was developed, reaffirmed, and reproduced. (I will elaborate on this in chapter 7.) Thus, sport became a popular means for men to reaffirm their masculinity and, hence, a powerful tool for maintaining patriarchal gender relations.

These social conditions made being both a woman and an athlete an anomaly in American life until the early 1970s. Women who participated in competitive sports faced social isolation and censure. By choosing the physically active life, a female was renouncing traditional female gender-role prescriptions. Female athletes did not suit society's ideal of femininity, and those who persisted in sport suffered various aversive sanctions, especially derogation and public ridicule.

Even into the late 1980s, public attitudes supported sport as a male preserve. One analyst articulately enumerated sport's role in advancing male hegemony: Sports "perpetuate patriarchy by reinforcing the sexual division of labor. By giving males exciting opportunities, preaching that the qualities they learn from them are 'masculine,' and preventing girls and women from learning in the same situations, sports confirm the prejudice that males are a breed apart. . . . By publicly celebrating the dramatic achievements of the best males, while marginalizing females as cheerleaders and spectators, they validate the male claim to the important positions in society."[15]

Another writer even argued that sport should be reserved solely for males: "Women should . . . be prohibited from sport: they are the true defenders of the humanist values that emanate from the household, the values of tenderness, nurture and compassion, and this most important role must not be confused by the military and political values inherent in sport. Likewise sport should not be muzzled by humanist values: it is the living arena for the great virtue of manliness."[16]

Shaping Gender Identities and Roles Through Sport

One's gender-role identity and beliefs are molded by a range of social forces, but the earliest and most persistent influence comes from parents, who typically behave differently toward sons and daughters from birth throughout life. The traditional American parental message has been that boys should be aggressive, independent, and achievement oriented, whereas girls should be passive, sociable, nurturing, and dependent.

Traditionally, parents overwhelmingly believed that sports are good training for developing desirable masculine characteristics, for making men out of boys, and for preparing boys for their future occupational life. It is under parental aegis that boys have been encouraged—even forced—into organized competitive sports. Parents have been the primary organizers and promoters of youth sport programs for their sons. At the same time, parents have traditionally discouraged their daughters from organized sports, especially after the girls reached adolescence. It is from experiences like these that children learn that sport is a male preserve. As one sport sociologist noted, "The fact is, boys are, to a greater or lesser extent, judged according to their ability, or lack of ability, in competitive sport."[17]

Gender socialization that begins in the home is extended in the symbols, rituals, and cultural practices that structure the daily life of adolescents. They reinforce and reproduce gender-differentiated identities, perceptions, and cultural visions that begin in the home. High school and college sport programs are testimony to the privilege of boys and men over girls and women.[18]

Because athletic events are the most popular social events of secondary schools and colleges, male athletes enjoy high visibility and prestige. Thus, high school and college sports have traditionally supported the status quo by reproducing images of masculinity and femininity that sustained asymmetrical gender relations in the larger society.

Adolescents are dedicated consumers of the mass media, and social representations, contexts, and descriptions of women in the mass media's sport coverage contribute additional support to the social construction of gender stereotyping and the perpetuation of female inequality. Mass media coverage of females in sport will be discussed more fully in chapter 8.

Early socialization is clearly a powerful force in shaping beliefs about appropriate male and female attitudes, values, and behaviors, and once established, these are resistant to change. Enlightened attitudes and beliefs during the past 20 years have improved social conditions for females. Still, through sport, along with other social practices, male hegemony remains part of our commonsense understanding of the world, legitimating not only inequities in sports but also patriarchal relations generally.[19]

Barriers to Female Access to Sport

Wherever structures of social inequality are found, there are typically norms and practices designed to deny particular groups equal access to and control over the rewards and resources of the social system. Since the latter 19th century, when sport began its rise to public prominence, one of the most persistent and widespread forms of discrimination in American society has been in women's lack of access to sport opportunities. Historically, females have been denied equal opportunity to sport in numerous ways. Not only have their opportunities and rewards been unequal, but their facilities and sport organizations—where they have existed—have been segregated from and inferior to men's. Even today, despite laws designed to provide equity in sport opportunity and improvements in access for females in sport, males still have access to more sport opportunities and public resources. Men continue to control most sport organizations, and numerous inequities remain.

The Olympic Games

The major international sporting event of the 20th century has been the Olympic Games. To participate in the Olympics is the dream of almost everyone who has ever considered herself or himself an athlete. But until 1932, women were all but excluded from taking part in the Games, primarily because the founder of the modern Olympic Games, Baron de Coubertin, opposed what he called the "indecency, ugliness and impropriety" of women in sports because women engaging in strenuous activities were destroying their feminine charm and hastening the downfall and degradation of sport.[20] De Coubertin, and sport leaders throughout the world, fought fiercely against female inroads into the Games.

Although the major barriers to female Olympic competition have gradually been challenged, the remnants of this heritage remain. There are still far fewer events for women than for men in the Olympic Games; at the 1996 Atlanta Summer Games, men competed in 63 more medal events than did women. Women constituted only 29 percent of the total participants at the 1994 Lillehammer Winter Olympic Games, the same percentage as the 1992 Barcelona Summer Games. At the 1996 Atlanta Games, 34 percent of the athletes were females. Of the American athletes who participated in the 1996 Olympics, 58 percent were male while only 42 percent were female; this was, however, the highest percentage of females ever achieved in Olympic Summer Games.[21]

High School and College Sports

Sport inequities for females in high schools and colleges were conspicuous and widespread before the mid-1970s. Several states actually had legislation prohibiting interscholastic sports for girls, and numerous colleges had minimal intercollegiate programs for women. But a veritable revolution in girls' and women's sport participation was unleashed with passage of the Education Amendments Act of 1972. Title IX, a key provision of this act, required, or at least it was widely interpreted as requiring, that educational institutions receiving federal funds must provide equivalent programs for males and females.

Title IX constituted a considerable weapon against sex discrimination in high school and intercollegiate athletics because about 16,000 school districts and more than 2,500 colleges and universities are recipients of federal funds. Within 10 years, the number of female high school athletes jumped from 294,000 to almost 2 million (see table 4.1 for statistics on female and male participants). By 1990, 35 percent of all high school participants were female, and the number of sports available to females had more than doubled.

Before the passage of Title IX, only about 15 percent of college athletes were women, and women's sport programs received only 2 percent of the money colleges spent on athletics. Facilities for female programs were customarily second-rate. The newer and larger gym routinely went to the men and the older gym to the women; where men and women used the same facilities, the women were expected to use them in the off-hours—during mealtimes, early in the morning, or late at night. Finally, the women got cheaper equipment than the men received, and they were expected to keep it longer. In the late 1990s, about 100,000 women competed on intercollegiate sports teams, and NCAA Division IA universities offered 20,000 scholarships to female athletes. Still, for every $1 spent on women's college sports, $3 is spent on men's.

One of the most remarkable transformations of the past generation has been the increased sporting opportunities for females. Sport is no longer an exclusive male domain. Still, gender equity is an ideal yet to be achieved rather than a condition that has been accomplished.

Table 4.1

Sport Participation Among High School Athletes Before and After Title IX

Year	Boy participants	Girl participants
1971	3,666,917	294,015
1979-80	3,517,829	1,750,264
1986-87	3,364,082	1,836,356
1990-91	3,406,355	1,892,316
1995-96	3,634,052	2,367,936

Reprinted with permission from National Federation of State High School Associations, 1996, *National Federation Handbook 1996-97.*

Male-controlled sport organizations only begrudgingly complied with Title IX, many contending that only those programs specifically receiving federal funds were bound by the law. In 1984 the U.S. Supreme Court ruled in the case of *Grove City College v. Bell* that the Title IX language applied only to specific programs or departments that receive federal funds, not to entire institutions. Although the *Grove City* case was not directly about sport, the effect of the Court's decision was to say that women could be denied equality in sports because no athletic programs received federal aid directly.

Within a year of the Court's decision, the Office of Civil Rights suspended 64 investigations, more than half involving college athletics. As one lawyer said, "The discrimination is so apparent, so blatant. Without the support and nourishment of the law, we see how fragile the support to maintain women's athletics really is."[22]

After the *Grove City* decision, various women's groups began to lobby Congress to pass legislation restoring civil rights weakened by the ruling. On March 22, 1988, both houses of Congress overrode President Reagan's veto, and the Civil Rights Restoration Act became law. One of its implications was the restoration of the original broad interpretation of Title IX.

Full compliance with Title IX and the achievement of gender equity in collegiate athletics have yet to be achieved. A 1997 *USA Today* survey found that although women made up more than 50 percent of the undergraduate students, only about one-third were varsity athletes, and female athletes received only 38 percent of the athletic scholarship funds and 25 percent of the operating budgets. The chairwoman of the NCAA's Committee on Women's Athletics said, "It is encouraging to see the increases for women but very discouraging to see that they are not really sharing equally in the money. The men's side of the ledger gets the vast amount of the money."[23]

In the past 10 years, dozens of lawsuits have been brought against universities by individuals and groups seeking gender equity in college sports. In most cases, the individual or groups bringing the charges of discrimination have won.[24] Significant strides have been made toward more equitable opportunities and rewards for high school girls and college women. But there is still room for improvement, and the issue of what constitutes gender equity is still a contentious issue that needs to be settled.

Professional Sports

Historically, professional sport opportunities for women have been severely restricted, and differential rewards the norm, with professional female athletes earning less money and public recognition than men do for their performances. But conditions have changed greatly in the past 20 years. Historically, the most popular professional sports for women have been individual ones, particularly golf and tennis, because they have been socially approved for women, especially among the affluent social classes. In 1978 there were fewer than 100 professional female tennis players and fewer than 100 female golfers; in 1998 there were more than 300 on the professional tours in each sport. Attendance, purses, and national television exposure have increased significantly for the top women's golf and tennis events. For example, in 1997 members of the LPGA tour played for a total purse of $30.2 million in 43 golf events, 31 of which were televised. However, overall, female professionals in both sports earn less than male professionals do for their performance.[25]

Professional sport opportunities for women have diversified greatly in the past two decades. Professional ice skating has provided a chance for a few skaters to make very high incomes; more than 100 women are doing well as jockeys in thoroughbred horse racing; and about 100 female distance runners, triathletes, and mountain bikers are making decent livings in their sports. Opportunities are increasing in professional sports officiating. Both of the women's professional basketball leagues are using female officials, and in the fall of 1997 two females were appointed to officiate in the NBA, a first for the male professional sports leagues.

Professional women's team sports have been less successful in the struggle for public support and acceptance. Professional leagues in softball, volleyball, and basketball have had an off-and-on existence. Three women's professional basketball leagues failed in the 1900s, so for several years top American female basketball players went to Europe and Asia to play in professional leagues.

A new women's professional basketball league, the American Basketball League (ABL), began play in fall 1996. Another league, the Women's National Basketball Association (WNBA), began play in summer 1997. Both leagues had successful first seasons. Building on interest generated from the U.S. women's softball and soccer triumphs in the 1996 Olympic Games, the Women's Professional Fastpitch (WPF) softball league was formed in summer 1997; the National Soccer Alliance is planning a first-ever women's professional soccer league season for 1998.

With the professionalization of the Olympic Games, opportunities have opened up for American Olympians to receive money. Several U.S. sport federations are paying women who train and compete for America's Olympic team.

Male Control in Sport Organizations

Men control sport. Almost every major professional, amateur, and educational sport organization in the United States is under the management and control of men. Despite federal law requiring that secondary schools and colleges treat the sexes equally in their sport programs, those who direct high school and intercollegiate sports have consolidated and entrenched male control. Developments in high school and intercollegiate athletics illustrate this point. Although participation opportunities for high school female athletes have greatly increased, women have lost ground in coaching and athletic administration. For example, in 1973-74 about 90 percent of high school girls' sports were coached by women; in 1988-89 women coached less than 50 percent of the teams in the most popular girls' sports. This situation has changed very little during the 1990s.

A common explanation for the increasing percentages of men coaching high school girls' teams is that males are hired because they are better qualified, with more extensive background in the sports they coach. Although this is sometimes true, it is not always the case. Several studies comparing the characteristics of male and female coaches of girls' high school basketball have found that the female coaches were actually more qualified than were the males.[26]

When Title IX was enacted in 1972, more than 90 percent of women's intercollegiate athletic teams were coached by females. This was the case because men's and women's athletics were administered separately. However, during the 1980s, men's and women's intercollegiate athletics programs were merged at most institutions, and the NCAA and the NAIA became the national governing bodies of all of intercollegiate athletics. Both developments left men in the powerful leadership positions in intercollegiate sports. By 1988, less than half the coaches of women's intercollegiate teams were women; in 1996 only 48 percent of the coaches of women's sports were women.[27] Figure 4.3 illustrates the decline of women coaching women's intercollegiate teams. What appears to have happened is that male hegemony has become one of the most pervasive influences on the hiring patterns of the past 15 years.

Female athletic administrators have been losing out, too. Women's intercollegiate athletic programs in the early 1970s were administered almost exclusively by women with the title of athletic director. Then, as women's programs grew under Title IX, and many colleges combined their men's and women's athletic departments into one, most mergers followed a pattern: after the merger, there was a male athletic director and several assistant directors, one usually a woman in charge of women's athletics or the less visible sports. In a survey of colleges and universities, investigators found that by 1988, 84 percent had placed women's athletic programs under male administrators.

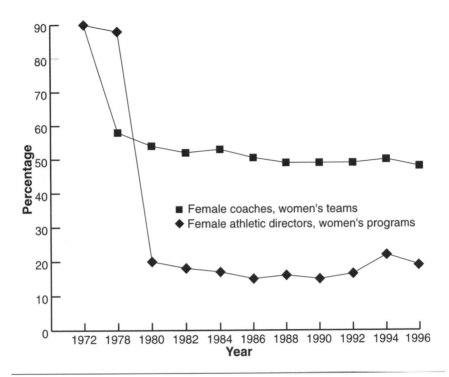

Figure 4.3   Percentage of women's college athletic programs coached or administered by women.

Reprinted with permission from R. Vivian Acosta and Linda J. Carpenter, 1996, "Women in Intercollegiate Sport: A Longitudinal Study—Nineteen Year Update, 1977-1996," (New York: Department of Physical Education, Brooklyn College).

Some 32 percent of all intercollegiate programs for women had no female involved in the administrative structure. In 1996 24 percent of all intercollegiate athletic programs lacked any female administrator, and 81 percent of women's athletic teams were under a male administrator.[28] Figure 4.3 illustrates the decline in the percentage of women running women's athletic programs.

Despite this rather dismal picture, progress is occurring. In 1997 five women—although none are African American or Hispanic— were serving as athletic directors at the nation's 111 NCAA Division IA schools, and the percentage of women in college athletic administration is increasing slowly.

The NCAA and the much smaller NAIA govern all intercollegiate sport. Women have never received equity in leadership in these associations. Over 15 years after the NCAA assumed control of women's collegiate sports, women have less than 38 percent representation on the NCAA Council and only 20 percent to 30 percent on other important NCAA councils and committees. Of the representatives casting institutional votes (each NCAA member institution has a single vote on convention issues) at NCAA conventions, about 95 percent are men.

Leadership in the Olympic movement offers little administrative opportunity for women. In 1997 only seven of the 106 members of the International Olympic Committee were women; one of them was an African American. Women have made little inroad into leadership positions on the U.S. Olympic Committee. In 1997, only about 20 percent of the members of the Board of Directors were women, 17 percent of the Executive Committee members were women, and 25 percent of the committee chairs and vice chairs were women. Few of these are minority women.

It is evident that the proportion of women in leadership and decision-making positions—those with power and influence—in American sport is quite small; far smaller, certainly, than would be expected based on the number of female sport participants. Significant shifts in the balance of gender power in sports is difficult to find.

Unresolved Issues of Gender Inequality in Sport

A great deal of change has occurred in gender relations, access, and distribution of rewards and resources in the world of sport during the past two decades. But a number of important unresolved issues need to be confronted.

Male Sports "Superiority"

One aspect of American sport works as a subtle but potent contributor to male hegemony and thus acts as an indirect weapon against females in sport. America's most popular sports favor achievement based on strength, power, height, and weight—and thus are biased toward biological male traits. Although there is considerable overlap in physical characteristics in the entire male and female populations, at the extremes of the distributions—from which come record-setting, idolized athletes—men are stronger, taller, and heavier. Thus, in sports where these traits are important, women's performance statistics tend to remain below men's. Some writers have argued that sports favoring male biological advantages provide insidious reinforcement for male "natural" superiority because male performance records in such sports appear to provide compelling "natural" evidence for male superiority.[29]

Various sport modifications for women—smaller basketballs, softball instead of baseball, shorter distances in golf, and three set matches in tennis championships instead of the men's five—also subtly promote and reproduce male hegemony. An unfortunate outcome of rule and equipment modifications for females is that some interpret that as confirming the assumption that "of course women are inferior to men." The modifications, then, turn out to confirm the idea of "natural female inferiority" in sports, at least in the eyes of some people.

Sexuality of Female Athletes

One of the most ominous weapons used to discourage women in sport is the claim that sport participation either changes the sexual orientation of females, converting them to lesbians, or attracts females who are lesbians. In either case, female athletes are portrayed as mostly lesbians. Because of the widespread homophobia (meaning fear, dislike, and intolerance of homosexuals) prevailing in American culture, such accusations have a profound stigmatizing effect on female athletes and inhibit some females who might want to become involved in sports. Olympian Jackie Joyner-Kersee describes the motivation behind the accusation: "It's something they do to keep you from playing sports. That's what it's about."[30] By portraying women in sport as lesbians, those who wish to maintain boundaries, with sport as a male domain, feel secure that the sports world "is not being invaded by 'real' women after all."[31]

The claim that sport "lesbianizes" females has been vigorously attacked not only for being totally without scientific evidence but also because of its clear ideological motive of maintaining traditional heterosexual privilege in gender relations. Furthermore, the whole issue of women's and men's sexual orientation is increasingly being viewed as irrelevant to their public lives, and it is becoming increasingly recognized and accepted that gays, lesbians, and bisexuals are a part of every domain of human life. Contemporary women and men are no longer willing to have traditional definitions of "appropriate sexuality" imposed on them, especially when such definitions prevent them from experiencing highly valued social activities. Diversity and difference are accepted; ignorance and narrow-mindedness are rejected.

Several top female professional athletes have openly acknowledged being lesbian in recent years. They have indicated that they will not be locked into outmoded role prescriptions and baseless assertions, especially those that limit their physical potential. Their efforts have helped to promote a dialogue that works toward creating an environment that accepts diversity and difference, while supporting positive identity development for all people.[32]

Male Gender Identity and Sport

Gender inequality, injustice, and issues about sexuality are not exclusive to females. Traditional gender-role prescriptions have caused problems for males as well as for females. Although various social barriers have discouraged females from becoming involved with sport to preserve their feminine identity, images of ideal masculinity have been closely associated with involvement is sport. The competition, physicality, and aggressiveness of sport have made it the perfect representation of traditional masculinity. Indeed, sports are said to "make men out of boys."

Males who are uninterested in sport, or who are unwilling to be forced into sport to fulfill dominant gender definitions of masculinity, often face harassment from both males and females. They are often the target of ridicule about their "effeminacy," and they are labeled "fags," "queers," and "fairies." In some cases, they are physically assaulted.

For males who do become involved in sports, one of the most profound things they learn through the sport culture is masculine sexuality. Uniformly, they learn that heterosexuality is good and is healthy. On the other hand, they learn that homosexuality is detestable. The sports world has often been seen as an arena in which males confirmed their masculinity, their heterosexuality, an arena that "proved" they were not homosexual. As one sport sociologist said, "The extent of homophobia in the sports world is staggering."[33] Even though it is now clear that gay athletes have competed, and continue to compete, at all levels of sport—mostly closeted—the sports world has remained steadfastly homophobic.

In recent years, several male professional and Olympic athletes have "come out" and acknowledged their homosexuality. When Olympic diving champion Greg Louganis revealed he was gay, a number of other gay athletes in other sports revealed they were gay also, illustrating that sport is no different from other sectors of life, despite the stigma about homosexuality in sport culture. A 1996 Associated Press release, carried in newspapers throughout North America, was titled "Sports Poised to End Taboo on Open Gays." That is probably too optimistic, but attitudes have been changing with respect to this issue.

Transforming Sport Culture Through Females in Sport

Female athletes and coaches have gained access to the sports world, but they have been victimized by the system as well. Many of the intercollegiate sports programs for women have become part of the commodified sport industry; that is, they are as commercialized as men's intercollegiate sports. Some of the less attractive aberrations of commercial intercollegiate sports at the big-time level are that female athletes' grades have begun to drift lower, that fewer female athletes are graduating, that eating disorders are rampant, especially in sports like gymnastics and swimming, that a number of athletes have been physically and sexually abused by coaches, and that the meaning of sport has become winning at all costs.[34]

Sport opportunities for girls and women have increased tremendously in recent years—mainly because of court decisions and federal laws—and sport for females is a fast-growing, fast-changing element in American society. But simply furnishing opportunities for equal participation is not enough to produce meaningful social changes. Although there is much to applaud about females gaining the right to participate in what has been an exclusive male preserve, some social analysts are asking, "What have women contributed to transforming sport, humanizing it?"

Women have become a significant voice and presence in sport, but recent observers have noted that when the women's sports movement began some 25 years ago, there seemed to be a serious commitment to exposing the root causes of patriarchy and to trying to formulate alternative sport structures; the Association for Intercollegiate Athletics for Women (AIAW) was one example. But today's female sport leaders have not maintained that focus. Instead, their efforts seem to be centered primarily on merely reducing inequities, while largely ignoring their root causes. Many in the women's sports movement appear to be accommodating themselves to dominant masculine sports meanings and practices for the opportunity to participate in that system.

Feminists keep hoping that when enough women acquire leadership positions in sport, things will change. But this expectation overlooks the fact that female sports leaders are just as constrained by economic silencing and just as compelled by the same set of rewards and punishments connected with the sport world as men are. It will be quite remarkable if female sports leaders actually lead a social transformation of the sports world because as coaches and administrators they have become part of the dominant hegemonic sport group—they are the major beneficiaries of the current social arrangements in sport.

Summary and Preview

Organized sport—from its beginnings in the late 19th century—has been one of the most powerful cultural practices for perpetuating the ideology of male superiority and dominance. It has been an important vehicle by which symbols and values that are institutionalized in patriarchy have been preserved and women's subordinate position in society has been maintained. Despite enormous changes since the mid-1970s, the world of sport still promotes and preserves traditional gender differences, and patriarchal ideology is still firmly entrenched in American institutions and social practices.

Fundamental social relations are not altered by courts and legislation, and culturally conditioned responses to gender ideology are ubiquitous and resistant to sudden changes. Although laws may force compliance in equality of opportunity for females in the world of sport, stratification continues, albeit in more subtle and insidious forms, as has been the case with racism (discussed in the next chapter). More females playing sports does not signify that a revolution has been won for women, not so long as the organization of sport promotes and sustains the dominance of men in social relations.

Suggested Readings

American Association of University Women. *How Schools Short-change Girls.* Washington, DC: AAUW Education Foundation, 1992.

Amott, Teresa, and Julie Matthaei. *Race, Gender, and Work: A Multicultural Economic History of Women in the United States.* Rev. ed. Boston: South End Press, 1996.

Birrell, Susan, and Cheryl L. Cole, eds. *Women, Sport, and Culture.* Champaign, IL: Human Kinetics, 1994.

Chambers, Marcia. *The Unplayable Lie: The Untold Story of Women and Discrimination in American Golf.* New York: Pocket Books, 1995.

Cahn, Susan K. *Coming on Strong: Gender and Sexuality in Twentieth-Century Women's Sport.* New York: Free Press, 1994.

Costa, D. Margaret, and Sharon R. Guthrie, eds. *Women and Sport: Interdisciplinary Perspectives.* Champaign, IL: Human Kinetics, 1994.

Dujon, Diane, and Ann Withorn, eds. *For Crying Out Loud: Women's Poverty in the United States.* Boston: South End Press, 1996.

Golombok, Susan, and Robyn Fivush. *Gender Development.* Cambridge: Cambridge University Press, 1994.

Griffin, Pat. *Strong Women, Deep Closets: Lesbians and Homophobia in Sport.* Champaign, IL: Human Kinetics, 1998.

Jacobs, Jerry. *Gender Inequality at Work.* Thousand Oaks, CA: Sage, 1995.

Kessler, Lauren. *Full Court Press: A Season in the Life of a Winning Basketball Team and the Women Who Made It Happen.* New York: Dutton, 1997.

Koss, Mary P., Lisa A. Goodman, Angela Browne, Louise F. Fitzgerald, Gwendolyn P. Keita, and Nancy F. Russo. *No Safe Haven: Male Violence Against Women at Home, at Work, and in the Community.* Washington, DC: American Psychological Association, 1994.

Messner, Michael A. *Power at Play: Sports and the Problem of Masculinity.* Boston: Beacon Press, 1992.

Nelson, Mariah B. *The Stronger Women Get, the More Men Love Football: Sexism and the American Culture of Sports.* New York: Harcourt Brace & Company, 1994.

Chapter 5

Structures of Social Inequality: Racial Inequality in Sport

The whirlwinds of revolt will continue to shake the foundations of our nation until the bright day of justice emerges. Injustice to anyone, anywhere, is injustice to everyone, everywhere.

Dr. Martin Luther King Jr.

The United States is characterized by the presence of multiple structures of inequality, each having its own qualities, contours, and consequences. The previous two chapters have examined two of these: social class and gender. Race is another of the traditional stratifying categories in American society. Racial inequality deprives people of color—African Americans particularly, as well as Hispanics and other non-Caucasians—of equal access to socially valued rewards and resources.

There are many racial and ethnic minorities in the United States, but my focus in this chapter is on African Americans. I want to emphasize, however, that African Americans are not the only group to have had to struggle against formidable odds for basic civil rights (e.g., personal freedom, the right to live where you want to, etc.). Native Americans, Hispanics, Asians, and other minority groups have had unique histories of struggle. Nor are African Americans the only minority racial group that has experienced discrimination in sport. Native Americans have had to suffer pernicious stereotyping through unflattering mascots and team names. Hispanics have had exclusionary sports practices employed against them. Jews, the Irish, Italians, and other ethnic groups have been the target of various forms of discrimination in sport at various times in American history.

I am focusing on the African American racial group for several reasons: first, it is the largest minority population (currently about 34 million, or 12.6 percent of the population; second, it is the only racial group to have been subjected to an extended period of slavery; and third, it is the only racial group to have had segregation laws passed against it that were supported and fully sanctioned by the U.S. Supreme Court.

Causes of Racial Inequality: Race or Economics?

During the past decade, influential conservative voices have sought to reformulate the debate over the causes of persisting racial inequality with arguments about the "declining significance of race" and "the end of racism." According to them, racial discrimination based on color has largely disappeared because of increased political, economic, and social opportunities available to African Americans. Current racial inequalities are seen as primarily attributable to social class and are thus grounded in economics rather than in color. When racial inequality is cast in class terms, the "equality of opportunity" logic used to explain and justify class inequalities in chapter 3 is also employed to explain racial inequalities. According to this logic, African Americans who are poor need to pull themselves up by their bootstraps, work hard, and stop whining about racism, and they too can achieve the American dream of financial success and happiness.

Although such arguments have achieved some credibility, they have come under intense attack by social analysts who, while acknowledging that racism is intertwined with class, see racial inequality as being created and maintained by institutionalized discrimination in the larger society and aggravated by callous attitudes toward minorities. From this perspective, racist ideology, zealously cultivated to legitimate the relations of domination in a plantation society, has continued to define the status of African Americans.[1]

Where racial inequality coexists with class stratification, as in the United States, there is compelling evidence that the racial discrimination is more basic to social structure and therefore the ultimate determinant of inequality between racial minorities and the dominant white majority. The basic fact is that much inequality and discrimination against African Americans continues, whether one measures income, employment rates, educational attainment, or political officeholding. African Americans remain among the most disadvantaged people in American society because institutional patterns and practices of racism are deeply ingrained in the structure of our society. Racial barriers block their achievement, not merely economic or class barriers.

The Legacy of Racial Inequality

Just as with class and gender inequality, racial inequality is a systematic power structure based on an ideology of white supremacy—racism—that keeps this power structure in place. Racism is not just individual random acts, it is systematic and institutionalized prejudice—attitude of superiority or bias—and discrimination—actual behaviors—against a group of people based on skin color and other facial and body features. The social dynamics by which racism is reinforced and reproduced are similar to other forms of prejudice and discrimination; this is illustrated in figure 5.1.

To understand the role of racism in American sport, we cannot perceive it apart from the larger cultural context in which it is situated. Thus, it is important to historically situate and culturally locate American racism—to develop a historical sensitivity to it.

More Than 200 Years of Slavery

American racial inequality is rooted deeply in America's early history. Black' slaves were first brought to colonial America in 1610. By the end of the 17th century, enslaved Africans became a major source of labor and were fundamental to colonial agricultural and commercial interests. Slaveholders of the preindustrial agricultural South, together with northern trading and shipping firms, created a racist social structure with blacks at the bottom.

Race relations are always developed, articulated, and understood within systems of power and privilege that define and structure those relations. Racial inequality was inscribed into the basic documents of the newly formed United States: the Declaration of Independence and the U.S. Constitution condoned racial subordination of and discrimination against African Americans. Despite their enlightened stance toward freedom and liberty, the framers of these documents saw no contradiction in espousing a liberal view of liberty for white males while denying it to blacks, who totaled 20 percent of the population when the United States began as an independent nation (and women). Indeed, slavery was sanctioned, and African Americans were denied all the rights of citizenship. The Constitution actually sanctioned the

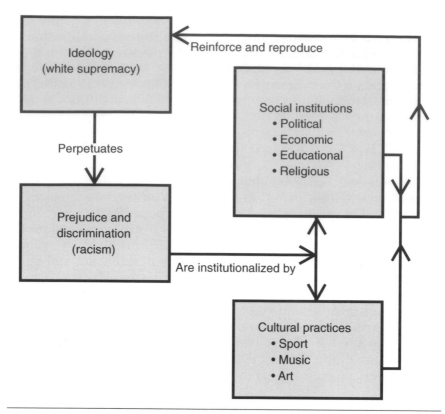

Figure 5.1 Social dynamics of racial inequality.

slave trade by prohibiting Congress from placing limitations on the importation or migration of slaves.

Although slavery was institutionalized during the colonial period, a formal ideology of racism did not emerge until the early 19th century. By the 1830s, influential writers had constructed and were defending theories of inherent racial differences, with the Caucasian race considered superior to all others. Although racist ideology had undisputed appeal for sanctioning slavery in the antebellum South, slavery as an institution increasingly came under attack throughout the other regions of the United States. Although many people in these other regions did not denounce racist ideology, they did consider human enslavement unacceptable. The issue of slavery was brought to a head by the Civil War.

Freedom Followed by Segregation

Slavery was abolished by the 13th Amendment to the U.S. Constitution in 1865, but governmental institutions spurned that opportunity to promote equality and justice. Jim Crow laws—segregation laws that legalized white domination and thus left racism essentially intact—and the "separate but equal" doctrine handed down by the Supreme Court in 1896 became even more efficient instruments of domination and oppression than slavery had been. It was not until 1954 that the "separate but equal" doctrine was declared unconstitutional, and only since the Civil Rights Acts of 1964, 1965, and 1968 that African American citizens have been protected by law.[3] But even though such laws are now in place and social norms have improved social relations and conditions in some private and public spheres, the domination and subordination of African Americans is still a basic attribute of American society, and race is a primary determinant of position in the social structure. People of color are still defined as humanly different by white groups and are singled out for a broad range of discrimination, including individual, institutionalized, and yes, even unconscious racism.[4]

Racial Inequality in Contemporary America

National opinion polls conducted in 1996 and 1997 by *USA Today* found that 72 percent of adult respondents think that racial discrimination against African Americans is somewhat to very serious, and 52 percent believe that the state of race relations in the United States is moderately to very bad. A broad range of evidence supports these beliefs. There are significant and persisting differences between white and black citizens in the economic, political, and social sectors of their lives, and in every case it is African Americans who are disadvantaged.

Economic Conditions for African Americans

Contrary to the perceptions of many Americans, the economic gap between whites and blacks has continued to widen. Black families have actually lost ground economically to whites over the past 25 years. The poverty rate among the nation's African Americans in 1998 was 33.1 percent, compared with 12.2 percent for whites. African Americans' household income was only 62 percent of whites' income, and it has changed very little during the 1990s. The jobless rate for African Americans has consistently been more than twice that of whites. Not only are African Americans twice as likely to be unemployed, but those who are employed are overrepresented in jobs whose pay, power, and prestige are low.

Although less common today than in the past, token integration in workplaces is more prevalent than demographic balance, even among occupations that are integrated. As one researcher noted, "Although there has been some erosion of white . . . advantages in the workplace over the last two decades, they remain substantial."[5] Racial discrimination undoubtedly accounts for this state of affairs. In 1991 the Urban League (a social service and civil rights organization) sent out carefully matched pairs of college graduates—one was white and one was black—to apply for the same jobs. The white applicants were hired 55 percent more often than were the black applicants. Later that same year, the ABC television program *PrimeTime Live* carried out the same experiment, with essentially the same results. In 1996 a firm that conducts employee training for *Fortune* 500 companies reported that from 18 percent to 36 percent of the African American employees said they had experienced blatant racism on their jobs; from 40 percent to 49 percent reported subtle discrimination, such as exclusion from business social functions; and from 30 percent to 50 percent of black employees said they heard racial jokes or slurs at least once a month on their jobs.

In the private sector of American business, only a smattering of African American managers have moved beyond middle levels of authority and control. Less than 3 percent of company senior management positions (vice president and above) are held by African Americans; there are no African American chief executive officers in *Fortune* 500 companies. Of 17 million U.S. business firms, only 2 percent are owned by African Americans. Less than 8 percent of the nation's physicians, dentists, and pharmacists are African American.

One social scientist recently noted: "All of the evidence points to the fact that the [economic] winners are predominantly White and the biggest losers are Black. A wealth of recent material demonstrates that Black Americans have lost out to such an extent as to make a mockery of free enterprise, and the gap between Black and White incomes, if anything, has widened."[6]

Political Conditions for African Americans

Political opportunities have opened up for African Americans during the past two decades. Many of the mayors of the largest cities are African American, and an increasing number of African Americans are being elected to state and federal legislative bodies. Although these are certainly promising trends, African Americans still trail far behind in terms of their proportion of the population. In 1998 for example, of the 100 U.S. senators, only one was African American; only 8 percent of the members of the U.S. House of Representatives were African American. Less than 1 percent of the members of the nation's state legislatures were African American, and blacks still hold less than 1.5 percent of the total elective offices in the United States.[7]

Violence Against African Americans

Racist ideology, in common with every bigoted ideology, is based on power, and that power is often manifested in violence. From 1885 to 1930, 3,256 lynchings of African Americans were carried out in southern states. Such despicable practices are part of America's past, but violence against African Americans is a part of contemporary American culture.[8] Documentation by the Southern Poverty Law Center (SPLC) shows that violence against African Americans in the 1990s is quite common. The SPLC monitors, reports, and litigates hundreds of incidents against African Americans each year, ranging from beatings to murders. Furthermore, the SPLC has documented that white supremacist groups have actually been growing throughout the country during the 1990s.[9]

In 1993 opinion analyst Louis Harris found that 75 percent of high school students indicated that they had seen or heard about a racial act with violent overtones, either very often or somewhat often, in the previous 12 months. Fifty-four percent of black high school students reported that they had been victims of a racial incident. The National Institute Against Prejudice and Violence, a group that monitors racist acts, reports that there are typically racial incidents on more than 50 college campuses each year (and college students are supposed to be the most enlightened sector of the population!).[10]

African Americans themselves commit numerous acts of violent crime each year, and leaders in the black communities across the nation have identified violence—to a great extent against other African Americans—as a major social problem. There are those who have rushed to accuse blacks of being more violent by nature than whites, but there is no scientific research to support that contention. What research does show is that the media report violent drug busts and other "street" crimes more often than they do other forms of criminal activity, and they use pictures of African Americans more often than they use pictures of whites to illustrate the stories. This has the potential to form public opinion about African Americans and violence. After social conditions, such as poverty, inner-city living conditions, unemployment, and other relevant social factors are controlled for, there is little difference in violent acts between the races. Still, violence committed by blacks plagues their struggle to wipe out stereotyping and racist ideology.

Despite Progress, Problems Remain

Although African Americans have made some gains economically, politically, educationally, and socially in the past three decades, many barriers to social equality remain. This period has been a time of African American hardship, with inner-city communities devastated by crime and drugs and national policies of retreat from efforts to increase opportunities for African Americans.[11] In the fall of 1996, revelations of a racist corporate culture at the highest levels at Texaco, Avis, and several other corporations vividly demonstrated that America has not yet conquered its heritage of racial inequality. Although there is less overt bigotry now, institutional racism persists, and Martin Luther King Jr.'s dream that "one day racism would end in America" still awaits fulfillment.

Racial Inequality in Sport

It is said that the history of sport is one that reveals all that has been bad as well as good throughout the history of the United States. This is true for African Americans in sport: sport has simultaneously been a powerful reinforcer of racist ideology and an instrument of opportunity for African Americans.

Unlike the patriarchal ideology that historically barred most women from sport, the ideology underlying racism has not been incompatible with African American sport participation, but it has dictated that African American athletes be subordinate and in certain times and places totally segregated from playing with whites. Still, despite pervasive and systematic discrimination against African Americans, they have played a continuing and significant role in every era of American history. Their involvement can be roughly divided into three stages: (1) largely exclusion before the Civil War, (2) breakthroughs immediately after the Civil War but segregation beginning in the last two decades of the 19th century continuing to the mid-20th century, and (3) integration during the latter 20th century.

The Era of Slavery

Social relations among African Americans during the more than 200 years of slavery involved a wide variety of games and sports played among themselves. Many plantation owners actually encouraged such use of leisure time because it was seen as preferable to other options such as drinking, fighting, and general mischief. They may have also encouraged games and sports to dissuade slaves from plotting acts of insurgency against plantation owners. Sporting social relations between whites and blacks during the slavery era (1619 to 1865) centered on two activities: boxing and horse racing. Holidays and special occasions in the colonial (1607-1789) and antebellum periods were often enlivened with sports and games, especially those on which people could wager. Many plantation owners selected—

and even trained—one or more male slaves to enter in boxing matches held in conjunction with festive occasions. The black boxers under such conditions were merely used to entertain their white "masters" and their friends.

Horse racing was another popular sporting event that allowed spectators to bet on the outcome. Horses were, of course, owned by whites, and training was done usually by whites, but African Americans were used as jockeys. There was little status and no significant material reward for jockeying because slave labor of any kind was unpaid; jockeying was viewed as basically mechanical, so slaves were trusted with a task that whites did not care to do anyway. Social relations, then, were seen as distant, with whites in control and African Americans in subordinate roles, pleasing the dominant white groups.

Latter 19th Century to Mid-20th Century

Emancipation had little effect on the social relations between African Americans and whites in sports. Although a number of African Americans played on professional baseball teams in the early years of the National League, Jim Crowism (segregation) gradually raised its ugly head. White players threatened to quit rather than share the diamond with black men. White opponents tried to spike African American players at every opportunity; pitchers aimed at their heads. Finally, in 1888 major league club owners made a gentlemen's agreement not to sign any more African American players. This unwritten law against hiring black players was not violated until 1945 when Branch Rickey, general manager of the Brooklyn Dodgers, signed Jackie Robinson to a contract.[12]

As other professional sports developed, African Americans were likewise barred from participation. This exclusion maintained the segregation of the wider society as well as the segregation of Major League Baseball. One of the many consequences of excluding African Americans from professional sports was to perpetuate privileges for white athletes, who did not have to compete with an entire segment of the population for sport jobs.

Excluding African Americans from white-only professional leagues did not stop them from forming their own teams and leagues. These so-called Negro baseball leagues (that is the term that was used) flourished for more than 40 years; they staged their own versions of the World Series and All-Star Games and produced their own heroes who were idolized in African American communities. All-black basketball teams and leagues succeeded in many cities of the Northeast and Midwest.[13]

African Americans were active in boxing throughout the time of slavery, but they found their aspirations for top prizes blocked when they tried to compete as free men after the Civil War. For example, when John L. Sullivan became the first American heavyweight boxing champion in 1882, he announced that he would fight any contender: "In this challenge, I include all fighters—first come, first served— who are white. I will not fight a Negro. I never have, and never shall." And he never did. One of the greatest heavyweight boxing champions of all time, Jack Dempsey, in his first public statement after he won the championship in 1919, said that he would not under any circumstances "pay any attention to Negro challengers."[14] Despite barriers like these, two African Americans—Jack Johnson and Joe Louis— managed to win the heavyweight championship during the first half of the 20th century.

During the late 19th and early 20th centuries, education in the South was totally segregated, so African American high school and intercollegiate athletes competed only against other African American athletes. Although not segregated, schools and colleges in other parts of the country managed to bar most African Americans from high school and college sports teams. Until the 1960s, most African American college athletes played at black colleges in black leagues (known as Negro colleges and Negro leagues), which existed because of institutionalized racial prejudice and discrimination.

Black colleges fielded teams in all the popular sports and played a leading role in promoting women's sports, especially in track and field—Tuskegee Institute (now Tuskegee University) and Tennessee State are prominent examples. They provided opportunities for women before such opportunities were available on predominantly white campuses. Although the educational system was segregated, the so-called Negro colleges provided an avenue of opportunity for many African American athletes—both men and women—though few were ever recognized outside the African American community.[15]

Latter 20th Century

The past 50 years has been a time of remarkable change for African Americans in sports. They have become a significant presence at every level of organized sports. From a condition of exclusion from "white" sports, they have passed through periods of tokenism, during which they were admitted in small numbers, to a period of "stacking," during which only specific positions on teams were thought appropriate for them (because racist ideology stereotyped them as having speed, quickness, and jumping ability, but not intellectual and complex thinking ability), to a period of open acceptance in many sports.

Professional Sports

African Americans have gradually assumed a remarkably prominent role in several professional sports. When Jackie Robinson took the field for the Brooklyn Dodgers in 1947, he broke the all-white exclusion barrier of Major League Baseball that had been in place for more than 50 years. The next 10 years was a period of tokenism by which most teams integrated by signing one or two African American players. By 1959, when the Boston Red Sox finally signed an African American player, every major league team was integrated, but even in the mid-1960s, less than 10 percent of all Major League Baseball players were African American. Most African American players were "stacked" at the outfield and infield corner positions of first and third base. Currently about 18 percent of Major League Baseball players are African American, and they are more widely distributed in the various playing positions.

Other popular professional team sports have passed through essentially the same phases as Major League Baseball. Exclusion was largely the situation in professional football before World War II. Then from the 1950s to well into the 1980s, periods of tokenism and "stacking" players into running back, wide receiver, and defensive back positions followed. African Americans have become dominant in the National Football League (NFL) in the 1990s; in 1998 68 percent of NFL players were African American, and they are distributed in all the playing positions (though very few are quarterbacks).

The most striking increase of African Americans in professional sports has taken place in basketball; in the late 1950s, only about 10 percent of National Basketball Association (NBA) players were black. Tokenism and stacking, while present for periods in basketball, were not as conspicuous as in baseball and football. At present, more than 80 percent of NBA players are African American; they dominate at all the positions.

When the two women's professional basketball leagues, the American Basketball League and the Women's National Basketball Association, began their inaugural seasons in 1996 and 1997, more than 75 percent of the players were African American. This reflects the prominent place that African American women have played during the past decade on intercollegiate and U.S. Olympic basketball teams, for it was from these teams that the professional leagues recruited their players.

Intercollegiate Sports

Intercollegiate sports at predominantly white institutions remained segregated, with isolated exceptions, until after World War II. At the University of Michigan, for example, from 1882 to 1945 there were only four black lettermen in football and none in basketball. The impact of World War II in opening up social and economic opportunities for African Americans, the 1954 Supreme Court decision forbidding racially separate educational facilities, and the growing commercialization of collegiate sports led more and more formerly white colleges and universities to recruit talented African American athletes to bolster their teams. Consequently, black colleges lost their monopoly on African American athletic talent. The best athletes found it advantageous to play at predominantly white schools because of greater visibility, especially on television, which boosted their chances for signing professional contracts at the conclusion of their eligibility. Athletic programs at black colleges were rapidly depleted, forcing several schools to drastically modify their athletic programs and some black leagues to disband.

In 1948 only 10 percent of predominately white college basketball teams had one or more African Americans on their rosters. This proportion increased to 45 percent of the teams in 1962 and 92 percent by 1975. Universities in the southern states maintained white-only teams until the latter 1960s. The conversion from segregated to integrated programs in the South is well illustrated by the University of Alabama: in 1968 there were no African Americans on any of its teams, but by 1975 its basketball team fielded an all-black starting lineup.

The percentage of African American athletes has exceeded the percentage of African American nonathletes in higher education for many years. In the late 1990s, less than 6 percent of all students at Division I universities are African American, while overall, 27.5 percent of the scholarship athletes in Division I institutions are African American; 60 percent of the men's basketball players, 37 percent of the women's basketball players, and 42 percent of the football players are African American.[16]

Remaining Barriers to Access

Despite the many opportunities now available in sport for African Americans that did not exist a generation ago, racial inequality in sport has not been eliminated. Many professional and college sports still have very few African American participants. Those sports most closely linked to upper-class patronage and with less spectator interest, and thus less economic impact, have been slow to provide access to African Americans. Both men's and women's professional tennis and golf have conspicuously few African Americans. But socially elite sports are not the only ones still lacking significant African American presence. Auto racing, ice hockey, and soccer are others. Laws that prevent African Americans from being kept out do not assure that they will get in. Ample evidence shows that those who control certain sports have created barriers to black participation, thus reproducing some of the more odious features of racial injustice.

It is important to understand that where barriers to access have been eliminated for African Americans in sports, these changes have not taken place purely from humanitarian concerns. Political, legal, and economic factors have played interlocking roles. The civil rights legislation of the 1960s opened up many sectors of life for African Americans, including sport. Sport opportunities for African Americans in professional sport grew only as discrimination became incompatible with good capitalist financial policy. It was in those team sports in which spectator appeal was strong and growing, and in which the profit motive was foremost, that African Americans were given a chance, and the valuable contributions of outstanding African American athletes in winning championships opened up further opportunities.

© Claus Andersen

African Americans' struggle for racial equality in American society has its equivalent in sport. The struggle in sport has evolved from exclusion, to segregation, to tokenism, to expanding opportunities. This struggle for racial equality has not been fully won in either the larger society or sport.

It is also important to understand that racism has not been eliminated in sport even though more sports opportunities are available and even though there is more equitable distribution of African Americans in professional and intercollegiate sports. Racial attitudes are not necessarily changed by laws or political and economic pressures. Prejudice, discrimination, and injustice remain, albeit in more subtle, even unconscious, forms. African American athletes, coaches, and sport administrators report that rarely a day goes by that they do not experience racial prejudice or discrimination of some kind. Their accounts have been corroborated by empirical research as well as by testimonials by their white teammates and friends.[17]

Leadership and Management Opportunities

Employment patterns in sports leadership for African Americans have been similar to that of female sport coaches and administrators. Access for black athletes has expanded greatly in recent years, but very few African Americans-—men or women—have been hired for positions high in the sport hierarchy. At the present time, blacks account for less than 5 percent of the key management positions in professional and intercollegiate sports. Racist ideology, stereotypes, and caricatures have portrayed African Americans as lacking the requisite intelligence and rational thinking capabilities for leadership. The same racist ideology claims that whites will not follow black leaders.

Another barrier to leadership positions in sport for African Americans is the dominance of the entrenched white "ol' boys" network. Those who control access to those higher levels can subtly insulate themselves against those with whom they do not wish to associate.[18] Of course, the extent to which any of these factors account for the hiring for any given sport leadership position is hard to determine, but the perpetuation of racial stereotypes and the dominant social network certainly are powerful forces.

In both professional and intercollegiate sports, coaching and administration jobs are under the control of those who have the power for determining who gets selected for the upper-level positions. Statements made by powerful persons in sport organizations suggest racist beliefs play a role in excluding African Americans from administrative positions. In 1987 Al Campanis, an executive for the Los Angeles Dodgers, appeared on the television program *Nightline* and was asked by host Ted Koppel why there are no black managers and general managers in Major League Baseball. Campanis replied that blacks "may not have some of the necessities to be . . . a field manager or perhaps a general manager." In 1992 Marge Schott, owner of the Cincinnati Reds, reportedly said she would rather "hire a trained monkey than a nigger" to work in her front office. These statements, and the hiring practices of those who make hiring decisions for sports organizations, clearly suggest that race has been a factor in those decisions.

As of 1998 there were only three black head coaches in the NFL, and conditions are not promising for improvement. During the 1997 season and before the 1998 season began, the NFL had 11 head coaching openings and none of the jobs was filled by an African American. Twenty-six percent of NFL assistant coaches in 1997 were black, and only four were offensive or defensive coordinators—the most responsible and prestigious coaching positions below head coaching. This in a league in which about 68 percent of the players are black.[19] Major League Baseball has had only a handful of black managers to date, and currently only about 18 percent of the coaches and one of the general managers are African American. In fall 1996, six Major League Baseball manager positions were open; no one was hired from the list of minority candidates. Professional basketball has had the most African American head coaches. In recent years, as many as seven blacks have held these positions at once, but this is in a league with more than 80 percent African American players.

African American coaches are equally scarce in intercollegiate athletics. The first African American to be hired as a head football coach at a major college was Ron Cooper at Eastern Michigan University in 1992. As of spring 1998, less than 8 of 112 head football coaches in NCAA Division IA are African American. Nearly all African American college coaches are assistants, and most coaching staffs have only one black. Of about 1,220 head coaching positions in NCAA Division I sports, not including the predominantly black colleges, in which African American athletes have a significant presence (football, basketball, track, baseball), less than 5 percent are held by African Americans.[20]

Executive positions in professional and intercollegiate sports continue to elude African Americans. In the commissioner's offices of pro sports, in the front offices of professional clubs, among the top-level NCAA administrators, and among university athletic directors, there are scandalously few African Americans. As of 1998, the NFL has had fewer than six black general managers, and about 10 NBA general managers have been African American. Of more than 20 new general managers hired by Major League Baseball from 1990 to 1998, one was African American. The one bright spot in this otherwise dim picture for baseball was the choice in February 1989 of Bill White, an African American, as the president of the National League.

In 1994 the NCAA's Minority Opportunity and Interests Committee reported that the proportion of black sport administrators at member institutions of the NCAA had changed little over the past four years.

Two years later, the situation was much the same. In 1998 only about 5 percent of the athletic directors at NCAA Division I institutions were African American.[21]

African American women who aspire to leadership positions in professional and intercollegiate sports are faced with two obstacles. First, they are victims of racist ideology that militates against their employment. Second, there are fewer women's sports than men's; the opportunities simply do not exist for females—white or black—to coach or manage in professional or intercollegiate sports. But where positions exist for which African American women might be employed, they are not being hired. Only one sport—women's intercollegiate basketball—has a significant number of black female coaches. In 1998 there were about a dozen NCAA Division I basketball teams coached by an African American woman.

The sports leadership situation for African Americans had became so disgraceful in the early 1990s that some of the sport governing bodies and civil rights groups formed committees and task forces to help seek out minorities for management and executive positions and to monitor team hiring. In 1993 the Rainbow Commission for Fairness in Athletics was created by the Reverend Jesse Jackson to reduce racism and gender barriers in the hiring practices of professional and collegiate sport. Substantial and meaningful results have been slow; the ranks of managers, head coaches, and front-office personnel continue to be filled by whites, sometimes using thinly disguised ploys that eliminate African Americans from serious consideration.

Social Mobility Through Sport for African Americans

It has often been contended that sport is one of the most responsive social practices for serving as an avenue of upward social mobility for African Americans; indeed, it has been argued that sport has done more in this regard than any other social practice or institution. Although it is certainly true that sport has provided some African American athletes with opportunities for social mobility denied them in other sectors of American life, and a few have become prominent figures in American life—Jackie Robinson, Muhammad Ali, Wilma Rudolph, "Magic" Johnson, Jackie Joyner-Kersee, and others—sport has not moved large numbers of African Americans into higher social-class standing. The rags-to-riches stories of individual, high-profile African American athletes disguise the actual reality of how little social mobility results from sports participation.

There are fewer than 3,400 male professional team sport athletes. There are about 50.2 million American males age 15 to 39 (the age range of most professional athletes), 6.2 million of whom are African Americans. So that makes the odds of an African American male becoming a professional athlete about one in 5,000 (see table 5.1). Meanwhile, there are 12 times more black lawyers and 15 times more black doctors than there are black professional athletes.

Sociologist Harry Edwards once remarked about an African American's chances of becoming a professional athlete: "You have a better chance of getting hit by a meteorite in the next 10 years than

Table 5.1

Odds of African American Males Attaining Professional Athlete Status in Major Professional Team Sports (expressed as a decimal)

Sport	Number of African American players and odds
Football	N=910
All males*	.00002
African American males**	.0001
Baseball	N=112
All males	.000002
African American males	.00002
Basketball	N=320
All males	.000006
African American males	.00005
Hockey	N=13
All males	.0000003
African American males	.000002
All four sports	N=1,355
All males	.00003
African American males	.0002

* Normed for all males age 15 to 39.

** Normed for all African American males age 15 to 39.

Adapted with permission from Wilbert M. Leonard II, 1996, "The Odds of Transiting From One Level of Sports Participation to Another," *Sociology of Sport Journal* 13 (3): 296.

getting work as an athlete." Henry Louis Gates Jr., professor of humanities at Harvard University and an African American, made a similar point: "An African American youngster has about as much chance of becoming a professional athlete as he or she does of winning the lottery. The tragedy for our people, however, is that few of us accept the truth.... The blind pursuit of attainment in sports is having a devastating effect on our people."[22] Still, many young African American athletes have bought into the myth that sport is the highway to financial success and upward social mobility. According to a national survey, 51 percent of African American high school athletes believe they can become professional athletes.[23]

African Americans have received an increasing number of athletic scholarships at predominantly white schools since the early 1970s, but this has been a mixed blessing. On one hand, a few athletically talented African Americans have been able to attend and graduate from colleges otherwise inaccessible to them, and this has allowed them to achieve upward social mobility. On the other hand, the evidence is clear and abundant that the athletic talent of many African American college athletes has been exploited by their schools. They have been recruited even though they lacked the academic background to succeed in higher education, and they have been advised into courses that keep them eligible but are dead-end choices for acquiring a college diploma. When their eligibility is used up or they become academically ineligible to compete for the team, they are discarded and ignored by the coaches who recruited them. From 55 percent to 75 percent of African American NCAA Division I football, basketball, and track athletes do not graduate. This represents a much lower rate of graduation than the overall graduation averages in those universities.[24]

The evidence is overwhelming that professional sport cannot provide much in the way of upward social mobility for large numbers of African Americans. Yes, the very few who become professional athletes make a lot of money and become wealthy for a time. But even for those who do become professional athletes, the average professional sports career is very short—less than five years. That's right. The average professional athlete remains at the top level of competition for less than five years.

An athletic scholarship has the potential to help an African American college student from a poor family earn a college diploma, which can then lead to a high-paying position in a professional field or business. But every year thousands of African American college athletes leave college without the diploma. For them, their future occupation will be determined by their educational achievement and by chance, just as it is for other men and women without a college degree.

Summary and Preview

Class, gender, and race stratification is a fundamental feature of American society, as revealed in the dominance, exploitation, and discrimination of capitalists over workers, of males over females, and of whites over blacks. These systems of stratification are interrelated and equally important as enduring forms of oppression, but each has its own unique forms and consequences, which sometimes act independently of the others but sometimes in conjunction with them. Moreover, each alone and all in combination are played out in the world of sport.

Analysis of any segment of American society—including sport—that does not account for the importance of class, gender, and race stratification forms an incomplete foundation for understanding our historical traditions and our contemporary social organizations and relationships.

The political institution—or the state, as it is called in the social science literature—is the most prominent social institution in modern societies. This is true not only because of its omnipresent role in the lives of its citizens, but also because it is vested with society's ultimate power. It is a widely held myth that there is no relationship between sport and the state, manifested in pleas to "keep politics out of sport." In chapter 6 I describe the naiveté of such admonitions and examine how the state intervenes in American sport and physical recreation.

Suggested Readings

Ashe, Arthur. *A Hard Road to Glory—Boxing: A History of the African American Athlete.* New York: Amistad, 1993.

Berry, Mary F. *Black Resistance, White Law.* Rev. ed. New York: Penguin, 1994.

Billet, Bret L., and Lance J. Formwalt. *America's National Pastime: A Study of Race and Merit in Professional Baseball.* Westport, CT: Praeger, 1995.

Brooks, Dana D., and Ronald C. Althouse, eds. *Racism in College Athletics: The African-American Athlete's Experience.* Morgantown, WV: Fitness Information Technology, 1993.

Gardner, Robert, and Dennis Shortelle. *The Forgotten Players: The Story of Black Baseball in America.* New York: Walker, 1993.

Gissendanner, Cindy Himes. "African-American Women and Competitive Sport, 1920-60." In *Women, Sport, and Culture,* edited by

Susan Birrell and Cheryl L. Cole, 81-92. Champaign, IL: Human Kinetics, 1994.

Hadjor, Kofi B. *Another America: The Politics of Race and Blame.* Boston: South End Press, 1995.

Hoberman, John. *Darwin's Athletes: How Sport Has Damaged Black America and Preserved the Myth of Race.* Boston: Houghton Mifflin, 1997.

Hochschild, Jennifer L. *Facing Up to the American Dream: Race, Class and the Soul of the Nation.* Princeton, NJ: Princeton University Press, 1995.

Peterson, Robert. *Only the Ball Was White: History of Legendary Black Players and All-Black Professional Teams.* New York: Oxford University Press, 1992.

Rust, Art Jr. *Get That Nigger Off the Field: The Oral History of the Negro Leagues.* Brooklyn: Book Mail Services, 1992.

Shropshire, Kenneth L. *In Black and White: Race and Sport in America.* New York: New York University Press, 1996.

Steinberg, Stephen. *Turning Back: The Retreat From Racial Justice in American Thought and Policy.* Boston: Beacon, 1995.

Wiggins, David K. *Glory Bound: Black Athletes in a White America.* Syracuse, NY: Syracuse University Press, 1997.

Wilson, Carter A. *Racism: From Slavery to Advanced Capitalism.* Thousand Oaks, CA: Sage, 1996.

Chapter 6

Sport and the State: The Political Economy of American Sport

Sport and politics always have been institutional partners . . . particularly where [a] society's reputation or national pride are at stake. Although in the United States the separation of sport and politics may be viewed as the appropriate relationship, it is not the practiced one.

Arthur T. Johnson, political scientist, and James H. Frey, sociologist

Every modern society has some system for promoting social order and general welfare. The preamble to the U.S. Constitution provides a written document articulating this system for our country. It states:

> We the People of the United States, in Order to form a more perfect Union, establish Justice, insure domestic Tranquility, provide for the common defense, promote the general Welfare, and secure the Blessings of Liberty to ourselves and our Posterity, do ordain and establish this Constitution for the United States of America.

The network of administrative and bureaucratic agencies that make up this system is often referred to by social scientists as "the state" (which is not to be confused with one of the 50 United States; each is a form of regional government). The state encompasses the government, the elected officeholders in all its branches and levels. Beyond that, the state is composed of a great variety of organizations, including hundreds of appointed officials, the military, and the police and the legal system, as well as the many public bureaucracies and agencies involved in opinion shaping and ideology formation. In effect, the state is an organized power structure, the functions of which are the management and control of society.

Most Americans think there is little about their nation that they do not already know, for they study "government" (sometimes called "civics") as a part of their basic education. But when this subject is taught and studied in schools, typically little effort is made to connect the state to other social institutions (the economy, education, religion, family) and cultural practices. However, the state is inseparably associated with all of America's social institutions and cultural life, as well as being part of a worldwide system of nation-states, so studying it as an isolated social institution provides an incomplete understanding of how it really works.

State Power and Capitalist Enterprise in America

The two images of society that were described in chapter 2—pluralism and hegemony—have much to say about the relationship between the American state and its citizens. Pluralists see the state as attaining consensus and preserving social order by adjudicating the conflicts and demands of numerous social groups through a continual sequence of bargaining processes. For pluralists, the state is equally accessible to all citizens and acts in the common interest, remaining outside particular interests but responding to diverse pressures. Pluralists often contend that the interests of the people and the policies of the state are the same. The state, then, is regarded as a benign and neutral set of agencies and bureaucracies that have no direct involvement in either furthering or hampering the functions of other social institutions or cultural practices. Such things are regarded as being of little consequence in the overall operations of the state.

The initial theoretician of hegemony theory, Antonio Gramsci, did not articulate a clear conception of the state in his writings about hegemony, but the modern capitalist state has become a subject of lively discussion for social thinkers with ties to the hegemonic tradition. An organizing theme of these analysts is the important changes that have occurred in western capitalist countries—including the United States—during the past century through the expanding role of the state into both social institutions and cultural practices.

One of the most astute social theorists of the latter 20th century, Ralph Miliband, described this trend:

> More than ever before men [and women] now live in the shadow of the state. What they want to achieve, individually or in groups, now mainly depends on the state's sanction and support. But since that sanction and support are not bestowed indiscriminately, they must, ever more directly, seek to influence and shape the state's power and purpose, or try and appropriate it altogether. It is for the state's attention, or for its control, that [persons] compete; and it is against the state that beat the waves of social conflict. It is to an ever greater degree the state which men [and women] encounter as they confront other men [and women]. This is why, as social beings, they are also political beings, whether they know it or not. It is possible not to be interested in what the state does; but it is not possible to be unaffected by it.[1]

In the hegemonic view, the state has enlarged its role in capitalist economies throughout the 20th century. In its expanded role, it is now indispensable in ensuring the reproduction of capitalist social relations, and the powers of the state are used to support and sustain the underlying economic and ideological framework of capitalist society. One consequence is that the state is intricately involved with supporting class differences and with protecting the overall continuity of dominant economic interests against those of other classes.

In the United States, although the capitalist class is the dominant social formation, it does not dictate the minutiae of state decision making. Nor does the state merely act at the command of capitalist leadership. There are too many complexities in state and economic operations to suggest that powerful economic interests are able to steer the state into complying with all their wishes. At times, however, they do employ pressure, and it is decisive because capitalist leadership has resources to successfully apply enormous pressure on state functionaries; but there are other times when it is not decisive. The point is that the notion that the state is reducible to the interests of the capitalist class is too simplistic. Furthermore, to maintain its own legitimacy, the state must be adept at continually integrating many of the interests of allied and even opposing interests under its banner.

Nevertheless, capitalist power, like all power, can be real without being omnipotent. Divisions and friction may exist within the capitalist class, but American society remains a class society with enormous differences in wealth and power, and the prevailing pattern of state actions is in reproducing the capitalist relations of production. One prominent form that state action takes on behalf of capitalist enterprise is in facilitating capital accumulation.[2]

Role of the State in Private Accumulation

Regardless of the measure of American state activity one uses, the importance of the state no longer lies in merely creating a basic governing structure and establishing an acceptable social order. Instead, the state is actively involved in subsidizing, supporting, and organizing private business and industrial activity. One social analyst elaborated on this point: "The state is more than a front for the economic interests it serves; it is the single most important instrument that corporate America has at its command."[3]

State intervention in the economy has largely been intervention for the purpose of supporting capitalist enterprise. This is done by providing conditions favorable to the accumulation of private capital by subsidizing it. Direct methods for doing this are through tax breaks, legal protection, protective tariffs, market regulation, and loans and credits with favorable conditions. Indirectly it is done by providing essential equipment and services, such as roads, energy, and transportation cheaply to capitalist firms. Private businesses are persistent and successful applicants for public subsidies. These proud advocates of the private enterprise system are beneficiaries of "corporate welfare" running into the hundreds of *billions* of dollars. A few examples will illustrate this point:

- In 1989 the federal government began a $166 *billion* bailout of the savings and loan industry—a bailout necessitated by widespread corruption, outright cheating, stealing, and general mismanagement by the powerful and wealthy owners and managers in this industry.
- $110 million is given annually by the federal government to corporations to advertise their products abroad (e.g., Sunkist, McDonald's, M&M/Mars).
- The federal government provides $200 million annually in subsidies to corporate farms having incomes of more than $5 million a year.
- The federal Office of Management and Budget estimated that subsidies in the form of tax credits, deductions, and exemptions to private corporations cost the government

(taxpayers) $440 *billion* in 1996. (This compares, for example, to $16 billion annual federal cost for child support programs.)

- Some corporations completely escape federal income taxes. Five to 10 corporations each year with total profits exceeding $1 billion pay no federal corporate taxes. Some of these companies receive refunds of past-year taxes of more than $100 million.[4]

Hundreds of similar examples could be given, but one fact is clear: the American state system at all levels favors corporate capital interests and is biased toward corporate ideology and goals.

Another of the major mechanisms by which the American capitalist class enjoys favorable treatment by the state, leading to enhanced capital accumulation, is through an interpenetration by members of the capitalist class into the state apparatus itself. In this way, economic wealth is translated into political power. Many elected politicians and top government officials are, in their primary occupations, business executives and lawyers who reflect the interests of the capitalist class. The highest levels of the state include many members of the corporate elite or people connected with them through kinship or social ties, all of which reflects the close relationship and community of interests between the state and the capitalist class.

One entrenched practice illustrates well the confraternity between private and government sectors. Thousands of former elected politicians and appointed government officials are regularly appointed to the boards of directors of corporations, hired as executives, or retained as lobbyists with the expectation that they will be able to help the private firm through their government connections. Two recent examples are Richard Darman, a former budget director, and James Baker III, a former secretary of state, both of whom were recruited by the Carlyle Group, a large Washington investment firm. Industries whose products are largely bought by the government employ this practice extensively. Examples are the weapons, shipbuilding, aircraft, and electronics industries.

A related mechanism of capitalist influence into the American state apparatus is through the economic resources of corporations to influence politics. There are numerous ways in which the economic power of big business is converted into political power. Pressure of economic interest groups is a pervasive condition under which the state must operate. A number of studies have shown that large corporations, wealthy elites, and "think tanks" and foundations funded by corporations and the wealthy work together to elect politicians who ensure that legislation and public policies will not depart from their interests. This practice is historically rooted in the American political economy. A late-19th-century Republican senator from Pennsylvania, Boies Penrose, articulated this symbiotic connection in a frank—if crude—manner. In addressing a group of corporate businessmen, he told them, "I believe in a division of labor. You send us to Congress; we pass the laws under which you make money . . . and out of your profits you further contribute to our campaign funds to send us back again to pass laws to enable you to make more money."[5] More recently, in a book titled *The Buying of the President*, the author asserts, "The presidential campaign in the United States has become . . . a giant auction, in which multimillion-dollar interests compete to influence and gain access to the candidates who would be president. . . . Before the first vote is cast in a presidential primary, a private referendum has already been conducted among the nation's financial elites as to which candidates shall earn his party's nomination."[6]

In 1996 Common Cause, a nonprofit, nonpartisan citizens' organization that works to improve the way federal and state governments operate, published a major report detailing how a group of corporations and superrich individuals finance the political parties, shaping the political agenda and reaping rewards with their huge money contributions. Corporate gifts dominated the large contributions to political candidates of both parties. These gifts, and donations by corporate political action committees (PACs), bring results through elected politicians' support of legislation favorable to the business elites. Thus, behind the slogan "we the people," the affluent and powerful influence legislation largely on their own behalf.[7]

The research reported in *The Buying of the President* and by Common Cause, and other similar research, does not suggest that the large business and wealthy elites are some kind of politically unified behemoth. Such a view is an oversimplification of a very complex system. However, corporate and individual wealthy elites do dominate American politics at the expense of the mass of citizens because average citizens are largely left out of the decision- and policy-making process.[8]

Despite the sobering degree to which big corporations and socially elite dominate American politics, it must be emphasized that the state is a contested terrain of conflict and compromise, which, although it largely serves to perpetuate the dominant social formations, does not simply obey their commands. As a result, working-class and underprivileged groups sometimes are able to wrest concessions from the state that are not supported by organized capital, as exemplified in legislation that provides for a minimum wage, Social Security, Medicare/Medicaid, and other social services. Laws also protect worker safety and civil rights.

Capital Accumulation and Sport

Professional sport in the United States is big business; it is structured to maximize profit. Those who own and control it are wealthy and powerful. As I noted in chapter 3, from 20 to 30 owners of professional sport teams are among the 400 wealthiest individuals in America, and a number of other owners are just a notch below this level. In addition to individual ownership, some professional sport teams are owned by large corporations (e.g., Ascent Entertainment Group owns the Colorado Avalanche and Denver Nuggets). These corporations bring their considerable resources of money and power into professional sports.[9]

From the very beginning of professional sport, team owners have benefited from actions of the state, sometimes by favorable legislation, sometimes by favorable court rulings, and sometimes through governmental policies and regulations. All have been important in defining the economic dynamics of professional sport. Because the state has played such a strategic role in the economy of sport, it is difficult to disentangle the two institutional strands.

The major means by which the state has protected the investments of professional team owners, and has advanced capital accumulation, has been through the courts and congressional legislation. From its beginnings, the professional sport industry has benefited from favorable court decisions that have enabled owners to monopolize their industry, and in cases in which their power has been threatened, they have joined forces with the courts to crush opposition.[10] All the professional sport leagues operate as cartels (groups of firms that organize together to control production, sales, and wages within an industry), with team owners making agreements on matters of mutual interest.

Such agreements violate the intent of antitrust laws and are illegal in most businesses, but the courts have consistently protected professional sport from antitrust accusations and have upheld its exemption from them. This protects each sport franchise from competition because the number of franchises is controlled by the team owners; no new franchise is allowed to locate in a given territory without approval of the owners. This protection from competition also eliminates price wars and frees owners to set ticket prices at will, thus maximizing their profits. Each league can also negotiate television contracts for the entire league without violating antitrust laws; indeed, this is protected by congressional action in the 1961 Sports Broadcast Act.[11]

Employment practices of owners in professional team sports have also been protected by the courts and congressional legislation, with the major results being the restraint of athletes' freedom of movement and of wages. Professional athletes in the team sports are drastically limited in choices of where they can play and in their bargaining power. An athlete who wants to play professionally in a particular sport must negotiate with the team that drafted him or her (or, in the case of veteran players, with the team that holds the contract). Team owners in all the professional sports have taken advantage of their immunity from antitrust laws to implement employment practices and structures that serve their own interests.

Baseball was the first sport to adopt what is known as the "reserve clause," but all the professional team sports have had some form of it. By the 1880s, all Major League Baseball owners used a provision in every player's contract that enabled the owners to control the player's job mobility. Once a player signed a contract with a club, that team had exclusive rights over him; he was no longer free to negotiate with other teams because his contract had a clause that "reserved" his services to his original team for the succeeding year.[12]

The reserve clause specified that the owner had the exclusive right to renew the player's contract annually, and thus the player was bound perpetually to negotiate with only one club; he became its property and could even be sold to another club without his own consent. In all succeeding years, then, the player had to sell his services solely to the club that owned his contract, unless the club released, sold, or traded him, or he chose to retire.

The reserve clause was an effective device for holding down salaries because players were denied an alternative market for their services. This caused a profound imbalance in bargaining power between owners and players, thus enabling owners to prosper. Meanwhile the players toiled for salaries far below what they would have received in a more competitive bargaining environment.

Resentment against the reserve clause was persistent from its beginnings, and on two occasions, challenges to its constitutionality reached the U.S. Supreme Court. In 1922 the Court upheld it, contending in essence that Major League Baseball was a sport, not a business, and therefore was entitled to immunity from antitrust laws. Again in 1972 when the reserve clause was challenged, the Court favored letting the 1922 decision stand. It was not until 1976 that the courts finally struck down the reserve clause, substituting in its place a limited player mobility plan.[13]

Athletes in the other professional team sports have found themselves in much the same position as baseball players. In each case, the player's freedom of movement was restricted by some type of reservation system. However, other professional sports have worked out various forms of compromise between owners and players, giving players limited control over their terms of employment, but still not the same freedom to choose their employers that workers in other industries enjoy.[14]

The extent to which professional athletes have struggled against the capital accumulation interests of those who own sport teams is illustrated in the various attempts that pro athletes have made to form player unions and engage in collective bargaining to have their concerns and grievances addressed. In all capitalist enterprise, ownership tries to minimize production costs by holding down wages and other expenses. As a means of redressing the balance of power between capitalists and workers, and protecting their material interests and working conditions, workers have formed unions. Unions of professional athletes go back to the 1885 creation of the National Brotherhood of Professional Ball Players. As other professional sports have emerged, most have formed players' unions, largely in response to wage issues and the restrictive player reserve systems.[15]

Although player unions and collective bargaining have had some significant successes, owners have used their considerable personal wealth and influence in Congress and the courts to minimize the effectiveness of the player unions. The unions have not possessed equivalent legal and legislative clout to secure many of their needs, so in effect the state has been able to preserve and protect the capital accumulation interests of those who own and control sports.

Another means through which capital accumulation accrues to professional sport owners is through tax abatements. Owners of professional franchises are given a number of ways to minimize taxable profits. One example is the depreciation of players. Most of the assets of a professional sport team are its players, so most of the cost of a franchise is player contracts. Owners can depreciate players the way farmers depreciate cattle and corporations depreciate company cars; the professional athletes' status is that of property. No other business in the United States is able to depreciate the value of human beings as part of its business costs. The obvious beneficiaries of such tax breaks are the wealthy team owners.

Social Costs of Private Enterprise

Another form of American state intervention into the economic institution is its assumption of a large share of the social costs of private enterprise. These are costs that are not paid for by individual private businesses but are instead shifted onto the public via the state. The expenses include, but are not limited to, air and water pollution cleanup; toxic waste disposal; and reclamation of wildlife, soils, and forest resources after their decimation for private profit.

The state also bears the social costs of private enterprise in accepting much of the cost of education for training skilled labor and in subsidizing scientific research, the findings of which often benefit private capital. Federal and state governments fund billions of dollars in research and development grants to private corporations who are then permitted to keep the resulting patents, technologies, and products for their own profit.

This has been the case for a wide range of products and advanced technologies. One political analyst said, "The computer industry was subsidized by the public through the military system during the costly phase of research and development, then turned loose for profit-making when sufficient progress had been made for a market to become available."[16] The United States would not have been the early world leader in semiconductor production without the support of the government. "The U.S. government . . . provided conditions that *could not otherwise have existed, . . .* in the crucial early years" of research and development, "and thereby got the [semiconductor] industry as a whole off the ground."[17]

In almost every type of business and industry, government provides various types of support, opportunities, and protections to subsidize private enterprise at public expense. There is very little research on the total national social costs of private enterprise. Recently, however, estimates of "the total social costs of business enterprise in the United States" were undertaken. The investigator reported that the total estimated annual costs were approximately $2,618 billion![18]

Corporate leaders demand this type of treatment. The chief executive officer for a large computer corporation asserted that "if the United States is to regain its competitive position, the public sector must encourage technical innovation, increased investment in research and development, and more emphasis on education of a highly trained workforce."[19]

Social Costs of Private Enterprise in Sport

State intervention has shifted a large share of the cost of professional sport to the taxpayers. Ubiquitous monuments to socializing the costs and privatizing the profits in sport are the numerous sport stadiums and arenas that have been built or renovated at public expense. More than 75 percent of these stadiums and arenas have been publicly financed at taxpayer expense since the 1970s, and more than 20 professional sports teams in the United States are planning to build new stadiums or arenas or remodel existing ones by the year 2002. These lavish structures have come to symbolize a city's willingness to undertake ambitious projects, and they provide visible evidence, at least to some, of big league status in the competitive world of civic pride. But civic pride can carry a high price tag. The average cost of one of these publicly subsidized facilities in the 1990s has exceeded $200 million, with actual costs ranging from a low of $125 million to a high of about $400 million.[20]

The reason that few pro sport team owners own the facilities in which their teams play is that when the local governmental jurisdiction owns them, the professional sport team owners are relieved of the burden of property taxes, insurance, and maintenance costs, not to mention construction. Team owners pay rent on the facilities, of course, but this usually covers only a fraction of overall operating expenses. Local taxpayers actually wind up subsidizing professional team owners.

Another reason that team owners do not own sport facilities is that they can easily move franchises to other cities should they become unhappy with existing financial arrangements (one sportswriter calls this "strip-mining" cities). In the 1980s, three NFL owners actually made such a move (the Oakland Raiders to Los Angeles, the Baltimore Colts to Indianapolis, and the St. Louis Cardinals to Phoenix), and the incidence of owner "extortion" appears to be increasing. In less than 24 months in 1995 and 1996, four NFL teams moved: the Los Angeles Raiders back to Oakland, the Los Angeles Rams to St. Louis, the Cleveland Browns to Baltimore, and the Houston Oilers to Nashville.

So much movement in the NFL has led to the league being derisively called "the league with franchises on wheels." With examples of franchise movement like these, team owners have very powerful leverage against a city and can extract very favorable leasing, concession, and parking agreements when they threaten to leave unless their demands are met.

The pressures that encourage public officials to campaign for the construction of stadiums and arenas at public expense come from various sources, but it is the pro sport franchise owners, supported by the local mass media, who create local interest in and demand for these facilities. The symbolic and public purposes of sport and civic imagery merge with private economic goals. When faced with such pressures, local voters, city councils, and legislatures frequently accede to the demands for quality facilities.[21]

To prevent the Chicago White Sox from moving its franchise to another city in 1988, the Illinois state legislature passed a bill that included financing the construction of a new stadium for the team. In the same year, funding for education in the state received a much lower increase than that which had been sought. Also during the latter 1980s and early 1990s, an incredible series of political machinations resulted in the commitment of more than $350 million of taxpayer money to build two sports stadiums in Baltimore to secure a long-term assurance from the Orioles baseball franchise to remain in Baltimore and to attract an NFL team to replace the Colts, who had moved to Indianapolis in 1984 (Baltimore succeeded in pirating the Browns from Cleveland in 1996). Also part of the Maryland package was $70 million to the billionaire owner of the Washington Redskins for infrastructural improvements around the stadium he is building in southern Maryland. This massive public subsidy to professional sports owners was made despite the fact that Baltimore has one of the worst urban social problems in any city in the United States, and the need for public money to address these problems is acute.

In 1990 Denver metropolitan district voters approved a sales tax increase to build a baseball stadium under the threat by Major League Baseball (MLB) that Denver would not get a franchise if the taxpayers did not pay for a new baseball-only facility. In Phoenix, taxpayers did not even get to vote on a tax increase to raise more than $200 million to build a baseball facility for the new MLB franchise, the Arizona Diamondbacks. Clever politicians committed the tax increase without ever consulting local citizens.[22]

There are times, however, when the state does not act at the behest of capitalist interests. On four occasions, San Francisco voters rejected public funding for a new baseball stadium for the Giants; as a result of citizen resistance, Giant owners had to privately finance the building of Pacific Bell Park. Demands by the New England Patriots for a new football stadium have garnered no support in that region. Citizen resistance to subsidizing professional sports owners appears to be growing throughout the country.

Professional sport team owners, and often local politicians, seek to rationalize the public expenditures in terms of public benefits, arguing that communities profit by increased revenues, business, and taxes. They also point to various intangible benefits, such as neighborhood redevelopment and enhanced civic pride. But these claims have never been well documented. In fact, most social and economic analyses have concluded that the prime beneficiaries of these sport facilities are a small group of wealthy individuals and that those who disproportionately bear the costs are low-income citizens.

Two economists who studied the various benefits and costs for stadiums and arenas concluded that "in most of the cases we have examined, calculation of the . . . enumerated direct costs and revenues result in a net loss for the municipal treasury." They further concluded that major league sports frequently have no significant positive impact on a city's economy, and in some ways may even drain funds from other municipal projects. Finally, with respect to the promised increased economic activity before and after building or renovating a sport facility, their research led them to conclude that "the positive impacts on area development touted by stadium promoters do not appear to be strong enough to show up in . . . measures of economic activity for individual cities that have built stadiums."[23] A study conducted by the Congressional Research Service found that the number of jobs created by subsidizing stadiums with taxpayer money costs $127,000 *per job created!* Those proclaiming economic benefit to a city appear to be blind to the myriad direct and auxiliary costs that diminish or eliminate positive economic impacts.

Urban policy researcher Mark S. Rosentraub supports these conclusions and argues that "sports teams can financially support themselves and do not deserve welfare." He further claims that "cities should not be held hostage to demands issued by team owners and players for subsidies that do not make sporting events more available to citizens but simply increase profits and salaries. It is time for cities, their taxpayers, and their civic leaders to recognize the leagues and sports for what they are . . . cartels that ensure profits and salaries."[24]

One final point needs to be made with regard to public funding of sports facilities. Even when local taxpayers agree to a tax to build professional sports facilities in a city, the tax-exempt bonds that are sold to build the facilities amount to a federal subsidy because the bondholders do not pay federal or state taxes on the interest they receive, thus costing taxpayers throughout the nation millions of dollars. In 1997 Senator Daniel Patrick Moynihan of New York introduced a bill that would prohibit the issuance of tax-exempt bonds for professional sports facilities. If Moynihan's bill becomes law, cities will not be able to issue tax-exempt bonds to build sports facilities. Communities wishing to sell bonds to fund sports facilities will have to sell them with a much higher yield, adding millions to local taxpayers' costs. Consequently, local taxpayers will likely be more reluctant to approve public funding of sports facilities. (See box, pp. 114-115.)

Coercing the public to bear the costs while privatizing the profits in sport is not limited to sport facilities. Another example of what amounts to a public subsidy for both sport franchises and private, nonsport businesses is the purchase of game tickets by corporations, part of which can be deducted from taxes as a business expense. A large proportion of the season tickets for professional sports are purchased by businesses. In effect, then, taxpayers are subsidizing the costs for corporate executives and their friends to see professional sporting events. When this deduction was threatened by the Internal Revenue Service, professional sports and businesses combined their lobbying efforts to retain the subsidy.

How You Pay $$$ For Stadiums Far, Far Away

Since 1990, owners of nearly 40 professional sports teams have tried to blackmail their communities into pouring public subsidies into new facilities for their teams. All but a few have succeeded. And it isn't only local taxpayers who pay.

Scratch beneath the surface, and you find sports moguls benefiting from an array of tax breaks, many of which are uniquely theirs. The cost is picked up by federal taxpayers, including those in the 26 states without a professional team. Here's how:

Loans

When states and cities issue bonds for stadiums and arenas, most are tax exempt to those who buy them, which allows for lower interest rates. But the Congressional Research Service has estimated the cost to the federal Treasury of such exemptions at $100 million a year in lost taxes. With new, higher-cost stadiums and arenas coming on line, that easily could triple.

Deductions

Luxury boxes are one reason owners demand new stadiums. Unlike general seating, almost all the money they earn goes to the home team. But they are expensive, up to $300 a seat per game. Thus most are sold to businesses which, by inviting clients, can deduct 50% of the cost from their income. Result: a 17% federal subsidy for wealthy people to watch games.

Depreciation

New owners can deduct half the price of purchasing a team against other income. That's possible because a loophole in the tax law allows them to depreciate the value of player contracts above their actual cost. With team prices skyrocketing, in part because of public stadium subsidies, the write-off can wipe out millions in tax liability.

Taken together, these tax advantages provide a hefty federal subsidy to owners. Federal taxpayers pick up 17% of stadium subsidies through the exemption for bonds alone, according to the CRS.

And for what? To make a few wealthy owners even richer.

Meanwhile, fans lose because ticket prices at new stadiums rise even faster than at the old ones. Most have fewer seats, thanks to luxury boxes, which limits public access even more.

Communities lose because the subsidies produce few jobs—and those at costs above $100,000 each, according to congressional studies. They also chew up a town's ability to fund other projects. If

Seattle voters approve $330 million in public financing June 17 for a new stadium for the Seahawks to go along with $440 million for the Mariners', the city's debt for sports facilities will equal a third of the total state debt.

And the nation gets no economic benefit. Franchises just shift around, infuriating fans and picking nonfans' pockets.

Source: *USA Today*, 5 June 1997, 14A. Copyright, *USA Today*. Reprinted with permission.

Ideological Role of the State

One of the traditional functions of the state is that of fostering and preserving social harmony. States have enforcement agencies, such as the police and the armed forces, that ensure social order is maintained, but they typically try to avoid using them because this often involves violence, which has the potential of antagonizing citizens and causing resentment and rebellion. Instead, social harmony is shaped through a common system of goals, values, and beliefs, and from this system a consensus is built that supplies the cohesion on which nation-states stand.

Social cohesion is formed and maintained through ideological inculcation, which socializes people to internalize and accept, even embrace, the prevailing social order. On this point, one political theorist explained that "the state cannot enshrine and reproduce political domination exclusively through repression, force, or 'naked' violence, but directly calls upon ideology to legitimize . . . and contribute to a consensus of those classes and fractions which are dominated from the point of view of political power."[25]

In every nation-state, education is a primary avenue for the state's hegemonic ideological work in socializing people to accept the existing social formation and to see the government and all its branches as right. Two notions underlie this educational promotion of hegemonic ideology: citizens must be taught loyalty and patriotism so that they will, one, support their political leaders and, two, be willing to fight to defend their country. In the United States, the school subjects through which these ideas are primarily taught are history and government (or civics), and both are required by law. Of course, the school (a state agency), through its own organization and social milieu, tends to sustain and reproduce the existing hegemonic relations.

Ideological work is actually carried out in several social institutions, not just the schools, with the encouragement, support, and approval of the state. For example, the mass media play a decisive role in the ideological sphere (this will be described in chapter 8).

Sport and the Promotion of National Ideology

Sport in modern societies is one of the means by which nation-states socialize their citizens, transmitting the symbolic codes of the dominant culture and inducing citizens toward conformity to beliefs and values that prevail in the wider society. At the same time, sport is one of the most salient molders of national collective identity.

© Chris Hamilton

Sport as an instrument for the promotion of national identity is highlighted through celebratory displays of a nation's flag by victorious athletes during international sporting events. Athletes' sporting success is often portrayed as symbolically representing a nation's achievements, thus bringing recognition and status to a country.

In the United States, sport inculcates values and norms that bolster the legitimacy of the American political system. National loyalty and patriotism are fostered through sport rituals and ceremonies that link sport and nationalism. National symbols and pageantry are often woven into sport events. Reciting the Pledge of Allegiance, singing the national anthem, performing patriotic halftime shows, and displaying emblems and insignias like flags all ideologically celebrate national identity and the legitimacy of the current social order.

Probably nothing provokes stronger nationalistic emotions than activities tied to patriotism. Important national and international events like the Super Bowl and the Olympic Games are incorporated into a panoply of patriotic ritual that serves to remind Americans of their common destiny. A specific example of patriotic symbolism occurred during the Persian Gulf War in 1991. Super Bowl XXV in Tampa Stadium was the epitome of patriotic imagery and display: the game was dedicated to the troops serving in the conflict, small American flags were distributed to each spectator, and nationalistic pageantry permeated pregame and halftime displays. Former NFL commissioner Pete Rozelle acknowledged "a conscious effort on our part to bring . . . patriotism into the Super Bowl."[26]

These events, and the spectacles surrounding them, help to create and support an effective dominant culture because they convey messages about norms, values, and dispositions that contribute to the ideological hegemony of dominant groups. They are also a means of social control in that the coaches, athletic directors, broadcasters, and so forth limit the exposition of ideological perspectives to those supportive of the prevailing political-economic system. Anything that is not in agreement with the reigning hegemony is censured; all that is seditious is removed or explicitly condemned.[27]

Most sport organizations and officials go to great lengths to foster national loyalty and patriotism, and in almost every political controversy, the sports establishment can be counted upon to line up behind the reigning political leaders. Any stand on social or political issues is typically supportive of the state's consensus about what to do about it. Police and military actions are virtually always supported, as are political positions claimed to be in the "national interest."

Occasionally, dominant political structures and values are contested in the sports world. Several of the more significant occasions of political resistance in the United States have centered on gender and racial politics. One of the most memorable political displays by athletes occurred at the 1968 Mexico City Olympic Games. As an attempt to call dramatic attention to America's pervasive racism, black American Olympic athletes Tommie Smith and John Carlos raised gloved, clenched fists and bowed their heads during the playing of the national anthem. They paid a heavy price for their commitment to racial justice. The U.S. Olympic Committee suspended them from the Olympic team and threw them out of the Olympic Village.

Title IX and the Civil Rights Restoration Act are examples of successful political resistance against the state in the area of gender equity. Title IX of the Education Amendments Act of 1972 opened up sport opportunities previously denied females in educational institutions. However, the Reagan administration and various branches of the government coordinated efforts to avoid enforcing Title IX. In 1984 the U.S. Supreme Court ruled that Title IX applied only to specific programs or departments receiving federal funds. At that point, numerous women's groups began lobbying Congress to pass legislation to restore the civil rights lost in the ruling. Their efforts were successful. In March 1988, Congress overrode President Reagan's veto and passed the Civil Rights Restoration Act.

The American State and International Affairs

Contemporary state interests extend far beyond national boundaries. Technological and industrial advances as well as political events of the past century have transformed relations between nations to the point at which people of the world are interdependent in unprecedented ways. We live in a world system of interacting and interdependent nations. Since World War II, the dominant features of this world system have been a struggle; first, an economic struggle between capitalism and communism, with each side trying to favorably influence the other as well as "uncommitted" countries, and, second, a geopolitical struggle in which the leading capitalist and the leading communist countries (the United States and the Soviet Union) were military adversaries, each fighting to get the advantage. With the breakup of the Soviet Union, the overthrow of communist governments in the Eastern bloc countries, and the turn to market economies in Asia, notably in China, capitalism has been able to move more rapidly toward a global economy.[28]

From its beginning, there has been an expanding character to capitalist production. One social scientist noted that capitalism is based on the fact that economic factors operate beyond an area that any political entity can fully control. Early merchant capitalism gave way to colonialism, which in turn in the 20th century has given way to postcolonialism, the current era of development of the world capitalist economy.[29]

The current period is so called because all the major territories subject to direct colonial rule have won their independence as new nations. The demise of direct colonial rule has been accompanied by a significant development in the nature of international capitalism: the rise of multinational corporations. This form of capitalist organization has become a leading influence in the world economy. Today, about 400 multinational corporations, out of millions of corporations around the world, control about 75 percent of the capital assets of the world. Some social scientists have called multinational corporations the modern colonial powers.[30]

Multinational corporations are privately owned firms unified by common ownership that have extended their marketing and production into countries outside their origins. Most of the world's multinationals are American in ownership and origin. As with any capitalist firm, the major driving force behind multinationalism is the profit motive.

Multinational corporations bring investment into countries throughout the world, thus stimulating the local economies and linking the economies of the world's nations, laying the groundwork for a world economy.

In their production and distribution operations, multinationals exploit many countries, especially those that are less developed, by many of the same methods of colonialism (paying low wages, not training local leadership, exporting local products, and returning profits to the modern country). Regardless of their other effects, multinational corporations are extremely profitable; some exceed in annual net income the gross national products of many countries.

For capitalism to grow and prosper worldwide, a congenial climate must be created to encourage other nations to purchase the products and services of this system. At the same time, capitalist states attempt to persuade other nations about the viability of their political-economic systems, spending significant state resources on ideologically based activities designed to demonstrate their indisputable superiority. Sport has played a significant role in the expanding international political economy.

Sport as an Instrument of International Politics and Diplomacy

One of the fastest growing and most popular cultural practices throughout the world is organized sport. The unmistakable preoccupation with sport is illustrated by the increasing number of national sport programs, which develop elite athletes for international competition in such events as the Olympic Games, the Pan-American

Games, the British Commonwealth Games, the Asian Games, the African Games, and the Third World Games. In all these events, and others, competition takes place in many different sports. In addition, each sport has its own world championship competition. The result of this worldwide interest and competition is a large, immensely popular international sport industry.

Commercialization and professionalization have firmly established themselves permanently in international sport, and competition among athletes representing different nations offers those countries free media publicity. Television has stimulated the incredible interest in the world's sport events and now binds them together. Because access to television is nearly universal, people in every part of the globe can follow the achievements of "their" athletes: billions of viewers throughout the world watch World Cup soccer play-offs, Olympic Games, and other international sport events. Sport has assumed significance in linking participants and observers world-wide. The past 25 years has brought a skyrocketing ascension for sport as an international cultural practice.

The high visibility of international sport events has fostered a favorable climate for state intervention. In the following sections, I examine the ways and means by which state intervention is used in the ideological construction of dominant group consensus. My focus is broader than just American involvement, for such a worldwide phenomenon is more appropriately examined from a wider vantage point. From this framework, American actions and policies can then become clearer.

Advancing National Unity Through Sport

Countries increasingly use sport to promote national unity and pride and to reflect the accomplishments of their political-economic systems. One way in which they do this is through the widespread use of sport on the international level to assert national prestige and promote a sense of national identity and unity. The United States and other large countries do not have to depend on sport for recognition and respect, but the achievements of their athletes serve as symbols of national unity and excellence and provide temporary emotional surges of national passion. These patriotic feelings are fueled by framing international sport competition in which American athletes compete in chauvinistic terms: American athletes vs._____, playing of the national anthem, and profuse displays of the flag. Anyone who has witnessed an American athlete's or team's Olympic victory over a heated rival has seen the wild flag-waving spectacle that often follows and can probably recall the feelings engendered and the outpouring of nationalistic emotion.

For the smaller, sometimes new, nations seeking national pride and recognition and respect in the world community, triumphs in international sport competition can serve this purpose well. A relatively unknown country can gain worldwide attention when one of its athletes or teams wins an important international sporting event. For a few days at least, a country can bask in the limelight of the world's mass media. Invariably, such achievements become a focus of conversation within a country, and feelings of national pride are enhanced as people sense a common bond, a collective identity, among the athletes, themselves, and their nation.

Before the reunification of Germany, East Germany, perhaps more than any small country, undertook a deliberate program to use sport as a means of gaining international recognition and prestige. Sport also played a significant role in creating a specific East German identity. A nation of only 17 million people (about the size of California), it placed third in the Summer Olympics in 1972, second in 1976 and 1980, and second in 1988 (with other communist countries, East Germany did not take part in the 1984 Games).

Canada and Australia are two countries small in population that have undertaken systematic programs to develop elite athletes for international competition. Their governmental actions began as efforts to provide greater opportunities for mass sport and physical fitness but turned rather quickly toward the promotion of high-performance sport because of its perceived potential for much more attractive political payoffs, especially in unifying nationalist needs. In a book about sport and politics in Canada, the authors describe the massive federally funded sports program as an instrument "to promote national unity."[31]

The most populous country in the world, the People's Republic of China, has revised its national sport policy from "friendship first, competition second," once advocated by Mao Tse-tung, to an all-out quest for global recognition and status. China's political and sport officials openly acknowledge that they view sport as one instrument for promoting national pride and identity, which is a primary motivation behind a huge expenditure of hundreds of millions of dollars annually for sports.[32]

Of course, when chauvinistic sentiment becomes wrapped up in sporting achievements, sports failures can bring national embarrassment. The poor showing by the U.S. team in Winter Olympic Games during the 1980s and 1990s has caused hand-wringing among political and sports officials and numerous mass media diatribes about the national disgrace of the quality of American sport. Even more embarrassing to Canada, though, was the ignominious disclosure that sprinter Ben Johnson, the gold medal winner of the 100-meter dash at the 1988 Seoul Summer Olympics, failed the postrace drug test. One

Canadian television announcer described it as "a tragedy for the country and the Canadian Olympic movement." And from a Canadian magazine publisher: "What he achieved . . . gave me a great deal of pride. Now I feel shame."[33]

International Dominance Through Sport

Historically, international political dominance has been pursued through military threat (or action), economic embargoes, increased tariffs, or severed diplomatic relations. But because international sport has such high visibility, it has become a strategic instrument for political dominance and diplomatic coercion. Actions taken against other countries gain worldwide attention, so countries have come to use sport to sanction recalcitrant nations and pressure them into complying with their wishes.

Official Recognition

When a nation's athletes are permitted to compete athletically with another, this is interpreted as a recognition of that country and its government. Conversely, refusing to engage in sport events with another country or denying its athletes visas or travel documents has become equivalent to severing diplomatic relations. The history of international sport, especially the Olympic Games, is filled with examples of this tactic. Germany and Austria were denied participation in the 1920 Olympics at Antwerp because of their role in World War 1. Germany, Japan, and Italy were banned from the 1948 Olympics because of their actions in World War II. The most long-standing and worldwide banning from international sport competition was enforced against South Africa for its state system of apartheid. South Africa was barred from the Olympic Games for more than 25 years; in fact, during that period, almost every major international sporting event denied South Africa participation. Although these actions were all officially taken by the International Olympic Committee, they were endorsed and supported by national governments; indeed, in some cases the actions were taken in direct response to governmental threats of various kinds.

Inviting countries into the world sport community, on the other hand, is a way of showing approval of their policies. Japan's hosting of the 1964 Olympics gave that country a chance to stage the Games while at the same time be welcomed back into the family of nations. Japan could show the world that it was a modern, peace-loving, democratic country and that it had put the legacy of World War II behind it. The 1972 Munich Olympic games did much the same for West Germany, although the Arab terrorist massacre of 11 Israeli athletes destroyed much of the positive image West Germany had hoped to receive from the Games.

Sport has occasionally been used to open channels of diplomatic recognition as well. The most well-known example of this is the "Ping-Pong diplomacy" carried out by the United States and the People's Republic of China in the early 1970s. From 1949, the beginning of the Mao socialist government in China, until 1971 the U.S. government had no diplomatic relations with China. By the early 1970s, it had become increasingly clear that this policy needed changing, so President Nixon arranged for groups of American and Chinese table tennis players to play a series of matches. This Ping-Pong diplomacy, as it came to be called, opened channels that ultimately resulted in the renewal of diplomatic relations between the two countries.[34]

Renewed or improved diplomatic relations are the harbinger of expanded economic relations. Multinational corporations are major beneficiaries of expanded international relations because new markets are opened up and capital accumulation is fostered for the products and services of these huge firms. Sport, then, serves to lubricate the international political economy.

Boycotts

The enormous popularity of sport ensures that much of the world's population will be aware of the existence, or lack, of sport competitions between particular countries. International athletic contests have thus become a public forum; countries can express disagreement with other countries' policies by refusing to compete with them. Governments have increasingly used the boycott to express political disapproval with other nations' policies.

The two most renowned incidents of boycotting are undoubtedly the U.S. boycott of the 1980 Moscow Olympic Games because of the Soviet Union's military intervention in Afghanistan and the Soviet Union's retaliation in boycotting the 1984 Los Angeles Games. Although these instances are well known, the boycott has been used frequently by other countries at various times.[35]

Promoting Political-Economic Systems Through Sport

Nations have increasingly forged direct propaganda links between sport triumphs and the viability of their political-economic systems. In this strategy, sport is an instrument of state policy that ties achievements of the nation's athletes to the country's political-economic system to promote the system's superiority. This has been called sports diplomacy, and the athletes used for this purpose have been labeled diplomats in sweat suits.

One of the early and blatant examples of sport as a platform for demonstrating political superiority was Adolf Hitler's use of the 1936

Olympic Games "to strengthen his control over the German people and to showcase Nazi culture to the entire world." The Games "were a dazzling charade that reinforced and mobilized the hysterical patriotism of the German masses."[36]

The major geopolitical dispute from the mid-1940s to the early 1990s was the disharmony formed around the two "superpowers," the United States and the Soviet Union. The two nations confronted each other throughout the world in what was called the cold war. But in place of armed conflict, the superpowers waged an ideological war in the form of political and diplomatic strategies designed to win support from the world community for their political economic system and to extend their influence worldwide. Both capitalist and communist countries used sport as a tool to promote their causes.

One sport historian claimed that the Soviet government viewed the successes of its athletes as having "particular political significance. . . . Each new victory is a victory for the Soviet form of society. . . . It provides irrefutable proof of the superiority of socialist culture over the decaying culture of capitalist states."[37] A similar ideological pride was found among Americans. Olympic fencer and modern pentathlete Rob Stull asserted that international sport sets the stage for "system versus system. And I believe we should show them that the capitalist system just beats the living hell out of [the communist] system."[38]

Funding International Sport in the United States

International sport has become a massive commercial business. Individual athletes and teams travel throughout the world to compete in sporting events. Because of the complex nature of the international sport industry, various public funding and private sponsoring systems exist. The focus here will be limited to the methods that are employed in the United States.

State Support

Compared with most countries of the world, the U.S. government has always had a more limited direct involvement in international sport. Many countries have a minister of sport (or a similar title) who has access to the country's top political leadership, just as the other ministers do, and has a direct funding source from the national treasury. In these countries, international-level sports are supported directly by the state.

Although the United States does not have such a system, the U.S. government and its many branches and agencies are nevertheless committed to using sport for the advancement of the American political-economic system. Indeed, concern about America's international image prompted former President Gerald Ford to create a

President's Commission on Olympic Sports. The commission's recommendations resulted in the Amateur Sports Act of 1978, reorganizing amateur sport and committing the government to a continuing investment in international sport. At the same time, the report strongly recommended that private sector firms provide the major funding for American sports, suggesting that it was in their interests to promote the American political economy throughout the world.

No specific American governmental agency oversees or funds America's international-level sports, but federal, state, and local governments use public money in various ways to support elite sports. A few examples will suffice to illustrate this point:

- Federal and state governments have contributed land, buildings, personnel, and support services to all the U.S. Olympic training centers.
- The 1993 World University Games in Buffalo, New York, had a task force assigned to the Games that included federal agencies such as the departments of Defense, State, and Transportation and the U.S. Information Agency that collectively put up $10 million.
- In all Olympic Games held in the United States, federal government money has been used in support of the venues and for security. Although the 1996 Atlanta Summer Games were privately funded, the federal government contributed an estimated $227 million for security, transportation, and so forth.
- The state of Georgia spent $150 million on public buildings that were used during the Atlanta Games. Atlanta and other local governments spent approximately $90 million on projects related to the Olympics.

These examples are a minute fraction of the total public support for America's international-level sports. It is actually impossible to determine how much government money is spent because much of it is spread out and hidden deep in the labyrinth of hundreds of agencies' and bureaucracies' budgets.

Corporate Support

A massive and growing corporate sponsorship for elite athletes and teams that compete in international sport can be seen as a response to the President's Commission on Olympic Sports report. It is especially noteworthy that many of the corporations that sponsor sports are multinationals (e.g., Coca-Cola, IBM, McDonald's). A number of benefits flow from their investment in sport. First, it supports the ongoing strategy of using sport to promote the American political economy. Second, corporate sponsorship offers companies image enhancement, high visibility, name recognition, and, perhaps, increased sales. As the athletes and teams who are sponsored compete worldwide, the sponsor's name becomes associated with the sports achievements; thus, assuming that consumer behavior is related to advertising, capital accumulation for the multinational firm is enhanced worldwide.

Political Economy of International Sport

Public and private support for international sport as an ideological instrument turns out, on close examination, to be solidly grounded in political economy. It integrates the interests of the dominant economic and political nexus in the United States. It is a particularly good way of stimulating capital accumulation in the gigantic world marketplace, which is driven to innovate new products, services, and industries. Moreover, manipulating competition among athletes to make it seem to represent competition among countries stimulates widespread interest in the events and their outcomes, while at the same time promoting collective national identity among Americans.

The enormous industry that has emerged to satisfy the needs of this competition includes building construction, transportation, clothing, sporting equipment, coaching, education, and medicine. It involves some of the world's largest multinational corporations, all to the end of staging sport competition among athletes from different countries. There are many material beneficiaries of this competition. But the sport entrepreneurs, managers, and executives who plan and stage the events and who own or manage the ancillary industries are certainly some of the major beneficiaries.

Money Well Spent or Money Wasted?

There are those who question pouring money and resources into the training and material welfare of elite athletes for international competition that could be used elsewhere. Every country has social problems involving the poor, hungry, homeless, sick, and oppressed. In the United States, for example, millions of poor and homeless people are in need of basic human necessities, and conditions are much worse in other countries, especially in those that are less developed. In the face of such reality, American expenditures of an estimated $1 billion per year for promoting elite sport raise the specter of distorted priorities.

It is possible that America's national prestige could be more appropriately promoted by raising the standard of living of the downtrodden. That would certainly contribute more to the advancement of the human condition and social health than does supplying sports entertainment to the masses, diverting their attention, however briefly, from their government's neglect.

Summary and Preview

This chapter highlights the partnership between the state, capital, and sport in American society—the political economy of sport. As the state has expanded its intervention into social institutions and cultural practices that were once fairly independent of the state, it has become a key link between corporate capitalism and modern organized sport. The state has nurtured and stimulated capital accumulation of sport business while using sport as an instrument of national policy, bolstering and consolidating the state's role in the management and control of American society.

On this foundation, I now take up a more extended analysis of commercialized sport. In chapter 7, the growth of commercialized sport over the past century is described and analyzed. An underlying theme is that with the commercialization of sport, hegemonic features have increasingly come to define and regulate our understandings of what sport is and how it should be played.

Suggested Readings

Baim, Dean. *The Sports Stadium as a Municipal Investment.* Westport, CT: Greenwood Press, 1994.

Chomsky, Noam. *On Power and Ideology.* Boston: South End Press, 1987.

Euchner, Charles C. *Playing the Field: Why Sports Teams Move and Cities Fight to Keep Them.* Baltimore: Johns Hopkins University Press, 1993.

Freedman, Warren. *Professional Sports and Antitrust.* New York: Quorum Books, 1987.

Lowenfish, Lee. *The Imperfect Diamond: A History of Baseball's Labor Wars.* Rev. ed. New York: Da Capo Press, 1991.

McDermott, John. *Corporate Society: Class, Property, and Contemporary Capitalism.* Boulder, CO: Westview, 1991.

Rosentraub, Mark S. *Major League Losers: The Real Cost of Sports and Who's Paying for It.* New York: Basic Books, 1997.

Sage, George H. "Stealing Home: Political, Economic, and Media Power and a Publicly-Funded Baseball Stadium in Denver." *Journal of Sport and Social Issues* 17 (August 1993): 110-24.

Shropshire, Kenneth L. *The Sports Franchise Game: Cities in Pursuit of Sports Franchises, Events, Stadiums, and Arenas.* Philadelphia: University of Pennsylvania Press, 1995.

Stefancic, Jean, and Richard Delgado. *No Mercy: How Conservative Think Tanks and Foundations Changed America's Social Agenda.* Philadelphia: Temple University Press, 1996.

Vinokur, Martin B. *More Than a Game: Sports and Politics.* New York: Praeger, 1988.

Vogel, David. *Fluctuating Fortunes: The Political Power of Business in America.* New York: Basic Books, 1989.

Wilson, John. *Playing by the Rules: Sport, Society, and the State.* Detroit: Wayne State University Press, 1994.

Zepezauer, Mark, and Arthur Naiman. *Take the Rich off Welfare.* Tucson, AZ: Odonian Press, 1996.

Chapter 7

Commercialization of Sport: From Informal to Corporate Organization

[Cultural practices, such as play, games, and sport,] have been vital, indeed necessary, features of human experience from earliest times. What distinguishes their situation in the industrial capitalist era . . . are the relentless and successful efforts to separate these elemental expressions of human creativity from their group and community origins for the purpose of selling them to those who can pay for them. . . . The common characteristics of cultural products [such as sporting practices] today are the utilization of paid labor, the private appropriation of labor's creative product, and its sale for profit.

Herbert I. Schiller, professor of communication

Every aspect of American culture is in the process of commodification and linkage to the sale of goods and services. (A commodity is something whose value is defined in monetary terms; commodity production is one in which goods and services are produced to be sold. *Commodification* means the buying and selling of goods and services, including labor power [such as hiring people for wages and salaries], to make a profit; something that has been *commodified* has become subject to this process.) The pervasive commodification in contemporary society is increasingly turning sport and leisure activities into commercial pursuits and away from their basic internal logic as sporting practices.

Demonstrating that contemporary American sport is a massive commodified enterprise poses little problem. The sport economy is the 11th largest in the United States, generating $152 billion in direct spending and ranking it ahead of industries such as chemicals, electronics, and food. Sports directly contribute more than 1 percent of the value of all goods and services produced in the United States. Figure 7.1 delineates some of the categories that make up the total sports industry and the estimated contributions of each.

The professional sport industry, with more than 150 major franchises spread throughout the country, a dozen professional sport tours (e.g., the PGA), and hundreds of sundry sports events (e.g., boxing), is perhaps the most salient aspect of commercialized sport. Franchises are owned by some of America's wealthiest persons, and professional athletes are some of the highest-paid wage earners in the world. Commercial sport stimulates various industries; for example, $1.7 billion was spent by Atlanta to prepare for and conduct the 1996 Summer Olympic Games.

Now, imagine your daily life without Major League Baseball, without the NFL, without the NBA, without the NHL, without the PGA and LPGA, without the Olympic Games—actually, without any organized sports. Although it might seem unbelievable to us today, that was the situation for Americans from George Washington's presidency to the presidency of Ulysses S. Grant. The first profes-

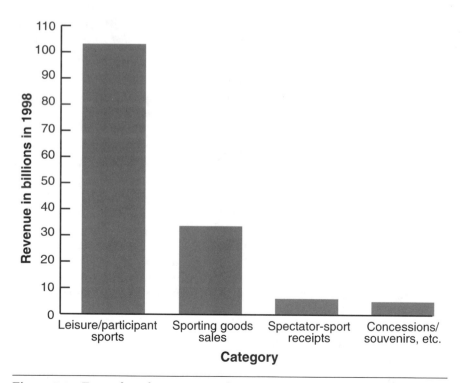

Figure 7.1   Examples of sports expenditures.

sional sport league, Major League Baseball, began in 1876, 87 years after Washington was sworn in as the first president of the United States.

Contemporary sport in American society needs to be understood as a historical moment; today's highly commercialized sport industry is not a cultural universal. It is the result of political, economic, and social events extending over the past two centuries, and it has evolved hand in hand with the growth of modern society. This in turn has occurred as an outgrowth of advances in technology, industrialization, urbanization, a population boom, and development of capitalist and wage-earning social classes.

Understanding and appreciating today's sports as cultural practices require forming a historical sensitivity—one of the components in the sociological imagination described in chapter 1—about contemporary sport. Having a historical sensitivity helps one grasp just how different sport once was and how dramatic have been its transformations. A historical review helps one realize that current sport practices and conditions are firmly rooted in events of the past.

Only a brief examination of the rise of modern sport will be presented in this volume. Readers can find a more detailed treatment in a number of excellent books.[1]

The Foundations of Modern American Sport

Economic, technological, and cultural changes since the mid-19th century have transformed the United States of 1790 from a preindustrial, largely rural nation of about 4 million people widely scattered along the eastern seaboard into a nation with a mostly urban population of 270 million; it now has one of the world's most modern and industrially advanced economies and one of its most highly commercialized sport industries.

The Colonial Legacy

Before the 19th century, the overwhelming proportion of America's working population consisted of independent farmers, with some skilled artisans and craftsmen, small retail shopkeepers and merchants, and shippers and traders. During the presidency of George Washington, about 80 percent of white families had property and worked for themselves. Day-to-day economic activities were structured around the regularity of seasons and harvests and bonds of social interdependence. A social aristocracy based on wealth (plantation owners in the South; large landholders, rich merchants, and shippers in the middle and northern colonies) occupied the top of the social ladder.

Sport in Colonial America

There were no organized participant or spectator sports during the colonial era of American history. Colonial settlers had little leisure time or opportunity to engage in sports activities. Wresting a living from the environment necessitated long and arduous work, and people who did not devote most of their efforts to it could not hope to survive. Moreover, religion was a powerful social institution in the American colonies, and all the religious groups strictly restricted games and sports, with the Puritans in New England being the most extreme.

Puritans attacked almost every form of amusement: dancing for its carnality; rough-and-tumble ball games for their violence; maypoles for their paganism; and sports in general because they were often played on the Sabbath. Honest labor was considered the greatest service to God and a moral duty; any form of play or amusement took on the badge of time wasting and idleness and was therefore defined as a vice.

Despite religious strictures against playful pursuits, they failed to eliminate the inclination of people to engage in play of various kinds. And during the latter 18th century, the harsh religious attitude toward sport gradually declined as a more secular and liberal spirit grew. Laws were also unsuccessful in extinguishing the desire to play. In defiance of local laws, people participated in games and sports for fun, sociability, and relaxation. Horse racing, shooting matches, cockfights, footraces, and wrestling matches were popular for breaking the monotony of life. Other popular recreations were those associated with the taverns. The tavern was a social center, primarily for drinking but also for all manner of popular pastimes, such as cards, billiards, bowling, and rifle and pistol shooting.

As the frontier moved west, religious strictures against sport were not very effective, and the frontiersmen enjoyed a variety of competitive events when they met at barbecues and camp meetings. They gambled on horse races, cockfights, and bearbaiting. The sports and games that marked these infrequent social gatherings were often rough and brutal.[2]

Industrialization and Urbanization in the 19th Century

Organized sport requires an infrastructure of large numbers of people living in close proximity with substantial amounts of discretionary time and money. These conditions did not exist at the beginning of the 19th century. But a series of technological inventions in England during the late 18th century began to transform the lives of Americans during the first decades of the 19th century. These inventions made possible the use of machines, large-scale manufacturing, and, gradually, business consolidation. They also ushered in two of the most significant developments in human history—industrialization and urbanization—and they laid the foundations for organized sport.

An industrial revolution had begun in England in the latter 18th century and quickly spread to the United States by the early 19th century. It involved technical innovations that when applied to the productive process resulted in a fundamental change in the system of production, changing human labor in important ways: first, the work process was organized into an extensive division of labor, separating the making of a product into simpler and simpler tasks; second, work operations increasingly were performed by machines; and third, vast amounts of nonhuman power were used to drive machinery.

The major characteristics and social consequences were that a capitalist mode of production grew in prominence and a factory system developed and quickly expanded. The initial impact of the industrial revolution was on the textile industry. Spinning thread and weaving cloth had traditionally been done at home on spinning wheels and hand looms, but these tasks were suddenly being done in factories by power-driven machinery. The sewing machine of Elias Howe revolutionized the making of clothes, shoes, and various leather goods.

Other industries quickly emerged. The successful smelting of iron with the aid of anthracite coal was perfected about 1830. By 1850 improved methods of making steel had been developed. Steel production became the harbinger of industrial development because the machinery for factories was made primarily from steel. Moreover, the rapidly growing railroad system depended on steel for track and for railcars. With water power, steam engines, and employment of a plentiful, cheap, and totally disarmed labor force, levels of production increased dramatically.

By the mid-19th century, a growing, flourishing industrial capitalism existed in the northeastern states. A rural society based on plantation slavery and cotton production characterized the South, and a society of farming, ranching, and mining spread out into the West. Both the South and West contributed raw materials and other necessities to keep industrialization expanding.

The gathering storm of dissension over slavery in the South eventually erupted into civil war in 1861. The stimulus the war gave to manufacturing and industrial expansion served as the economic basis for subsequent rapid advances in industrialization and urbanization during the latter 19th century. Before 1860, U.S. industry was largely concentrated in New England and the mid-Atlantic states, but after the Civil War, industrialization and manufacturing spread to all parts of the country. Especially noteworthy was the movement of industry westward. The meat-packing industry developed in Chicago and Kansas City, while in the western states, mining and raising cattle and farm crops became prominent.

Developments in one field stimulated changes and growth in others. As noted, the steel industry was enhanced by the expanding railroad network that used steel rails for the lines being built in the West. Railroads, in turn, were stimulated by the need of the steel industry for iron ore, coal, and other materials that had to be transported by rail to the factories. From 1869 until 1873, the length of completed railroad lines increased by 50 percent. Railroad development encouraged the westward movement, and new and fertile areas of the West produced coal, other minerals, farm crops, and cattle that required transporting to markets, further stimulating railroad building. Simultaneously, industry produced the farm machinery that made it possible to raise more crops. Finally, the new methods of communication promoted the growth of all kinds of businesses and were in turn stimulated by that growth.

Industrialized production needed a plentiful supply of labor near plants and factories, so population shifts from rural to urban areas began to change American demographics. In the first U.S. census (taken in 1790), only about 6 percent of the population was classified as urban; by 1850 about 23 percent was urban, and by 1900, 35 percent. So as technology increased the means of industrial production, more and more people descended on towns and cities to work in the proliferating factories and offices. They were joined by a seemingly endless stream of immigrants who sought a better life in North America; indeed, after 1840 75 percent of industrial wage workers were immigrants or children of immigrants. Factories multiplied, and towns and cities grew rapidly, and by 1880 some 22 percent of the population lived in cities of 10,000 or more. Chicago's population tripled in just 20 years (from 1880 to 1900), as did Boston's—from 177,840 to 560,892 between 1860 and 1900. From 1860 to 1910, the number of American cities with populations of more than 100,000 increased from nine to 50. New forms of social, economic, political, and intellectual organization evolved from these trends.

By the 1890s, corporations produced nearly three-fourths of the total value of manufactured products in the United States. The large corporations were able to develop mass-production methods and mass sales, the bases of big business, because of the huge amounts of money that they controlled. Consequently they were able to drive out small businesses and acquire control over production and the price of goods and services in particular fields. For example, by 1880, the Standard Oil Company controlled 90 percent of the country's petroleum business. At the same time, Cornelius Vanderbilt, the railroad magnate, secured a monopoly of the railroads. Near the turn of the century, the U.S. Steel Corporation controlled some 60 percent of the iron and steel production of the nation—from mining the ore to distributing the finished products.

Capitalism and the Social Relations of Production

Any discussion of the industrial revolution is incomplete without considering the two major social class configurations that arose from it because the basic elements of those class structures are present in contemporary society. The major social classes created by the industrial revolution were an industrial capitalist class and an industrial working class.

During the first half of the 19th century, factories were small, and the most common forms of business organization were the partnership (two or more owners) and the proprietorship (a single owner). But as the factory system took root, an industrial capitalist class began to emerge, eclipsing former business configurations. Labor power to run the factories and carry out the semiskilled and manual tasks that kept industries growing was supplied by wage workers, who became the backbone of the modern working class.

The American capitalist class had its origins in the landed gentry, merchants, shipowners, and moneylenders who dominated commerce during the colonial era and the first few decades of the 1800s. During the Civil War and in its aftermath, a new generation of capitalists formed and asserted itself. Capitalists built the framework for monopolistic control of the economy and became a powerful influence over cultural practices, a development that has characterized American capitalism throughout the 20th century.

Before the 1840s, most manufactured goods were produced in the home or by individual artisans and craftspeople paced by their own motivation and work habits. But the introduction of machinery housed in factories meant that workers employed by owners of the productive forces had to be brought to the factories to carry out the work. Many farmers and their families left the farms to work in the factories and city businesses that were being created. The proportion of the labor force engaged in wage labor steadily increased from approximately 20 percent in 1840 to 52 percent in 1870 and 72 percent in 1910.[3] Major consequences of the industrial productive process were long hours—60- to 70-hour workweeks were not un-usual—and harsh working conditions, as capitalist owners strove to best the competition in the various expanding commodity markets.

The backbone of industrial capitalist enterprises was (and still is) workers with no material goods, only their labor power, to sell. Their labor, in effect, is a commodity they sell to capitalists to get money to live. From the beginnings of industrial organization, workers labored under the direction, supervision, and control of capitalists. Directions and orders in the production process were communicated to workers from above. There was a hierarchical organization between those who had power (the capitalists) and those who did not (the workers); Karl Marx, an astute analyst of the 19th-century industrial workplace, described this relationship as the despotism of the workplace. Capitalists held power over workers because they had purchased the right to dispose of the workers' ability to perform labor. Workers had no property rights in the production of whatever resulted from their activity. They were only a means to an end—the growth of capital.

Industrial laborers "were employed with the intention of extracting the maximum" from their labor, "and it was in conditions of misery and unbearable oppression that the original core of the modern working class was formed. This movement was an extension of what had begun in England during the previous century, but with a definite acceleration" in the United States after 1860.[4]

The development of industrial capitalism ensured as priorities the economic, the instrumental, and the technical to the point that it involved every aspect of social institutional patterns and cultural practices.

The Rise of Modern Sport

As an integral component of culture, sporting practices are closely linked with cultural trends, and such was the case in 19th-century America. The economic and cultural transformations provided the infrastructure for the rise of modern commodified sport.

In the first few decades of the 19th century, Americans enjoyed essentially the same recreation and sports as they had during the colonial period. But industrial expansion brought about dramatic changes in daily life as the working class accommodated to factory exigencies, the long workday, and urban living. As conditions changed from a rural to an urban population, there was neither the space nor the opportunity to engage in traditional forms of leisure. Urban dwellers, especially the working class, progressively turned to watching sports for entertainment, especially horse racing, rowing, prize-fighting, footracing, and similar activities. The occasional, informal, and social community form of sport participation diminished as highly organized commercial spectator sports became the structural and cultural principle in the period after the Civil War, setting the stage for revolutionary developments in leisure pursuits, mass popular sport (sport played by large numbers of people), and professional sport.

By the latter three decades of the 19th century, an orchestration of expanding industrialization and urbanization, enhanced by the revolutionary transformations in communication, transportation, and other technological advances, provided the framework for the rise of commercial sport. No transformation in the recreational scene was more startling than the sudden burgeoning of sports, which diffused from the wealthy and upper classes down to the middle and working classes.

In addition to the long-standing interest in horse racing, yachting, and prizefighting, new sports gained popularity. Lawn tennis, croquet, golf, and polo were pioneered by the wealthy as games for "polite society." But none of these sports grew as rapidly as baseball and American football. From an informal children's game in the early 18th century, baseball developed codified rules in the 1840s, and groups of upper-class men organized clubs, taking care to keep out those of the lower social class. The Civil War tended to wipe out this upper-class patronage of the game, and a broad base of popularity existed in 1869 when the first professional baseball team was formed. This was followed in 1876 by the organization of the first major league, and baseball became firmly entrenched as a popular spectator sport—indeed, the national pastime—by the end of the century.[5]

American football owed its origins and popularity to higher education. Intercollegiate athletics began in 1852 with a rowing match between Harvard and Yale, but it was not until the 1870s and 1880s that intercollegiate sports became an established part of higher education and contributed to the enthusiasm for athletic and sporting diversions. During this era, football was a sport for the upper classes rather than for the masses because it largely reflected the interests of the college crowd; nevertheless, the sport developed into a national one by 1900.[6]

Towns and cities were natural centers for organizing sports. The wealthy who took up yachting, young ladies of upper and middle class who turned to cycling, and prizefighting enthusiasts who backed their favorite challengers were largely from urban areas. In the cities, better public transportation, a higher standard of living, more available funds for the purchase of sporting goods, and the greater ease with which leagues and teams could be formed all contributed to the rise of commercial sport.

The popular sport of horse racing centered in New York; Charleston, South Carolina; Louisville, Kentucky; and New Orleans; while the first organized baseball clubs were founded in such communities as New York, Boston, Chicago, St. Louis, and Toronto. Yachting and rowing regattas, footraces, billiard matches, and even the main agricultural fairs were held in or near the larger cities.

One of the ways city dwellers replaced some of the traditional social functions of the village community and the church was through voluntary associations, in which they could interact and form friendships with people of common interests. The sport club, as one type of voluntary association, was one of the main ways certain groups established subcommunities within the larger society. Sport clubs were, then, an important catalyst to the growth of organized sport.

Some of these urban sport clubs were founded and patronized by ethnic groups—the Scottish Caledonian clubs and the German Turner societies are examples—and others were organized on the basis of social status and patronized by the wealthy commercial, professional, and social elite. These latter clubs were the predecessors of country clubs, which began to flourish in the early 1900s. Although clubs were overwhelmingly dominated by men, they were also on the forefront of providing expanded sport opportunities for women. It was, of course, a very restricted menu of sports for women—golf, tennis, archery, and croquet.

One major purpose of the metropolitan sport clubs was social rather than competitive, but during the late 19th and early 20th centuries, they became a dominating force in amateur sports. The Amateur Athletic Union (AAU) and the U.S. Olympic movement were both primarily under the sponsorship of socially elite members of sport clubs.

Opportunities for participatory sport and leisure for the growing urban working class were restricted in several ways. Space was at a premium; city building closed off open play areas at an alarming pace. Long workweeks left little time for physical recreation. Ideological discourse by religious and capitalist leaders often promoted a hostility toward the concept of free time and disparaged sport and playful activities for the working class. Local laws often prevented the playing of sports at certain times.

As more and more people became involved in sports, mass production of goods and corporate organization developed in sport just as in other industries. The first major sporting goods corporation was formed by Albert G. Spalding, a former pitcher for the Boston and Chicago baseball clubs, in 1876. Beginning with baseball equipment, he branched out into various sports, and by the end of the century, the A.G. Spalding and Brothers Company had a virtual monopoly in athletic goods. Spalding was the king of the business in the latter years of the century, but department stores also began carrying sporting goods on a large scale in the early 1880s, led by Macy's of New York City. Sears, Roebuck & Co., one of the largest department stores in the latter 19th century, devoted 80 pages of its 1895 catalog to sporting equipment.

The Cult of Manliness

Along with the social and occupational changes of the 19th century arose a concern about the impact of modernization on male roles and behavior. Rapid change was altering institutions of socialization and drastically eroding traditional male roles and responsibilities. Writers, educators, and influential national leaders expressed fear that men were losing "masculine" traits like courage, ruggedness, and hardiness to effeminacy. There was even concern about the future of the nation if men lost their traditional characteristics. A host of organizations—the Boy Scouts, the YMCA, and athletic clubs—arose to promote a broadly based devotion to manly ideals, to toughen up boys for life's ordeals.

Within this context, sport, with its demands for individual competition and physical challenge, was promoted as an important proving ground for manhood. As towns and cities spread over the continent, sport blossomed as an escape hatch for what many men saw as the "feminization" of American civilization, a kind of sanctuary from the world of female gentility; it catered to men who felt a need to certify their manhood. Involvement in sports became a principal source for male identity and a primary basis for gender division.

The cult of manliness became widely pervasive in the upper and middle classes and rapidly trickled down to working-class social life. "The frequency with which writers began to assert that sport could serve as a means of promoting manliness was in direct response to both the impact of modernization on urban society and the role of modernization in redefining the masculine role and creating a new middle-class view of proper sexual behavior."[7]

Cult of Manliness and Women in Sport

Defining sport as an inculcator of manliness had the obvious effect of excluding women from all but a few sports, and those only when done in moderation. Although women were encouraged to participate in recreational sports for health reasons, they were given no rationale for competing with one another. Indeed, women who wished to participate in competitive sports and remain "feminine" faced almost certain social isolation and censure. "Since competitive sport was a place where manhood was earned, women had nothing to gain and everything to lose by trying to join in."[8]

Of course, it was not just the cult of manliness that discouraged female involvement in sport. Responsibility for domestic labor and child rearing weighed heavily against women's engaging in sport as either participants or spectators. Victorian attitudes and religious moral codes also militated against sport for women. The net effect of all these influences on the concept of femininity was to demand docility, domesticity, and subordination of women.

Despite these obstacles, upper-class and college women were often ardent participants in croquet, archery, lawn tennis, rowing, and bicycling. In fact, the bicycle was an important agent of social change, revolutionizing lifestyles for women, especially middle-class women, who were denied by social status, money, and lack of leisure time from participating in most physical recreation. It was one of the most significant factors in liberating attitudes of women and men toward the capabilities and needs of females. To comfortably ride bicycles, women were allowed to experiment with shorter skirts or some type of "bloomer" costume—both very daring for that period—which gave them a new sense of freedom. Bicycling also gave young women opportunities to escape ever-present parents or chaperones and to test independent social relationships.[9]

Marginalization of African Americans

As noted in chapter 5, despite the conditions under which they lived, African American slaves engaged in a wide variety of games and sports among themselves. Beyond that, plantation owners often trained slaves in the sport of boxing so they could pit them against the slaves of other plantations owners for entertainment during festive occasions. Plantation owners also frequently used slaves as jockeys during horse races. Both sports gave the plantation owners and their friends an opportunity to wager on the outcome of the bouts and races.

In 1865 the 13th Amendment to the U.S. Constitution abolished slavery, but during the post–Civil War era, American society became racially segregated. Although African Americans made some notable achievements in sports, they were largely barred from most sports or relegated to segregated participation. For example, after allowing African American baseball players to play in the early years of Major League Baseball, league owners, conforming to pressure from segregationists, made a "gentlemen's agreement" not to sign any more African American players. That agreement remained in place until 1945.

American Sport in the 20th Century

Multifaceted changes took place at a bewildering pace in America during the 20th century, changes greater than in any other period in human history. Scientific discoveries and the new technologies they spawned were appropriated by business interests to build new industries and reorganize old ones, especially in transportation, communication, and electronics. These industries and others did much to shape 20th-century society. They were fundamental to what has been called the "scientific-technical revolution" by some and the "second industrial revolution" by others. Regardless of the name, they were fundamental to the social, economic, and cultural trends of the 20th century.

As important as the steam engine was to improving transportation and stimulating industrialization, its impact on the social life and transportation habits of Americans was slight compared with that of the internal combustion engine. This invention made possible the automobile and the airplane, modes of transportation that completely revolutionized travel and numerous other aspects of American life. The automobile and airplane created totally new industries, involving billions of dollars of annual capital and employing millions of workers. Together they spawned the growth of many ancillary industries (including oil, rubber, and steel) and occupations. Garages, filling stations, hotels, airports, and numerous highway businesses are a few of the myriad by-products of the motor age.

The automobile also changed social habits; cities were expanded by suburbs, allowing people to live away from commercial and manufacturing centers of the city, and the automobile gave them greater opportunity for personal travel. The airplane has become the most common means of long-distance transportation. Air travel has in effect shrunk our world.

Improvements in communication kept pace with developments in transportation. The telegraph and telephone, inventions of the 19th century, were supplemented by radio and then television. Commercial radio broadcasting began in 1920, and by 1940 broadcasting companies claimed that 98 percent of American homes had at least one radio. The television boom began in the early 1950s; by the mid-1960s, TV sets were a fixture in almost every American home, and many households now have two or more TV sets.

The electronics industry was another revolutionizing force in the 20th century. Electricity turns the wheels of industry; without it the gigantic increases in industrial output would be impossible. Electricity lights up everything from homes to billboards to computers, and it has led to the production of countless new manufactured products, many of them labor-saving ones.

From Entrepreneurial Capitalism to Monopoly Capitalism

Before 1860 American industry was largely concentrated in New England and the mid-Atlantic states, but by 1900 industrialization and manufacturing spread out to all parts of the country, and the United States had become the world's leading industrial nation. Entrepreneurial capitalism was overshadowed by monopoly capitalism in the latter 19th and early 20th centuries. The first was characterized by ownership of business by an individual or partnership who organized and managed the enterprise; in the monopoly corporate model, the functions of ownership and management tend to be separated, and the primary agents of capital accumulation become salaried managers who replace the self-made entrepreneurs.

Growth of corporate monopolies gradually wiped out large sectors of independent business, and by the early 20th century, large percentages of American industries were represented by huge corporations,

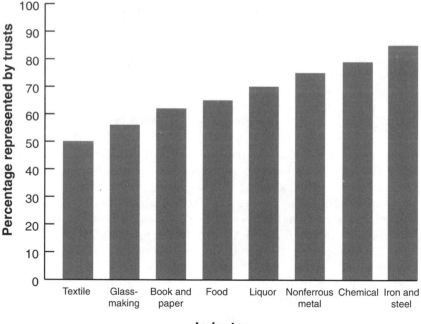

Figure 7.2   Percentage of industries controlled by trusts in 1900.

called trusts (see figure 7.2). Large corporations expanded and extended into virtually every form of goods and service industry.

A major feature of the past half century is a continuation of the trend of concentrations of economic wealth and power by fewer and fewer megacorporations. In 1998, the 100 largest corporations, out of more than 230,000, controlled more than 65 percent of the total assets held by all the corporations, an increase from 39.8 percent in 1950 (see figure 7.3). Dominance of corporations is also evident in that in 1998, about 91 percent of total sales receipts of American businesses were from corporations, and the largest corporations have annual revenues of $100 billion to $170 billion, more than the gross national product of most countries of the world.[10]

Decisions of the megacorporations influence prices, unemployment, prosperity, and the very character of the work and occupational structure in the United States. Although these corporations operate in a competitive capitalistic infrastructure, they monopolize their industries and are able to monopolize supply; through their large-scale advertising and other sophisticated marketing techniques, they create consumer demands for their goods and services. Thus, much of the freedom of choice people believe they have is merely the freedom to

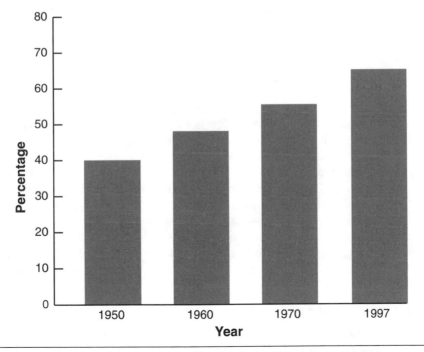

Figure 7.3   Industrial assets controlled by the 100 largest corporations.

buy commodities to satisfy needs that have been artificially created by corporations.[11]

An economic mutation of monopoly capitalism has been the advent of a national consumer-goods market. The combination of cheap raw materials, cheap energy, cheap labor, and mass production methods has enabled capitalist enterprises to keep prices relatively low and still make good profits. Thus millions of Americans can afford automobiles, radios, refrigerators, television sets, and hundreds of other consumer items. Of course, unless millions of consumers keep buying, these products cannot be made in great quantities, be sold at such low prices, or bring in such attractive profits. To hold and extend their markets, companies spend tremendous sums on nationwide advertising and skillful sales techniques. Installment buying—buying out of future income—has been widely encouraged. This dependence on the mass consumption of goods and services by both consumers and producers (who are actually workers who in turn become consumers) has become a way of life that has spawned what social scientists call a consumer culture.[12]

The consumer culture has moved the source of social relations, culture, and ideology away from a class culture centered on work and occupation. Because most American workers feel powerless and isolated from the products they make, their work and occupation is now perceived as merely a way to support their consumer-based lifestyle away from work. For most workers, then, the domain for self-expression and pleasure has come to be away-from-work activities and consumerism rather than one's occupation.[13]

Modern Urbanized Society

Developments in the economic sector during the 20th century led to increased need for workers and further centralization of production. This in turn led to further urban development. In 1890 about 35 percent of the population lived in cities or towns; a little over a hundred years later, 1998, the proportion of urban dwellers had grown to about 85 percent. Urbanization irrevocably changed institutions and cultural values and practices. Modern cities have a vastly different social texture from preindustrial towns and cities, which were more of a collection of neighborhoods than industrial labor markets. Modern cities tend to be places to live in order to find work rather than places to live one's life; a sense of community, though present in varying degrees, tends to have declined in importance.[14]

Corporate Monopoly Power and Sport

Monopoly capitalism in the last half of the 20th century, with its concentration of power, wealth, and influence in corporate giants that

© Unicorn/Joseph Sohm

Contemporary sport is a vast commodified industry that is part sport, part entertainment, and part commercial advertising, with each element grounded in the profit motive.

dominate economic life in their incessant search for markets and profits, also dominates cultural practices. Sport and mass informal leisure have been transformed into a huge, commodified industry that more and more dominates the everyday life of the average American. As one sociologist noted, "The most significant structural change in modern sports is the gradual and continuing commodification of sports. This means that the social, psychological, physical, and cultural uses of sport are assimilated to the commercial needs of advanced monopoly capital."[15]

Most people are dependent on the marketplace as a source of gratification, providing increased incentive for the full-scale commodification of sports. Working people are enjoined to purchase much of their sport and leisure involvement with their own wages.

The commodification of sport and other leisure activities has transferred the profit motive into cultural practices.

The 20th-Century Workforce

Occupational trends that began under entrepreneurial capitalism in the 1800s continued under monopoly capitalism. Whereas early in the 19th century 10 percent of working people were employed as wage workers (meaning that more than 90 percent were farmers or self-employed), currently about 90 percent of workers are nonmanagerial wage and salary employees, sellers of their labor-power in the labor market, increasingly in service occupations.

The average worker has always been rather powerless in the capitalist occupational structure because inherent in capitalist ownership of property is legal control over its use. Workers without material goods to sell or the material means of producing goods are left to sell their labor power, their ability to work. This system of relations results in workers having no property rights in the products that result from their labor. Although the principle of democracy rules over workers' political lives, the structure of their economic lives remains autocratic. As two political economists observe, "[T]he work place [is] governed by the laws of private property, not the Bill of Rights."[16]

The rise of capitalist production processes brought authoritarian, bureaucratic, and rational organization, standardization, and impersonality to the workplace. Under this system of organization, goals are to be achieved as completely and cheaply as possible. Human needs and interests are not the hallmark of bureaucratic and rational organizations; instead, they are designed to minimize the discretionary behavior of individuals by making organizational processes more routine and predictable.

Central to capitalist production is the belief that employers hold the right to decision making and that workers must subordinate their wills to the organization. Because the central ideology supports technology and the domination of humans and their environment by bureaucratic techniques, science, organization, and planning are all prime values.

Preindustrial social processes of labor, emphasizing kinship, family patterns, and personal relationships, were gradually transformed by the systematic adoption of rationalization in the workplace. This was a highly structured bureaucratic approach to production, emphasizing specialization within the division of labor and rigid control by management.

As part of a program of capitalist economic hegemony, in the first few decades of the 20th century, capitalists reorganized the workplace according to the principles of what was called "scientific management," with far-reaching social and economic implications for workers. The scientific management movement, which emerged from the studies and writings of Frederick Taylor, was based on cost efficiency in the productive process. The mass production assembly line exemplifies the Taylorist approach to production.

Taylor believed that an organization could reach its production goals only by achieving an optimal cost-efficiency ratio. The resulting system of management treated workers as a tool, assuming that they would cooperate and work only when forced to do so. Workers were reduced to an instrument of the organization, functioning under a hierarchical authority relationship.

Relations between managers and workers were closed and inflexible; there was little opportunity for change initiated by the workers.[17] The collective consequences of these processes were the cultural devaluation of the status of labor as the major constituent of class experience and the enhancement of consumerism as a primary tool for shaping consciousness and representing capitalist hegemony.

Rationalization, Bureaucracy, and Sport

The values and norms of the rationalized and bureaucratic work world have increasingly come to define and characterize the sport world. This is a trend that could have been anticipated, given German sociologist Max Weber's insightful analysis of bureaucratic organization. For Weber, the expansion of capitalism is closely linked with bureaucratic administration. He argued that large, industrial, capitalist firms depend on training the workforce to accept strict control and discipline to enhance production and maximize profit. Furthermore, he suggested that because social life under capitalism is dominated by it, this bureaucratic model of rational discipline would extend beyond the boundaries of the workplace.[18]

The fulfillment of Weber's prophecy is evident in contemporary sport. Even the language of the bureaucratic work world has become prominent in sport—productivity, hard work, sacrifice, loyalty. Some critics of modern sport contend that it has increasingly come to resemble a workplace. One observer has argued that sport has become a sector for the rationalization of work—a copy of the world of work—and that individual athletes have become merely objects in the production of sports performance.[19] According to another, commodified sport mirrors industry, with the same formal functional rules and standards of valuation.[20] It is revealing that when coaches want to praise an athlete, they call him a "hard worker," or they say she has a good "work ethic."

The influence of corporate power is so strong and so pervasive that the values and behaviors that corporate power engenders have become core ones for American society. They so permeate the fabric of every social institution that the socialization process is largely devoted to conditioning youth—particularly males—to this ideology. As commodified sport has grown prominent and powerful, it has clearly adopted the assumptions and values of large private and public organizations.

Play, games, and sport have historically functioned as rituals and practices of self-expression, creativity, and sociability, but the rise of modern sport has been in large part the transition from informal play and games to bureaucratized sport, from player-controlled games to management-controlled organized sport. There has been a decreasing degree of autonomy for athletes, whose role at one time was a more or less independent participant. That role has been largely supplanted by the trained athlete under the strict discipline of coaches. This rigid bureaucratization in sport is not limited to professional sport. It has diffused into collegiate and high school sports, and even into the adult-controlled, highly organized youth sports.

The emergence of a bureaucratic ethos in sport has been dependent on many of the same factors that were responsible for its growth in other areas of organizational life; for example, the expansion of a money economy, larger administrative units, the growth of occupational specialization, and the prominence of the profit motive.

Organized sport at all levels has assumed an acceptance of the priorities of sport organizations and a belief that individuals must subordinate their wills to them. Individual players are expected to do their best to meet the needs of the organization. This is vividly exemplified by a popular locker-room slogan: "There is no 'I' in team." Systems of incentives and rewards (e.g., letter awards, helmet decals, player-of-the-week designations) are instituted to motivate athletes to perform. Decisions are made by the management (the coach) after a thorough cost-efficiency analysis, and the players are expected to carry out the will of the coach for the accomplishment of organizational goals.

In sport, as in other complex organizations, authority is rigid. Strict hierarchies control more and more of workers' and athletes' lives both on and off the job or the field of play. "The bureaucratization of top-level sports implies a system of social roles like that existing in the world of work," argues one sociologist.[21] He continues, "Within a sports [team], as in an industrial enterprise, every active person acquires a rank that fixes his area of activity. . . . Every social role is linked on the basis of objective determinations to expected behavior on the part of those who fill the role. Top-level sports have copied this model of ordered status and roles in their elementary forms of social organization."[22]

Coaches typically structure relationships with athletes along authoritarian lines; they analyze and structure team positions for precise specialization, and they endeavor to control player behavior not only in practices and contests but also around the clock, with rules for grooming, training, dating behavior, and so forth. Under this form of management, the athletes are the instruments of organizational goals. In most cases they are not consulted about team membership, practice methods, strategy, or any of the other dynamic functions of a team. In a biting critique of contemporary sport, one social analyst argued that modern sport is fundamentally a mechanization of the body and is governed by the principle of maximizing performance. The athlete is "engineered" to sustain prolonged effort and pain. Indeed, the popular sport slogan "No pain, no gain" institutionalizes this attitude. In the guise of a play form, which is supposed to be undertaken for fun and self-expression, sport in fact reproduces the world of the employed worker.[23]

Because coaches are the authorities of organized sport teams, athletes learn dominant-subordinate relationships within the social relations of the sport productive process. Thus the structure of contemporary corporate society is learned by athletes through understanding the hierarchy of power within the structure of modern sport. At the same time, the production and reproduction of a modern workforce are facilitated by cultural activities, such as sport, which are grounded in the logic of rationalization, productivity, and the "naturalness" of discipline and achievement-oriented behavior.

The Commercial Imperative in 20th-Century Sport

The prosperous years before World War I and the tumultuous 1920s are considered the "takeoff" years in the rise of commercial sport. The growth of the city and the rising standard of living were important social forces that combined with numerous other conditions to promote the expansion of organized sport at an unprecedented rate. Shorter working hours and higher wages resulted in discretionary time and money for leisure pursuits, one form of which was sport.

Commercial spectator sport became one of the most engrossing of all social interests. By the 1920s, it was a bandwagon around which rallied business and transportation interests, students and alumni, advertising and amusement industries, and the mass media. The 1920s are still looked upon by some as sport's golden age. A number of America's most famous athletes were at the height of their careers during those years: Babe Ruth, the "Sultan of Swat," in baseball;

Knute Rockne and the "Four Horsemen of Notre Dame" in college football; Jack Dempsey, "the Manassa Mauler," heavyweight boxing champion; Bill Tilden and Helen Wills Moody in tennis; and Bobby Jones and Glenna Collett in golf.

From the 1920s onward, the objective character of modern sport is its existence as a commodity. That is, it is made by wage labor, and its purpose is exchange value, thus uniting it with almost everything else in capitalism. Two major trends have characterized recent commercial sport development: the phenomenal expansion of amateur and professional spectator sports and the boom in participatory sports.

Youth sport, high school sport, and college programs are the backbone of amateur sport. Although these programs are all classified as amateur, they are closely tied to the spread and penetration of capital production, and they have grown at an astounding pace in recent years. Baseball and football were once about the only sports sponsored for youngsters, but there are now more than 25 organized youth sport programs—from swimming to motorcycling—and it is possible for children as young as age 6 to win national championships. And high school and collegiate programs once limited to a handful of sports for males only have expanded to 12 to 15 sports for both males and females.

The professional sport industry has been one of the most successful growth industries in recent decades. Indeed, professional team sports have such a dominating presence in America that I devote an entire chapter (chapter 9) to this industry.

Participatory sport, the second major trend of the past generation, has been the product of increased leisure and income and of a concerned awareness about sedentary lifestyles and related health problems. National polls report that approximately seven in 10 American adults engage in some form of exercise or sport each week. It is estimated that 56 million people exercise walk, 61 million people swim, 47 million bicycle, almost 23 million play golf, and 40 million bowl. Other sports have their devotees as well. Perhaps most remarkable is the running/jogging boom that has swept the nation during the past two decades; it is estimated that 20 million to 22 million participate in this activity regularly.

The growth of sport participation is also closely linked to the commodity world of goods and services. Equipment, facilities, and sundry services are provided for participants by sport industries as diverse as sporting goods manufacturers and conditioning spas. Participatory sports have been penetrated by diverse and aggressive businesses whose primary goal is selling their products and generating profits, and they have been successful. Approximately $104 billion is spent annually in leisure and participant sports. This commercialization of participatory sport is one aspect of the wider consumer culture, structured in accordance with the priorities of capitalist interests that promote and profit from it.[24]

Commodifying Every Moving Body

So aggressive is the capitalist system that many informal, anonymous, or unorganized sports are often rapidly incorporated into the market. The running boom provides a good example. It began with the desire of individuals who had been excluded from high performance, elitist sport to enjoy a simple form of exercise on their own terms for their own health. Within a few years, a massive commercial "running industry" was created, with multinational firms merchandising running shoes and other accessories. Moreover, running for fun became overshadowed by marathon races, triathlons, and "ironman" competitions, many sponsored by large corporations, and winners of these events were paid for their achievements. Thus individual leisure and group fun-runs have become incorporated into commercial sport structures and the quest for victories and winning money.

Aerobic exercise, beach volleyball, in-line skating, and 3-on-3 basketball have all followed on the same trajectory in recent years. Aerobic exercise, which began as a movement to improve the cardiovascular condition of people who were overweight, underexercised, and of high coronary risk, and who initially worked out in simple shorts and T-shirts, has spawned industries in aerobic centers, aerobic shoes, and aerobic clothing. Even this activity—originally a noncompetitive one focused on self-improvement—has become competitive, with participants now able to compete for a national aerobic championship!

Beach volleyball, played for many years as part of an afternoon outing at the beach, became organized as a sport with corporate sponsorships a few years ago and became an Olympic sport in the 1996 Atlanta Summer Olympic Games. Similar patterns of the transition from informal fun and exercise to expensive equipment, commercial sponsorships, and national championships can be seen in other sports as well.

It is not just active sport participants and spectators who are engulfed by the commercial sport imperative. Consumers of sportswear become advertisers for sporting goods firms. Almost every sporting goods company has adopted logos and slogans for advertising purposes. The Nike swoosh, the Adidas trefoil, Nike's "Just Do It" and "I can," and Reebok's "Life Is Short, Play Hard" are examples. These logos and slogans are emblazoned on the products that consumers purchase and wear. Every young boy and girl or every man and woman wearing products with these logos and slogans becomes an unwitting walking advertisement for these companies. It is interesting that no resentment is expressed by consumers about the use of their bodies for commercial advertising. This is probably because people have become so accustomed to seeing commercial logos and advertising on everything else that they see nothing amiss about having their bodies used for this purpose.

Forms of the Commodified Sport Industry

The industry of commodified sport has multiplied into a variety of organizations and occupations. The forms that I describe in this section represent only part of this multifaceted industry.

First, a significant portion of the sporting industry is organized as profit-maximizing enterprises. Here, capital investors own, organize, and control a business with a goal toward capital accumulation. An example of this is the professional sport industry, composed of owners, athletes, coaches, and ancillary workers.

A second form of the sport industry is organized with all the trappings of commercialism but does not function strictly for profit; the objective is to balance the books so as to seem to be breaking even. Examples of this are high school and intercollegiate athletic programs and some elite amateur programs. To maintain a nonprofit status with the Internal Revenue Service, these programs must give the appearance—in their accounting practices—of not making a profit. In reality, many members of these organizations profit handsomely. Coaches, administrators, and sundry personnel in these programs are often paid extravagantly. This is one of the ways in which profits are disposed of.

A third aspect of the commercial sport industry involves markets for associated goods and services. Here, businesses accumulate capital indirectly by providing those goods and services. Examples of this are the sporting goods industry (mostly manufacturers and retailers), the sport component of the mass media (including television, newspapers, and magazines), businesses that benefit from sport events (hotels, airlines, restaurants), and advertisers (those buying sport advertising or sponsoring events). A less-clear example is gambling; although one's immediate response may be that gambling and sport are unrelated, this is wrong. Untold billions of dollars worth of sports bets are handled annually through bookies and betting syndicates.

Meanings and Ethos of Sport as a Commodity

Capitalist firms exist to pursue their own profit maximization, not the collective aspirations of people. Most of the commercial sport industry seeks to organize events on strict market principles—namely, the pursuit of capital accumulation—rather than on the satisfaction of individual personal and social needs. Although the sport industry goes to great lengths in its advertising and public relations to make the public think it is nurturing play forms and traditional values, it actually has little to do with the human play impulse and traditional conceptions of personal development, family, and community.

Sporting practices have been seized by commercial interests as tools for marketing, and the imperatives of the market have squeezed out the play elements in sporting endeavors. One recreation expert noted that "the continued growth of spectator sports, involving the buying and selling of athletes, and of franchises, have undercut much of the genuine meaning behind athletics as a form of recreation or entertainment."[25]

Social analyst Harry Braverman's observations about how monopoly capitalism has transformed all social practices into a huge marketplace illuminate those observations. He said:

> In a society where labor power is purchased and sold, working time becomes sharply and antagonistically divided from nonworking time, and the worker places an extraordinary value upon this 'free time,' while on-the-job time is regarded as lost or wasted. Work ceases to be a natural function and becomes an extorted activity, and the antagonism to it expresses itself in a drive for the shortening of hours on the one side, and the popularity of labor-saving devices for the home, which the market hastens to supply, on the other. But the atrophy of community and the sharp division from the natural environment leaves a void when it comes to the 'free' hours. Thus the filling of the time away from the job also becomes dependent upon the market, which develops to an enormous degree those passive amusements, entertainments, and spectacles that suit the restricted circumstances of the city and are offered as substitutes for life itself. Since they become the means of filling all the hours of 'free' time, they flow profusely from corporate institutions which have transformed every means of entertainment and 'sport' into a production process for the enlargement of capital. . . . So enterprising is capital that even where the effort is made by one or another section of the population to find a way to nurture sport . . . through personal activity . . . these activities are rapidly incorporated into the market so far as is possible.[26]

Compelling historical evidence shows that as human practices undergo changes in form and content, they inevitably experience transformations in meaning, and this has certainly been the case with modern leisure and sport. One of the cultural transformations of the past century is the diminution of traditional forms of industrial working-class sport and recreation and the rise of privatized sport and recreation that are related to the products of the cultural industries. Playful activities emphasizing autonomous and nonutilitarian values in sport have been increasingly incorporated into the instrumental culture of capitalism. Social relations of sport and leisure have become grounded in relations of capital domination, with individuals cast in the role of consumers by businesses that shape them to promote their own interests. A survey of the leisure activities of suburbanites concluded that sport and physical recreation have to a large extent become regarded as commodities to be purchased instead of experiences to be lived.

Even when people do pursue active leisure, they cannot break free of the values of the hegemonic culture. When Americans engage in leisure activities on their own, they "shape their free time so it becomes as much like work as possible—segmented, mechanical, purposeful, busy, and routinized. They commit themselves to a host of scheduled classes, leagues, rehearsals and meetings and beyond this, often see leisure as a means of gaining status by doing things that are popular or that contribute to career success."[27]

Hegemonic influence is mediated through various ideological avenues throughout the social formation (e.g., schools, mass media); these avenues are the means of transmitting and elaborating on the dominant ideology. In commodified enterprises, the ethics and standards of profit making dominate. This is nicely characterized by the term "the bottom line," which in business language defines the ultimate consideration: Is it profitable? The same value is manifested in commodified sport by the common attitude that "winning isn't everything, it's the only thing." An American Olympic Greco-Roman wrestler illustrates this one-sided view of sport. When he lost his opportunity to win a medal at the 1996 Atlanta Olympic Games, he said, "It's hard to compete at something you're not the best at. If I can't find the key to be No. 1, I'm not going to be doing it just to do it."[28] Nike displayed a billboard at the 1996 Atlanta Olympic Games that claimed "You Don't Win Silver, You Lose Gold"—a blatant perversion of the Olympic ideal. But, after all, the Olympic movement has become the epitome of commodified sport.

Several scholars who study the historical trends in sport have noted that commodified sport has subverted the ethics of play with an ethics of work. Although both center on competition, they are worlds apart. In competitive play, one strives to win within the rules of the game and to perform to the best of one's abilities, whereas in competitive work one pursues a very different goal, namely, striving to succeed by whatever means are necessary. One educator says, "In an ethics of play, competing to win does not mean that winning is everything. In play, the test is ultimately more important than the contest. But in an ethics of work, competing to win does mean that winning is everything."[29] The ethical consequence of the latter is illustrated in this incident: During a National Football League game between the Minnesota Vikings and the Denver Broncos, a replay clearly showed an offensive lineman deliberately holding a defensive lineman—a violation of the rules—but the illegal action was not seen by an official. When the replay ended, one of the sportscasters commented: "I'd hold too. If you don't get caught, it's not holding."

Commercialization of the Female Body

The contours and meanings of commercialized sport are quite different for men and for women. Although there were progressive changes in attitudes toward female involvement in sport and physical recreation in the first two decades of the 20th century, the dominant viewpoints about the female body did not change dramatically. In the 1920s, American women slowly pushed into competitive sports; some became noted in such arenas as tennis, golf, ice skating, and swimming. In the 1930s, the presence of women in the Olympics became acceptable. Title IX of the Education Amendments Act of 1972 and the women's movement over the past 25 years have opened up sport for women at every level of competition.

The emergence of competitive female athletes has represented a changing conception of women's bodies. But, this enlightened awareness of women's physical potential also has another dimension. The active female form has been sexually encoded with messages to make it a commercially useful and marketable item, and it is used to sell numerous products and services. Although the commercialization of women's sports has provided a cultural opening for women's sports as an industry, active female bodies have been sexualized through advertising to sell all manner of products and services.

Female athletes are often used—reflecting traditional patriarchal stereotypes of women as sex objects—as yet another tool for the generation of capital accumulation rather than being accepted for their sports achievements. Nevertheless, although women's physical marketability does yield profit in commercial markets, the opportunity for women to compete in a range of sports has created a limited means of liberation through an expanded use of their bodies.

Scientization and Technology[30]

Just as science and technology were appropriated by dominant economic interests to create new and influential industries, they have been appropriated to serve commodified sport interests. There is a flourishing industry of so-called sport sciences whose primary goal tends to be performance enhancement—getting athletes to run faster, jump higher, and throw farther.

These sport sciences tend to treat the bodies of individual athletes as machines or as though they ought to be machines. Training methods are designed to achieve maximum performance from the human body. When athletic performance is not up to expectations, solutions are sought in science and its companion technology.

High-performance sport has increasingly become a project in human engineering whose objective is producing levels of performance with seemingly little understanding of—or even interest in—what the consequences may be for the personal and social development of the athlete. This approach to sport tends to implicitly validate enhancing performance, employing scientific findings and using technological approaches as unproblematic; there is an unreflecting and uncritical attitude about ends in sport.

A manipulative solution seems possible for every problem athletes might encounter. Athletes who suffer from anxiety are taught stress-management techniques. If motivation seems to be languishing from months of hard training, a behavioral modification program is employed to reward athletes for meeting the coach's goals of performance, or a goal-setting program is established whereby the coach can manipulate athletes to set goals for themselves that are congruent with the coach's goals. Drugs (legal and illegal) and nutritional supplements are administered to elicit sustained training regimens that would not be possible without them.

Sport scientists, and coaches who employ their techniques, seem to be unconcerned with the social consequences of their programs and socially naive about the complexities and contradictions of contemporary sport. They seem unaware of the connection between sport and the broader society, especially as it is manifested in ideological, political, and economic arenas. Although sport scientists may not believe that their field lies within the political and economic contexts of modern society, this does not exempt their work from ideological meaning.

Some observers have noted how few outspoken critiques of modern sport have been made by sport scientists—critiques of coaches who psychologically and physically abuse athletes, of dangerous equipment, of unproven psychological intervention techniques, or of the ethos of performance enhancement. One observer said, "Look at those aspects of domestic sport that American discourse avoids recognizing and talking about: the denial of individual personhood to athletes in favor of making them abstract embodiments of sociopolitical ideology; the absence of ordinary civil and political rights among them; the power of large organizations over them; anorexia/bulimia, emotional disorders, steroid abuse, and blood-doping tied directly to the pressure for sport success and either directly encouraged by or insufficiently discouraged by coaches and officials; the concealing of medical data, the social approval, and desire for family advancement which lead . . . to the victimization of their own children by dominant class and status groups."[31]

Although sport scientists can rightly claim that they are not solely responsible for all of these practices and that they cannot be held fully accountable, few speak out forcefully against any of them. In their desire for status, recognition, and entry into the rarefied environment of elite sports, sport scientists have been unwilling to criticize what coaches and athletes are doing in the name of achieving records and winning championships.

Relevant oppositional perspectives to the thrust of scientization in sport are difficult to muster. We should be honest enough to understand that our civilization provides us with little in popular culture that matches the performance principle in popular appeal. The fundamental logic of the performance principle demands improved performances. This in turn leads to the use of scientific techniques that threaten traditional ideas about what humans are and what they should remain.

Although the popularity of high-performance sport will undoubtedly continue to pressure sport scientists to help coaches, trainers, and athletes achieve new performance records, one might hope for a contrary disposition among some to direct their efforts toward studying, supporting, and promoting athletic participation that is evaluated by qualitative criteria rather than by quantitative efficiency criteria.

Although any real critique of the dominant ethos of commodified sport interests has been very minimal and spasmodic up to now, there is hope on the horizon. An awareness of this dominant ethos and a desire to stem its influence are growing, and various forms of resistance are beginning to mobilize in word and in deed. These are discussed in chapter 12.

Summary and Preview

Contemporary sport and physical recreational forms in the United States are historically and culturally rooted in the development of America since its birth. Traditional play and games of preindustrial

American life were community-based expressions of pleasure and ceremony. They were unorganized, episodic, and localized, and they were governed by particularistic rules and customs; they were, of course, racially segregated and embedded in class and gender relations. Today, a massive commercial industry is the driving force behind sport and physical recreation forms. Sport has experienced a transformation in meaning as it has undergone changes in form and content; hegemonic features and dominating interests in commercialized sport have increasingly come to define and regulate our understandings of what sport is and how it should be played.

A major pillar—one could say the lifeblood—of commercial sport is the mass media. The media are the main advertising forum for modern sports, but at the same time commercial sports are an important source of revenue for the media. The various connections and mutual dependencies between the mass media and contemporary sport are examined in the next chapter.

Suggested Readings

Adelman, Melvin L. *A Sporting Time*. Urbana, IL: University of Illinois Press, 1986.

Frank, Robert H., and Philip J. Cook. *The Winner-Take-All Society*. New York: Free Press, 1995.

Harrison, Bennett. *Lean and Mean: The Changing Landscape of Corporate Power in the Age of Flexibility*. New York: Basic Books, 1994.

Hoberman, John. *Mortal Engines: The Science of Performance and the Dehumanization of Sport*. New York: Free Press, 1992.

Ingham, Alan G., and John W. Loy, eds. *Sport in Social Development: Traditions, Transitions, and Transformations*. Champaign, IL: Human Kinetics, 1993.

Rader, Benjamin G. *American Sports: From the Age of Folk Games to the Age of Televised Sports*. 3rd ed. Englewood Cliffs, NJ: Prentice Hall, 1996.

Roberts, Randy, and James Olson. *Winning Is the Only Thing: Sport in America Since 1945*. Baltimore: Johns Hopkins University Press, 1989.

Wiggins, David K., ed. *Sport in America*. Champaign, IL: Human Kinetics, 1995.

Chapter 8

Mass Media and Sport: Managing Images, Impressions, and Ideology

Sports, perhaps more than any other aspect of American life, has been changed by television. TV has made sports a multibillion-dollar industry. In the process, athletes have been transformed from mere heroic figures . . . into highly skilled, highly paid commodities, props to boost ratings and sell advertising.

Stephen Seplow and Jonathan Storm, journalists

The term *mass media* refers to all the technically organized means of communication that reach large numbers of people quickly and effectively. This system of communication falls into two major groupings: print media, such as newspapers, magazines, and books, and electronic media, such as radio, television, and movies. The mass media are a social institution with a dual social identity. They have both economic and cultural functions; they are private profit-making businesses while at the same time they are narrators of events, producers of meaning, and creators of social consciousness. Each media form has unique features, and although most attention in this chapter is devoted to newspapers and television, considerations specific to other media are discussed where appropriate.

Power and Ideological Control of the American Mass Media

The mass media comprise one of the most powerful social institutions in American society. Their power is derived from four main sources: constitutional protection, universal access to the public, corporate organization, and ability to construct ideology.

Constitutional Protection

The First Amendment of the United States Constitution, granting freedom of the press (which has come to include the electronic media), gives the media almost unlimited public license. Freedom of the press is unarguably fundamental to the maintenance of a free and open society; in fact, the protection granted by the First Amendment is an acknowledgment of the importance of the media to a democratic society. However, because the media have direct access to the public and are instrumental in directing attentions and shaping attitudes, values, and beliefs, there is always the possibility that the enormous power in this freedom will be abused.

Universal Access to the Public

The mass media are the primary source of public information, and with more than 25,000 media outlets and a television set in more than 98 percent of American homes, the mass media literally have universal access to every person in the nation on a daily basis. One media analyst called the mass media "the national narrator of record."[1]

Corporate Organization

In addition to their constitutional power and universal access, those who own the media hold the power inherent in their ownership. With the exception of the Public Broadcasting System (PBS) and National Public Radio (NPR), all the major mass media in the United States are privately owned. But the forms of ownership and management have changed dramatically during the past century. The trend during the past few decades has been for fewer and fewer companies to acquire control over media firms. Despite the fact that there are more than 25,000 mass media outlets—newspapers, magazines, radio stations, television stations, book publishers, and movie companies—fewer than 25 corporations control more than 50 percent of the entire media industry. As a consequence, most media firms are now owned by giant corporate conglomerates that are actually not media companies in a strict sense.[2]

At the beginning of the 20th century, most newspapers were owned by individuals or partnerships, and publishers were not particularly wealthy. At midcentury, more than 80 percent of the daily newspapers were independently owned; by 1996 less than 25 percent were independently owned. Today the prevailing pattern for newspapers is corporate ownership. Indeed, of the approximately 1,600 daily newspapers, the 15 largest newspaper chains control more than 50 percent of the U.S. newspaper circulation. The Gannett Corporation, publisher of *USA Today,* is the largest newspaper chain in the United States; Gannett publishes 89 daily newspapers. Other large chains include Scripps-Howard and Times Mirror.

Concentration of power in the newspaper industry is reflected in another way. Behind most of the news in our hundreds of newspapers are but a few highly centralized organizations that feed stories to the local papers—the wire services of the Associated Press (AP), United Press International (UPI), the *New York Times,* the *Los Angeles Times,* and the *Washington Post.*

The broadcasting industry displays a similar trend. Television and radio networks are part of massive corporate conglomerates. Table 8.1 shows the ownership pattern of the major broadcasting networks and their annual revenues, which illustrate the economic size of these corporations. General Electric, owner of NBC, is one of America's 10 largest corporations; Walt Disney Corporation, owner of ABC, is a leader in the entertainment industry; Westinghouse Electric Corporation, owner of CBS, is the nation's largest broadcaster with 15 TV

Table 0.1

Ownership of Television and Radio Networks and Annual Revenues

Network	Owner	Annual revenues (1996)
NBC	General Electric	$79 billion
ABC	Walt Disney	$19 billion
Turner Broadcasting	Time Warner	$10 billion
CBS	Westinghouse Electric	$9 billion
Fox	News Corporation	$9 billion

stations and 83 radio stations. Time Warner, owner of Turner Broad-casting, has far-flung enterprises in entertainment and retail sales; Fox Network, owned by billionaire Rupert Murdoch's News Corpora-tion, is a transnational media conglomerate. It is quite obvious that control of what we see, read, and hear flows from a small, but powerful handful of corporations.[3]

Freedom of the press is granted to those who own the means of public communication, or, as the critic A.J. Liebling once said, "Freedom of the press is guaranteed only to those who own one." Ownership of newspapers, magazines, books, and radio and TV programming and the like is, in theory, open to all, but in fact access to mass media communication is limited to those who have the financial resources to afford the costs involved. In the present era, those who have the necessary resources are extremely wealthy individuals and increasingly large conglomerate corporations. It is they who are the power holders of the media, and it is they who fashion the dominant discourses of the day through that ownership.

The concentration of ownership and centralized control of the mass media parallel that in other sectors of the American economy, and, collectively, the mass media are a forum for the most powerful corporate interests in the United States. Because of inadequate public funding support, even the Public Broadcasting System has increas-ingly become tied to corporate interests.

Overlap of the mass media ownership and the corporate economic elite is considerable, with perhaps as many as half their members being part of both groups. Even those only in the media have characteristics resembling the economic elite. One social analyst noted that "the media represent the same interests that control the state and private economy, and it is therefore not very surprising to discover that they generally act to confine public discussion and understanding to the needs of the powerful and privileged. . . . Their top management (editors, etc.) is drawn from the ranks of wealthy professionals who tend naturally to share the perceptions of the privileged and powerful, and who have achieved their position, and maintain it, by having demonstrated their efficiency in the task of serving the needs of dominant elites."[4]

Together, then, the economic and media elite largely represent the same dominant class interests. As a result, this class exerts a major influence on the mass media, directly through ownership and indi-rectly through buying advertising.[5]

Ideological Hegemony

That the mass media comprise one of the most salient cultural sources of information and public debate on matters of national importance is illustrated by the fact that there are 1,532 daily newspapers; that 98 percent of all American homes have television sets and the TV set is on an average of 7 hours and 51 minutes a day; and that radios (home and automobile) are on for more than 6 hours per day.[6] The media, then, are part and parcel of our daily life, investing it with particular meanings. They have become an extremely powerful source for forming values and beliefs and for organizing consensus within American society; indeed, the media have often been labeled "the consciousness industry." Television, especially "through its use of a powerful language comprising images, words, gestures, clothing, settings, music, and sounds, has become one of our society's principal repositories of ideologies/ideology."[7]

Basic to hegemonic theory is the premise that access to the means of mass public communication is access to the minds of the public—to public attitudes, values, and beliefs. According to one social theorist, "If we learn anything from Gramsci's *Prison Notebooks,* it is that capitalism is held together by consent from within a populace . . . rather than through coercion. The main organ of this consensus in our contemporary period is the mass-media communications systems."[8]

Because concentration of ownership of the media is in the hands of large corporations, which in turn are owned by wealthy stockholders and run by managers, the dominant class tends to have privileged access to the mass media. Through its privileged access, the dominant class is in a favorable position to influence important societal resources that shape the beliefs and thought patterns that explain and justify existing social arrangements. A noted communications scholar said that "all of broadcast and printed news is pulled by a dominant current into a continuous flow of business conservatism. . . . The main news mostly ignores or obscures the true 'other side,' the social and economic realities that most Americans live with. . . . The result is that American news is overwhelmingly the world as seen from the top down and negligibly the world as seen from the bottom up."[9] Such conditions give the dominant class not only a privileged position for the inculcation of its values but also the ability to define the parameters of legitimate discourse and debate over alternative beliefs, values, and worldviews.[10]

A great deal of the mass media's ideological work is impression management. One of the primary portrayals the mass media like to draw of themselves is that they are looking out for all of us. The slogan of the *New York Times,* for example, is "All the news that's fit to print." A second impression purports that media versions of events are unfiltered, objective reality; witness common slogans like "And that's the way it is," "Eyewitness news," and "Brought to you live." Another favorite media cliché is that they write and broadcast what the public wants. According to a top executive officer at CBS, "All TV does is reflect the taste of the American public."[11]

Actually, mass media claims of looking out for everyone, reproducing reality, and giving the public what it wants are questionable—one might even argue dangerous and misleading—half-truths that conceal how the media actually constrain and shape public impressions and beliefs. For example, a publication titled *CENSORED! The News That Didn't Make the News and Why* is published yearly by Project Censored. It provides news and information on important political, economic, and social issues not published nor broadcast by the mainstream media in America.[12]

Mass media also engage in the social construction of information that conveys and promotes dominant political-ideological agendas—agendas that appear to be the authoritative interpretation of events, persons, and values. The techniques used to carry this out are numerous and complex. One in particular is frequently used in news reporting: the "expert." Supposed experts commonly are quoted to shape the authoritative view of issues and events; some radio and television networks have experts in areas like business, politics, military affairs, foreign affairs, and so forth. The impression meant to be conveyed is that the "experts" and "specialists" have access to more accurate or more specialized information than the average person and therefore they will tell us what is good, right, or true. But even where these experts and specialists are indeed knowledgeable, they tend to be the minions of the media industry, largely elaborating and defining the dominant consensus. So-called experts on political, military, and economic topics cited, quoted, and interviewed by the media are overwhelmingly drawn from conservative think tanks.[13]

The ideological role the media play in shaping people's understanding of the world has been analyzed by social scientists from several theoretical standpoints. Most have found that the media are biased toward maintaining the status quo and promoting dominant group interests.[14] They suggest that our cultural norms and values, and our knowledge and understanding of the world, are derived more and more through our experiences with the mass media. By shaping our picture of the world, the media determine what we think, how we feel, and what we do about our social and political environment. In producing their definition of social reality, the media tend to construct an image of society that represents dominant class interests as the interests of all members of society.

In attempting to connect the economic realities to the ideological potential of the mass media, it is easy to discern their inherent capacities for hegemonic work because they are the forum for the most influential commercial interests in America. Contrary to conventional wisdom and the claims of the media industry, media messages are not a neutral product. Indeed, the media industry is not a neutral communicator of messages in any of its forms. It is instead an industry of complex organizations involved in the everyday production and marketing of mass cultural products. Its traditions, norms, and practices belong to a broad system for interpreting and promoting culture and consciousness.[15]

Thus, the broad pluralistic range of voices that the media claim they represent is actually a range within certain narrow ideological limits. Actually, the choice of media content is made by advertising and stockholder-conscious editors and publishers, filtering the news through a profit motive. A careful analysis of the news pages and broadcast programs reveals lamentably little outside the mainstream of public discourse.

Image Versus Reality

Because the media are such a powerful force in the presentation and interpretation of information, they help to shape our perceptions of social reality. The message of the media is distinctive and deviates from "reality" in several compelling ways. Evidence has been compiled through content analysis of American television that shows persistent and consistent distortions of reality in the areas of the family, education, sex roles, work roles, aging, death and dying, and

© Beth Schneider

The mass media and sport—especially television—have formed a symbiotic relationship. The enormous popularity of sport is due largely to the media; conversely, the media benefit from sales, circulation, and advertising money generated by sports events.

violence and crime. An explicit implication of this research is that the media industry "produces its goods, tailoring them to particular markets and organizing their content so that they are packaged to be compatible with the dominant values and mode of discourse."[16]

Even though the mediated images may be distortions of reality, we eventually come to believe them as truth because the media relentlessly present them as such. However, many people do see the mass media as objective reporters of the news and events that are worthy of note. They are unaware of the highly mediated and ideological nature of the process by which information is conceived, produced, and disseminated in reaching us. Media content that is perceived as objective news or simply innocent entertainment will not be understood as laden with hegemonic ideology. Thus, in addition to wielding the power inherent in the enormous economic foundations of the mass media, the media—especially television—are American culture's most potent instrument for articulating the dominant ideology. By reproducing and sustaining specific definitions of reality that favor the powerful, the media serve a larger system of social control.

Ideology as a Contingent Process

The media tend to reinforce the established social order and reigning consensus, not necessarily out of a cynical self-interest or subservience to particular group interests, but certainly as an instrument for the promotion of dominant meanings and ideas. However, the media do not merely dispatch the ideology of the dominant class in a conspiratorial manner—the control of ideology in society is a much more contingent process than that.

Moreover, media credibility and legitimacy are maintained by their lack of complete agreement on all issues and controversies and by their occasionally even opposing the dominant political and economic perspectives. But the media's structural affinity with the economically and politically powerful plays a key role in propagating the definitions of dominant groups.[17] As emphasized in several other places in this book, securing consent for the dominant ideology does not necessarily require force or threats of force because it is flexible enough to assimilate, co-opt, undermine, or override potentially contradictory notions; this is its genius.

The Role of Print and Electronic Media in Sport

Both print and broadcast media devote significant attention to sport issues and events. Daily newspapers have sizable sport sections to report on local and national news, and sports events are broadcast on television and radio with interpretive commentary; sport has spawned myriad specialty publications to offer even more extensive coverage.

Newspapers

Although it is difficult for those under 40 years of age to imagine, prior to 1950 there were no home television sets, and only 30 years earlier, no home radios. So it is only during the past two generations that television has been a part of daily living. The only prior mass medium was print—newspapers, magazines, and books—until radio emerged in the 1920s.

In the mid-19th century, American newspapers began periodic coverage of sport events, but it was not until the 1890s that a sports section first became a regular newspaper feature. William Randolph Hearst, publisher of the *New York Journal,* developed the modern sports section. Today, about 30 percent of the public say they buy the newspaper for the sports section. In some of the most popular newspapers, almost 50 percent of the nonadvertising space (a sizable proportion of any paper) is devoted to sports, which has five times the readership of any other section.

A recent innovation is the symbiosis of newspapers and sport in the establishment of some newspapers as the "official newspaper" of a particular professional sport team (e.g., the *Rocky Mountain News* is "the official newspaper" sponsor of the Denver Nuggets). This is a highly unusual development in the journalism industry because a business connection between a newspaper and a sport franchise eliminates any claim that the newspaper has to be objective and unbiased when reporting about that team, its players, and coaches— the newspaper and the sport franchise have become business partners.[18]

Electronic Media

Wireless transmission of information was developed in the 1890s, and in the early 1920s, radio broadcasting began. Reports and broadcasts of sport events quickly became one of radio's most popular functions. Today, radio stations broadcast more than 500,000 hours of sport annually. The newest innovation in radio is 24-hour sport stations, by which serious fans can stay abreast of what is happening in sport. In 1998 there were about 160 all-sports stations, and the number is increasing.

The technology to produce telecasts was developed during the 1930s, but large-scale growth was delayed until after World War II. In the early 1950s, commercial television, developed by private capital in the context of an expanding consumer culture, immediately made a union with sport. Since that time the two industries have developed a symbiosis; indeed, it is often claimed—and with good reason—that commercial sport could not exist without television and that television would have a much tougher time generating revenue without commercialized sport.

Spectators consume sport to a far greater extent indirectly through television than directly through personal attendance at events. More than 2,100 hours of televised sport is programmed per year by the four major networks, and cable television provides an additional 6,000 hours. The Entertainment and Sports Programming Network (ESPN, ESPN2), which reaches 70 percent of American homes with televisions, alone broadcasts more than 8,000 hours of live sports each year. Regional sport cable networks and direct satellite broadcasts are growing rapidly, and they broadcast countless thousands of hours of sport each year. Finally, pay-per-view (PPV) seems poised to become an increasingly popular form of sports telecasting.

More than half of the 25 top-rated television programs of all time are sport events. Super Bowl telecasts usually attract from 60 percent to 71 percent of the households watching television. Television audience viewership was an estimated 6 billion people worldwide during the 1996 Atlanta Summer Olympic Games. The 1994 World Cup in the United States, involving 24 soccer teams playing 52 games in a month-long tournament, drew 32 billion TV viewers worldwide.

The newest innovation in sports television is the all-sports news channels. These channels do not carry live sports events. Instead they telecast only sports *news*. ESPNews and CNN/SI began this form of 24-hour sports coverage in fall 1996.

The Lucrative Association Between Television and Sport

The first objective of the mass media is profit. They have no inherent interest in sport; sport is merely a means for profit making. Likewise, commercialized sport is a profit-making business as well, and much of its revenue is generated through the media. For newspapers and magazines, sport coverage helps sell the publications because many people like to read about sports. At the same time, media coverage helps to promote and popularize sport. For radio and TV, sport attracts listeners and viewers to the events that sport organizations (such as the NFL or the New York Yankees) have sold the rights to broadcast to the media; the media, in turn, have sold time to corporations to show their commercials. This reciprocal process may sound complicated, but it is quite simple, and I shall explain it more fully with a focus on television.

Sport and television have become mutual beneficiaries in one of capitalism's most lucrative associations. The nexus between the television industry and the sport industry works like this: The product of commercial sport is a sporting event. This product is sold to customers who pay admission fees to see sporting events. The product is also sold to television networks in the form of broadcast rights fees to the sports events. In fact, the search for TV rights revenues dominates the structure of the professional sport industry.

The sport industry has been successful at negotiating large contracts with media networks for the rights to televise events, which in turn helps make commercial sport wealthy. Take a few examples:

• In 1998, the rights to televise NFL games, as well as the Super Bowl, were sold to several networks for eight years for $17.6 billion. (All NFL TV money is split evenly among the teams; this averages $73.3 million per year for each of 30 teams.) About 65 percent of all revenues of NFL teams come from the sale of television rights.

• In 1995 the national TV rights to Major League Baseball were sold to NBC, Fox, and ESPN for $1.7 billion over five years, making the annual income for each team from these contracts more than $12 million. More than half the teams can pay their entire annual player payrolls just from national TV revenues. This does not include local broadcast rights, which total more than $200 million annually.

• During the fall of 1997, NBC and the Turner networks signed a four-year contract of $2.64 billion for the rights to telecast NBA games.

• NBC paid $456 million in rights fees to televise the 1996 Atlanta Summer Olympic Games, $715 million for the 2000 Sydney Summer Olympic Games, and $545 million for the 2002 Salt Lake City Winter Olympics.

• In 1994 CBS signed a seven-year TV broadcast rights contract with the NCAA for $1.725 billion for the Division I men's basketball tournament; this was an increase of 70 percent over the previous contract.

Contracts like these have made the commercial sports industry very wealthy, resulting in expanded franchises, higher salaries, and all-round plush lifestyles for many in the industry. They also demonstrate the extent to which television subsidizes the commercial sports industry.

It is advertising that is the key to the economic function of the mass media. After television networks have bought the rights to broadcast specific sports events, they then sell advertising time to these events to corporations who are selling a product and wish to advertise it. Some media analysts view what television networks sell a little differently. They claim that what the networks are really selling to advertisers is audiences—the viewers.

Regardless of how it is viewed, media networks sell a great deal of advertising for sport events. As a percentage of all network TV, advertising by corporations during sports events accounts for about 25 percent. Because TV sports are extremely popular, the networks have been able to set phenomenal advertising fees—the larger the anticipated audience, the larger the ad fee. For example, NBC sold time for the 1998 Super Bowl for an average of $1.3 million per 30-second commercial—$43,333 per second! Advertising sales to sporting events provide substantial profits for the television industry; NBC's advertising sales exceeded $680 million just for the 1996 Atlanta Olympics.

Corporations are willing to spend huge sums of money on advertising during sports events—more than $3 billion annually— to create demand for and sell their products. Because so many people are interested in sports, sporting events attract viewers, so they are a natural setting for advertising. The beauty, excitement, and drama of sport are immensely popular, generating large audiences. TV broadcasts, in effect, rent their viewers' attention to sell advertisers' products. Those audiences hear and see the broadcast commercials, and many become consumers of the products and thus help the advertisers to realize a profit.

Other Linkages in the Media-Sport Relationship

In its association with the media, commercial sport receives an enormous amount of free publicity. Media exposure is in itself enough to promote sports, but typically the sports are reported in a blatantly booster fashion designed to hype interest in the athletes and teams. Newspaper sports sections are, in many ways, an advertising section for sports; the radio and television sports news segment, accompanying the national and international news and the weather forecast, is basically an advertising commercial for sports. Indeed, many sports news announcers literally act like cheerleaders for the local professional sports teams. For the commercial sport industry, no other privately owned, profit-making industry receives as much free publicity for its product. Of course, the reciprocal nature of this is quite clear: the more interest is generated in sport, the greater the profits for the mass media.[19]

Before the marriage of television and professional sports, pro sport franchises were considered to be permanent fixtures in a city. In the

Table 8.2
Media Corporations That Have Ownership in Professional Sport Teams

Corporation	Teams
Walt Disney	NHL Mightly Ducks, MLB Anaheim Angels
Ascent Entertainment	NBA Denver Nuggets, NHL Colorado Avalanche
Time Warner	MLB Atlanta Braves, NBA Atlanta Hawks
Comcast	NBA Philadelphia 76ers, NHL Philadelphia Flyers
Tribune Co.	MLB Chicago Cubs
Cablevision	NBA New York Knicks, NHL New York Rangers
Paul Allen Group	NBA Portland Trail Blazers, NFL Seattle Seahawks
Ackerley Group	NBA Seattle SuperSonics

past 25 years, however, franchise jumping has become commonplace. One reason in almost every case has been the potential for additional TV revenues in the new city (see chapter 9 for more detail). This is especially true in the NHL. NHL franchises, historically based in Canada where ice hockey is the national sport, have been gradually moving to the United States, largely because of the enhanced opportunity for greater media exposure and income.

The relationship between the media and professional sports goes beyond mutual business interests; the media and sports have intimate ownership connections. Several owners of professional sport teams are also owners, or major shareholders, of media corporations. A few examples will suffice. These examples, shown in table 8.2, illustrate well the close business ownership associations between the media and sport.[20]

Another linkage between professional sport and capital arises from the employment by the broadcast networks of former professional athletes. A growing pattern is to hire former sport stars to report play-by-play coverage or serve as commentators for sport events. Some of these former athletes have even ascended to management positions in the networks.

Sport Adaptations for Television

To enhance spectator appeal and accommodate programming needs, the television industry has been increasingly permitted to manipulate the structures and processes of sport. In NFL football, certain rule changes—moving the sideline hash marks and the kickoff spot, reducing defensive backs' contact with receivers, liberalizing offensive holding—have been implemented to open up the game and make it more attractive to television viewers. The sudden-death tiebreaking rule and the extended play-off system are further means of increasing TV viewer interest. Other modifications have been introduced to permit more commercials—official time-outs at the end of each quarter, time-outs at the discretion of television officials, and, of course, the two-minute warning (a TV time-out).

In both professional and collegiate basketball, the shot clock, the slam dunk, and the three-point shot have been adopted to enhance viewer interest. In televised golf, match play, in which the golfers compete hole by hole with the golfer winning the most holes being the winner, has been completely replaced by medal play, in which golfers play the field and the one with the lowest score over the course wins, and the Skins Game (a variation of match play in which large sums of money ride on the outcome of each hole) because these forms of play are more compatible with television coverage. To accommodate television scheduling, tennis executives established a tiebreaker system of scoring when sets reach six games for each contestant, thus making it easier to complete matches within a designated time.

For the same reason of viewer interest, Major League Baseball introduced the designated hitter and lowered the strike zone, and there is strong suspicion—denied by baseball executives and ball manufacturers—that in recent years the baseball itself has been modified to make it more lively. These changes have stemmed from a view toward producing what spectators like to see: a steady barrage of extra-base hits and home runs. The time-honored afternoon World Series and All-Star games have been switched to evenings to accommodate the interests of television. The 1988 addition of lights at Chicago's Wrigley Field was a pure and simple concession to television.

Another bow to television has involved rescheduling events in recent Olympic Games. To maximize its revenue from the sale of television rights, the International Olympic Committee has agreed to reschedule championship events to accommodate NBC's desire to show them during prime-time viewing hours in the United States. Moreover, much of the Olympic Games' TV coverage is now shown after the events are completed, but the events are presented to television viewers without informing them of this fact, leading them to believe they are actually seeing events as they occur.

These and other sport adaptations, modifications, and concessions are tied directly to enhancing the action for the television viewers so that a bigger audience will see the commercials being shown. This illustrates how capital-accumulation priorities go hand in hand with cultural practices that have become commodified.

Made-for-Television Sports and Alternative Sports

One of the most unpleasant influences of televised sport for those who cherish traditional sport forms has been the creation of various made-for-television sports events, popularly known as trash sports. Made-for-television sports began in the mid-1970s with an ABC program in which outstanding athletes competed in events other than their specialty. The idea was to find the "best" athlete and discover which sports had the "best" athletes. Once this event became a television success, other made-for-television sports followed: "Challenge of the Sexes," in which top male athletes competed against top female athletes, with the males given handicaps to heighten the uncertainty of the outcomes, and "Super Teams," in which members of professional teams in two different sports competed in contrived events.

These particular sports have disappeared from the TV sports menu, but with the popularity of almost any kind of competitive event, and with all-sports channels needing to fill time with programming, numerous made-for-television and alternative sporting events now appear. Many of these sports do not have large numbers of actual participants, but when telecast, nearly every aspect of them is aimed at making them appealing to viewers and thus to corporate advertisers and sponsors.

Ideological Hegemony, the Media, and Sport

Media sport plays two major roles: economic (profit making) and ideological (shaping attitudes, values, and beliefs). The economic role has been emphasized in previous sections; this section will address the ideological role. Although the televising of sport events may seem to be a neutral activity, it is in reality a forum laden with opportunity for dominant interests to shape the very meaning of sport and to cultivate their ideology among generally unsuspecting viewers. Sport telecasts, carefully chosen and orchestrated, have become symbol bearers, with the choices of what is shown and how it is shown being guided by a specific agenda.

Hegemonic Work

In principle, a broadcast sports event has no manifest ideological content. Basically, it is a tool for attracting listeners and viewers so the media can broadcast the commercials during the time slots they have sold to advertisers. Common assumptions of the public are that a broadcast sport event is an objective mirror of the reality of the contest and that, in television for example, the camera angles and commentary are neutral conduits for presenting "the facts" of the event. But actually a broadcast game is a commodified entertainment spectacle sold in the marketplace. Sportscasters and the entire apparatus involved in producing programs have become the definers of the subculture of sport, the interpreters of its meanings, and, most important, a crucial means by which hegemonic ideology is propagated and reproduced.

Broadcast sports events are mediated experiences for listeners and viewers. Ostensibly, sportscasters simply keep listeners and viewers apprised of essential information. But they do much more. Because of sportscasters' mediation, a game becomes a media-defined event, a collage of happenings and thus a "reality" socially constructed by the sportscasters, who decide what to reveal to listeners and viewers and how. This supposed reality becomes, in effect, the "event," and the way listeners and viewers experience it becomes their reference point for its very existence—but it is a manufactured version of reality.

In a televised sport event, between the viewers and the event are the cameras, camera angles, producers' choices of focus, and sportscasters' interpretations—which are the invisible apparatus of a media presentation. Viewers never see the entire event; instead, they see only those parts that are sifted and filtered through the presentation process. Viewers are located in a very different position than are spectators at the event itself. Spectators in a stadium or arena perceive the event as is, but TV viewers experience a "media event" that is the product of a team of professional gatekeepers and dramatic embellishers.

The public has many options as to what to listen to and watch, and media networks compete fiercely for listeners and viewers. So broadcast sports events are formed and framed with the major purpose of attracting listeners and viewers, and a variety of techniques are used to accomplish this. Attracting listeners and viewers is a major part of the mediating process of media sport.

Hooking Listeners and Viewers

One of the first tasks of media sport is to "hook" listeners and viewers to the broadcasts of sporting events. That the broadcast sport event is mediated and different from the actual event is illustrated through pregame shows that at one level are mostly a contrived mix of hoopla, banal interviews, network promos, and puff pieces (e.g., theme building, "matchups"). The rhetoric focuses listener and viewer attention on the overall importance of the competition, individual athletes' (and coaches') personalities, statistics, records, and team styles of play. Integrated with this, however, is the major purpose of these programs—to frame and contextualize the game by artificially building dramatic tension and solidifying allegiances, thus persuading listeners and viewers to stay glued to their sets and preparing them for how they should hear, see, and understand the contest.

Selection

In the process of mediating sports events, the broadcast media define the meaning of sport in many ways, but one of the most prominent is through selection—the decisions both to broadcast some sports and not others and to accentuate certain aspects of the sporting event for listeners and viewers and not others. In doing this, radio and TV coverage constructs viewer interests, attitudes, and beliefs about sport. One insightful description of this selection process deserves to be quoted at length:

> [Television] selects *between* sports for those which make "good television," and it selects *within* a particular event, it highlights particular aspects for the viewers. This selective highlighting is not "natural" or inevitable—it is based on certain criteria, certain media assumptions about what is "good television." But the media do not only select, they also provide us with definitions of what has been selected. They interpret events for us, provide us with frameworks of meaning in which to make sense of the event. To put it simply, television does not merely consist of pictures, but also involves commentary on the pictures—a commentary which explains to us what we are seeing. . . . These selections are socially constructed—they involve decisions about what to reveal to the viewers. The presentation of sport through the media involves an active process of re-presentation: what we see is not the event, but the event transformed into something else—a media event. This transformation is not arbitrary, but governed by criteria of

selection, which concentrate and focus the audience's attention, and, secondly, those values which are involved in the conventions of television presentation: concentration and *conventionalism*.[21]

Two examples of media selection can illustrate the ideological shaping of sports interests and attitudes. First, the media's practice of emphasizing male sporting events coverage has played an important role in reinforcing cultural attitudes about gender specificity in sport and gender appropriateness of sports. Second, a preponderance of team sports are broadcast. Thus, male team sports are television's and radio's "authorized sports"—they are the sports with media network contracts—so in many ways the media have advanced the popularity of male team sports at the expense of other forms of sport. From these two methods of selection, listeners and viewers learn that male sports are more important than female sports and some sports are more important than others. Thus, social value is conveyed through particular choices made by the media's selective coverage.

The selecting, screening, and filtering of sport events by television professionals through the images shown and the commentary given have the effect of presenting games as entertainment, and in essence that is what broadcast sport is all about—commodified entertainment.

Consequently, one outcome of the selection process is that the basis for interest in sport is changed from the traditional appreciation of the beauty and style, the skill, and the technical accomplishments of the performers to a primary concern for provocative excitement and productive action, usually meaning scoring.

The selective processes of the media also constructs meaning in sport by what is left out. For example, in the women's team gymnastic competition during 1996 Atlanta Summer Olympics, one of the American gymnasts, Kerri Strug, injured an ankle in a landing during the vault competition. Despite obvious pain, Strug ran down the runway and completed her second vault. A courageous act, but at the time of her second vault there was no way of determining how her score would affect the overall outcome of the competition. However, in the delayed telecast of the meet, NBC revised the sequence of the competition and selected her performance as the last for the vaulters, and thus the culminating factor in the overall competition. Television viewers were led to believe not only that the televised event was live but also that the competition took place in exactly that sequence.[22]

So television does not merely nonchalantly report sport events. TV sport selection and presentation are the culmination of a complex process of sorting and selecting events and topics according to a socially constructed set of values and assumptions.

Winning Is the Only Goal

The spontaneous, creative motive to participate for the love of the sport has been overshadowed in media sport by an obsession with victory above all else. Success in media sport is defined by one criterion: Who won? Broadcast sports tend to be unbridled odes to winning; we frequently hear sportscasters admiringly say that an athlete will do "whatever it takes to win." Almost any action in the pursuit of victory is justified; indeed, athletes sometimes are lionized for illegal play. In one NFL play-off game, instant replay showed an offensive lineman clearly and deliberately throwing a vicious elbow into the face of an opponent, which was followed by a comment from one of the sportscasters: "Nobody said this was going to be a tea party!"

No sacrifice is too great in the interest of winning. During another NFL game, one of the cameras zoomed in on the heavily taped right arm of a defensive lineman. One of the sportscasters then explained that the player had incurred a compound fracture of one of his fingers—meaning the bone was sticking out of the skin. The player had gone to the bench, shoved the bone back in, taped up the finger, and returned to the game. The sportscaster then said, in a thoroughly approving manner, "It just goes to show how badly these guys want to win." In another example, during an NFL game, one of the sportscasters applauded a quarterback by saying, "Here's a guy that probably had to take a painkiller shot in his lower back so he could play tonight."

The competition is waged not only against opponents but also against the rules—to see how often and how thoroughly they can be stretched and outright violated, in letter and spirit, without getting penalized, all in the pursuit of victory. Baseball players who are caught with illegal cork embedded in their bats are lauded for their resourcefulness, and basketball players observed illegally holding or obstructing opponents are praised for their cleverness; indeed, almost any athlete who uses illegal tactics is praised for his or her willingness to do "whatever it takes to win."

Camera crews and sportscasters are not attuned to the aesthetic nuances of a well-executed play; instead, they are focused on the score—who's winning and who's losing. Thus, definitions, values, and practices of the media are privileged and made to sound as if they are actually enlightened ways of thinking about the meaning of sport. They become the "commonsense" constructions about sport that grow out of the production of media sport.

One result of this selection process is that spectators become less interested in the beauty, elegance, and movement artistics of the games they watch. Instead, they become more sensation minded, focusing on the issue of winners and losers. Thus, specific meanings about sport are constructed through mediated presentations.

Sportscasters: Narrators of Mediated Sport

As important as the other aspects of forming and framing the media sport event are, sportscasters are perhaps the most important ingredient because they are the "tutors" for what listeners and viewers should hear, see, and believe about sport. Sportscasters are carefully selected with an eye to their ability to command credibility; indeed, the media rely heavily on the personas of these men and women. So former professional and elite amateur athletes with high name recognition are most often selected.

Presenting accredited "experts" is a prime purpose behind this selection process, as it is in other departments of the media, because their statements will convey objectivity and authority. Once the expertise of these sportscasters is established, the impression conveyed to viewers is that they have privileged access to knowledgeable opinion about the event and preferred interpretation of its meanings. The fact that most sportscasters are male contributes to the impression of authority and expertise American society continues to associate with men.

Consumers of media sport are expected to rely on the judgment of these "experts" and to accept their opinions as absolute. They are part of the media star system whose insights and interpretations listeners and viewers are supposed to admire and in whom they should confidently believe. Thus, exclusive access through certified experts serves to legitimize media interpretations. Although employing former athletes to describe the technical skills, strategy, and tactics used during a game may seem reasonable enough, it is important to understand that sportscasters do not act only to report on the action of the contest. Perhaps more important, they also act "to prescribe moral values and to comment prescriptively on social relationships."[23]

Former sport stars are uniquely qualified for this task because they are survivors—even models—of the competitive meritocracy. By and large their social consciousness is congruent with hegemonic perspectives; they are fully integrated into the dominant value and belief system.

A main concern of broadcast media producers is to prevent listener or viewer boredom, so one of the basic jobs of sportscasters is to attract and maintain listeners and viewers for the broadcast. They must provide a commentary that heightens the drama of the event. One of the favorite ways of doing this is by framing themes, such as "These teams hate each other" or "This is a grudge game." The message in both cases is that viewers and listeners should expect lots of violent play. Another favorite tactic of sportscasters is to frequently point to "matchups" between players on opposite teams. This constructs a kind of mano a mano competition that listeners and viewers can focus on. A third technique is framing the game as an extremely crucial game for both teams (even if they are both in last place); heightening the significance of the game enhances viewer interest (or so it is believed). Other sportscaster techniques are personal interest stories, recitation of statistics and records, anticipation of what to expect, dramatic embellishments of the action, and second-guessing. All this commentary is designed to keep listeners and viewers tuned in to the broadcast.

Another basic job of sportscasters is to sell the sport organization they are broadcasting for; they essentially advertise the league and the sport for which they are broadcasting. Much game commentary is actually commercial hype for the league and sport being broadcast. For example, sportscasters use slogans to develop name recognition and get viewers to identify with teams or athletes— for example, "America's Team."

By and large, the audience is unaware that it is being subjected to advertising—advertising for the league and sport—that is independent of product commercials for which a break occurs periodically during the program. One media analyst contends that an appropriate description for sportscasters would be "sport public relations agents."[24]

Political and Moral Ideology and Media Sport

The media are an ideological system of symbols sharply honed to promote political hegemony. The strong relationship that has evolved between sport and the mass media has not merely enhanced the mass appeal and popularity of sport but has also bolstered both the range and depth of sport's influence on political consciousness. One sport analyst has contended that "in their working assumptions and practices—the type of commentary, the use of verbal and visual imagery— the media re-dramatize and re-present what are already potent dramatic spectacles within a framework of interpretation, which facilitates the passing of ideologically coded messages, that is, preferred ways of seeing sport and society." He further notes that "media sport often reads like a handbook of conventional wisdom on social order and control. There are homilies on good firm management, justice, the nature of law, duty and obligation, correct attitudes to authority, the handling of disputes, what constitutes reasonable and civilized behavior, on law and order and on the state of society generally."[25]

The annual Super Bowl, for example, uses numerous symbols— technology, competition, individual achievement, flag, nation—within this one event for a national celebration of the "American way of life."[26] One social analyst observed, "By making a fetish of ritualized sport, a political regime may thereby draw a veil over the realities of the manipulation of people's imaginations and so make opaque what would clearly be seen as intolerable if social relations were transparent. A society in which the popular media supply the public with enough pabulum of pseudo-events and plastic personalities in the field of phony sport can therefore operate by consensus."[27]

Even though the mass media have no inherent interest in sport per se, they become the definers of its subculture, the interpreters of its meanings, and thus the crucial means by which the normative culture is transmitted. Although TV sport bears little resemblance to the real world, this does not detract from its symbolic usefulness in spreading information about meanings and moral boundaries in sport and in the wider society. Sport media's influence ranges far and wide, communicating messages with hidden content. The hidden, or latent, content is something that has to be consciously sought to be identified.

Gender, Race, and the Mass Media

Social analysts and researchers have focused on several persistent issues as they relate to gender and race in media sport. One of these is the ideological role of media sport in reproducing hegemonic masculinity and racial stereotypes. Another is the role of sport in the promotion of traditional gender relations, especially through its coverage, or lack of coverage, of males, females, and African Americans. A third has been the restricted opportunities afforded women and African Americans as journalists and broadcasters.

Reproduction of Hegemonic Masculinity in Media Sport

A number of scholars have analyzed how the male body is used ideologically in media sports. In this work, media representations— verbal and visual—of the male athletic body are interpreted as a key source in reinforcing the dominant definitions of masculinity as well as general masculine hegemony in American society. Although this is accomplished in all media sport presentations, media sport presentations of football are where we find reproductions of hegemonic masculinity most frequent and most vivid. Two sport analysts note that "football's historical prominence in sport media and folk culture has sustained a hegemonic model of masculinity that prioritizes competitiveness, asceticism, success (winning), aggression, violence, superiority to women, and respect for and compliance with male authority."[28]

One researcher examined how traditional images of masculinity are reproduced in *Monday Night Football* telecasts. The evidence was compelling in showing that three images of the male body—as instrument, weapon, and object of gaze—were regularly reproduced in those telecasts. The investigator said, "Football is a kind of work, organized in accordance with military images, that require the body to be used as an instrument of sanctioned aggression and violence. Television transforms these weaponlike bodies into objects of fascination and the aggressive and violent acts they perform into graceful gestures that can be appreciated aesthetically, even erotically. . . . American football reproduces hegemonic masculinity by demonstrating that the male body is most powerful when it is used for work and violence, and when it performs in a homosocial (but heterosexual) environment."[29]

He concluded that hegemonic masculinity reinforced in media sport has serious costs for both women and men. For women, it marginalizes, subordinates, and symbolically annihilates them; for men, it marginalizes nontraditional images of masculinity, especially nonwhite and nonheterosexual images.

Media Sport and Women

The first thing that has to be said about conditions for women in sport is that a great deal of improvement has been made in the past 10 years toward more equitable treatment. Still, gender inequality is widespread and deeply rooted, and media sport is one of the foremost arenas for the reproduction of dominant traditional gender images.

Because the media are influential in organizing the ways in which we come to know and understand gender relations, they contribute to constructing public consensus about what is considered male and female. As I noted in chapter 4, females were marginalized in the world of organized sport until the 1970s, for sport was considered to be an exclusive male domain. Consequently, there was little in the way of female sports for the media to cover, so sports in which females were involved were rarely seen in either the print or the broadcast media. With the women's movement and passage of Title IX during the 1970s, women increasingly became a presence in sports at all levels.

According to two media researchers, two themes have characterized the media's treatment of female athleticism during the past 20 years: "(1) Compared to male athletes, female athletes have been grossly underrepresented in terms of overall coverage, and (2) the coverage women [have] received emphasizes their femininity and sexual attractiveness significantly more than their athleticism."[30]

With respect to the first theme—underrepresentation in media coverage—women's sports have not achieved parity with coverage of men's sports in any of the media forms. Numerous studies of the contents of newspapers and magazines consistently show that stories and photos of women's sports constitute from 15 percent to 30 percent of the coverage; stories and photos of men's sports dominate the print media. Although the proportion of feature articles about females in athletic roles has increased, many articles written about females still focus on "sex-appropriate" sports (tennis, golf, figure skating) rather than "sex-inappropriate" ones (basketball, softball, weightlifting), revealing a continued conventional and restricted view of female athletic participation.

In the mid-1980s, researchers' fieldwork at one U.S. newspaper found that the limited coverage devoted to females was not simply due to journalists' bias against women's sports but that sports news was defined as "news about men's sports."[31] In other words, the "commonsense" consciousness of the journalists was that women's sports were unimportant and thus unworthy of coverage. Attitudes and practices have changed at many newspapers during the 1990s, but the coverage of women's sports at some newspapers suggests there is still a strong residue of the attitudes of the past.

Perhaps the most promising trend for women's sports coverage in the print media is the creation of several magazines devoted exclusively (or almost exclusively) to women's sport and fitness. *Women's Sports & Fitness* and *Sports Illustrated Women/Sport* are two magazines with growing circulations. These magazines provide comprehensive coverage of women's sport activities, focusing on individual female athletes, women's teams, and women's sport organizations, and they also examine issues and problems in women's sports.

In the broadcast media, conditions are much the same as they are in the print media. In radio and television, women's sports continue to struggle for coverage. With the exception of women's professional tennis and golf, there is little regular national network programming of women's sports. Until 1996, no women's professional team sport league had ever secured a major national TV network contract. Undoubtedly, there were multiple reasons for this, but certainly a major one was that advertisers were not convinced that women would watch women's sports, and because they buy sports programming to reach a targeted audience, they did not buy sports programming.

This pattern was broken in fall 1996 when the new American Basketball League secured a national cable network contract; in 1997 when the Women's National Basketball Association league began play, a network television contract was in place. Furthermore, network radio and TV coverage of women's college basketball is increasing rapidly.

With respect to the second theme of the media's portrayal of women's sports—that of selecting and framing meanings that overemphasize femininity and sexual attractiveness and thus the "otherness" of female athleticism—reportorial and pictorial images of females and female athletes often belittle and trivialize their athletic efforts and achievements. Sports journalists have contributed to the condescending attitudes and stereotyping of female athletes; when females do get media attention, the emphasis is frequently on them as sex objects. Recent manifestations of this have been the selection by the media of a "sweetheart" in multisport events like the Olympics or an emphasis on female athletes in their roles as wives, mothers, or girlfriends rather than as skilled performers.[32]

In the early 1990s, studies found that newspapers and sport magazines focused on personalities as opposed to athletic abilities and used sexist language to portray female athletes, and an overwhelming number of articles were still reinforcing a hegemonic masculinity; finally, the image of female athletes was largely constructed by male journalists and broadcasters. Although significant strides have been made for women in media sport, their accomplishments will mean little as long as sportswriters and broadcasters trivialize and minimize women's performances through sexist commentaries.[33]

Trivializing women's athletic achievements or treating them differently from men's achievements promotes and reproduces traditional cultural gender relationships. Signs that the marginalization and trivialization of female athletes by the media are diminishing and that media recognition of female athletes is increasing may turn out to be a mixed blessing. As females increasingly compete in sports, their performances can be objectively measured against males. Because the major media sports "are organized around the most extreme potentialities of the male body, 'equal opportunity' as the sports media's dominant framework of meaning for presenting the athletic performances of women athletes is likely to become a new means of solidifying the ideological hegemony of male superiority."[34] In this context, equal opportunity will provide compelling evidence for the "natural" superiority of male performances, thus justifying the predominant coverage of male sport by the media.

Female Sport Journalists and Broadcasters

Women have had a presence in the mass media throughout American history, but it has been a decidedly secondary presence. As recently as 1996, less than 42 percent of newspaper staffs were made up of women, and only 16 percent of the television network stories were reported by women. In recent years, conditions have improved for women in media occupations, but they still must struggle against an entrenched male-dominated network of power.

Women who wished to have careers in sports journalism and sports broadcasting have had an arduous struggle. From virtually no presence in media sports 20 years ago, women now hold important positions in both print and broadcast media sports. In the late 1970s and in the 1980s, despite experiencing indignities and discrimination, the number of female sports journalists gradually increased, and they acquired access to press boxes, locker rooms, and other facilities pertaining to their work.

During their struggle, women have had many trials and tribulations. They have often faced harassment and abuse from male athletes and coaches. In one celebrated case, Melissa Ludtke, a young female reporter for *Sports Illustrated,* brought a suit claiming that her exclusion from locker rooms was based solely on her sex and thus violated her right to pursue her profession under the equal-protection and due-process clauses of the 14th Amendment of the U.S. Constitution. But perhaps the most notorious event concerning women in locker rooms took place in 1990 when a female sports reporter was harassed and subjected to humiliation by naked football players in the New England Patriots' locker room.[35]

The appointment of LeAnne Schreiber as the first female sports editor in the history of the *New York Times* in 1978 and the election of the first female president by the Association of Sports Press Editors in 1993 were both significant events in legitimizing the role of women in the media sport profession. New breakthroughs occur each year, as women continue their struggle for equality in sports journalism.

Women in sports broadcasting have had their breakthroughs as well. In the late 1980s, Gayle Gardner was hired by NBC as the first full-time female sports anchor, and Gayle Sierens became the first woman to do play-by-play broadcasting in NFL history. Notwithstanding the increase in women in sports journalism and broadcasting, the Association for Women in Sport Media (AWSM, pronounced awesome) reports that only about 8 percent of the working sports journalists and broadcasters are women. Furthermore, the women in these positions do not receive equal pay for equal work; the highest paid men receive up to five times the salary of the highest paid women.[36]

Media Sport and Race

Because African American and minority male athletes are male, their presence in sports is considered legitimate, at least in the patriarchal scheme of things, so they have not suffered the same marginalization as female athletes by media sport. Moreover, the long history of outstanding African American and minority male athletes in American sports has established a tradition of reporting their performances in the mass media. However, African American sportswomen have suffered the same discrimination in media sport that other female sportswomen have experienced, with the additional burden of racism that all black athletes, coaches, and sundry sport personnel have endured.

Although African American athletes have had a presence in American sport, subtle racial stereotyping has been present in all the media forms. The most blatant examples are the frequent attributions of black athletes' achievements to their "natural" abilities to run fast and jump high and their "instincts" to react fast; at the same time—and sometimes during the same game—white athletes' achievements are typically attributed to their "intelligence" and superior "thinking ability." Historical stereotypes of African Americans are coded into characterizations of this kind.

In light of the limited personal contact between most whites and African Americans in American society, the media, rather than personal contact, become the primary "source of information shaping the identity of each group. Unfortunately, the media's depiction [of African-Americans]. . . assists in institutionalizing the social and information gap between whites and blacks."[37]

African American Sport Journalists and Broadcasters

Closely mirroring the hierarchical racial division of labor so evident in the broader American occupational structure, journalism and broadcasting have been largely white male professions. A 1997 American Society of Newspaper Editors study found that African Americans, who comprise about 13 percent of the population, account for just 5.4 percent of the newsroom workforce.

Except for publications and broadcasts targeted specifically to blacks, sports journalism and broadcasting were virtually all-white occupations until the late 1980s. As recently as 1997, there were no African Americans serving as sports editors in the U.S. cities that had at least one professional sport team. In 1995 *Sports Illustrated,* the nation's most prominent sports magazine, had only five African Americans listed on its masthead out of 102 editors, department heads, writers, reporters, and copyeditors. Of those, four were writers-reporters and one was a copyeditor; no African Americans were department heads or editors.[38]

In 1998 68 percent of the NFL players were black, but only 9 percent of the radio and television broadcasters covering the league were African Americans; 4 percent of the radio and TV broadcasters covering Major League Baseball were black. The percentage of Latino radio and TV broadcasters was higher in both sports: 19 percent and 13 percent, respectively.

Many barriers have fallen by the wayside as blacks have gained increasing respect for their sports-reporting and broadcasting skills, but one fact is clear: there are still very few African Americans in this profession. The percentages of those working in sports journalism and broadcasting are a poor reflection of the proportion of African American and minority athletes playing sports at any level. The subordination of African Americans in media sport continues, and each new breakthrough requires concerted struggle against the persistent, white-dominated division of labor in media sport.

Summary and Preview

A symbiosis exists between the mass media and contemporary sport. Media sport is another arena for accumulation of capital and expenditures for leisure. But media sport is not just about the economic interests of the corporations that own the media. Because the media are effective and powerful organizations for promoting hegemonic ideology, media sport is also an arena for the advancement and reproduction of dominant interests.

The mass media are the financial foundation of professional sports. Without the television rights fees paid to the various professional sports, they could not continue to function in their accustomed manner. Professional team sports are among America's major cultural industries, and the focus of chapter 9 is on professional team sports.

Suggested Readings

Bagdikian, Ben H. *The Media Monopoly.* 5th ed. Boston: Beacon, 1997.

Cohen, Greta L. "Media Portrayals of the Female Athlete." In *Women in Sport: Issues and Controversies,* edited by Greta L. Cohen, 171-84. Newbury Park, CA: Sage, 1993.

Cramer, Judith A. "Conversations With Women Sports Journalists." In *Women, Media and Sport,* edited by Pamela J. Creedon, 159-80. Thousand Oaks, CA: Sage, 1994.

Dates, Jannette L., and William Barlow, eds. *Split Image: African Americans in the Mass Media.* 2nd ed. Washington, DC: Howard University Press, 1993.

Davis, Laurel. *The Swimsuit Issue and Sport: Hegemonic Masculinity in Sports Illustrated.* Albany, NY: SUNY Press, 1997.

Duncan, Margaret C., Michael Messner, Linda Williams, and Kerry Jensen. "Gender Stereotyping in Sports." In *Women, Sport, and Culture,* edited by Susan Birrell and Cheryl L. Cole, 249-72. Champaign, IL: Human Kinetics, 1994.

Fallows, James. *Breaking the News: How the Media Undermine American Democracy.* New York: Pantheon, 1996.

Fornoff, Susan. *Lady in the Locker Room.* Champaign, IL: Sagamore Publishing, 1993.

Himmelstein, Hal. *Television Myth and the American Mind.* 2nd ed. Westport, CT: Praeger, 1994.

Kane, Mary Jo, and Lisa J. Disch. "Sexual Violence and the Reproduction of Male Power in the Locker Room: The 'Lisa Olson Incident.'" *Sociology of Sport Journal* 10, no. 4 (1993): 331-52.

McAllister, Matthew P. *The Commercialization of American Culture: New Advertising, Control and Democracy.* Thousand Oaks, CA: Sage, 1996.

Sage, George H. "Patriotic Images and Capitalist Profit: Contradictions of Professional Team Sports Licensed Merchandise." *Sociology of Sport Journal* 13, no. 1 (1996): 1-11.

Schiller, Herbert I. *Culture Inc.: The Corporate Takeover of Public Expression.* New York: Oxford University Press, 1989.

Thomas, Ron. "Black Faces Still Rare in the Press Box." In *Sport in Society: Equal Opportunity or Business as Usual?* edited by Richard E. Lapchick, 212-33. Thousand Oaks, CA: Sage, 1996.

Trujillo, Nick. "Machines, Missiles, and Men: Images of the Male Body on ABC's *Monday Night Football.*" *Sociology of Sport Journal* 12, no. 4 (1995): 403-423.

Chapter 9

The Professional Team Sports Industry

Sport ... has become one more site for capital accumulation and leisure expenditure. ... This new dominant social definition of sports practice—and the full incorporation of professional sport as a part of sport's modern institutional structure—has become a constitutive part of the consolidation of capitalist hegemony in the modern world.

Richard S. Gruneau, sport sociologist

Professional team sports comprise a commercial industry with a commanding place in contemporary American life. They dominate significant portions of our lives through print, radio, television, and just daily conversation. Following the fortunes (and misfortunes) of one's favorite teams is one of the most popular forms of leisure and entertainment for many Americans. Seventeen million people attend National Football League games each year, and 71 million attend Major League Baseball games; the National Hockey League has averaged 16 million in recent years and the National Basketball Association, 19 million.

But television is the medium through which most people are directly involved with professional sports. Up to 40 hours of professional team sports are beamed to home television sets per week by the major networks, and hundreds of additional hours are provided by cable networks spread across the country. Some of the most popular programs are professional sport events—the Super Bowl, the World

Series, the Stanley Cup play-offs, and the NBA World Championship Finals. The Super Bowl is usually the highest-rated single television program each year.

Professional Team Sports as an Industry

Professional athletes and coaches are some of the best-known celebrities in the United States, and they are admired as role models by many people, young and old. Becoming a professional athlete is something to which millions of young boys—and increasingly girls— aspire because pro athletes are viewed as society's heroes by many.

The professional team sport industry is one in which capitalist productive relations hold sway. The overall logic of pro sports is grounded in the principles of buying and selling goods, services, and labor. The premise of capital accumulation is the foundation on which this industry is built: professional team ownership is privatized, and team owners want to make money. In many ways, professional team sports reflect, but also promote and legitimize, the material and ideological foundations of capitalism in American social and economic life. Thus, the sport industry is both an economic and an ideological force.

Competition within this industry, though present, is primarily against other forms of popular entertainment; in effect, competition among team owners within a league is intentionally muted (more on this later) so that franchises within a professional league do not compete directly against one another. Professional team sport leagues and team owners want a minimum of government interference, while at the same time they lobby for and receive unique local and national government protections of their controlled competition with one another.

In understanding the professional team sport industry, it is important to recognize that it is a business—a component of the economic processes of production and consumption. Professional sport franchises are incorporated enterprises whose major purpose is the accumulation of profits. A sport corporation like the New York Yankees or the Denver Broncos is as real a business as General Motors, Exxon, or Warner Brothers, and the profit motive that drives the auto industry, the gas and oil industry, or the movie industry is the same profit motive driving professional sport. The products in the case of professional sport are sport events, just as the products in the auto industry are automobiles and the products in the movie industry are films. In owning or controlling the means of athletic production, team owners, commissioners, and league organizers represent the interests of the dominant class, through acting as agents of it as well as belonging to it.

Not Just Fun and Games

The average American does not view or perhaps refuses to view professional sport as a business. Instead, professional teams are seen by many as a kind of extension of the local high school team, with the players thought of as a group of local boys who, through their achievements, boost civic pride and promote solidarity and imagined community.[1] A local professional team is viewed as having been brought to the city by a public-spirited citizen, instead of a wealthy entrepreneur, or corporation, making another investment. Because most people do not understand the pecuniary driving forces of professional sport, the pro sport owners, the league commissioners, and the mass media nurture the public's gullibility about professional sport franchises because such an attitude is good for the pro sport business.

Not only is professional sport concerned with business, but its leaders go to great lengths to conceal this fact from the public. They do this by what is called appropriating community, meaning they locate themselves as representatives of the larger community (all of us), meanwhile mystifying their real interests—profit. Jerry Jones, owner of the Dallas Cowboys, said, "I don't feel I own the Dallas Cowboys. . . . All I . . . do is use my talents to husband the Cowboys for our fans. That's who owns the Dallas Cowboys."[2] The Dallas Cowboy organization refers to the team as "America's Team." Professional teams are named after cities, states, or regions rather than owners solely for commercial purposes. These examples of appropriating community are used to suggest that the local professional sport team is owned by the public and operated on its behalf.

Team advertising and hype from the mass media sell civic identity and community involvement through terms like "Your Denver Nuggets," beguiling people into believing the team is really *theirs!*—that the team is a community venture and is providing a philanthropic service to the public. In reality, a pro sport team is no more "yours" than is Sears or Wal-Mart. But through such tactics, professional sport mimics other forms of capitalist enterprise that employ ideological techniques to provide socially sanctioned justifications that legitimate money making.

Actually, celebrating the successes of a privately owned, profit-making business that calls itself by a city's, state's, or region's name is naive. But residents take very seriously the assertion that they are the owners of pro teams in their areas, and the real owners consider it essential to encourage this belief—after all, it is good for business. This public attitude has enabled professional sport team owners to extract very favorable subsidies for their businesses from the public sector (as was described in chapter 6).

Economic Importance of Professional Teams

There is no question that professional team sport is an enormously popular form of entertainment. But despite the frequent claims of franchise owners, politicians, the mass media, and business interests that a professional franchise is an economic engine for a city or region, especially when a city is trying to attract a franchise or is seeking public funding for a new facility, the fact is a sport franchise is actually just a small business when compared with other industries in an urban area. As one urban policy analyst noted, professional team sport "is really 'small potatoes' in terms of the economy of the United States, the economy of any region, and the economy of virtually any city. . . . [I]t is not an 'engine' that drives any economy." He goes on to say, "In no county in the United States do sports account for more than one-half of 1 percent of all jobs or all payroll dollars, and the most financially successful sports teams have budgets that would be less than one-third of the expenditures made by a typical urban university. Sports may attract a great deal of attention, but they are not an economic engine, they will not generate a great number of jobs, and they will not revitalize a city's economy."[3]

Development of Professional Team Sports

Owners of capital, from early merchants to contemporary corporate magnates, have promoted the conversion of all potential products of human labor—including labor power itself—into commodities that can be bought and sold for profit so their own assets can be expanded. This pattern can be seen with sport. The human labor of amateur sports has been converted into the human labor of professional sports—a thoroughly commodified industry. The evolution from an amateur model of sports to commercial professional team sports has occurred at a different time and different pace in each of the four major men's sports. Professional sport teams have existed for more than 100 years, but the rise of professional sport to its present visible, powerful, dominant position in American life is a development of only the past 40 years. In every case, the process has produced franchise owners who are dependent on paying spectators and television for the growth and health of their financial interests.

No attempt will be made to create a detailed chronicle of the development of American professional team sports. But a brief account of the growth and change of the most popular professional team sports will be undertaken to provide a foundation for understanding the current social issues and problems in the professional team sport industry. As I indicated in chapter 1, C. Wright Mills was quite emphatic about the importance of historically situating social phenomena when pursuing sociological analyses.

Major League Baseball

American professional team sports had their beginnings just before the Civil War with the formation of the National Association of Base Ball Players, but it was during the last three decades of the 19th century that professional baseball boomed. From 1869 until 1900, about 850 professional baseball clubs were founded; most perished within two years. Only the Cincinnati Red Stockings, launched in 1869, survived from the era before the establishment of the National League in 1876. The Cincinnati team was a touring team—there was no professional league—that traveled throughout the country playing local teams. The Red Stockings established an enviable record in their inaugural year, winning 64 of their 65 games.[4]

Within two years of the Red Stockings' initial season, a group of baseball players formed the National Association of Professional Baseball Players, and in summer 1871 the association began operating as professional baseball's first major league. This "players' league" lasted five years before it folded, to be replaced in summer 1876 with the National League. A second league, the American League, began in 1900, completing the two leagues, with eight teams in each league. The two leagues became known as Major League Baseball (MLB).

No new franchises were added to MLB until 1961; in the 1960s and 1970s, the American League added six teams and the National League added four. There were no new franchises in the 1980s, but two were added to the National League in 1993, and two additional teams begin play in 1998.

National Football League

What is now the sport of football had its beginnings in the elite colleges of the northeastern United States in the latter 1800s. The first intercollegiate game was played in 1869, and football quickly gained popularity in colleges. During the 1890s and through the 1920s, noncollege, semiprofessional football games were played in which the players were paid. Most of these semiprofessional teams represented a town or city, and most players came from the local community, supplemented by current and former collegiate players who were paid by the game to play. There were no leagues and no regular schedule of games. However, in 1921 a group of interested parties organized the American Professional Football Association, with membership set at $100. A year later, the association was reorganized and the name was changed to the National Football League (NFL).[5]

From its beginnings, private commercial interests have had a hand in the development of the NFL. The Acme Packing Company in Green Bay, Wisconsin, sponsored a local team, fittingly called the Packers; and in Decatur, Illinois, the A.E. Staley Manufacturing Company started the team now known as the Chicago Bears. In the mid-1950s, the NFL was a modest sandlot league of 12 teams. From these humble beginnings, professional football has become a billion-dollar-a-year business, and the average franchise in the NFL is worth $160 million. The editors of the business magazine *Financial World* estimated (1997) that the total value of the 30 franchises in the league is $6.14 billion![6]

National Hockey League

Professional ice hockey paralleled the development of professional football in many ways, but its early development took place in Canada. By the end of the 19th century, it was played throughout Canada. The first professional hockey team was formed in 1903; soon after, other professional teams were organized and the first professional league, the International Professional Hockey League, was formed in 1904. In 1917 the National Hockey League (NHL) was organized.[7]

All the original NHL franchises were in eastern Canada, but in 1924 a franchise was granted to the city of Boston, thus making professional ice hockey available to American audiences. Two years later, New York, Chicago, and Detroit gained franchises.

After World War II, the NHL settled into a league composed of six teams. In 1967 a major expansion took place and the league doubled the number of franchises; by 1972 it had expanded to 16 teams, and there were 26 teams in the late 1990s. Expansion plans will add four new franchises by 2000—Nashville (1998), Atlanta (1999), and Columbus, Ohio, and Minneapolis-St. Paul (2000). Despite the fact that only six Canadian franchises—out of 26—remain in the NHL in the late 1990s, Canadian players continue to vastly outnumber American players.

National Basketball Association

The sport of basketball was born in 1891 when James Naismith wrote a set of rules for the game and had his students at Springfield College (called the YMCA Training School at the time) play it for the first time. The sport caught on immediately in colleges, especially women's colleges, and by World War I there were teams made up of players who were professional in the sense that they received money for playing; in most cases they were getting a portion of the gate receipts. After a number of false starts between the world wars a professional league was founded as the Basketball Association of America in 1946; before the 1949-1950 season the league changed its name to the National Basketball Association.

During its history, the NBA has had a great deal of unrest, especially with franchise relocations. At first, some NBA franchises were in smaller cities, including Sheboygan, Wisconsin, and Waterloo, Iowa, with limited potential for generating the necessary revenue to support a professional sport team. As NBA franchises moved to larger cities during the 1950s, the popularity of professional basketball grew, and increased gate receipts throughout the league consolidated its stability.

During the 1960s, the NBA was confronted by two rival leagues, the American Basketball League (ABL) and the American Basketball Association (ABA). The ABL lasted only two years; the ABA merged with the NBA in 1976. During the past 22 years, the NBA has added several franchises and was composed of 29 franchises in the latter 1990s.

Growth of New Professional Team Sports

The four professional team sports described here have dominated the industry for more than 50 years, with really little opposition. Each of the sports has had rival leagues attempt to compete against it. But in every case, the rival league either folded or was incorporated into the existing league. The existing leagues have simply had too much power, influence, money, and control of the media for the rival leagues to be successful.

What is surprising to the rest of the world is that professional soccer has not been the most popular professional sport in the United States. After all, professional soccer leagues are found all over the world, and in most countries, professional soccer is the most popular professional team sport by far. The North American Soccer League (NASL) was formed in 1968, but without a major network television contract and little spectator support, it folded in the early 1980s. Indoor professional soccer has struggled for recognition for years; again, without a major TV network contract, it has achieved little public popularity. In spring 1996, hoping to capitalize on the American public's exposure to soccer during the 1994 World Cup held in the United States, a diverse group of investors launched a 10-team professional soccer league called Major League Soccer (MLS). MLS surprised practically everyone with good attendance in its first two seasons, leading it to expand to 12 teams in 1998. But the jury is still out as to whether MLS will be able to survive the competition from the other professional sports and a public that is still not very knowledgeable about the sport of soccer.[8]

Although male professional team sports have been a growth indus-try over the past four decades, women's professional team sports have been unsuccessful. As noted in chapter 4, the most popular profes-sional sports for women have been individual sports, especially golf and tennis. Several women's professional softball, volleyball, and basketball leagues tried and failed in the 1960-to-1990 era. The only women's professional team sport with any success in the early 1990s was volleyball.

Until 1996 female basketball athletes had to play in foreign profes-sional basketball leagues. But during fall 1996, the American Basket-ball League (ABL), a women's professional league, began play with eight teams. A second league, the Women's National Basketball Association (WNBA), a pro basketball league backed by the NBA, began play in June 1997. So, ironically, two women's basketball leagues are competing with each other for fans' allegiance. Unfortu-nately, it will be difficult to sustain two leagues—even though they are playing at different times of the year—for the same reasons that rival leagues in men's professional team sports have failed.[9]

One of the unique features of the ABL, WNBA, and MLS is that they all began with a single-entity ownership system—the teams are owned by the league—not with individual private owners, which is the case for the other professional leagues. This form of organization raises leaguewide monopoly/cartel control (more on this in the next section) to a new level. The MLS Players' Association has already filed an antitrust lawsuit against this system in that league.

Cartel Organization of Professional Sports Leagues

The basic organizational unit of professional sport teams is the league, not the individual franchise. As such, professional sport leagues are effectively cartels. A cartel is a group of firms that organize together to control production, sales, and wages within an industry. Commenting on the organization of professional team sports, one sport economist noted that they "have in general operated apart from normal business considerations, and their rules of business conduct have not been subject to governmental scrutiny to the same extent as any ordinary business."[10]

Obviously, cartels increase the benefits for the powerful few at the expense of the many. In professional team sports, the purpose of cartel organization is that of restricting competition for athletes (the labor force) and dividing markets among franchises in the industry. What-ever other functions a professional sport league performs, it serves as a network of power.

A cartel acts to constrain individuals to behave in the interests of the group of firms as a whole. The actual consequences of cartelized industries are varied and complex, depending upon such factors as the commodity produced and sold and the amount of the market actually under the control of the cartel. But in most cases, the negative consequences affect labor and consumers most adversely. With respect to labor, cartels are able to hold down wages, and with respect to consumers, cartels typically restrict production and control sales and thus can set prices as high as they wish.[11]

The beneficiaries of cartelwide control of wages and production should be obvious. The major benefits accrue to owners of individual firms through the maximization of joint profits. In the case of professional team sports, the cartel members are the owners of the various team franchises, and all the owners are wealthy. One does not have to be an economist to understand that the advantages of cartel organization in sport go overwhelmingly to the powerful owners, while the laborers (athletes) and consumers suffer the burdens of such organization.

Professional sports leagues operate as cartels in three major ways:

1. They restrict interteam competition for players by controlling the rights of workers (players) through player drafts, contracts, and trades, thereby reducing competitive bidding among teams for player services.

2. They act in concert to admit or deny new teams, and they control the location and relocation of teams.

3. They divide local and regional media markets, as well as negotiate, as a single entity, national media rights fees.

Most people recognize the economic and political power inherent in collective corporate organization, and they believe that there are laws prohibiting cartels, monopolies, and trusts. It is true that beginning in the late 19th century, the U.S. government took steps to thwart large corporations that organized to restrict trade through such tactics. The Sherman Antitrust Act of 1890 forbade every contract, combination in the form of trust, or conspiracy in restraint of trade and all attempts to monopolize any part of an industry. Since then, much additional legislation has been passed in the government's effort to outlaw corporate conspiracies. Unfortunately, it has had limited effect in the corporate world. And, more important, in the case of professional team sports, it has been judged generally not to apply.

Despite numerous challenges to cartelization by athletes and rival leagues during the 20th century, professional sports have been able to sustain their position that a sport league is a single entity—some have called it a joint venture—and that there can be no restraint of trade as defined by the Sherman Act because that would require two independent firms.[12] Several arguments have also been consistently advanced to justify collective organization:

- Teams have to cooperate in scheduling and playing games.
- Commercial sport events must involve fairly evenly matched teams to maintain uncertainty about the outcome of games and league championships (without evenly matched teams there will be no marketable competition, so the league needs control over the distribution of athletic talent).
- Revenue sharing is necessary to regulate economic competition among teams and to equalize the distribution of money, thus enabling resources to be similar among the various franchises and equalizing competition on the field.[13]

Former NFL Commissioner Pete Rozelle articulated the need for a cartel system in professional team sports. "On the playing field, member clubs are clearly competitors—and every effort must be made to promote this. But in their business operations, member clubs of a league are less competitors than they are partners or participants in a joint venture. There is nothing comparable to this relationship elsewhere on the American scene. Because of it, the application of ordinary antitrust principles to sports league operations is more likely to produce confusions and distortions than sound results."[14]

Although there are certainly ways in which professional team sports differ from most business enterprises and thus need to structure their organization differently, it is the enormous advantages in terms of power and accumulation of profits that really foster cartelized arrangements.

Restriction of Interteam Competition for Players

When the first professional team sport—baseball—was in its formative stages, team owners and promoters competed with one another in an open market, vying for athletes and spectators. But gradually a few promoters and potential owners of professional baseball teams came to view such competition as counterproductive to the interests of controlling sport labor and capital accumulation. They realized that labor and consumer issues could be better stabilized and joint profits more consistently realized by a collective, or cartel. Accordingly, they took the lead in bringing order from the chaos with the formation of the National League, which set a precedent for business organization in professional sports that ultimately became the standard.

Founders of the National League established cartelized practices in the marketplace, and within a few years they expanded these practices to include what economists call monopsony, which merely means a one-buyer market. In the case of professional baseball, this meant that all rights to a player were held by one team and one team only. Once a player signed a National League standard player contract with a team, he was bound to that team for his entire playing career unless it sold him. Under this reserve clause system (which was described in chapter 6), competitive bidding among teams for player services was forbidden. The reserve system was, then, basically an agreement among owners not to compete with one another for players.[15]

A 1922 challenge to the reserve clause, standard in major league contracts, was settled by a U.S. Supreme Court ruling in favor of the baseball owners. The Court's decision was written by Justice Oliver Wendell Holmes, who wrote that Major League Baseball "is giving exhibitions of baseball, which are purely state affairs. . . . Personal effort, not related to production, is not a subject of commerce."[16] In other words, MLB was given an exemption from the federal antitrust laws on the ground that it was not engaged in interstate commerce or trade, and MLB was, in effect, not a commercial activity!

By default, other professional team sports have used that decision, and more recent ones, to define their own special legal and economic positions. This "cartelization scenario has been played out not only in baseball, but also in basketball, football, hockey, and soccer."[17]

The Professional Team Sport Franchise Market

Control of the number and location of franchises is one of the important advantages of cartel organization in professional sports; all the leagues have policies that allow the owners to do this. By controlling the number of franchises within a league, the owners make them scarce commodities, which means their worth appreciates much faster than other investments. Table 9.1 shows the values of several of the franchises in MLB and the NFL, along with the incredible appreciation that has occurred with them from 1991 to 1997.

For the NBA, the value of the average team has increased 81.4 percent from 1988 to 1997, and NHL franchises have increased in value 68.2 percent in the same time period.

If the annual profit of the franchises is added to the appreciation values, it is well above that of the 500 largest industrial corporations, whose annual profit as a percentage of sales (revenues) has ranged

Table 9.1

Approximate Values of Selected Professional Team Sport Franchises in 1991 and 1997

Team	Value (millions of $)	
	1991	1997
Major League Baseball		
New York Yankees	225	241
Baltimore Orioles	200	207
Atlanta Braves	74	199
Los Angeles Dodgers	110	178
Chicago Cubs	125	165
National Football League		
Dallas Cowboys	180	320
San Francisco 49ers	150	218
New York Giants	150	211
Kansas City Chiefs	122	204
Atlanta Falcons	113	191
Denver Broncos	113	182

from 4 percent to 6 percent during the past 20 years. Predictions are that the values of franchises will continue to appreciate rapidly into the first decade of the 21st century.

Franchise Expansion

Cartel organization allows team owners to exercise great control over league expansion. Applicants for new franchises must secure the permission of three-fourths of the existing owners in a particular league. Such permission is difficult to obtain because owners are typically reluctant to expand the league and further share athletic talent and profits. Moreover, the scarcity of existing franchises and the difficulty of securing permission for a new franchise drive up the cost of expansion franchises—when they are approved. For example, each applicant for the two newest Major League Baseball franchises—Tampa Bay Devil Rays and Arizona Diamondbacks—had to pay $140 million to obtain a franchise. The cost is made more burdensome for applicants because they are often required to pay an indemnity fee if the new franchise is to be located near an existing one.

The only alternative for someone who wants to establish a professional sport franchise is to start a new league, and all four established professional team sports have experienced challenges from upstart rivals. The established leagues have used their enormous political and economic power to either destroy the new league or incorporate some of the teams into the established league on terms that were very favorable to the established team owners. In 1986 the United States Football League (USFL), a rival to the NFL, brought a suit against the NFL challenging several of the monopolistic advantages the NFL enjoyed over any new league. Although the Supreme Court ruled that the NFL was indeed a self-regulating monopoly committed to crushing rival leagues, it set damages at $3, making it clear that it had no intention of changing this antitrust exemption.[18]

Franchise Relocation

In addition to controlling the number of franchises within a league, each league has policies about the movement of franchises. The basic policy is that a franchise may not be moved without the approval of at least three-fourths of the owners. All the leagues have fought fiercely to maintain control over franchise movement or relocation. The reasons for this are described by one pro sport analyst: "The stability of each franchise is important to the overall financial success. If franchises were permitted to move freely, such as a move into an existing franchise market or to a distant franchise market, the franchise movement or relocation could jeopardize the existing financial security of all professional teams in that league. Stability of franchise operations is also important to cities and states which support those franchises; public bonds are often utilized to construct stadiums and arenas for use of professional sports teams."[19]

Although these may sound like good defenses, the fact is that when faced with economic considerations, the hypothetically valid reasons for franchise stability have frequently been jettisoned. Since 1953 there have been more than 70 franchise relocations in Major League Baseball, the National Football League, the National Basketball Association, and the National Hockey League, attesting to the leagues' power to accomplish what they consider beneficial to the business of professional sports. In less than one year during the mid-1990s, efforts by fans of football's Cleveland Browns, Los Angeles Raiders, Los Angeles Rams, and Houston Oilers to petition and plead to keep "their" teams fell on deaf (but powerful) ears—they all moved. The actions led one NFL owner to dub the league the National Floating

League, while a sports reporter suggested the name Nomad Football League.

At the same time, the Quebec Nordiques of the NHL moved to Denver to become the Colorado Avalanche, and the Winnipeg Jets, also of the NHL, reached an agreement to move to Phoenix. This mobility of franchises vividly reveals the lie in the "your team" rhetoric advanced by pro team owners, thus blatantly exposing the community facade promoted by the professional sport industry.

The dynamics of franchise movement are quite complex, involving owners, politicians, business leaders, and the mass media, to name only the major participants. In each specific situation, at the heart of the phenomenon is the exercise of subtle power by different combinations of these groups. Furthermore, the threat to move is especially ominous because communities know that it will be extremely difficult to secure another franchise if one is lost. All in all, then, owners have considerable leverage for extracting concessions from cities desperate to retain their franchises. That leverage rests on the most basic economic premise: where demand exceeds supply, the supplier (in this case franchise owners) sets the price.[20]

Add to the instability of franchise location the fact that some cities have appointed commissions whose sole task is to try to lure professional franchises. These commissions and their backers resort to an incredible array of enticements that exacerbate sport-franchise hopscotch. Encouraged by the success of Indianapolis, which built sports facilities before it had a professional sport franchise and which, once they were built, went out and lured a pro sports franchise to move there, other cities are constructing facilities—most are publicly financed—as bait to attract sport franchises.[21]

Publicly Owned Facilities

The issue of public subsidies for professional sport owners was discussed in some detail in chapter 6, but a few additional points deserve elaboration here. A frequent underlying issue in franchise relocation, or threats of relocation, is the complaint by an owner that existing facilities are inadequate or that financial arrangements with the city for facility rental, division of concessions, and parking are unacceptable. Owner complaints are usually accompanied by threats to move the franchise: "Build a new facility/improve the existing one/ give us a better financial package, or we will move" is the way the demands and threats are usually phrased. Sportswriters have begun to refer to this tactic as sportmail (a play on the term blackmail). Whatever it is called, it must be taken seriously by cities housing professional teams because there exists many examples of the mobility of professional sport franchises.

From 1993 to 1996, U.S. taxpayers throughout the country spent more than a billion dollars to subsidize pro sport facilities for professional sport team owners. In MLB only the Cleveland Indians played in a publicly owned stadium in 1950. By the late 1990s, 92 percent of MLB stadiums, 93 percent of NFL stadiums, 50 percent of NBA arenas, and 50 percent of NHL facilities had been built with public funds. In 1998, 44 professional sports teams were seeking or building a new venue. It is estimated that public money will be used to pay two-thirds to three-fourths of stadium project costs, while the teams will receive most of the millions in annual revenue. One journalist calls this "sports welfare."

Many cities are financially burdened with debt on municipal facilities built to accommodate local pro sport franchises. Most of these publicly built sport facilities have become a financial liability. Rental income from pro teams typically covers only a fraction of the actual maintenance and construction costs. When a professional franchise leaves a city, an additional load is thrust on taxpayers by a facility with no tenant to provide income. A public trust given to franchise owners through provision of a playing facility comes back to burden the taxpayers, who all along have been subsidizing the accumulation of private capital by owners.[22]

Cities throughout the nation are also burdened with a plethora of pressing needs, and taxpayers are being asked to shoulder more and more taxes. While this is happening, taxpayer-funded sport facilities are transferring tax dollars to wealthy beneficiaries: franchise owners, pro athletes, the corporate media, and the corporate sponsors who use the product (the sport event) to advertise their products. In effect, the taxpayer-funded facilities deplete social capital needed for a variety of community needs. In Denver, the owner of the Broncos has insisted that Mile High Stadium is no longer usable for NFL games (despite his having signed a contract to play there through 2017). In 1998, taxpayers in a six-county area around Denver will be asked to vote on a $180-million subsidy for a new stadium. The *Denver Post* calculated what else $180 million could buy for the Denver metropolitan community.[23] (See box, pp. 204–205.) Although some items on the list compiled by the *Denver Post* are specific to the Denver metro area, the sheer volume of goods and services that could be purchased is similar throughout the nation.

Professional Sport Team Owners

With few exceptions, professional sports teams have always been owned and controlled by private interests. In the early years of professional baseball, football, hockey, and later basketball, franchise

What else could you buy for $180 million?

A football stadium board is studying the financing of a new Broncos stadium. If the board decides it's cost-effective to build a new venue, residents in the six-county area will be asked in [1998] whether the 0.1 percent sales tax that is paying for Coors Field should be extended to help pay for a new Broncos' stadium. The taxpayers' contribution would be capped at $180 million. The Denver Post asked several local agencies what $180 million could buy.

Education

In the Cherry Creek School District, $180 million would cover the cost of:

- 2 high schools.
- 2 middle schools.
- 4 elementary schools.
- Computer equipment for all 37,000 students.
- Making all the district's schools more energy-efficient.

Or

- In Denver Public Schools, it could pay for salaries for all 4,000 teachers for one year (not counting benefits).

Municipal

The City of Englewood could pay for:

- Redeveloping Cinderella City mall site.
- Building a new city hall, library, and performing arts center.
- Upgrading water plant.
- Paving every alley, replacing every cracked sidewalk, and facelifting South Broadway.
- And all urban renewal debts.

Transportation

The Colorado Department of Transportation could pay for:

- The widening of a 15-mile stretch on Interstate 25 from Lafayette to Longmont from four to six lanes.

The Regional Transportation District could pay for:
- The agency's entire annual operating budget.

Or
- The 8.7-mile southwest extension of light rail from the I-25/ Broadway station to Mineral Avenue in Littleton.
- And the purchase of 19 light rail train cars.

Environment

Great Outdoors Colorado could pay for:
- 166 state park outdoor recreation projects.
- 218 wildlife protection and education projects.
- 136 open space conservation projects.
- 237 projects to plan for future open space and recreation.
- 311 community park, outdoor recreation, and environmental education projects.
- 294 trail projects.
- And 14 legacy projects.

Reprinted with permission from Alan Snel, 24 November 1996, "'A Matter of Pride' or `Extortion'?" *The Denver Post,* 13A.

owners included a menagerie of promoters, local politicians, small manufacturers, and local businessmen. Most owners have been white males with considerable accumulated wealth, through either inheritance or their own financial investments.[24]

At the present time, professional sport team owners are definitely among America's capitalist elite. Each year *Forbes* magazine compiles a list of the nation's 400 wealthiest individuals. In recent years, from 20 to 30 of the *"Forbes* 400" have owned or had stakes in professional sports franchises. In 1997 the richest sports owner was Paul Allen, cofounder of Microsoft and owner of the NBA Portland Trail Blazers and the NFL Seattle Seahawks; *Forbes* lists his wealth at $17 billion—making him the third-richest American. Owners with an estimated worth of more than $3 billion were Philip Anschutz, owner of the NHL Los Angeles Kings and the MLS Denver Rapids and Chicago Fire; and Ted Turner, owner of the MLB Atlanta Braves and NBA Atlanta Hawks. *Forbes* estimates the wealth of H. Wayne Huizenga, owner of the Miami Dolphins of the NFL, Florida Marlins of MLB, and Florida Panthers of the NHL, as well over $1.7 billion. In 1997 10 of the 30 NFL owners, or majority owners, had personal fortunes estimated to be at least $500 million. The *average* net worth of all the owners of professional team sports franchises is about $600 million.

The Green Bay Packers are the major exception to the overwhelming pattern of private ownership in professional sports. The Packers have been a publicly owned nonprofit franchise since 1922. Between 1950 and 1997 about 1,900 stockholders owned some 4,650 shares of stock, and no individual owned more than 200 shares. The stock paid no dividends and was redeemable only for the original purchase price of $25, and shareholders had no special privileges. Stock ownership entitled one to attend the annual stockholders' meeting, which elected the team's board of directors and conducted general oversight of team business. In November 1997 Green Bay Packers stockholders approved a plan to raise up to $80 million in the first sale by the publicly held team since 1950. Each share of Packer stock was sold for $200. All of the former restrictions on stockholders remained in effect.

The NBA's Boston Celtics and the NHL's Florida Panthers are publicly traded sports franchises. But they are both privately owned, and the traded shares collectively constitute less that 50 percent

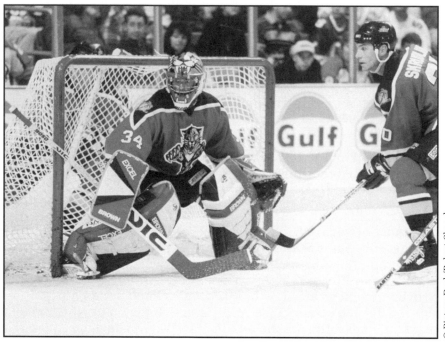

© Picture Desk/Robert Skeoch

Professional team sports is one of the most successful commercial industries as well as one of the most popular forms of mass entertainment. Owners of team franchises are some of the wealthiest Americans. They also have enormous power; they have control over the number and location of franchises as well as substantial control over player mobility within a league.

interest in the teams. So the franchise owners maintain control over both teams' operations.

The Trend Toward Corporate Ownership

Until the past decade, ownership of professional sport teams has been almost totally by individuals or partnerships, but increasingly corporations have begun purchasing sport franchises. Indeed, in early 1997, when Peter O'Malley announced that his family's Los Angeles Dodgers were for sale, he called family ownership "a dying breed." At the time of O'Malley's announcement, more than 50 corporations, especially entertainment and media corporations, had stakes in franchises. Several examples of media and entertainment ownership in professional sports are shown in chapter 8, table 8.2.

The ownership connection between professional sport and entertainment/media corporations is, in a way, an understandable tie because professional sports are, after all, a form of popular entertainment. But the motives behind this connection are more than common interests. The major motivation is the concentration of power and resources into fewer and fewer hands for maximizing profits. It is a form of concentration of ownership that is taking place throughout the corporate world. One professional sports executive argues that a major consequence of corporate ownership is "less interest in what happens on the field and more interest in synergistic interests of the corporation."[25]

Lack of Diversity
in Professional Sports Ownership

As I noted in chapter 5, African American athletes are highly overrepresented, in terms of their proportion to the general U.S. population, in professional baseball, football, and basketball, but they are highly underrepresented in leadership positions in professional team sports. As for professional sport franchise ownership, African Americans are almost totally absent. A sports law researcher states that "in 1994 . . . of the 275 individuals with ownership interests in the professional sports leagues of baseball, football, and basketball, only seven of these owners were African Americans."[26] Little has changed since then. That is, only 2.5 percent of the total ownership in pro team sports is African American.

Many obstacles prevent African Americans from breaking into the ownership of professional sports, but, as the researcher just cited notes, "The greatest obstacles are not financial but structural." League commissioners, coaches, even the athletes can play more active, more affirmative leadership roles in increasing minority participation in franchise ownership. "The key barrier to change is the legally protected clubbiness of the owners."[27]

Women, Asians, and Hispanics are almost nonexistent in the ownership of professional team sports. Two women, Joan Kroc (San Diego Padres) and Georgia Frontiere (St. Louis Rams), inherited ownership of professional sports franchises upon the deaths of their husbands. Marge Schott bought into the Cincinnati Reds as a limited partner in 1981. But that has been the extent of female ownership of the major league professional sport teams. Several years ago, the offer of Hiroshi Yamauchi, a Japanese billionaire, to buy the Seattle Mariners franchise created a national outcry against ownership by a foreigner; to allay the xenophobic reactions, a deal was worked out in which a group of local investors, backed by Yamauchi, bought the franchise.

Motivations for Owning a Professional Team

Several analyses of the motivations of those who invest in professional sport franchises suggest two basic motives: fun and capital accumulation. Those who own professional sport teams frequently go into the venture with the intention of having fun. Owners are often superfans rather than merely prudent financial investors. Pat Bowlen, owner of the Denver Broncos, agrees; he was quoted as saying, "A lot of people who own sports teams live vicariously through their players. I get a lot of thrills from this. Making money is one thing, having fun is something else."[28]

Even though owners may seek the fun factor of being a part of the immensely popular world of pro sports, once owners acquire franchises, they also want to make a profit. Franchise owners have been successful in business, and they are not accustomed to, nor comfortable with, losing money in business ventures. They expect to succeed financially with their sport investment even though their motive for investing in sport was primarily nonpecuniary.

It turns out that there are various ways in which sport team owners can add to their already considerable wealth. First, a number of tax advantages are available to them; one of the most significant is depreciation allowances. Second, there are direct profits from annual revenues and, more important, resale of the franchise. Finally, important promotional opportunities enhance profits and the value of other investments the owners have.

Player Depreciation

Sport franchise owners can depreciate professional athletes just like ranchers and manufacturers depreciate cattle or aging machinery; from the standpoint of pro sport owners, and supported by rulings by the Internal Revenue Service, an athlete is like a piece of equipment, with a useful life like any piece of equipment. One sportswriter said in reference to the Boston Celtics that "the Celtics write off their players like a hot dog maker writes off packaging machines."[29] Professional athletes are typically depreciated over four to five years. So a player valued at $5 million, depreciated over five years, gives the team owners a tax write-off of $1 million for each of those years. A *Denver Post* business writer noted that the Colorado Rockies' owners paid Major League Baseball $95 million for the franchise. Because the tax code permits a sport team owner to depreciate players, "half of the franchise fee—$50 million or so—could be written off over a five-year period at a rate of $10 million a year."[30] Depreciation is, of course, subtracted from a team's gross income, so the owner pays less in taxes. It can be seen that player depreciation is indeed a significant tax shelter for owners.

Annual Profits and Resale

Figures on annual profits of professional teams are extremely difficult to obtain because ownership is private, and financial statements do not have to be opened to the public (with a few exceptions to be described later). Because professional sport is one of the most secretive industries in the country, very limited information is available about the actual annual profits or losses of the various franchises. One thing is certain: when owners do make their financial reports public, they cannot be viewed as accurate. Economics professors who have testified at trials and hearings of various kinds involving owners have consistently reported that the owners understate revenue because of the way owners do their books. For example, one economist found that teams record certain money as operating costs to make themselves look less profitable. In one case, an NFL owner paid himself a salary of $7.5 million and recorded it as a general expense, when it should have been counted as profit for that owner. Other owners use similar ploys, according to economists.

The Green Bay Packers are a publicly owned corporation and are required by law to reveal their figures. Annual profits reported by Green Bay in the 1990s have ranged from $3 million to $7 million. In 1986 the Boston Celtics basketball team began a public sale of its stock, and its financial statements reveal that the team has made between $5 million and $16 million in annual profit during most of the years since going public. The owner of the Florida Panthers of the NHL took his team public in 1996 amid plans to build an arena for the team; the franchise has had an estimated annual operating income of about $3 million in recent years.

Professional sport franchise owners have historically complained that they either are just scraping by or are losing money. But independent economists and financial analysts consistently argue that the owners are being deceitful, and they are actually doing quite well. During litigation proceedings between the NFL and the players' union in the early 1990s, union officials claimed that the average annual profit for NFL teams exceeded $3.5 million. In 1997, *Financial World* reported that all NFL teams combined averaged about $6 million profit in 1996. The same magazine estimated that MLB's Colorado Rockies made $12.7 million in its first year in the league. One economist who has studied professional team sports claims that revenues have risen about 12 percent a year during the past 20 years. All in all, then, claims from team owners about losing enormous amounts of money must be viewed with skepticism.

Investors in pro franchises do not buy for tax benefits and annual profits only. The history of sport franchises is unmistakably clear about one thing: the biggest financial benefit to a franchise owner accrues when the franchise is sold. According to an attorney whose law firm serves as counsel to one sport franchise owner, when owners go into sports, they don't go in to make a lot of money; when they sell, they sell to make a lot of money. Two economists who have made a detailed analysis of the annual rate of increase in franchise values reported that "baseball and NFL franchise prices were increasing at around 20 percent per year during the 1980s, while NBA franchises were increasing at a faster rate, around 30 percent per year."[31] Professional sport franchises have continued to appreciate in the 1990s. Between 1996 and 1997 MLB franchise values increased 17 percent, NFL 18 percent, NBA 17 percent, and NHL 22 percent.

Other Investments of Franchise Owners

Sport team owners do not acquire their wealth through their investment in teams; one must be wealthy to be able to buy a professional team. Beyond the direct financial rewards of sport ownership already described, such ownership opens up numerous business opportunities that can integrate sport with owners' diversified corporate interests. This sometimes allows owners to take advantage of tax laws that enable them to lower their personal tax obligation.

As noted in a previous section of this chapter, the most common ownership link that has emerged among sports owners is with the entertainment and mass media industries. The symbiosis between sport and entertainment/media cannot be more complete than with common ownership in these industries. Moreover, this kind of organizational diversification is characteristic of corporate capitalism throughout American business, enabling a few giant firms to maintain their economic and political power.

Alternatives to Private Team Ownership

Private sport team ownership dominates professional sport so overwhelmingly that few people have even considered that there might be alternatives. For the few who have, there is little understanding of how such alternatives might work. Several years ago sports journalist Matthew Goodman described how community ownership of a professional team franchise (similar to Green Bay's) might operate. He deserves to be quoted at length, if only to stimulate thinking about the issue of sport team ownership in light of the increasing mobility of franchises and the public demands for expansion of professional sports.

> Here's how a buy out might work: Fans within a community could set up a corporation and issue public stock. The corporation would then negotiate with the team's owners on purchase of the franchise, using the capital raised from the stock drive as a down payment. The host city might float general obligation bonds to back up the rest of the purchase price, or the corporation might buy special revenue bonds, using—to take just one example—a 10 percent tax on tickets as a revenue stream to guarantee long-term payments. . . . A few important principles would have to be maintained. . . . Stock ownership must be broadly dispersed; there must be no speculative profits available on shares; management must be delegated, so that the franchise can run on a day-to-day basis like any other club; the charter of incorporation must prohibit the team from moving. . . . The sports commissioners have already made clear their opposition to this type of ownership. Not only does it reek of socialism, more importantly it would require that the team open its books, and this has been anathema to owners and commissioners alike. . . . In the long run, professional sports might be rescued from the present system of ownership, in which city is pitted against city by men and women whose fortunes are often outstripped only by their own egos.[32]

In their frustration over losing a professional sport franchise or their inability to secure local ownership for an existing franchise, politicians and citizens' groups in several cities have explored community ownership of professional teams. One of the avenues that has been investigated is the possibility of the city using its power of eminent domain to seize the name of the team on behalf of the citizens, just as it does when it condemns land for a new street, paying the owner fair compensation. Of course, the team is the property of its owners, and the league may lay claim to the team's name, but some legal experts believe there is a legal basis, through eminent domain law, for a city preventing an owner from actually relocating a franchise.[33]

Little has come of such efforts. Two major obstacles confront those who wish to change the current ownership structure: first, convincing local taxpayers that an investment of this kind is a good use of their money would be an enormous task; second, the opposition of current team owners would be vigorous. The owners would view community ownership as a threat to the private enterprise structure of professional sport (NFL bylaws prohibit ownership by public trusts or municipalities; Green Bay has been granted an exception). Indeed, that is exactly what happened in 1990 when Joan Kroc, owner of the San Diego Padres, "offered to *give* the Padres to the city of San Diego, along with a $100 million trust fund to finance the continued operation of the ball club."[34] For its part, the city was willing to consummate the deal, but MLB owners refused to even consider Kroc's proposal, citing the bad precedent that community control would set. She was forced to sell the franchise to a group of private investors. But the prospect of public ownership arose again in 1997. The Pohlad family, owners of 90 percent of Major League Baseball's Minnesota Twins, offered 49 percent of the team to the state of Minnesota in exchange for most of the funding for a new stadium. In November 1997 the Minnesota state legislature voted against funding for a new baseball stadium for the Twins.

Professional Athletes and the Social Relations of Their Production

Because of the immense popularity of professional sports and the incredible social prestige of the players, almost everyone who has ever hit a baseball, shot a basket, caught a pass, or slapped a puck has imagined becoming a pro. But the enormous trivia disseminated about professional athletes contrasts markedly with the little knowledge the public has of them as a social group and in relationship to the power structure of the professional sport industry.

Every productive enterprise has people who are the actual producers of the goods or services. The productive labor force of professional sports is the athletes. Without the athletes, there would be no sport event—no product. Professional athletes are laborers who have acquired salable skills, and indeed that is what they do—sell their labor as an occupation and a livelihood. As such, they also are a commodity themselves, a commodity that can be arbitrarily traded, sold, and moved according to the whims and impulses of team owners. As one MLB superstar said, upon learning that the owner was considering trading him, "I'm just an employee. If management wants to move me, I have no control over it." When Deion Sanders became a free agent with the San Francisco 49ers, he received criticism from a 49er player for signing a lucrative contract with the Dallas Cowboys. Sanders replied to the criticism, saying, "This is a business world," meaning the NFL. Jerry Reinsdorf, owner of the Chicago Bulls, when asked, "What is your current thinking about Scottie Pippen?" replied, "Scottie's been a great player for the Bulls, and he's done everything that anybody ever could have asked him. . . . But . . . our obligation . . . is to put the best possible team out there that we can. Which means that players come and players go."[35] And, of course, both players and owners are absolutely right. These are accurate portrayals of the social relationship of production in professional sports.

Athletes' labor is crucial to professional sport as a commodity because it is their performances that attract the public and the mass media; their labor makes the economy of sport possible. The social relations of pro athletes as employees place them in a position that is completely driven by capitalist relations, and they work under a historically specific set of production relations. Professional athletes do not own or control the means of producing their athletic labor power because they have no access to professional sport leagues except through the sale of their labor power to franchise owners. Under the cartelized organization of professional team sport, leagues control athletes' contracts, mobility, and working conditions, and the cumulative effects increase profits for the owners. Despite their subordinate status in pro sport, the athletes are both the machinery and the product. They are not just part of the game: they are the game.

The specific effects of the cartel organization enjoyed by owners on athletes are difficult to delineate, but the best example of their impact on salaries is vividly demonstrated whenever a rival league begins operating in a sport. Player salaries have consistently risen with the creation of new leagues and fallen with their demise. Basketball and hockey salaries almost doubled with the formation of the American Basketball Association and World Hockey Association in the 1970s. This is, of course, the main reason why the established professional leagues have always fought so fiercely against every rival league.

Are Pro Athletes' Salaries So Outrageous?

As much as the public dotes on professional athletes, there is often resentment about the money pro athletes make. Why is there this resentment, aside from a probably natural envy of people with more money? There are several reasons. In the first place, the average American has never really fully understood—or at least accepted—that professional sport is a business. Instead, professional teams are commonly perceived as a sort of extension of one's high school athletic team, and pro athletes as the lucky stiffs who get to go on having a great time playing games while everyone else had to go to work to earn a living.

It is easy enough to understand why people think this way about pro sports, given its similarities to youth and school sport teams: game rules are basically the same, players wear the same type of uniforms, teams are led by coaches, and teams participate in similar rituals and use similar mascots. With so many similarities, it is perhaps understandable that the average person has difficulty seeing pro sport as a business and athletes as skilled workers.

Much of this resentment would probably diminish if people more adequately understood the *business* of professional sport. The celebrated salaries of athletes need to be seen in the light of factors like the scarcity of talent, the average length of pro sport careers, job-related injuries, comparison with other professions, and the profitability of franchises. For instance, most Americans subscribe to the talent principle of pay, that those who have rare talent should be paid for it—the good old supply-and-demand economic principle of capitalism.

The athletic talent necessary to play a professional sport at the highest level is extremely rare; pro athletes are an exceptionally skilled group. There are only about 750 Major League Baseball players, 1,600 NFL players, 400 NBA players, and 600 NHL players. With a total of fewer than 3,400 athletes in the team sport leagues, each player represents one in 10,000 of the 23 million adult men in the United States in the 20-to-30 age group. As I noted in chapter 3, professional sports provide a livelihood for very few.[36] In fact, there are more brain surgeons than there are professional team sport athletes!

The acclaimed high salaries of professional sport workers need to be put in the context of a total career pattern. Most adults work in the same occupation until retirement; there may be job changes, to be sure, but they are usually within the same line of work. Professional team sport careers, by contrast, are very short. Indeed, the average age of NFL, NBA, NHL, and MLB players is 27; their average career length is about five years! This average is for those who actually make a major team roster; it does not include players who sign a pro contract but are cut before the season begins. So the few who have the rare ability to become pros remain at that level of sport for only a brief time. Their high salaries end when they can no longer make the team.

Stripped of the public adulation and media hype, professional athletes are entertainers. When the salaries of pro athletes are compared with others in the entertainment business, athletic salaries are not particularly impressive. The following list is the 1997 median salaries (half make more, half make less—a more meaningful measure of the salary structure than the mean, which is the "average" usually given in media accounts of players' salaries) of athletes in the top four team sports.

National Basketball Association	$1,700,000
Major League Baseball	$400,000
National Football League	$400,000
National Hockey League	$500,000

At the beginning of 1998, the highest single-year salary in all of professional team sports was Michael Jordan's $33 million. But there is a steep drop-off from there. The highest annual salaries in these four sports are from $4 million to $14 million. About nine NBA players are in that range; about 30 MLB players had salaries of $6 million to $10 million; about 12 NFL and four NHL players had salaries in the $4-million to $5-million range. A few superstar athletes earn additional millions of dollars in endorsement and public appearance fees. Thus, an elite handful of players has the salaries that are featured in the news, but the median salaries in the leagues are much less, as the figures here show.

These are unquestionably impressive salaries, but what about other entertainers? Each year *Forbes* magazine publishes the earnings of the top American entertainers. Its report for 1997 listed these figures:

Oprah Winfrey (talk-show host)	$104 million
Michael Crichton (writer)	$65 million
Jerry Seinfeld (comedian, actor)	$66 million
David Copperfield (illusionist)	$45 million
Tom Cruise (actor)	$55 million

The top 20 entertainers all reportedly had earnings of more than $20 million. What is clear, then, is that as entertainers, professional athletes' earnings are not exorbitant; in fact, one could argue that they are underpaid, as several economists do claim (more on this later).

Professional athletes can also be viewed as workers who are tops in their field, and their salaries can be compared with those of business executives considered the best in their field, the chief executive officers of American corporations. *Forbes* magazine publishes an annual report of the total compensation of CEOs of American business firms. Some of the top earners in *Forbes* 1997 report included the following:

Millare Drexler (Gap)	$104,822,000
Lawrence Coss (Green Tree Financial)	$102,449,000
Andrew Grove (INTEL)	$97,937,000
Sanford Weill (Travelers Group)	$91,565,000
Theodore Waitt (Gateway 2000)	$81,326,000
Anthony O'Reilly (H.J. Heinz)	$64,236,000

Again, what is indelibly clear is that professional athletes' salaries are not out of line with others who are at the top of particular professions. On the other hand, many highly skilled professionals in teaching, social work, nursing, and so forth make less than 10 percent of the annual salary of a professional athlete. Pay inequalities are endemic in a capitalist society; there is no standard of what constitutes a socially just or "legitimate" salary.

Professional team owners always spend less on athlete salaries than they expect to earn in revenue. Occasionally, it is possible to demonstrate a rather direct relationship between the salary paid to hire an athlete and the income he generates. And invariably the business acumen of owners is proved sound: the athlete actually generates more money for the team than he is being paid.

In recent years, several economists have used sophisticated statistical models to connect team performance and individual player statistics. One economist calculated the discrepancies between what some professional athletes are paid and what they are worth, in terms of the revenue their performances generate for their teams. The results for several 1993 Major League Baseball players are as follows:[37]

Professional Athlete	Actual Player Salary	Revenue Player Generated
Len Dykstra	$2.87 million	$10.69 million
Barry Bonds	$4.2 million	$ 9.83 million
Cecil Fielder	$4.26 million	$ 7.52 million
Steve Avery	$560,000	$ 2.94 million

Two other academicians constructed statistical models for estimating how much money a player generates for his team. Their equations take into account the player's performance and his team's record and revenue reports. They report that in almost every case, the player was actually underpaid.

Another factor that needs to be considered in relation to pro athletes' work is the dangers of the job and its effects on career and postcareer health and well-being. Professional athletes' work has become more difficult and dangerous in all professional team sports mainly because of longer seasons and higher and higher performance standards. Injuries are common, especially in football and hockey, where they are considered part of the job. In fact, injuries are so numerous in the NFL that the league publishes a weekly list of injured players—a casualty list. As one NFL running back told an ESPN interviewer, "Almost every time I run the ball, I'm lucky if I don't get injured somewhere on my body. The fans see me get hit and get up, get hit and get up. They don't see me the days following the game, when I can hardly get out of bed and am in constant pain from injuries."

Injuries have cut short the playing careers of many professional athletes, and for a few players, injuries have brought permanent physical disability. In a survey of 440 former NFL players, 78 percent said they suffered continuing football-related disabilities, 54 percent admitted to having psychological adjustment problems, and 66 percent said that they believed that playing had shortened their life expectancy.[38]

What about the postcareer incomes of professional athletes? A widely held scenario shows many attractive jobs waiting for professional athletes when their playing careers are over. This impression stems principally from the few former athletes who move into sport broadcasting and the filling of the professional coaching and managerial ranks with former pros. But these are the exceptions, the elite, of former players. Large-scale studies of former pro athletes are scarce, but the pattern seems to be that most move into occupations commensurate with their educational levels. Athletes with college degrees tend to wind up in occupations occupied by college graduates; those with only a high school education (many baseball and hockey players go right from high school into the pros) tend to enter jobs like those held by other high school graduates.

Collusion by Owners

Evidence that owners pay professional athletes only what they believe they have to, and that they will resort to illegal anticompetitive tactics if they think it is necessary, is found in the rulings of three impartial arbitrators involving MLB owners. The iron lock of the reserve system was broken in the mid-1970s when professional baseball's arbitrator ruled in favor of two players who had challenged the reserve system. His ruling modified the reserve system and created "free agency," which allows professional athletes to negotiate with owners of other teams under certain circumstances (free agency came later in other leagues and its features vary from league to league; they are complex and will not be described in this volume). After the decision by the arbitrator, a wave of spending on free agents swept

MLB. Consequently, a great disparity in spending arose, with teams like the New York Yankees and the California Angels spending lavishly while the Cincinnati Reds and Toronto Blue Jays spent little.

After several years, great animosity developed among the owners. Not only were the free agent player salaries escalating rapidly, and more and more players becoming free agents each year, but the salaries were causing the overall salary structure of baseball to rise sharply. This open labor market was welcomed by the players but understandably despised by the owners, so the owners struck back. In 1985 free agents found that owners would not engage in legitimate bidding for players still coveted by their former teams. The same thing occurred in two subsequent years. These actions were so patently obvious to the players and constituted such a flagrant violation of one of the contract provisions between the MLB Players' Association and the owners ("Players shall not act in concert with other Players and Clubs shall not act in concert with other Clubs") that the players' union filed a grievance against the owners. During the next two years, the players' union filed two more collusion grievances. After several years of testimony, two of the arbitrators found the owners had engaged in a clear and deliberate pattern of collusion to hold down player salaries, and thus there was no vestige of a free market. The third arbitrator found that the owners shared salary offers in an information bank. In all three cases, the actions by the owners were blatant violations of the owners-players' contract. The owners had to pay $280 million in damages; more than a dozen players were given another opportunity to test the free agency market.[39]

Effects of Monopsony on Salaries

As I noted earlier in this chapter, monopsony is a situation in which there is only one buyer in a market. In pro sports, this has meant that only one franchise owner could negotiate with a player and a player could negotiate with only that owner, thus restricting player freedom and mobility. For years the NFL Players' Association (NFLPA) squabbled with owners over free agency, even striking over the issue on two occasions (1982 and 1987), but to no avail. The attitude of some owners was succinctly expressed by the president of the Dallas Cowboys: "No free agency; not now, not ever." But in spring 1989, facing litigation from the NFLPA over restraints on player movement, the owners established their own form of free agency. Under it, each team protected 37 players—presumably its best—from free agency while exposing the rest to the open market. The result? More than 225 players were signed by other teams; their salaries rose 78 percent and signing bonuses averaged $40,000! In the last year before free agency was won by the NFLPA, the 167 players who switched teams under the owners' form of free agency received an average 53 percent increase in salary!

Here was clear and unambiguous evidence of the adverse economic impact of monopsonistic practices on professional athletes. It also dramatized the effects of movement restriction for those 37 players on each team who were not given free agency. If players considered expendable could increase their salaries so dramatically, imagine what the best could do in an open market. When the NFL players finally won free agency in 1993, imagination was not needed; the reality was that salaries shot up.

Professional Sports Players' Unions

To mitigate working conditions under capitalism, American workers have joined in unions designed to deal collectively, rather than individually, with management. Such organization began in the mid-19th century, originally to address the interests of workers for increased wages, shorter working hours, safer and more humane working conditions, and benefits such as health plans. The union movement in the United States has had a checkered history spanning glorious successes and desperate failures. From 11.6 percent of all employees in 1930 to a high of 34.5 percent immediately after World War II, union membership has declined to only 15 percent of employed Americans in the late 1990s. Unionization rates in the United States rank at the bottom of all capitalist countries.

In a comprehensive analysis of the American working class, two sociologists concluded that weaknesses in the union movement and in working-class consciousness in general are not a product of working-class indifference or of the generosity and goodwill of capital, but rather that throughout the history of American capitalism, private capital has enjoyed "unchallenged control in almost every sector of the economy." They further said that there are good reasons to conclude that U.S. capital "has had more power than the capitalist class of other Western democracies. In the face of this overwhelming power, the U.S. working class has had a more difficult time constructing political and class organizations to defend its interests."[40] Failures in the union movement largely represent, then, the successful application of political and economic repression by the dominant class.

The response of professional athletes to monopsony, abridgment of individual rights, and other job restrictions has been unionization, collective bargaining, and strikes. The first organizing effort of professional athletes was the founding of the National Brotherhood of Baseball Players in 1885, and the Brotherhood actually formed its own league in 1890. In that year, the Players' League successfully conducted a season of baseball, but a poor financial base and intense attacks by powerful forces within the National League forced it to disband.[41]

The modern era for collectivization of professional athletes began in the mid-1950s with the Major League Baseball Players' Association, as major league ballplayers attempted to establish some power against the hegemony of the owners; it was not until the mid-1960s, however, that they emerged with real powers. The NBA Players' Association was established in 1952 but did not become an authentic force until the mid-1960s. In 1956 the NFL Players' Association was formed, but it had to wait more than 12 years for full recognition by the league. Several attempts were made in the 1950s to organize NHL players, but it was not until the late 1960s that the National Hockey League Players' Association received formal recognition from team owners.

The organization of players' unions within professional sports needs to be seen in terms of the relations of production within a capitalist enterprise. As sociologist Anthony Giddens has noted, "A distinctive feature of the capitalist labour contract . . . is that it is purely economic, a monetary relation. The worker is not accorded any rights of participation in the policies which govern the nature of the labour task or other aspects of the work setting. The formation of unions, one major aspect of class conflict . . . represents an attempt of workers to gain a measure of control over the conditions of their labour."[42]

Try as they might to gain some control of the productive relations in professional sports, the players' unions have never been particularly strong. There are several reasons for this:

- Because most pro athletes' careers are less than five years long and because athletes have to compete intensely to maintain their jobs, many see no conspicuous advantages in joining and supporting unions. The result is that pro athletes usually lack the commitment to solidarity that is needed to challenge the power of the higher levels of the sport hierarchy.

- Pro athletes are isolated from the mainline working class and so cannot benefit from the experiences of organized labor nor draw support from it.

- The emphasis on individual achievement deeply embedded in the typical professional athlete militates against collective responses to the league system.

- The ethos of the sports world—a world most pro athletes have been part of since their youth—is extremely conservative and teaches obedience to superiors; thus many pro athletes have developed personal political philosophies that oppose (or at least are very lukewarm toward) unions.

- The awesome power of the league and its owners tends to foster antiunion sentiments among athletes. Building upon players' naive understanding of the economic oppressions they face (i.e., their underdeveloped class consciousness), owners have brought hegemonic ideology to bear through the various communications channels they control. Thus team owners not only control the productive process to accumulate wealth, they also dominate the belief system of professional athletes, thus reproducing owner rule.

As a consequence of these weakening forces, pro players' unions have not functioned like trade or labor unions, and the scope of their interests has been extremely narrow. For example, the players' unions have shown no interest in trying to organize among pro sports' underclass—the minor leagues in the various sports—nor have they used their high visibility to promote broader economic, social, or political issues which are of concern to the larger labor movement.

Despite the fact that the organization of professional players' unions has generally been rudimentary and inadequate, the unions have challenged the powerful interests that own and control the pro sport industry, and they have gradually gained some important concessions. For example, the Major League Baseball Players' Association has won seven labor disputes in the past 20 years, forcing baseball's owners to cede a variety of concessions. The National Football League Players' Association even had to take the drastic step of decertifying (giving up its right to bargain as a labor union) to allow its players to sue the NFL. The strategy worked, and NFL players won free agency. The NFLPA was then reorganized.

Owner response to the players' union movement has been predictable: annoyed and angered by unionization, which has aroused their unbridled wrath, they have fought it consistently. Players' unions are perceived not merely as an economic threat to owners but as an enemy to be destroyed. Team owners, like most members of the capitalist class, tend to view union activity as antithetical to their social and political agendas.

But beyond that is a more pervasive ideological view—a plantation mentality—of professional sport, manifested in owners not wanting "their" athletes to struggle against the paternalistic structure underlying professional sport. This is also called a neutrality vision of sport—that is, sport is thought of as an isolated world unconcerned with political, economic, and cultural phenomena. Such a view of sport is not limited to team owners; it permeates American society as well. The owners' consensus is to keep "inappropriate" matters, such as union organization (as well as issues of race, gender, politics, etc.), out of professional sport. The problem with this view is that it leaves no forum for confronting the so-called inappropriate issues.

Clearly, the purpose of this hegemonic ideological perspective is to prevent any kind of progressive reform. The message of the neutrality argument is that political, economic, and social reform has no place in professional sport. But such a strategy obscures the real social and material exploitation in professional sport.

The most overt example of the vulnerability of unionized players to coercion by owners is seen in the treatment of players who have served as representatives to their unions. Each players' union has a committee of player representatives, elected by their teammates, which makes major decisions about union activities. Although these representatives are commonly among a team's better players, many of them are traded or are forced to retire by the owners. Such actions are particularly conspicuous immediately after a strike or other acrimonious dispute between owners and the union.

Summary and Preview

Professional team sport is a significant component of the commercial sport industry. There are similarities to other capitalist industries— ownership of the means of production is privatized, and workers, in this case athletes, produce the product (the sporting event)—but professional team sports have a number of unique characteristics.

The professional sports discussed in this chapter are not the only form of commercialized sports in the United States. Intercollegiate athletics, which began as student-sponsored and student-run physical recreation in American colleges and universities (and still are in most parts of the world) have become a commercialized sport industry. Under the guise of educational and amateur sport, major universities across the nation are engaged in a massive commercial entertainment enterprise. The peculiar aspects of intercollegiate athletics are examined in chapter 10.

Suggested Readings

Anderson, Benedict. *Imagined Communities: Reflections on the Origin and Spread of Nationalism.* Rev. ed. New York: Verso, 1991.

Baim, Dean. *The Sport Stadium as a Municipal Investment.* Westport, CT: Greenwood Press, 1994.

Danielson, Michael N. *Home Team: Professional Sports and the American Metropolis.* Princeton, NJ: Princeton University Press, 1997.

Euchner, Charles C. *Playing the Field: Why Sports Teams Move and Cities Fight to Keep Them.* Baltimore: Johns Hopkins University Press, 1993.

Freedman, Warren. *Professional Sports and Antitrust.* New York: Quorum Books, 1987.

Gorman, Jerry, and Kirk Calhoun. *The Name of the Game: The Business of Sport.* New York: Wiley, 1994.

Leifer, Eric M. *Making the Majors: The Transformation of Team Sports in America.* Cambridge: Harvard University Press, 1995.

Lowe, Stephen R. *The Kid on the Sandlot: Congress and Professional Sports, 1910-1992.* Bowling Green, OH: Bowling Green State University Popular Press, 1995.

Noll, Roger, and Andrew Zimbalist, eds. *Sports Jobs and Tax: Economic Impact of Sports Teams and Facilities.* Washington, DC: Brookings Institute, 1997.

Quirk, James, and Rodney D. Fort. *Pay Dirt: The Business of Professional Team Sports.* Princeton, NJ: Princeton University Press, 1992.

Rosentraub, Mark S. *Major League Losers: The Real Cost of Sports and Who's Paying for It.* New York: Basic Books, 1997.

Scully, Gerald W. *The Market Structure of Sports.* Chicago: University of Chicago Press, 1995.

Shropshire, Kenneth L. *The Sports Franchise Game: Cities in Pursuit of Sport Franchises, Events, Stadiums, and Arenas.* Philadelphia: University of Pennsylvania Press, 1995.

Vincent, Ted. *The Rise & Fall of American Sport: Mudville's Revenge.* Lincoln: University of Nebraska Press, 1997.

Zimbalist, Andrew. *Baseball and Billions.* New York: Basic Books, 1992.

Chapter 10

Power and Ideology in Intercollegiate Sport

The first intercollegiate competition in the United States was conceived and organized by students in the mid-1850s. . . . This all came about through student initiative and effort. The students set in place the underlying structure for college sports. Today, professional coaches, professional managers and money-minded presidents have total control. It is time to give back to the students who play sports the freedoms they deserve. At a minimum, they are entitled to freedoms enjoyed by their fellow students.

Walter Byers, former executive director of the NCAA

Sport is an enormously popular form of physical recreation on every college campus in the nation. Campus recreation facilities overflow with students playing pickup games of basketball, racquetball, volleyball, and half a dozen other sports. More than 60 percent of college students participate in campus intramural sports programs. Sport club teams—teams that athletic departments refuse to fund—are provided money by college student governments and compete against other institutions. Finally, on most campuses there is a formal intercollegiate athletic program.

The characteristics of formal intercollegiate sports programs vary widely. At one extreme, there are the programs in which the student-athletes are an integral part of the student body, receiving no "athletic scholarships" for playing their sports. In these institutions, intercollegiate sports are primarily funded from general institutional accounts, games are played against colleges within the region, and spectator attendance at games is typically small, consisting mostly of students, parents of students, and alumni. These programs are classified by the National Collegiate Athletic Association (NCAA), the major controlling body of intercollegiate sports, as Division III.[1] At the other extreme are "big-time" intercollegiate sports, or Division I by the NCAA classification. This form of intercollegiate sports, especially the sports of football and basketball, will be the focus of this chapter because it is what John Thelin, author of a book titled *Games Colleges Play,* calls American higher education's "peculiar institution."[2]

Big-Time Intercollegiate Athletics Is Big Business

Big-time intercollegiate sport is called "peculiar" by Thelin because there is nothing quite like it in other countries of the world. It is also "peculiar" because it is part of the nation's larger commodified cultural industry. Big-time college sports events are accompanied by marching bands, cheerleaders, pompon groups, tailgate parties, and so forth. But the pageantry and hoopla tend to mask the underlying profit-oriented structure—the explicit fact that college sport is a big commercial business.

The following statements by various people associated with big-time college sports confirm that at least some of them are willing to describe big-time collegiate sport as it really is. The former athletic director at the University of Michigan said, "This is a business, a big business. Anyone who hasn't figured that out by now is a damned fool." The University of Arizona athletic director concurred, saying, "I think it's important for people to realize that [NCAA Division I] sports is . . . a big business." Indiana University's basketball coach Bobby Knight echoed those of the athletic directors', asserting that major college athletic programs "are business programs, and they have to be run that way." A former University of Minnesota president told a special convention of the NCAA, "We in Division I are in an entertainment business and we can't fool ourselves." When introducing a bill making some items of intercollegiate sport revenue taxable income, Congressman Paul Henry of Michigan said, "Intercollegiate athletics have little to do with the educational mission of the universities which sponsor them. . . . [T]hese programs are large-scale businesses, operating under the golden dome of higher education."[3]

For anyone who doubts the big-business aspects of big-time intercollegiate sports, consider the following:

- Many major universities have athletic budgets exceeding $25 million.
- NCAA-sanctioned football bowl games generate more than $55 million each year to participating institutions.

- In 1994 the NCAA signed a $1.725 billion, seven-year contract permitting CBS the rights to televise the men's basketball tournament. Thus, nearly $247 million in revenue is generated for the NCAA and the universities each year, with universities selected for the men's basketball tournament netting from $300,000 to $500,000.

- The NCAA has an annual total revenue in excess of $270 million and has reported multimillion-dollar profits annually in recent years.

- Corporate sponsorship of individual university athletic programs, basketball tournaments, and football bowl games has become a common feature of big-time college athletics.

- In a book titled *Keeping Score: The Economics of Big-Time Sports,* the author reports the results of an economic analysis of how big-time college sports teams stack up in terms of financial value against professional sports franchises (recognizing, of course, that college programs, unlike pro franchises, cannot be sold). In ranking the 25 most valuable sports organizations, the Dallas Cowboys lead the field, but four college programs are among the top 25.[4]

The big-time collegiate sport industry organizes athletics not, as one might expect, to meet students' personal and social needs for physical recreation, but strictly on market principles (the pursuit of capital accumulation). College sports' nonprofit status does not mean that schools cannot make money but rather that any earnings— "excess revenues" or year-end "surplus" in nonprofit accounting jargon—must be spent to further the purpose of the organization. The Internal Revenue Service generally allows a tax-exempt organization to avoid taxes on business income as long as the business is "substantially related" to the organization's founding purpose. In the case of intercollegiate sport, the NCAA and individual colleges argue that because the institutions themselves are tax exempt, and intercollegiate sports programs are performing a valuable services for the institutions, the intercollegiate sports programs have a legitimate claim to the educational linkage between them and the universities.

Regardless of the amount of their excess revenues, athletic departments find ways to spend the money (higher staff salaries, new staff positions, facilities, equipment, recruiting, etc.) to avoid any appearance of profit. For example, it is common practice for universities participating in football bowl games and the Final Four basketball tournament to spend more than $150,000 treating guests (governors, state legislators, college administrators, big donors, and the like) to free trips to the events out of bowl or tournament payouts. This money, of course, is "excess revenue," and it would have to be declared as profit by any ordinary business.[5]

Images of Big-Time College Sports as Just Fun and Games

Most people do not think of college sport as a commercial industry. The prevalent images of college athletics in the public's mind are of bright and bouncy cheerleaders urging their fellow classmates/athletes to victory over a rival, of alumni tailgate parties, of eager young student-athletes giving their all for their school, of universities upholding the ideals of good, clean, amateur athletics. But more accurately, college athletics on the NCAA Division I level (the focus of this chapter) are about capital accumulation and the bottom line. They are about economic exploitation, dominance, power, and control by one segment of the college sport industry and the powerlessness and subordination of another. They are also about employing ideological hegemony to sustain existing social arrangements.[6]

Many people deny the possibility of any relationship between intercollegiate athletics and power, dominance, and exploitation. Their attitude is, How could power wielding be possible in such a seemingly benign activity? Such an idea challenges the integrity of a practice that, for many people, exemplifies some of the most admired values and standards of American life and that is the source of much exciting entertainment. Ironically, it is precisely this naive perspective that plays a compelling, albeit unintentional, role in perpetuating the relations of power and dominance in collegiate athletics. Although there is much potential good in college sport, the existing social arrangements in big-time collegiate football and basketball are inherently exploitative and unstable and harbor flagrant inequality.[7]

Reams of literature and analyses are regularly published about intercollegiate athletics, but they rarely situate college sport in a structural context of power, dominance, and ideology, as must happen if we are to really understand this enormously popular cultural practice. This contextualization must begin with C. Wright Mills's notion of establishing a historical sensitivity by tracing the evolution of college athletics from a spontaneous student recreation to their present form.

Shift From Student Games to Big-Time Sport

Intercollegiate athletics did not always have the look they have today. They began quietly enough—the year was 1852—when a group of

Yale and Harvard rowers engaged in a boat race. It took place on a lake in New Hampshire, and this was America's first intercollegiate athletic contest. But the entire affair was regarded as a "jolly lark" by the crewmen. A writer for the *New York Tribune* commented that although the race was amusing and momentarily diverted the attention of participants and spectators from mundane matters, intercollegiate sport would "make little stir in the busy world." Of course, subsequent events over more than a century certainly have proved this prophet wrong. College sports have made a very big stir in the busy worlds of higher education and commercial entertainment.

In 1859 baseball, popular among upper-class young men in that decade, became the second intercollegiate sport when Amherst and Williams Colleges organized a game (in which final score was 66-32!). After an interruption by the Civil War, most colleges in the late 1860s and early 1870s formed baseball teams, and the sport was quickly established as the most popular one on many campuses.

An 1869 game between Princeton and Rutgers is considered the first intercollegiate football contest, but there were no established rules like those in baseball, and the team captains at the first game—and subsequent games for several years—spent considerable time haggling over the rules under which it would be played. The last two decades of the 1800s witnessed growing numbers of sports being played on campuses throughout the country. By the turn of the century, many had taken their place as intercollegiate sports, and college athletics were indeed making themselves known.

Era of Student Initiative and Control

Collegiate sports were founded upon student initiative, unassisted and unsupported by faculties, administration, or alumni. As legendary Yale football coach Walter Camp put it, "Neither the faculties nor other critics assisted in building the structure of college athletics. . . . It is a structure which students unaided have built, and with pride they point to their labor, and love it more dearly for its difficulties."[8]

This original form of governance was modeled after the well-established sports in the private secondary schools of England. In the British model, the sports were for the students, and as student recreations, they were expected to be organized, administered, and coached through student initiative, not adult intervention. Much of 19th-century British school life in general featured student self-government—students supervising and governing one another—and in no part of the school life was self-government more highly developed than in games and sports. This feature of sport still persists in British secondary schools and universities.[9]

Just as with British school sports, early American intercollegiate sports were governed by the students themselves. Faculty members refrained from interfering, viewing the games as a good expenditure of energy and adopting the British attitude that the games were valuable for the qualities of character that they brought out. It was believed that the best environment for nurturing good character traits was one in which students were in control.

Management of the business end of intercollegiate programs was initially in the hands of students, organized in athletic associations. Most associations scheduled games, cared for fields, and handled other necessary transactions pertinent to the business; when hiring of professional coaches began, the associations did this, too. The most pressing purpose of these associations was finding ways and means of financing their teams. From 1870 until 1900, nearly every college formed a student athletic association to garner financial and student support for its teams.[10]

The thrust for some form of collective governance arose as early as the second intercollegiate contest (the 1855 Harvard-Yale boat race), when the eligibility of a Harvard coxswain became an issue. It was from this impetus that the first intercollegiate governing body emerged at a meeting in New Haven, Connecticut, and the College Union Regatta was formed. Regulated competition grew, and athletic clubs from different campuses formed intercollegiate associations to govern their competition. The earliest governing associations, then, were initiated and run by students. An association's mission was generally threefold: to sponsor and conduct competition, outline playing rules, and determine eligibility criteria.

Decline of Student Control

A gradual transformation in governance began during the late 1870s; student control began to diminish and was eventually eliminated. The process began as university administrations, faculties, and alumni sought greater participation in the management of college athletics. All three groups agreed that the job was becoming too large for students to handle. Administrators and faculty members thought that college students ought to be restrained from pursuing goals that appeared increasingly incongruent with higher education; they expressed alarm about growing professionalism, mismanagement of finances, lack of sportsmanship, glorification of athletics over academics, and other problems. Alumni, on the other hand, desired to bring greater competence to the pursuit of gate receipts and championships.[11]

Concerns like these led to the formation of faculty athletic committees, which either worked closely with the student associations or took them over completely. By 1900 nearly every college had an athletic committee that either gave the institution sole power to regulate athletics or divided the power with the students and alumni. They were the harbingers of faculty-controlled athletic conferences.

The expansion of collegiate athletics was so great after 1880 and the practices attending them were so varied that conferences of colleges were formed to standardize athletic procedures among schools in one geographic area. These conferences, usually made up of colleges with similar enrollments, academic requirements, and financial standings, made rules and regulations concerning athletic eligibility, provided a means of enforcing conference rules, and drew up playing schedules.

Not until 1905, however, did colleges formulate a collective national solution to the issue of interinstitutional governance. The impetus for this action was a crisis that developed in football. During the 1905 season, there were 18 deaths and 149 serious injuries attributable to football. A public outcry about the brutality of the game led President Theodore Roosevelt to threaten to abolish it on college campuses unless rule changes were made. Within a few months, colleges had banded together, modified the rules, and in the process formed the Intercollegiate Athletic Association of the United States. This name was changed in 1910 to the National Collegiate Athletic Association. From its inception, the NCAA stood for institutional control and order; the control has been sustained with little opposition, but the search for order has been elusive throughout the association's history.[12]

Throughout these early years, students complained about the intrusions into their domain, but to no avail. By 1910 they had lost most of their authority to various governing groups and alumni. The students clearly were no longer masters of their own product. By the mid-1920s, the structure of collegiate athletics as it exists today had been established. Its foundation was built on institutional control, with two main approaches to college sport. One views athletics as an integral part of student life and physical recreation; this is currently codified in NCAA Division III (smaller school) athletics. The second approach runs collegiate sport as an entertainment business and a training ground for professional and elite amateur athletes; this is currently codified in NCAA Division I (big-time college sports). Division II is a hybrid of the other two.

Control of Women's Intercollegiate Sports

Governance of college athletics for women took quite a different course in its founding and early development. It was fully under faculty control from its beginnings because female students never established their own athletic networks. Instead, early women's sports were advised and directed by female faculty. Sponsorship began with female physical educators and remained that way until the early 1970s. From this model, a course was charted to deliberately avoid the problems of the commercialized men's programs. Promotion of educational goals and philosophies was the guiding principle, but the success of this model came at the expense of not sponsoring high-level skill development.[13]

Women's collegiate sport took a dramatic change of course in the early 1970s with the founding of the Association for Intercollegiate Athletics for Women (AIAW). The former purposes and philosophies were renounced because influential leaders in women's intercollegiate athletics were won over by the quest for high-level competition, records, championships, and public recognition. Women's athletics began to model the men's programs. The change became complete in 1981 when the NCAA began scheduling national championship events for women's collegiate sports. Within a year, the AIAW was destroyed; women's athletics came under the jurisdiction of the NCAA and have come to mirror the men's system in almost every detail. In 1997 a *USA Today* analysis found that approximately 116,000 women were participating in college athletics, 44,000 in NCAA Division I universities. Female athletes receive from 35 percent to 40 percent of athletic scholarships at Division I schools. The women's Division I basketball tournament has the same format as the men's; and in the 1995-96 school year, the University of Connecticut women's basketball program reported nearly $1.4 million in revenues. Female athletes as well as male athletes are part of big-time college sports.

Big-Time College Sport and Amateur Sport Ideology

Some commercialism was present in collegiate sport from its beginnings, but while control was in student hands, the extent of commercialization was minimal. But once institutional control was solidified, college presidents, alumni, and business interests forged a coalition and plunged wholeheartedly into the professionalization of intercollegiate athletics. In a quest to acquire increasing private and public financial support, college administrators envisioned the potential of their teams for advertising and for generating alumni interest and contributions. They also presumed that the achievements of a college's athletic teams and the attending publicity would help attract students, thus raising enrollments. For their part, the alumni and public viewed intercollegiate athletics as good entertainment.

The result of these various interests was expanding commercialization. By the 1950s the course was set. A national mania had grown up around college football especially, "and its future would be linked with the development of mass entertainment in a growing industrial society."[14]

Although commercialized collegiate athletics were a growing industry before midcentury, financial domination of big-time collegiate football and basketball is a phenomenon of the past 50 years. Many factors have contributed to this phenomenon: the expansion of the mass media and especially the enormous television revenues, rapid and convenient air transportation making possible interregional rivalries, increased leisure time and discretionary income, and the advent of college sports information departments and their widely successful advertising efforts. These factors—and undoubtedly others—directly or indirectly increased interest in commodified forms of intercollegiate athletics.

As almost all the earmarks of capitalist enterprise have come to characterize the business of big-time collegiate athletics, enormous inequalities and conflicts of interests have arisen, not the least of which is the social relationship of student-athletes to the commercial enterprise. As college sports have become imbued with commercial values and modes of operation, the original commitment to amateur sport—meaning sport played for the personal, social, and emotional gratification of the participants—has been jettisoned in the process.

The single exception is that student-athletes, the major labor force in producing the product of commercial college sporting events, are still defined by the NCAA and its member universities as amateurs, and they are not paid wages or salaries based on market considerations. The collegiate sport industry does this through an ingenious deployment of ideological hegemony codified in the *NCAA Manual*. In it is a declaration that student-athletes must be amateurs "and their participation should be motivated primarily by education and by the physical, mental, and social benefits to be derived. . . . [S]tudent-athletes should be protected from exploitation by professional and commercial enterprises."[15] Such a statement implies that amateurism is a higher form of sport than commercial sport, but even more remarkable, it completely discounts, even denies, the blatant commercialized nature of big-time intercollegiate athletics. By declaring that college sports are a form of amateur sports, the NCAA and its membership are able to mystify the reality of big-time college sports as professional and commercial and are able to manufacture support for the economic exploitation of student-athletes.

Ideological Hegemony in Big-Time College Sports

Renowned philosopher Bertrand Russell said that "the fundamental concept in social science is Power, in the same sense in which Energy is the fundamental concept in physics."[16] Social organizations tend to be stratified on the basis of power, with those holding the power possessing an unequal share of the benefits of that system. Power tends to get translated into a structure of dominance enabling the powerful to write their advantages into the system's very structure. Of course, the interests of a dominant group rarely appear pretentious; they are protected by laws, nurtured by the media, and fortified and elaborated by ideology. Ideology is the social lubricant of dominant groups—in this case, the NCAA and its member universities.

The enormously successful commercial entertainment business that has emerged from major college football and basketball is actually a popular cultural form of the same genre as theater, cinema, popular music, and, of course, professional sport. In each case, people talented and well trained in their specialties provide amusement and entertainment for audiences who pay to watch the performances. Although all these forms of popular entertainment have a formal business organizational structure, they all, except for big-time college sports, operate throughout as commercial entities with an unambiguous labor market orientation; all employees are paid at least a minimum wage, and they are free to negotiate for more money with other employers in the industry. Even in the case of big-time collegiate sport, all employees—athletic directors, coaches, athletic trainers, sports information directors, and sundry support staff—make a good living and are free to seek other employment if they are dissatisfied at a particular university. Some athletic directors and coaches earn annual salaries in excess of $500,000, and with TV contracts, equipment endorsements, and speaking fees, a few have incomes of more than $1 million.

Only the athlete is without a salary; indeed, the collegiate sport industry prevents universities from paying the athlete an outright salary and prohibits the athlete from accepting offers of salary or any other money under penalty of permanent banishment from collegiate sport participation. Instead, the athlete gets what is euphemistically called an "athletic scholarship," worth about $10,000 per year at a state university (in 1998), and said to be a "free ride" to a college education. Reggie Rivers, a former college football player and NFL running back, has this to say about the term "free ride": "A federal grant provides a 'free' education. A scholarship from a local bank with no strings attached, provides a 'free' education. A rich uncle provides a free education. There is nothing 'free' about a football scholarship ... when you calculate all the hours spent during summer two-a-days, meetings, practices, travel and off-season workouts."[17]

This clever use of the term "free ride" by the NCAA and individual universities projects an image of student-athletes as the beneficiaries of a generous philanthropy from institutions of higher education. But in fact these student-athletes are laborers whose work (sports performance) generates the income for thousands of employees of the big-time intercollegiate athletic industry, the mass media, and corporations that advertise through college sports.

The power brokers of big-time college sport are able to maintain this arrangement because the public image they have successfully constructed portrays college athletics as student-athletes competing for the love of sport while their classmates cheer on their beloved heroes. Tutored by the NCAA, the public accepts the premise that college athletes must remain amateurs, untainted by money. In the most recent legal decisions, courts have held that the athletes were not employees under a labor contract. That is, of course, exactly the

© Terry Wild Studio/Chris Stutz

Even though the NCAA and its member universities maintain that big-time college athletes are "amateur" athletes, the commodified nature of big-time college sport belies such a claim. The athletes themselves know they are part of a business industry, but they are powerless to change NCAA policies.

interpretation the sport establishment—NCAA executives, university administrators, and coaches—wants. However, athletes at major universities quickly understand what big-time college sport is really all about. As one noted, "It's a business here. We're here to make money for [the university]. When we're not useful for [the coaches] they don't pay as much attention to us."[18]

Basis for the Amateur Ideology in College Sport

It is normal for those dominant in an organization to interpret reality and create normative prescriptions so as to serve their interests, and the NCAA and its member universities have done this with the amateur ideology. These molders of American intercollegiate athletics have taken a 19th-century upper-class doctrine of amateur sport and welded it to a distorted idea of ancient Greek athletes competing for the love and excitement of the sporting experience. They have made their case so persuasively that alternative images have been made to seem unthinkable.

Analysts of social inequality and group consciousness view ideology as integral to relations of inequality because the dominant group typically uses it as a form of engineering of consent to promote its interests. Use of ideology to secure consent does not, it must be emphasized, necessarily require force or threats of force. Judiciously used, it molds, manipulates, and persuades potentially opposing factions. The ability of those in control of collegiate sport to justify existing conditions and power relationships hinges considerably on the promotion of an amateur ideology.[19]

This process of legitimation has been so successful that amateurism is widely accepted as a given, the natural and most just form of collegiate athletics. Thus, the institutionally powerful groups in collegiate sport have created an interpretation of reality that successfully serves their interests; they have made their advantage part of the very structure of their enterprise.

To fully understand amateurism, two points must be made. First, amateurism is one aspect of a 19th-century socially elitist approach to sport as a casual practice, which flourished first among the upper social classes in England. Social traditions and ideals among America's social elite were greatly affected by British customs and standards, and amateurism was introduced to the United States in the last two decades of the 19th century. Second, amateurism is founded upon a myth that ancient Greek athletes competed solely for fame and honor.

Amateurism arose in Britain as an elitist mechanism designed to exclude the working class from competition, and it was an upper-class prejudice that disdained professional athletes, the product of a Victorian doctrine that work and play must be preserved as separate entities. This notion was readily congruent with the British history of upper-social-class rule and traditions of deference.

In the latter 19th century, athletic clubs that limited their membership to upper-class gentlemen grew, at first in England but soon after in the United States, explicitly separating their sport events from the working class. The words *gentleman* and *amateur* were synonymous, while *professional* meant working class. The question of social separation was clearly outlined in membership regulations for competition. The rules for the Henley Regatta, a popular British sporting event for the socially elite, stated, "No person shall be considered an amateur . . . who is or has been by trade or employment for wages a mechanic, artisan, or labourer, or engaged in any menial duty."[20] At first, then, amateurism was a question of social class; indeed, amateur rules were instruments of class warfare.

By the 1880s, amateurism was redefined, forbidding amateurs to accept money for their sport participation or achievements. Although social distinctions were dropped, working-class persons were effectively excluded because they could not devote the time necessary to train and compete without remuneration. Thus social exclusivity was retained.

With the growth of American college sport from 1880 to 1900, prizes and cash awards were occasionally given, but objections surfaced immediately. Upper-class interests dominated American higher education during this period. Administrators and faculty members, though not necessarily wealthy, were socially elite and held the values of that social stratum. Students, especially those at the prestigious colleges where sport was popular, were overwhelmingly from upper-social-class families. American universities, eager to model themselves after the much-admired British universities, adopted many of the elitist trappings then fashionable, one of which was the amateur sport ideology.

Influential supporters of the view that American intercollegiate sport should remain strictly amateur solidified this doctrine for the public through their writings and speeches. Walter Camp, the Yale University football coach for many years and often called the father of American football, as well as one of the most respected representatives of college sport, counseled college men in his book *Walter Camp's Book of College Sports:*

> Be each, pray God, a gentleman! It is an easy word, and a pleasant one. I don't doubt but that you all pronounce it trippingly enough, and have each one his own high ideal of what a gentleman should be. Do you live up to it? Or are you letting it come down a little here and there; so little, perhaps, that you hardly notice it until you make

comparison? A gentleman against a gentleman always plays to win. There is a tacit agreement between them that each shall do his best, and the best man shall win. A gentleman does not make his living, however, from his athletic prowess. He does not earn anything by his victories except glory and satisfaction. . . . A gentleman never competes for money, directly or indirectly. Make no mistake about this. No matter how winding the road may be that eventually brings [money] into the pocket, it is the price of what should be dearer to you than anything else—your honor.[21]

Such a statement makes explicit what is implicit in the amateur sport ideology.

Capt. Palmer Pierce of the U.S. Military Academy, one of the leading forces in the organization of the NCAA, claimed in a speech to the 1907 NCAA convention that

this Association does not require acceptance of any particular set of eligibility rules. It does, however, bind its members to line up to the well-known principles of amateur sport. . . . In a word, this is a league of educated gentlemen who are trying to exercise a wise control over college athletics.[22]

A final example comes from Casper Whitney, the powerful editor of *Outing,* one of the most popular sporting magazines of the late 19th and early 20th centuries. Whitney, who was an influential doctrinaire of amateur sport and an advocate of college athletics during this era, made emphatic the place of amateurism. He argued that it should be reserved for the upper classes: "The laboring classes are all right in their way; let them go their way in peace, and have their athletics in whatsoever manner suits their inclinations . . . [but] let us have our own sport among the refined elements."[23] It is quite clear, then, that the early molders of intercollegiate sport promoted an ideology-based doctrine of the adequacy and legitimacy of amateurism.

We now turn to the second point with respect to understanding the amateur sport ideology in intercollegiate athletics, which is the myth that ancient Greek athletes competed solely for fame and honor. Formal organization of college athletics was achieved in the latter 19th and early 20th centuries, at the same time that the Olympic Games were revived. The Olympic movement adopted rules of amateurism largely for two reasons: first, its founder and early leaders were aristocrats who enthusiastically embraced the amateur doctrine.[24] Second, influential historians had persuasively written that ancient Greek athletes were amateurs during Greece's Golden Age, competing only for fame and honor. Promoters of the modern Olympics, wishing to represent Greek athletics as a precedent for the Games they were establishing, adopted amateurism as a formal requirement for participation. But, it turns out, the Greek athlete-as-amateur is a historical hoax. One historian, after a thorough study of these athletes, stated:

> I can find no mention of amateurism in Greek sources, no reference to amateur athletes—no evidence that the concept "amateurism" was even known in antiquity. The truth is that "amateur" is one thing for which the ancient Greeks never even had a word. . . . With respect to money and the so-called "Ancient Greek amateurism," the results are hardly indecisive. . . . There is abundant proof, direct and indirect, in contemporary documents and later reports, to show that athletes could and did win large amounts of money.[25]

The founders of the NCAA, many of whom were also leaders in the American Olympic Games movement or had close social contacts with those leaders, were adamant about maintaining college sport "on an ethical plane in keeping with the dignity and high purpose of education." But events over the past generation make quite clear that in big-time collegiate athletics, amateur ideals have been replaced by marketplace priorities driven by a prominent and undisguised profit motive. Thus, amateurism in big-time collegiate sports is not a moral issue; it is, in the words of former NCAA Executive Director Walter Byers, "an economic camouflage for monopoly practice."[26] Big-time intercollegiate athletics are more akin to the values of modern corporations or professional sports than to the basic values of amateurism.

The Beneficiaries of Amateur Ideology

In light of the fact that big-time college football and basketball are commodified activities, the practice of maintaining an amateur sport ideology is obviously not founded on any interest in amateurism per se. Valorization of amateurism by the NCAA and its member institutions is merely a subterfuge to avoid paying the athletes a legitimate wage. By providing student-athletes with athletic scholarships instead of a wage, the NCAA and its member colleges have used a highly valued source of human capital—a college education (which can be obtained at a rather moderate cost)—as the sole compensation for college athletes.

In reality, the athletic scholarship is nothing but a work contract. What colleges are really doing is hiring entertainers. The deceit of claiming that educational purposes preclude salaried compensation for athletic performance is testimony to the extensive attempts of the collegiate sport establishment to avoid its financial obligations. Athletic scholarships are actually a form of economic exploitation, the establishment of a wage below poverty level for student-athlete-entertainers who directly produce millions of dollars for athletic departments.

Stripped of the rhetoric used to convince athletes and the public that athletic scholarships are philanthropic free rides to a college education, the NCAA athletic scholarship is first and foremost a conspiracy to hold down athletes' "wages." College student-athletes, a group one journalist called "the arms and legs and breathing hearts of the big business of college sports," are caught in the clutches of the NCAA. They cannot sell their skills on the open market to the highest bidder because of the rules against wage payments that all universities must observe even though some collegiate athletes generate 10 to 20 (and a few as high as 100!) times the amount of their scholarships in income for their schools.[27]

Meanwhile payouts to the college football teams that play in bowl games are more than $55 million a year, and it is customary for the coaches of bowl teams to receive a "bonus" of several thousand dollars when the team qualifies for a bowl. Teams get to bowl games through the hard work of both coaches and athletes, but athletes of bowl teams earn no bonuses. Similarly, participating institutions in the NCAA Division I men's basketball tournament make about $400,000 after expenses, and coaches whose teams qualify for the tournament typically receive bonuses and healthy boosts in their new contracts as a reward. But student-athletes on those same teams make no more than the NCAA scholarship allows.[28]

The benefits of this "wage-fixing" for the NCAA and the universities are quite evident: the lower the payouts to the student-athletes (the major workforce in this industry), the greater the profits for the NCAA and universities. In effect, then, employment of an amateur sport ideology in intercollegiate athletics makes the labor of many into the wealth of a few. The NCAA appropriates the labor of student-athletes and uses the athletes' names and images in its marketing. At the same time, it restricts the amount of remuneration to student-athletes.

But it is only the student-athletes, the ones generating the financial empire of big-time college sports, who are singled out for restraint. There is no restraint on the money and benefits that others in the big-time college sports industry can receive. Tom McMillen, a former high school All-American basketball player, an All-American at the University of Maryland, and a U.S. congressman, had this comment about big-time college sports: "The NCAA's concept of amateurism is anachronistic. . . . With huge sums being raked in by all parties except the athletes, the present system reeks of exploitation." Former Duke University basketball player Dick DeVenzio has argued that "athletes need a Bill of Rights, or at least the opportunity to receive deferred compensation through trust funds. There is no educational purpose being served by keeping athletes penniless while universities engage fully in the billion dollar sports entertainment industry." Even Walter Byers noted, "It is a disservice to these young people to remain committed to an outmoded code of amateurism for economic controls."[29]

Paying as little as possible to operate a business is called keeping overhead low; it is what every business owner strives to do. The NCAA and major universities have mastered this principle. No other American business operates so pretentiously, making huge sums of money but insisting the enterprise be viewed as an educational service. Even though athletes, the only students who generate money for a university, are the key to the financial success of college sports through their indispensability in the sport-production process, they do not receive compensation commensurate with their contributions.

One of the principles of capitalism is that market forces will determine wages. There is no inherent reason that college athletes should not be subject to market forces like all other laborers and free to realize their actual market value. If big-time collegiate athletics must be granted their commercial orientation, then they should be held accountable to those whose labor creates the product, for without them there would be no sport event. Continuing to define big-time college athletes as amateurs can legitimately be viewed as an evasion of a moral responsibility that universities have to either treat athletes as equal members of a commercial enterprise (big-time college sport) or withdraw from commodified sport and return to promoting an educational model of college sports and using sport as a medium for the personal development of participants.[30]

Amateur Sport Ideology Legitimates Other Restraints

The athletic scholarship is only one of the many NCAA regulations designed to restrain athletes and boost revenue for NCAA members. Student-athletes who enroll and participate in sport at one NCAA institution and then subsequently transfer to another—switch jobs, as it were—are ineligible for competition at the second school for a full year. Such a rule seriously reduces the interorganizational mobility of collegiate athletes, thus stabilizing the labor market and saving the universities untold dollars that might otherwise be spent in competitive bidding for the best players.

The major beneficiaries of this restriction on college athletes' mobility are obvious—the colleges and the NCAA. On the one hand, the NCAA promotes and sells competition through sport, but it severely restricts competition for wage labor within its own industry with the complex rules and practices it has adopted. Athletic directors and coaches are fond of expounding on the virtues of competition, but they have formulated nationwide regulations to avoid competing for those who actually produce their product—the sports event.

But it is only the athletes whose mobility is restricted. The NCAA does not apply such restrictions to others involved in the college sports production industry (athletic directors, coaches, athletic trainers, etc.). Indeed, "jumping" contracts is so common among college coaches that it has almost become an annual ritual in the college sports business. Again, student-athletes are the ones who suffer. Many student-athletes experience serious feelings of betrayal when a coach resigns after recruiting them (many athletes choose to play at a university just because of a particular coach). They are exhorted to demonstrate loyalty to their institution, and they lose a year of eligibility if they transfer to another university, but if the offer of a better job looks good to a coach, he or she can leave without penalty.

Collegiate athletes cannot endorse products or engage in any commercialization of their athletic talent or name recognition. Meanwhile, coaches can engage in an incredible variety of commercial activities to supplement their salaries. Some of the perks common for major college coaches are television and radio shows (worth up to $400,000), free use of a car, university housing, and use of university facilities for summer camps. A few coaches also have lucrative sporting equipment endorsement contracts. For some coaches, the perks and benefits push their annual incomes above $1 million.[31]

Universities have capitalized on the popularity of college athletics to license and sell sport equipment and souvenirs. Collegiate Licensing Company of Atlanta estimates that the licensing market for college sports paraphernalia is worth about $2.5 billion! Universities with the biggest licensing programs earn $600,000 to $800,000 a year. Marketing opportunities of these kinds exist primarily because of the interest in intercollegiate sports generated by talented and skilled student-athletes. Unlike athletes in professional sports, college athletes get no money from the revenue universities derive from this market.

The newest major revenue source for big-time collegiate sports programs is corporate equipment and sponsorship contracts that universities are signing with sporting goods firms such as Nike, Reebok, and Converse. For example, in the mid-1990s, the following sponsorship deals were struck: University of Colorado, $5.6 million for six years; Florida State, five years for $6 million; and University of Michigan, six years for $5.7 million. Student-athletes at colleges where these contracts exist must wear the sporting goods logos (the Nike swoosh, for example) on their uniforms to advertise the products, but they receive no income from these sponsorship deals—not a penny.[32]

So while the NCAA preaches the virtues of amateurism and a Spartan existence to student-athletes, it winks at the lavish lifestyles of coaches and athletic directors and condones the university licensing market in equipment and souvenirs. Indeed, the NCAA itself has formed NCAA Football USA, a licensing program that coordinates millions of dollars in sport merchandising efforts. Inconsistencies like these in the NCAA rules brought this comment from economist Thomas Sowell: "If General Motors or Exxon formed a cartel to treat their workers even half as badly as college athletes are treated, there would be antitrust suits across the country and whole armies of executives would be led away in handcuffs."[33]

The rules and regulations cited in this chapter do not exhaust all the guidelines the NCAA and its member universities apply to student-athletes. The effect of all these rules and regulations is to restrain competition and reduce costs among NCAA members to the disadvantage of collegiate athletes; taken together, these rules constitute a formidable assault on athletes. When one analyzes the NCAA rules and regulations for athletes from the standpoint of who benefits, the pattern is clear: the prime beneficiaries are the NCAA and its member universities.

It seems rather obvious, then, that although the official ideology of the NCAA proclaims a promotion of amateur sport, its operative goals involve maximizing power and oppression over student-athletes. As a structure of domination, the NCAA is organized to achieve the commands of those who control it. Student-athletes are expected to comply with the formally rational expectations of their roles. At the same time, they are excluded from participation in substantive decisions by the NCAA about them.

Scandals and Reform in Big-Time College Sport

Most people are aware that numerous scandals have beset major university football and basketball programs during the past few years. Despite a continuing parade of committees, commissions, and task forces whose purpose has been to reform big-time college sport, a steady stream of horror stories continues involving violations of NCAA rules, reports of how few football and basketball athletes graduate at some universities, and disclosures of athletes receiving illegal money from boosters. Scandals develop with a frequency that is astonishing even to the most cynical of observers; one ignominious episode is followed by another of greater proportions. Each revelation is followed by righteous promises from university authorities and the NCAA that change is on the way, that collegiate athletics are going to be cleaned up. But the NCAA has been unable to stop these violations or the conditions from which they breed.[34]

The two most recent NCAA attempts to address the endemic problems of major college sport have been the NCAA Presidents' Commission and the Knight Foundation Commission on Intercollegiate Athletics (also called the Knight Foundation Commission). The former promised to reform and redirect intercollegiate athletics. But it floundered badly; its results can best be characterized as a little tinkering with the system while leaving intact the existing distribution of powers. Little more could have been expected, when the chairman of the Presidents' Commission was quoted as saying its job would "be more a matter of fine-tuning and adjusting than making major changes."[35]

The most recent reform group was the Knight Foundation Commission. In 1989, the trustees of the Knight Foundation, concerned with the abuses in intercollegiate athletics, created the commission and directed it to propose a reform agenda for college sports. During more than three years of work, and spending some $3 million, the commission produced three reports placing less emphasis on specific solutions for abuses in college sports and more on establishing a structure for reform.[36]

But little has changed. For all the chest pounding about reform by the Presidents' Commission and the Knight Foundation Commission, an analysis of changes that have been made or proposed over the years shows that most are cost-containment measures directed primarily at athletes (reducing scholarships, dropping sports, or making promises to hold athletes to tougher academic standards). Any attempt to reorganize existing structural relations is conspicuously absent from reform in intercollegiate athletics. The *structure* of big-time, commercial college athletics—a structure that is largely responsible for the pervasive corruption and abuses—has been left intact, with no substantive changes. Hope for meaningful reform by the NCAA so that it would better serve the interests and needs of all college athletes is nowhere to be found. Byers claims, "College athletics reform movements spanning 90 years have been remarkably consistent.

They never reformed much of anything." Dale Brown, former basketball coach at Louisiana State University, was more blunt in assessing NCAA reforms: He said NCAA reforms don't "solve the problems; they keep throwing talcum powder on [the] cancer."[37]

In saying that the structure of college athletic programs has been left intact by all the reform initiatives, I am referring to the pressures brought to bear by mass media attention and the expectations of alumni and boosters who demand championship teams. I am referring to universities who use athletes as public relations agents. This is the essential structure of major university football and basketball programs that reform initiatives have not touched.

Beyond those features, I am also referring to the common practice of keeping student-athletes involved in one way or another with their sport during the season for 40 to 60 hours per week. Analyses of the time that average major college football and basketball players devote to their sports suggest that football players devote about 55 hours per week and basketball players 50 hours per week during their respective seasons. That time is devoted to practicing, weight training, watching films, traveling to games, and being away from campus and missing classes. A study of Notre Dame football players who later played NFL football reported that playing at Notre Dame was as physically and psychologically demanding as professional football.[38]

Time devoted to their sports does not end with the last game; indeed, student-athletes are expected to remain in training year-round. Big-time college football and basketball student-athletes report devoting up to 18 hours per week to training during the off-season.

Blaming the Victim

Instead of addressing structural issues that perpetuate scandals, most of the NCAA reform efforts have labeled student-athletes as the major cause of the continuing scandals suffered by collegiate sports, and various forms of rules and regulations have been passed by the NCAA that are designed to convince the public that the NCAA is taking corrective actions for these problems. Defining certain individuals (student-athletes, in this case) as the source of a social problem is a tactic frequently used by dominant groups seeking to divert attention from social structural problems. It is called blaming the victim.

Blaming the victim is an ideological process, meaning it is a more or less integrated set of ideas and practices promulgated by a dominant social group about how things should and do work. "Victim blaming is cloaked in kindness and concern, and . . . it is obscured by a perfumed haze of humanitarianism."[39] Rather than addressing the inherent structural problems that plague big-time collegiate sports, the college sport establishment disguises the fundamental issues by repeatedly blaming the victim, in this case student-athletes.

Through the rules they have enacted to further control and restrict student-athletes, the NCAA and university authorities claim to be attempting to solve the problems of big-time college sport. What they have done instead is to blame the student-athlete for their own failure to address the real causes of corruption, cheating, and unethical behavior that are now well documented. They have engaged, clearly and directly, in a classic display of blaming the victim. Moreover, they have fashioned an ostensible legitimacy for their actions so that alternative images have become unthinkable. In doing this, athletic authorities have sought to co-opt, undermine, and marginalize alternatives that might address the deep-seated problems of big-time college sport.

Academic Scapegoating

The NCAA's Propositions 48 and 42 are good examples of focusing the blame for problems in big-time college sport on student-athletes. Proposition 48 (currently called Proposition 16) set minimum academic standards for incoming freshman athletes. Those who failed to meet grade-point and SAT or ACT minimums were ineligible for an athletic scholarship, practice, or competition their freshman year, and they lost one year of college eligibility (this last provision was dropped in 1997). Proposition 42 revised Proposition 48 (this policy has been revised several times), setting even higher standards of eligibility for an athletic scholarship. By requiring that student-athletes achieve certain minimum high school grades and standardized test scores to be eligible for participation and an athletic scholarship, the NCAA can appear to legitimize its supposed insistence upon having qualified students as college athletes.[40]

Of course, no rational person can really quarrel with holding athletes to academic standards. Even many African American leaders who recognized the unequal and adverse effects that Proposition 48 would have on African American student-athletes supported the passage of this legislation because to have opposed it would imply that they did not favor academic standards. But focusing on athletes' academic achievement—something around which everyone can rally—and seemingly showing how athletes are being held to academic standards, while ignoring the system of power, privilege, and exploitation, serve to suggest to the public that some social pathology within the student-athletes is the reason for the recurring scandals in collegiate athletics, not the social structure of which they are a part. Such actions also deflect questions away from the more endemic social structural problems of big-time college sports, such as the appropriateness of a commercialized sport system that does not pay its main workforce a livable wage operating on university campuses.

The one main reason for an academic standards problem in big-time college sport is that coaches and other university officials have admitted—indeed, have recruited—academically unqualified students, and through various ingenious methods have been able to keep them eligible for one purpose: to help the university athletic teams maintain competitive success in the world of commercialized sport. According to the NCAA, about 20 percent of football and basketball players enter through "special admit" programs. Yet only about 3 percent of all students enter under such programs. For student-athletes who are academically qualified and genuinely interested in pursuing college degrees, the intensity and structure of major college sport force many of them to choose between academic performance and athletic performance.

The most prominent responses of the NCAA and universities to the various reform initiatives have involved reaction and retrenchment within existing forms and a rather arrogant attitude of impunity to any serious challenge to their policies. Their practice of enacting rules and regulations that focus on the control, restrictions, monitoring, and punishment of student-athletes is a strategy for diverting attention from the real sources of the fundamental problems and for justifying a perverse system of social organization and action. Far from desiring to change the basic commercial and exploitative structure of major college sports, the NCAA and member universities seem to be striving for a change by means of which existing patterns will be made as tolerable and comfortable as possible. Meanwhile the larger course of reform is charted along paths compatible with corporate values and goals, and meaningful reform remains largely a false promise. Thus, the exploitation and victimization of collegiate athletes continue unabated.

Some observers pointed to the abolishment of football—the so-called death penalty—imposed on Southern Methodist University (SMU) in 1987 by the NCAA as an example that serious reform was on the way. This action was taken by the NCAA after administrators, boosters, and coaches at SMU had repeatedly violated NCAA rules over many years. Although the term "death penalty" sounds severe, it actually has done little to reform big-time college sport. First, this action did not address in any way the endemic structural problems of big-time collegiate athletics. Second, it was done only after SMU quite literally forced such a course of action by continued flagrant violation of NCAA rules. And third, it appears to have been a one-shot effort to scare other universities into temporary compliance with NCAA policies; it has not been employed again in more than 10 years, despite flagrant violations of NCAA policies by more than a dozen universities.

Absence of Student-Athlete Protest to the Lack of Reform

A question may be raised about the lack of protest from intercollegiate athletes about the prevailing conditions under which they labor. In one way it can be expected that the student-athletes would not find anything to question. For most of them, the opportunity to play big-time college sports is a dream come true. It is also exciting to play at the top level of competition before large crowds of spectators. Furthermore, a great deal of social status accompanies being an athlete at a major university. So most college athletes are faithful spokespersons for the system of college sport.

There are other reasons as well. Most college athletes have been involved in playing organized sports for six to 10 years, and they have been thoroughly conditioned through organized sport involvement to unquestioned obedience to athletic authorities. As a group, athletes tend to be resigned to domination from the college sport leadership because, at least partly, the institutional structure of athletics is essentially hostile to independence of mind. Moreover, student-athletes tend to take the existing order for granted, not questioning it because they are preoccupied with their own jobs of making the team and perhaps gaining national recognition.

Hence, athletes are willing participants whose self-worth and self-esteem have largely become synonymous with their athletic prowess. Their main impulse is to mind their own business while striving to be successful as athletes. In the work world, this is referred to as pragmatic role acceptance.

Awareness, Opposition, and Potential Reform

The NCAA's proposals for reform bring into question whether it will ever solve, or is even capable of solving, the problems of big-time intercollegiate sport. However, opposition to the present collegiate sport order has been persistent in various quarters, and the raised consciousness and sustained critical questioning about the current situation give hope for bringing about meaningful change. Hardly a week goes by without some public figure in politics, business, law, education, or the media expressing dismay with the current system of big-time college sport.

Ten years ago, there was no support in any sector of public life for paying salaries to college athletes. By the late 1990s, a growing number of college presidents, coaches, student-athletes, and public figures were calling for outright payment to athletes. The University of Washington president argued, "At the core of the existing regulatory structure [of the NCAA] is the idea that having college athletes 'play for pay' is obviously wrong for society and wrong for them. I'm less and less sure about such matters, and I'm even less sure as I contemplate the obvious fact that so many of the most gifted athletes are economically and educationally disadvantaged blacks."[41] Byers, who served as the executive director of the NCAA from 1951 to 1987, published a book in 1995 in which he vigorously advocated the payment of athletes playing big-time college football and basketball.[42] In at least two states, bills have been introduced into the legislatures calling for the outright payment of college athletes.

Beyond the issue of social justice for student-athletes, there are many other problems facing big-time college sport. Effecting change will undoubtedly require continued efforts to critically interpret the social reality of big-time college athletics accurately. Although the reality is that dominant economic interests make major university athletics virtually impenetrable, it is not necessary to concede that inequities in the distribution of money, violations of basic human rights, and victimization of athletes are legitimate.

The absence of critical commentary is a precondition to all forms of domination. Ignoring or retreating from criticism of the NCAA not only renders its current forms of domination natural and acceptable, it also hinders meaningful reform to alleviate conditions of those who are victimized by that system. Nothing about the current system is natural or universal. All social arrangements are human creations. Built and sustained by humans, they can also be changed by humans.[43] Byers has proposed the development of a Bill of Rights for college athletes (see box, p. 250).

Summary and Preview

Big-time intercollegiate athletics have become another part of the massive commodified sport industry, a part that plays a significant role in the overall entertainment business. As collegiate athletics have grown from student-sponsored, student-run campus recreation, they have taken on most of the trappings of conventional capitalist entertainment enterprises. The major exception to the typical business model is that the workers who produce the product—the sport event—are paid no wages or salaries. Universities avoid direct

A College Athletes' Bill of Rights

Congress should enact and the president should sign a comprehensive College Athletes' Bill of Rights. This is *not* a suggestion for new government controls; on the contrary, it is an argument that the federal government should require deregulation of a monopoly business operated by not-for-profit institutions contracting together to achieve maximum financial returns. . . . The Bill of Rights should deal with five issues of freedom and welfare:

1. Repeal the rule that establishes the NCAA as national arbiter of the term, value, and conditions of an athlete's "scholarship" and as controller of the athlete's outside income during his or her collegiate tenure. Whereas the NCAA defends its policies in the name of amateurism and level playing fields, they actually are a device to divert the money elsewhere.

2. End the NCAA ban that prevents players from holding a job during the school year.

3. Require repeal of the transfer rule, which unreasonably binds athletes to their current colleges. This restriction once had an academic purpose. When freshmen were required to wait one year before competing in varsity sports, it was argued that transfer students also needed a one-year adjustment period free from the pressures of varsity competition. The rule, however, has become a player control measure in the hands of the coach, a sort of option clause.

4. Force the NCAA to allow players to consult agents in making sports career choices.

5. State legislatures should amend state workmen's compensation laws to require that major colleges and universities provide coverage for varsity athletes and other students engaged in auxiliary enterprises.

Adapted with permission from Walter Byers, 1995, *Unsportsmanlike Conduct: Exploiting College Athletes* (Ann Arbor, MI: University of Michigan Press), 374-84.

payments to student athletes by proclaiming collegiate sport as an integral component of the educational mission of the university and by applying the ideology of amateurism to college sport.

Chapter 11 moves one level lower in the sport hierarchy to high school and youth sports. It is in these programs that most people first become involved in organized sport, and they are the forms of organized sport with the greatest active participation.

"Building character" is frequently cited as a major purpose and achievement of high school and youth sport programs. In chapter 11, I analyze the ideological meanings of this seemingly innocent goal and examine the growing commodification and its consequences in these forms of sports.

Suggested Readings

Bailey, Wilford S., and Taylor D. Littleton. *Athletics and Academe: An Anatomy of Abuses and a Prescription for Reform.* New York: American Council on Education/Macmillan, 1991.

Byers, Walter. *Unsportsmanlike Conduct: Exploiting College Athletes.* Ann Arbor: University of Michigan Press, 1995.

Davis, Timothy. "A Model of Institutional Governance for Intercollegiate Athletics." *Wisconsin Law Review,* no. 3 (1995): 599-645.

Fleisher, Arthur A., III, Brian L. Goff, and Robert D. Tollison. *The National Collegiate Athlete Association: A Study in Cartel Behavior.* Chicago: The University of Chicago Press, 1992.

McMillen, Tom. *Out of Bounds.* New York: Simon & Schuster, 1992.

Sheehan, Richard. *Keeping Score: The Economics of Big-Time Sports.* South Bend, IN: Diamond Communications, 1996.

Smith, Ronald A. *Sport & Freedom.* New York: Oxford University Press, 1988.

Sperber, Murray. *College Sports Inc.: The Athletic Department Vs the University.* New York: Henry Holt, 1990.

Telander, Rick. *The Hundred Yard Lie.* New York: Simon & Schuster, 1989.

Thelin, John R. *Games Colleges Play: Scandal and Reform in Intercollegiate Athletics.* Baltimore: Johns Hopkins University Press, 1994.

Yaeger, Don. *Undue Process: The NCAA's Injustice for All.* Champaign, IL: Sagamore Publishing, 1991.

Young, David. *The Olympic Myth of Greek Amateur Athletes.* Chicago: Ares, 1984.

Chapter 11

Building Character Through Youth and School Sport

Assessing the sport-builds-character issue requires more than collecting anecdotes of athletes who believe that sport has taught them how to be successful or saved them from a life of crime and drugs.

Andrew Miracle Jr. and C. Roger Rees, professors of anthropology and sport studies

Americans participate in sport more during childhood and adolescence than during any other time in their lives. The informal sandlot games of yesteryear—though they are still played occasionally today—have given way to highly organized youth sports, which have become one of the most popular cultural practices in American life. About 30 million boys and girls are involved in community-sponsored youth sport programs each year.

Little League baseball is the largest of the youth sport organizations, with about 2 million participants. In addition, more than 3,000 YMCAs provide about 2 million boys and girls the opportunity to play organized sports, and the Junior Olympics Sports Program sponsors more than 2,000 local, state, regional, and national events in more than 20 sports. But it is local community recreation departments that organize the largest number of competitive sports for young boys and girls.

High schools throughout the nation take over the sponsorship of organized sports for older adolescents. Approximately 5.8 million adolescents participate on interscholastic athletic teams annually—some 3.5 million boys and 2.3 million girls. It is not an exaggeration, then, to say that sport plays a central role in the lives of millions of young boys and girls.

Although the popular impression of sport for children and adolescents is that it provides them an opportunity to learn and enjoy organized games—which is true—there is another firmly held belief that sport experiences help youngsters learn valuable social skills, cultural values, and behaviors that are useful in other spheres of life. It is this belief that is the focus in this chapter. As with the other aspects of sport examined in this book, an accurate analysis requires maintaining a sociological imagination and thus historically situating and culturally locating community-based youth sport and interscholastic athletics.

Growth of Public Education and Organized Sport

A new industrial era emerged in America after the Civil War. The years from 1875 to 1910 saw the most rapid expansion of capital and industry of any period in American history. As industrial jobs boomed, many people left their farms and small towns and converged on the growing industrial cities. These migrations, along with an influx of millions of immigrants, flooded the cities and formed a growing urban industrial workforce. In the first 10 years of the 20th century, 8.8 million immigrants entered the United States, representing more than half of America's population increase. In 1909, 58 percent of the industrial workers in manufacturing were foreign; of the immigrant male heads of households from non-English-speaking countries living in cities, only 45 percent could speak English.[1]

The rapid transformation from rural to urban lifestyles, the mass of foreign immigrants, and the conversion from agricultural to industrial occupational roles created a host of social problems; one of the major ones was raising and educating children. The traditional context for doing so within the family became unsuitable in an industrialized society, in which one or both parents worked outside the home and children were away from home more often (either playing in the streets or working part time). In addition, immigrant children needed a way to learn the English language and American values and customs. So traditional, informal education was gradually taken over by public schools, churches, and other social organizations, and in these settings, children learned about living as citizens, workers, and consumers in American society.[2]

As with many spheres of modern American society, the state has taken an increasingly larger role in education, and the growth of public education during the past 100 years illustrates the expansion of the state into the former role of the family. In 1890 only about half the children age 5 to 17 were in some type of public school; by 1930 this had grown to 81 percent and by 1990, to about 92 percent. In 1890 about 7 million children attended public schools; by the mid-1990s, there were some 65 million students. From 1930 to 1998, the percentage of 17-year-olds in high school grew from 29 percent to more than 83 percent. These figures give impressive testimony to the public school's expanding responsibility for socializing American youth, and they signify that passage through the school system has become an important initiation rite for preparing to become an adult member of the American community.[3]

Public school growth went hand in hand with the expansion of industrial capitalism. At the end of the Civil War, the industrial output of the United States was small compared with that of Great Britain. But by 1900, the United States had surpassed Britain in the quantity and value of its manufactured products and had become the world's foremost industrial nation. Corporate capitalism was a stalwart supporter of public education, regarding it as important for providing both support for capitalist enterprise and skilled workers for increasingly specialized jobs.

As the American system of education has grown, it has become organized in ways consistent with the needs of dominant political and economic interests, shaping students' attitudes and values to conform to the demands of hierarchical models of authority and producing graduates fitted for their places in corporate and government bureaucracies. The reigning hegemonic ideology has stressed the importance of the schools for teaching discipline, obedience, orderly work habits, respect for authority, and an uncompromising admiration for the reigning social, political, and economic order. Its influence has consistently won out over proponents of more progressive educational ideas, and most educational reform movements have consistently focused on accommodating economic interests and student adjustment to the prevailing social norms and values.

Thus, schools are a fundamental part of the hegemonic power framework, structurally and ideologically dedicated to the political and economic forces that nourish them. By serving as an agent of legitimation, public education, then, has become central in the reproduction of labor power, as well as the class, gender, and race structures of American society. This role does not mean, however, that schools are merely instruments of reproduction; this would be much too simplistic a view. The American education system is a complex institution, serving many interests and having various constituencies.[4]

Still, social control is at the heart of public education, despite its many roles and purposes. Controlling and channeling students is crucial to training them in the skills and discipline for holding jobs in modern capitalism and also to infusing them with broader values of morality, patriotism, and loyalty. A citizenry compliant to authority and with established laws and customs is considered essential by hegemonic groups to making a political democracy work.

The Rise of Interscholastic Athletics

As public education expanded and modified its curriculum to meet changing social and student needs at the beginning of the 20th century, various extracurricular activities, such as debate teams and student government, began to grow. One of the activities that quickly gained a commanding popularity among high school students was athletics. Colleges had begun playing intercollegiate sports shortly before the Civil War, and by the beginning of the 20th century, intercollegiate athletics had achieved a prominent place in college life. In the meantime, high school students had begun to organize their own athletic contests.

Writing about the growth of school sports in Boston, one sport historian said that by 1888, several area high schools were fielding football teams and had formed an Interscholastic Football Association. Furthermore, "within two decades, baseball, track, basketball, and ice hockey leagues operated among the city's secondary schools. . . . By the turn of the century, interscholastic sports had become a fixture. The daily newspapers carried not only regular coverage of the competition, but also feature articles on the prominent schoolboy stars and the prospects of each team for the upcoming season."[5]

In New York City, a Public Schools Athletic League was started in 1903, and surveys of secondary school athletics in 1905 and 1907 showed that most high schools fielded teams in at least one sport. The 1905 survey found that football was played in 78 percent of the schools; the figures for baseball and basketball were 65 percent and 58 percent, respectively. The 1907 survey indicated that all of the 225 responding public high schools had some form of interscholastic competition.[6]

At first, school faculty members and administrators either discouraged or ignored these student-organized and student-controlled activities, but eventually they began to see potential in them for serving some of the schools' purposes. Seeking to capitalize on the popularity of sports, school administrators gradually and inevitably wrested control of school athletics from the students.

Educators had come to accept "the notion that schools should convey to students the specific skills, behavior, and values necessary to a productive life in the new industrial order," and in athletics they presumed that "the lessons of teamwork, self-sacrifice, and discipline were . . . transferable from the playing field to the business world or the factory." Even more significant, it was believed that the qualities thought to be developed by school sport—competitiveness, individualism, respect for authority, work discipline—were those "upon which rested the greatness of America's cities and corporations."[7] By the 1920s, high school athletics were firmly under the control of school authorities, with teams supervised by coaches hired as full-time faculty. Little change has occurred in the organizational structural arrangements of high school athletics since that time.

Organized Sports Sponsored by Nonschool Agencies

In conjunction with the expansion of the public school system, nonschool social agencies concerned with youth experienced enormous growth. Many of the early 20th-century social reformers were concerned with play, and almost every social reform organization was involved in assisting the rise of organized play in one way or another.

Games and Sports at Public Parks and Playgrounds

Like schools, parks and playgrounds were regarded as resources for replacing the socializing influence of family life, which was seemingly being suppressed with the growth of urban America. Beginning with private, uncoordinated, and voluntary efforts that gradually gave way to various public agencies, play opportunities were increasingly provided for youngsters. From 1890 to 1910, city and state governments nationwide organized recreation programs, built parks, formed playgrounds, and hired leaders to direct programs and maintain facilities. Even private business groups began to sponsor organized play opportunities for youngsters.

The play movement was a product of the desire among social reformers, educators, and concerned business interests to protect children from the harmful effects of city life and to supply a mechanism for supervising the process of socialization. In addition to providing recreation and physical activity, organized play was regarded as a forum for teaching good habits, such as group loyalty, common ideals, self-discipline, and subordination of self to the group. Another major goal was a desire to reduce juvenile crime.

Recounting the drive for community support for playgrounds in Massachusetts, sport historian Stephen Hardy wrote this description: "When the Massachusetts Civic League barnstormed the state to drum up support for a referendum on playgrounds, they found a ready audience among businessmen who agreed that organized play promoted qualities that were fundamental to the successful worker. Among them were the capacity for teamwork, good health, enthusiasm . . . honesty, clean play, temperance, and imagination."[8]

Social reformer Jacob Riis envisioned an even broader purpose. He said, "The problem of the children is the problem of the State. As we mold the children of the toiling masses in our cities, so we shape the destiny of the State."[9]

The Rise of Community-Sponsored Youth Sports

High school athletic programs were enthusiastically endorsed by educators and community leaders, and the same was true of the park and playground movement, but neither high schools nor recreation programs provided organized sport opportunities for preadolescent youth. In fact, educators and community leaders discouraged such activity. Sport historian Jack Berryman said, "The policy statements of professional physical education and recreation groups as well as other leading educators . . . illustrated their discouragement of highly competitive sports for children."[10] But preadolescent youngsters (mostly boys) and their parents clamored more and more for organized sport opportunities, and some community leaders advocated the value of sport experiences for the same reasons that high schools had adopted them.

Finally, "the belief that a boy busy with sports had little time to get into trouble influenced many organizations in local communities to begin sponsoring boys' competitive sports."[11] Community business leaders and service organizations, and some municipal recreation departments as well, stepped forward and began to provide money and leadership for organized preadolescent sport competition. From its beginnings, this form of organized sport has been popular, and it has continued to grow unabated.

Community-sponsored youth sports were primarily under the direction of municipal recreation departments or national youth sport organizations, such as Little League. Participants competed largely with youngsters within their own community. But in the past two decades, a professionalized form of youth sport has been growing. There has been a significant increase in programs that train young athletes for careers in professional sport, with athletes in sports such as tennis, gymnastics, and figure skating competing in national and international sporting events as early as age 13. Here young athletes are developed as commodities that are then sold to audiences through-out the world.[12]

Youth and School Sports as Agents of Social and Moral Development

As part of the movement in the public high schools and community youth agencies to prepare youth for their places in a rapidly expand-ing industrial society, community and school authorities began to envision that well-organized sport programs could also promote social and moral attributes and thus contribute to the goal of a particular interpretation of good citizenship. In both the schools and the community-based programs, structured sporting activities were linked to moral development. Community youth sport programs and high school athletics were gradually colonized as ideological instru-ments for socializing American youth to the formation of a common consciousness, to a sense of common allegiance, and for different positions in the social, economic, and occupational hierarchy.

Organized sport for young people began to receive recognition as an educational medium for transmitting advanced capitalist ideology in the name of building character.[13] Formal sport programs, then, were not solely organized to provide an outlet for human expression and self-fulfillment. According to one educational historian, "Educa-tional administrators and leading physical educators saw athletics as a valuable means of developing those characteristics associated with efficient citizenship in a modern industrial society. Through orga-nized sport, they sought to inculcate a conception of citizenship with a high degree of corporate consciousness.... Citizenship in twentieth century America required a strong sense of cooperation, institutional national loyalty, and a willingness to subordinate personal interests to those of the group."[14]

Thus, athletics were praised as an important medium for instilling young participants with common ideals, particular modes of think-ing, and social cohesion in the service of the instrumental culture of capitalism. In short, sport was viewed as a mechanism for producing a social consciousness willing to accept, and even embrace, condi-tions of structural social inequality. Community youth and school sports, then, became agents in the maintenance and reproduction of the reigning politically and economically powerful and dominant groups in American society. The norms, values, and dispositions of the sport subculture provided legitimation for their ideology.

A slogan emerged that became a powerful image of the supposed outcome of sport for children and adolescents: "Sport builds character."

This assertion was, and still is, frequently made by community leaders, school officials, parents, and even average citizens when a discussion turns to the purpose of organized sport for children and adolescents. Sport, it is argued, provides a social environment for acquiring culturally valued personal and social attitudes, values, and behaviors; moreover, it is implied that what is learned in the sport setting transfers to other spheres of life. So this creed canonizes a widespread faith in sport as an agent of social development and a medium for the formation of a particular ideological consciousness.[15]

Until the early 1970s, high school and youth sport programs were overwhelmingly for boys only, and the character traits usually identified as expected outcomes of organized sport experiences were those typically valued as masculine. Thus, school and nonschool sports reinforced traditional gender-role differentiation. Excluding females from these programs kept them from being socialized into the traits presumed to bring success in American public life. Thus one of the most persistent arguments advanced during the past 20 years for equal opportunities in sport for females is that the lack of sport experiences deprives females of experiences that develop traits that bring conventional definitions of success in American society.

Social Origins of Sport as a Builder of Character

How did the notion that sport builds character develop? To understand this creed's ideological dimensions, we must understand its origins and evolution. The idea of positive social outcomes through sport participation grew slowly in the United States during the 19th century. Sport historian Donald Mrozek contends that "at the beginning of the 19th century, there was no obvious merit in sport—certainly no clear social value to it and no sense that it contributed to the improvement of the individual's character."[16]

But in England, a tradition arose in the mid-1800s that was to profoundly influence sporting practice in the United States. With the emergence of student sport teams in British private secondary boarding schools, school sports won recognition as a medium for socialization, enculturation, and social control, and they became imbued with a moralistic ideology that came to be known as athleticism.[17]

Although British school authorities first disdained as frivolous the sports played by the students, sports gradually came to be valued by the headmasters (school principals), more for the qualities of social character they were presumed to develop than for the physical exercise they provided. In a description of British boarding school sports, sociologist Christopher Armstrong observed that they were considered an excellent way to develop "moral authority and exemplary character in England's evolving ruling class. . . . Here the ideal was intended to allow boys to prove themselves as potential leaders on the playing fields through moral courage, devoted team work, and group spirit."[18]

In 1864 the British Royal Commission on Schools succinctly identified the purpose of school sports: "The cricket and football fields . . . are not merely places of exercise or amusement; they help to form some of the most valuable social qualities and manly virtues, and they hold, like the classroom and the boarding house, a distinct and important place in . . . school education."[19] These school sports, "were the wheel around which moral values turned. They were the pre-eminent instrument for the training of a boy's character."[20]

The notion that school sports developed character was pragmatically related to the expansion of the British Empire, which required self-confident soldiers, administrators, and businessmen capable of withstanding the physical and psychological demands of their occupations. Graduates of the British private boarding schools became leaders in many spheres of life—government, the military, the domestic industry, commerce—throughout the British Empire. These young men were destined to govern and control.

So a tradition of self-government was seen as foundational in these schools because the British believed that experiences in controlling self and governing others were good training for future leadership. The school sports were almost totally governed by the students themselves. Games were lively and competition was spirited, but there was an emphasis on fellowship, sacrifice, cooperation, sportsmanship, and a willingness to accept defeat graciously. How one played the game was more important than the outcome of the contest; indeed, there was a sense that how one played was an indicator of how one would later behave, and that is why team sports were valued so highly.

Although no one ever empirically verified the social-developmental effects of school sport, belief that sport did build character was unshakable in Britain. A popular saying that "the Battle of Waterloo was won on the playing fields of Eton" (a private boarding school) suggested that Arthur Wellington, the victorious British general at the Battle of Waterloo, had acquired skills and values while playing sports at Eton that prepared him to defeat Napoleon. (In fact, though, there is compelling evidence that as an adolescent attending Eton, Wellington did not play sports. There were no compulsory, organized games at Eton while he was there, and even the most casual cricket or boating contest did not attract his participation.)[21]

Importing the Sport-Builds-Character Theme

Like so many ideas and practices of the British upper-class, athleticism and its accompanying character-building theme were imported to

America with little thought of the profound differences in cultural conditions and circumstances. Consequently, character development has been proclaimed as a goal and an outcome for organized school and preadolescent sports in the United States for a century, even though the cultural milieu and social meanings that prevailed in British private schools did not and do not underlie American sport programs.

Whereas British schools were preparing a socially elite group of young men for leadership positions in government, business, and the military, American youth and school sports were popularized in the first half of the 20th century when educational programs were increasingly directed at lower- and middle-class youth (except in private boarding schools). This was a time of great social transformation. Vast numbers of immigrants and their children needed to be educated; rapid urbanization stretched community housing, sanitation, health care, and employment resources; city crime became a major social problem; and the growth of monopoly corporate enterprise revolutionized the labor market and working conditions.

The kind of character formation needed in America was quite different from that considered indispensable for the leaders of the British Empire. Social conformity, obedience, and respect for authority seemed more congruent with future roles in America than did leadership, initiative, and self-discipline.

Ideological Dimensions of Sport as a Character Builder

A major task facing dominant groups that wish to maintain their status and power is to mold a common consciousness among the people, animate it with the appropriate ethics, and use it to shape attitudes, habits, and lifestyles. As I have repeatedly stressed, dominant elites do not usually exercise hegemony in direct, overt ways. Instead, their methods are diffuse, circumspect, and suffused by a complex of ideological techniques that permeate the social institutions and practices of society, including cultural and leisure activities. Thought of in this way, hegemonic ideology is like a protective wrapping around the structures and processes of domination and exploitation; it legitimates and encourages patterns of activity that ensure that a particular set of social relations is sustained and reproduced. Ideological work in this context preserves the prevailing practices and visions while proclaiming them as universal.

Dominant groups use various institutional and cultural resources to legitimate and disseminate their ideologies and interests. As I have

Youth sport has the potential to enable boys and girls to experience positive personal-social growth and development. But there is increasing concern that this cannot be accomplished in youth sport programs dominated by adult intrusion and where children are increasingly used as sports entertainers.

shown throughout this book, modern sport forms are cultural practices that are part of the terrain on which the dominant ideology is built and sustained. Here, as in other spheres, systems of symbols, such as mottoes, slogans, and clichés, are used to shape attitudes and values and to engineer consent in the service of socially powerful interests.

The motto "sport builds character" must be seen in light of its ideological intent. It is not an empirical statement of fact, nor neutral commentary. Like other slogans and mottoes, it expresses much more than its intrinsic content, and it embodies and represents wider patterns of meaning, expressing and sustaining established patterns of activity and beliefs. It is an instrument of ideology.

Patriarchal Ideology and Character Development

Another ideological aspect of youth and school sport needs to be addressed—namely, its contributions to patriarchy. A prime reason that patriarchal practices continue is that so many American cultural institutions and practices are based on relations between men and women, and sport is one of the most prominent. Part of the ideological content in the idea that sport builds character conceals a subtle message that reinforces, through intention and innuendo, male power and superiority. It fosters gender inequality by promoting the building of character traits traditionally associated with masculinity.

In the ideology of athleticism fashioned in Great Britain in the 19th century, manliness was an intricate link in the presumed character development achieved by athletic competition. Team sports such as rugby and cricket became closely associated with moral training, and the games provided the laboratory for the outward display and the reinforcement of manly traits. This ideology was incorporated in the United States, and character building and moral education for masculine traits were the key concepts justifying athletics for young boys.

Patriarchal features and the roles they play in supporting male privilege have been central to youth and school sport programs. Despite the greater opportunities available to females in youth and school sports, these activities continue to be in large part an arena for the inculcation of traditional masculine characteristics, while grudgingly conceding a place for females in sport. This is illustrated by the vigorous and persistent resistance of male-dominated sport organizations to female inroads into sport during the past 20 years.

Although male-dominated youth and school sports programs have gradually conceded a place for females, they have conceded little else. Females who wish to participate in these programs are overwhelmingly coached by males who propagate the traditional male sport model to female athletes: autocratic leadership, lengthy, regimented practices, an emphasis on hard work and the subordination of the individual to the team, and winning seen as the only measure of pleasure or criterion for success. Thus increasing opportunities for young females in youth and school sport have meant that females have had to assimilate into the male sport system in exchange for an opportunity to participate. Therefore, they have been able to contribute little to transforming sport.

Character Development and the Social Structure of Youth and School Sport

Formal and objective aspects of sport and the mottoes and slogans popularized by the sport culture capture only a fragment of the day-to-day social relationships of the sporting experience. Sports have immense power to shape consciousness, values, and beliefs of athletes and to pass on selected aspects of the dominant culture. Indeed, the distinctiveness of the sporting experience is to be found not in learning skills or in teamwork but in the social relations of the sporting encounter—the relationships between coaches and athletes, athletes and athletes, and athletes and their sport tasks. When viewed from this perspective, organized youth and school sport not only meets the physical expressive needs of youngsters, but it also serves the self-interests of particular institutionalized groups—coaches, parents, business community, and so forth.

The structure of social relations in youth and school sport programs introduces the hierarchy and authoritarianism of the larger society to participants. This characteristic of sport programs is exemplified in rules and routine, the prominence of a work orientation over play, and the unquestioned coach's authority within and beyond the sport realm. This structure has penetrated into high school sports and even into the adult-controlled, highly organized youth sports programs.

Some analysts have suggested that sport for young athletes has become a form of "anticipatory productive labor." By this they mean that it socializes young athletes to accept authoritarian leadership and the norms of segmented labor and rationalization in the playplace. Coaches are the autocratic center of the young athletes' world—mirroring the hierarchical capitalist workplace setting; they set the standards of excellence and prescribe methods for attaining them. This total authority is justified as necessary to achieve the team's objectives and is vividly evident in popular locker-room slogans: "My way or the highway"; "There is no 'I' in team"; "A player doesn't make the team, the team makes the player." From the youth leagues through high school, aspiring athletes learn to please their coaches; if they wish to play organized sports, they must play the social-acquiescence game properly or they will be weeded out.

In terms of segmented labor and rationalization, youth and school sport programs are structured to familiarize athletes with a model and an actual system in which persons slated for specialized roles of varying prestige and importance learn to cooperate for the good of the organization. Individual athletes are expected to do what is thought best for the team. One sport analyst contends that when carefully scrutinized, the discourse of building character through sport turns out to emphasize forming traits admired in the capitalist workplace. He argues that youth and school sport tends to prepare "young men [and women] to take for granted the norms of the capitalist workplace; and central among these is that every aspect of the process is necessarily geared to the 'natural' goal of increasing productivity. Never can player (or worker) satisfaction, let alone the possibility of restructuring the 'relations of production' so as to afford opportunities for personal growth, take precedence over the imperative of building a winner."[22]

After three years of direct observation of the role of adults—coaches, umpires, parents—in structuring Little League baseball, sociologist Gary Fine concluded, "There are components of the playing of Little League baseball that can usefully be seen as 'work,' at least in a moral sense. Coaches and many players expect the participants to adhere to a Puritan work ethic, preparing themselves for adult life. When they don't, moral disparagement is seen as warranted and is judiciously applied."[23]

Thus a collective consciousness is fostered, strengthened by myths and slogans and infused with the virtues of conformity, obedience, work discipline, respect for external rewards, and unquestioned loyalty. These are the character traits that are labeled desirable. In this way, it can be seen, dominant group hegemony is maintained and reproduced not only through the diffusion of ideas but also in the routines and rituals of sport involvement and in its system of rewards and punishments.

The tightly managed organizational arrangement of the world of youth and school sport will be encountered again in the occupational world. Presumably those who have been athletes will be well trained for it because hierarchical structures that stress relations of control, obedience, and conformity give rise to a distinct socialization that tends to reproduce itself.[24] A major achievement of organized youth and school sport programs, then, is training participants to accept the prevailing social structure and their fate as future workers in advanced capitalist society.

Commodified Interscholastic Athletics

Increasingly, interscholastic sport has taken on many of the trappings of the commodified sport industry, seen in meritocracy, the endorsement of the performance principle, overemphasis on winning, assault on records, and the intensifying use of high school athletes as public entertainers. In a position statement about interscholastic athletes, the National Association for Sport and Physical Education declared: "The exploitation of athletes, so commonly associated with intercollegiate athletics, is currently so pervasive in interscholastic programs that State Activity Associations are compelled to devote a substantial portion of their rules and regulations to the prohibition of such violations as illegal recruiting, ineligibility, undue influence, excessive awards, extended practices and seasons, and inter-state all-star and post-season contests. The increasing commercialization of interscholastic athletics, exemplified by the televising of high school contests, regional and national all-star games, and the dependence of professional fund-raisers for the support of the interscholastic programs, all testify to the vulnerability of the interscholastic athlete to exploitation by those who have little or no interest in her/his academic achievement."[25]

Elite Youth Athletes

As I noted in a previous section of this chapter, a thriving commercial sport industry has developed in which young athletes are the commodities. Investigative reporter Joan Ryan has documented in explicit detail the story behind the making of elite young female gymnasts and figure skaters. What she found, she says, was a "story about legal, even celebrated, child abuse." She goes on to say,

> "In the dark troughs along the road to the Olympics lay the bodies of the girls who stumbled on the way, broken by the work, pressure and humiliation. I found a girl whose father left the family when she quit gymnastics at age thirteen, who scraped her arms and legs with razors to dull her emotional pain and who needed a two-hour pass from a psychiatric hospital to attend her high school graduation. Girls who broke their necks and backs. One who so desperately sought the perfect, weightless gymnastics body that she starved herself to death. . . . I found a girl who felt such shame at not making the Olympic team that she slit her wrists. . . . A father who handed custody of his daughter over to her coach so she could keep skating. . . . A mother who hid her child's chicken pox with makeup so she could compete. Coaches who motivated their athletes by calling them imbeciles, idiots, pigs, cows."[26]

But elite young athletes are not all females, nor are gymnastics and figure skating the only sports in which elite youth athletes compete in the commercial marketplace (nor is sport the only place where children are used as commercial commodities—for example, children's beauty pageants, child music protégés). Swimming, skiing, tennis (involving both males and females), and ice hockey are only a few of the sports in which elite young athletes are groomed for national and international competition in venues seating thousands of spectators before television audiences numbering in the billions.

Fun and Excitement in Youth and School Sport?

The description of the current social structural features of youth and school sports in this chapter is not meant to suggest that young sport participants never experience fun or excitement from their sport experiences; indeed, many of them do, and many youth and school sport participants cherish their sport experiences, often considering them the most memorable times of their young lives. However, young athletes have little awareness of how the very real experienced emotions evoked in their sporting experiences are effective tools for legitimizing the forms and features of youth and school sport while at the same time inculcating dominant values.

Evidence for Sport as a Character Builder

In presenting the origins and evolution of the slogan and belief that sport builds character, I have begged the obvious: Does it? Let me address this question.

Although many Americans take this motto for granted, few well-conceived and implemented empirical research studies have been conducted on the effects of organized sport involvement on the social development of young athletes. There are several reasons for this. First, the word "character" is vague; character is a socially constructed concept amenable to a variety of meanings and interpretations. When left unspecified, there is no way of knowing which meaning or interpretation is intended. To be amenable to verification, the definition of character needs to be anchored to a set of specific attitudes, values, and behaviors. Second, cultural ideas differ about which character traits are considered "good." After all, the exhibition of a particular behavior or trait in a specific situation might be considered a demonstration of good character in one culture but bad character in another.

Third, even if one clearly defines what one means by character in a given setting, it is extremely difficult to empirically verify the character-building effects of sport involvement. Traditional experimental designs are impractical because it is almost impossible to arrange the necessary controlled conditions for relevant data collecting. Cross-sectional research designs, which provide data about relationships between variables, are worthless to substantiate causal effects. Some studies have attempted to analyze the effects of sport involvement on a single discrete variable, such as courage or self-discipline, but this type of analysis is at the expense of almost trivializing the symbolic interactions that occur in a complex social setting like sport. So such an approach is too simple to yield anything meaningful.

Because statistically verifying that sport builds character is so difficult, those who argue for this theme are left to relating anecdotes such as how particular athletes displayed courage, perseverance, or self-discipline in the course of a game or how a team showed dedication and teamwork. But a perusal of the nation's newspapers on any given day will reveal stories of courage, loyalty, perseverance, and so on by people who have never participated in sport. So character qualities often attributed to athletes are neither confined to nor peculiar to them.

Another common form of anecdotal evidence is the personal account of "what sport did for me." Such testimonials are often made by former athletes who attribute their postplaying achievements to their sport experiences. Regardless of the form, of course, anecdotal evidence is unacceptable as scientific proof.

To these problems we can add questions of whether the "character" displayed by athletes or former athletes was present before they played organized sport or whether their particular preexisting character dispositions may actually have predisposed them to take up sport in the first place. Several sport-studies researchers have suggested such possibilities.

My comments about the problems of empirically supporting claims that sport builds character should not be misunderstood. I am not asserting that sport experiences have no effect on the personal-social development of participants. Indeed, there is convincing, empirically grounded knowledge that salient social experiences are powerful socializers. Sport involvement is an exciting form of human expression; many people find sport a source of great fun, joy, and self-satisfaction, and young athletes' values and beliefs are undoubtedly shaped by their experiences. But the exact effects of sport on attitudes, values, and behaviors (character) depend greatly on the social contextual conditions of the sporting experience, and the social contexts in which sports take place vary widely. Moreover, perhaps the sport setting is merely a particularly good setting for enabling persons to exhibit preexisting character traits; that some athletes or former athletes display culturally valued personal and social characteristics cannot be wholly attributed to their sport experiences without an enormous leap of faith.[27]

The summary of the evidence that I have provided concerning the theme of sport as a builder of character is shared by social scientists who have devoted many years of study to this topic. As to whether sport participation does or does not develop character, two University of California social psychologists state that "research does not support either position in the debate over sport building character. If any conclusion is justified, it is that the question as posed is too simplistic. The term *character* is vague. . . . More important, sport experience is far from uniform. . . . [T]he social interactions that are fostered by the sport experience . . . [vary] from sport to sport, from team to team, from one geographical region to another, from one level of competition to another, and so on."[28]

Two other social scientists who have made an intensive study of the claim that sport builds character agree with the previous scholars. They conclude, "The consensus of the research presented . . . and the conclusion of other researchers who have reviewed the research in this area, is that there is no evidence to support the claim that sport builds character in high school" sports "or anywhere else."[29]

Recent research actually suggests that contrary to building character, organized sport for youth may actually be detrimental to moral development, a key component of character regardless of how it is defined. Two researchers set out to analyze high school student-athletes' cognitive moral reasoning compared with their nonathletic peer population. They collected data on more than 1,300 high school students, ninth through 12th grades. Among their findings were (1) athletes scored lower on moral development than their nonathlete peers and (2) moral-reasoning scores for athletes steadily declined from the ninth grade through high school, whereas scores for nonathletes tended to increase.[30]

Ethos of Youth and School Sport

Every cultural practice has the potential to tutor its participants about values and actions, and, as I have emphasized earlier in this chapter, that is the deliberate objective of organized youth and school sports. But though social experiences do affect attitudes, values, and behaviors, there tends to be a cultish assumption that sport transmits only universally admired ethical and moral attributes. But little serious thought seems to be given to the well-known principle that whatever attitudes, values, and beliefs that will be acquired by young athletes will be strongly related to the values, actions, and morality that are displayed, admired, and rewarded in the social environment in which sport participation takes place.

That being the case, we can ask, "Just what is the ethos of youth and school programs?" Well, certainly many do emphasize lessons about fair play, self-discipline, cooperation, and respect for human rights and dignity. But there is a growing element in contemporary sport that is detrimental to the development of higher-order ethical and moral attributes: an emphasis on the view that anything goes in the pursuit of winning. All kinds of slogans in the sport culture exalt winning, such as "Winning isn't everything, it's the only thing," "If you're not a winner, you're a loser," "Whatever it takes to win." Meanwhile, among the numerous denigrations for losing are "Lose is a four-letter word," "Show me a good loser, and I'll show you a loser," "Second place is for losers."

By watching televised sport and hearing the commentary, by reading about sport in newspapers and magazines, and by listening to and observing their own coaches and parents, many young athletes learn that cheating and violating basic codes of moral conduct in big and little ways are often acceptable in sport. In a *USA Today* commentary, Tim Green, a former NFL player, claimed that in football "you cheat to win, and because you can . . . You're not wrong unless you're caught." He approvingly cited a slogan one of his coaches used: If you ain't cheatin' you ain't tryin'. It is understandable, then, that young sport participants may interpret some of what they see and hear to mean that anything goes in sport as long as you do not get caught. If one accepts the notion that youth can learn culturally valued beliefs and behaviors from sport, and if one agrees that an ethos of "winning is the only thing" is prevalent in the American sport culture, then it becomes clear that sport experiences may be providing patterned reinforcement of attitudes, values, and behaviors that are actually antithetical to character-building ideals of fair play and the morality of justice.[31]

A survey of men's college basketball players conducted by *Sports Illustrated* asked players to respond "agree" or "disagree" to a series of statements. One of those statements was, "My teammates would expect me to cheat if it meant the difference in winning a game." Forty-seven percent of NCAA Division I athletes responded with "agree." Forty-six percent agreed with the statement, "Trash talking is an acceptable part of being competitive." Although it is true that these were college athletes, and not youth and school athletes, college basketball players are products of youth and school sport programs, programs in which they learned not only the skills, tactics, and strategy of basketball but also the norms and values to sport.

Certainly young athletes learn more from sport than how to cheat and to disrespect moral codes. But one social analyst of sport has expressed serious misgivings about the moral and social lessons often promulgated in organized sport for youth: "As far as moral character in . . . competitive sports in general, one must wonder whether that particular character is, indeed, an ideal to be adopted. The widespread cheating by coaches and players, the envy, disappointment, cynicism and hypocrisy entailed in commercialized competitive sports, as well as the abusive and profane behavior of the fans, leave one in doubt about the psychological benefits accruing from and calling for such social investments."[32]

Transformative Potential of Youth and School Sport

Youth and school sport is certainly not merely an ideological mirror of the dominant social alliances in our society, nor is all the talk about sport building character a conscious hegemonic conspiracy. Furthermore, no assemblage of ideological practices and meanings and no set of social and institutional arrangements can totally eliminate countervailing tendencies and oppositional practices. Young athletes are not human sponges, passively soaking up every command, instruction, example, or slogan that comes within sight or hearing. Like all humans, they can and do resist enculturation in subtle and overt ways; they often contradict and partly transform modes of control into opportunities for resistance, and they maintain their own informal norms that guide the sport process. As one sport sociologist has argued, "[C]ritics of youth sport underestimate the capacities of young people to act creatively and define spaces of autonomous expression and resistance even in the most repressive of sport settings."[33] Some correspondence between sport and the social conditions in which participants live is unmistakable, but the social context of sport does not warrant linking it inextricably to the larger social world in which participants live.

Organized youth and school sport can be transformative as well as socially reproductive. A genuine, widespread public interest in truly promoting youth and school sport as a medium for personal enrichment and development, enabling participants to acquire and practice the universal moral qualities for which sport has been valorized, would certainly promote its transformative potential. But for this to happen, large-scale public debate and commitment to change would have to take place with a vision of substantially transforming the current purposes and forms of sport for the younger generation.

Rather than relying on slogans about the outcomes of organized sport for children and youth, an assertion like sport building character would be better problematized so that serious efforts can be undertaken toward creating sports experiences that will actually bring about favorable educational, developmental, and liberating outcomes. As a beginning, that will require seriously undertaking an alignment of agreed-upon personal-social characteristics and sports programs in which attitudes, values, and actions that are commensurate with such characteristics are displayed, admired, and rewarded. Sociologist D. Stanley Eitzen expresses this idea well in the box on page 273.

Where is such activity going on today? Who is challenging the present assumptions and practices about youth and school sport? The reality is that critical commentary about current youth and school sport structures and processes is almost nonexistent. Judging from prevalent trends, the attitudes, values, and behaviors with the greatest currency in sport have little to do with the expressive and creative potential or with the advancement of humane morality in sport.

Although sport for young athletes does have many problems, few viable alternatives are available for filling the substantial free time of

Ennobling Sports

Sport has the potential to ennoble its participants. Athletes strain, strive, and sacrifice to excel. But if sport is to exalt the human spirit, it must be practiced within a context guided by fairness and humane considerations. Sports competition is great, but it can go too far. . . . Competition has gone too far when a high-school league in Southern California eliminates the mandatory postgame handshake because trash talking in the handshake line leads to shoving and fistfights. Competition has gone too far when the quest to win corrupts organizations, coaches, and players.

Sports teach, participants learn. But in the current sports climate what is often being taught is disrespect for opponents and that using unfair means trumps those who play by the rules. When those involved step over moral boundaries, then rather than achieving its ennobling potential sport has the contrary effect. If sport is to achieve its promise, then those involved must be guided by the fundamental premise that to win by going outside the rules and the spirit of fair play is not really to win at all.

Reprinted with permission from D. Stanley Eitzen, "The Paradox of Sport: The Contradictory Lessons Learned," *The World and I* (July 1996): 321.

young people. Pleas for a return to the good old days are largely utopian cries against current arrangements; they are typically not followed up with actions. Parents and other adults have come to accept organized sport for young boys and girls as a feeder system that exists in an atmosphere of capital and labor. They see little in the way of alternative models to the dominant sport forms that now prevail. But there is a growing literature that discusses ways in which parents and coaches can enrich the quality of youth and school sport, and the American Sport Education Program (ASEP) is an educational package that helps parents and coaches teach the skills and strategies of sports while emphasizing the personal and developmental needs of young athletes.[34]

Summary and Preview

I have focused in this chapter on the connections between school and youth sport and other sectors of American life in terms of production and cultural reproduction and on the contradictions that exist in this system of sport. It is a rare youngster who is not touched in some way by school and youth sport in passing through childhood and adolescence, and these programs are a powerful means for inculcating social norms, values, and beliefs. As a cultural practice, organized youth and school sport is closely connected to other sectors of American society, and its forms and functions are grounded in and contoured by dominant political, economic, and cultural interests of the wider community.

The next and final chapter turns to examining the broad issues of the oppositional and transformative potential in contemporary sport. Sport is analyzed as a terrain in which different means and ends are contested, as a site for struggle and resistance against dominant definitions and meanings, and as an arena for human emancipation and freedom.

Suggested Readings

Armstrong, Christopher F. "The Lessons of Sports: Class Socialization in British and American Boarding Schools." *Sociology of Sport Journal* 1 (December 1984): 314-31.

Berryman, Jack W. "The Rise of Highly Organized Sports for Preadolescent Boys." In *Children in Sport,* edited by Frank L. Smoll, Richard A. Magill, and Michael J. Ash, 3-16. 3rd ed. Champaign, IL: Human Kinetics, 1988.

Brennan, Christine. *Inside Edge: A Revealing Journey Into the Secret World of Figure Skating.* New York: Scribner, 1996.

Fine, Gary. *With the Boys: Little League Baseball and Preadolescent Culture.* Chicago: University of Chicago Press, 1987.

Hardy, Stephen. *How Boston Played.* Boston: Northeastern University Press, 1982.

Lumpkin, Angela, Sharon K. Stoll, and Jennifer M. Beller. *Sport Ethics: Applications for Fair Play.* St. Louis: Mosby, 1994.

Mangan, J.A. *The Games Ethic and Imperialism.* New York: Viking Penguin, 1986.

Miracle, Andrew W., Jr., and C. Roger Rees. *Lessons of the Locker Room: The Myth of School Sports.* Amherst, NY: Prometheus Books, 1994.

Ryan, Joan. *Little Girls in Pretty Boxes: The Making and Breaking of Elite Gymnasts and Figure Skaters.* New York: Doubleday, 1995.

Shields, David Lyle Light, and Brenda Jo Light Bredemeier. *Character Development and Physical Activity.* Champaign, IL: Human Kinetics, 1995.

Smoll, Frank, and Ronald E. Smith, eds. *Children and Youth in Sport: A Biopsychosocial Perspective*. Madison, WI: Brown & Benchmark, 1996.

Thompson, Jim. *Positive Coaching: Building Character and Self-Esteem Through Sports*. Dubuque, IA: Brown & Benchmark, 1993.

Tyack, David B. *Tinkering Toward Utopia: A Century of Public School Reform*. Cambridge: Harvard University Press, 1995.

Chapter 12

Sport as a Site for Agency: Resistance and Transformation

Each time a man [or woman] stands up for an idea, or acts to improve the lot of others, or strikes out against injustice, they send forth a tiny ripple of hope, and crossing each other from a million different centers of energy and daring, those ripples build a current that can sweep down the mightiest wall of oppression. . . . Few are willing to brave the disapproval of their fellows, the censure of their colleagues, the wrath of their society. Moral courage is a rarer commodity than bravery in battle or great intelligence. Yet it is the one essential, vital quality for those who seek to change a world that yields most painfully to change.

Robert F. Kennedy

I have sought in this book to introduce you to a new perspective for analyzing American sport—a critical social perspective. This perspective attempts to reveal the social structural conditions in American society as they exist, especially conditions of oppression, exploitation, and social injustice. Its purpose is to increase one's awareness of ideology, values, and conditions that are concealed or hidden by everyday definitions of social reality perpetrated by dominant groups.

I have employed hegemony theory—an approach relying on insights about the historical construction of dominance and the roles of political, economic, and cultural institutions in society. According to this approach, privileged, elite social groups that control the critically important economic, political, and cultural sectors of a society also have principal access to the fundamental ideological apparatus. Privileged access to the ideological machinery allows these groups to write society's rules in the form of norms, values, and beliefs, and the rules they write enable them to continue to write the rules, reinforcing and reproducing their structural advantages.

I have used selected aspects of the theory of hegemony to examine power, domination, and ideology and their intersections to social class, gender, and race as they are related to sport. In addition, I have analyzed the role of the state, the economic system, the mass media, and education in American sporting practices. Finally, I have scrutinized the role of institutionalized sport in promoting conformity to the dominant cultural consensus. My overall purpose has been to challenge readers to see beyond the clichés, myths, slogans, and dominant discourse disseminated about sporting practices in American culture.

One of the fundamental outcomes of applying a hegemonic image to the study of American sport is the development of an understanding of how sport serves as an important cultural practice for the reinforcement and reproduction of the ideology of dominant social alliances. Despite the efforts of pluralists to cloak sport in an aura of unreality—of just innocent play—in fact one of the most compelling roles of contemporary sport is the promotion of activities that help fashion the instruments of economic, political, and cultural hegemony of dominant groups. Sport's social importance, then, is rooted in its power to structure and promote social relations in accordance with the requirements of the dominant interests that control or own it. As a type of cultural practice and as a direct reflection of dominant group interests, sport can be seen as promoting and supporting various forms of social inequality in American society. It can also be seen as having been transformed from an informal folk play and leisure cultural practice to a largely commodified industry that is one component of the more comprehensive capitalist consumer culture.[1]

Issues relevant to analyzing sport from a hegemonic perspective address how sport is associated with social class, race, and gender and with the control, production, and distribution of economic and cultural power. Because the social practices and relations of American sport are structured by the culture in which they exist, any adequate account of them must be rooted in an understanding of the social, economic, political, and cultural context of American society. As one social analyst has argued, "The *dramatizations* of social life that are provided by games and sports are far from innocent individual and collective experiences; rather they represent a powerful affirmation of the legitimacy of existing social conditions and thereby tend to reinforce these conditions."[2] The key to understanding sport as a cultural phenomenon, then, is found in the nature of its relationship to broader societal forces of which it is a part.

A consequence of the transformation of sport to a commodified productive enterprise is that many opportunities exist for dominant groups to associate themselves with sport and use it to further their own interests: commercialized sport is mediated by the mass media, the government intervenes in it, and it plays an important role in the educational system. Meanwhile, spontaneously initiated, informal, and creative sport and leisure have steadily diminished. Every effort to nurture informal, anonymous, unorganized sport is quickly incorporated into the marketplace by the drive for capital.

The characteristics of commodified sports and their widespread popularity make it easy for them to penetrate everyday life and to represent and reproduce the dominant ideology. This does not mean, however, that there is only passive compliance with hegemonic domination in sport or any arena; resistance to, evasion of, and challenges to the oppressive measures of hegemony are constantly taking place in the everyday actions of people, including cultural practices like sport.

In summary, then, sport is one of various cultural settings in which the hegemonic structure of power and privilege in capitalist society is continually fortified. Learning to see sport through the prism of hegemony theory enables one to be more aware of the role sport plays in producing and reproducing relationships of power and dominance. One becomes skeptical of assertions about the naturalness of contemporary sporting practices and events and more open to alternatives that would elevate personal development and social justice through sport. This may form a critical self-consciousness and empower one to seek alternatives to the present sport system.

Challenging Hegemony in Sport

The persistence of any pattern of domination is always problematic. Antonio Gramsci's theory of hegemony implies an ongoing struggle against ideological domination through various forms of resistance because hegemony is never secured, nor is it ever fully consolidated. Every society experiences numerous points in which subordinate groups resist the total domination that is hegemony's aim. The disempowered and oppressed oppose and resist, even transform, in various ways. So despite the enormous power and resources of dominant groups, hegemony always has elements of uncertainty and changing balance. As one social theorist has persuasively argued, hegemony "does not just passively exist as a form of dominance. It has continually to be renewed, recreated, defended, and modified. It is also continually resisted, limited, altered, challenged by pressures not at all its own."[3]

The point made in that quotation emphasizes that social life is not solely determined by hegemonic social structure. Individual human agency—meaning the capacity of individuals to construct and reconstruct their world—empowers individuals to change social structure. Consequently, dominant groups must work hard to sustain their power through an active process of accommodation and compromise.

Resistance, opposition, and struggle—acts of agency—against abuses of power, discrimination, inequality, social injustice, and autocratic control are pervasive features of human history. Well-established traditions of popular evasion of and resistance to programs and policies of dominant groups on the part of subordinate groups show that hegemony and compliance can never be assured. No set of social institutional arrangements and no collection of hegemonic practices and meanings can completely eliminate initiatives of agency. Political scientist James C. Scott has written extensively about the wide variety of resistance tactics that have been used. He distinguishes between the open, declared forms of resistance, which attract most attention, and the disguised, low-profile, undeclared resistance that constitutes the domain of what Scott calls infrapolitics, which is actually the most common form of opposition and resistance (see table 12.1). Scott emphasizes that opposition and resistance of subordinate groups "is to be found neither in overt collective defiance of power holders nor in complete hegemonic compliance, but in the vast territory between those two polar opposites."[4]

Resistance and Acts of Agency in American History

In the United States during the latter 19th and early 20th centuries, citizen movements ended slavery, secured the right to vote for women, won the eight-hour day for workers, and ended child labor. During the past two generations, sit-ins, protests, boycotts, and other actions by brave African American (as well as white) men and women prompted passage of the Civil Rights Acts of the 1960s. The women's movement of the 1960s and 1970s launched a successful struggle for basic citizen/human rights for females. Within the past 20 years, in communities throughout the United States, citizen groups have successfully struggled against corporate interest and government insensitivity. They opposed the nuclear industry because of their fear of radioactive fuels and wastes, and they have had successes in fighting giant corporations and the government to preserve and protect their rights to privacy, personal property, nonrenewable resources conservation, and clean water and air.[5]

Cultural activities are often on the forefront of opposition and resistance to hegemonic structures and practices. Historical traditions of the theater, the arts, and literature show them to be common

Table 12.1
Domination and Resistance

	Material domination	Status domination	Ideological domination
Practices of domination	Appropriation of labor	Humiliation, insults, assaults	Justification by ruling group for privilege (e.g., slavery)
Forms of public declared resistance	Demonstrations, boycotts, strikes, open revolts	Public assertion of worth by gestures, dress, speech	Public counter-ideologies (e.g., propagating equality or negating the ruling ideology)
Forms of disguised and low-profile resistance, infrapolitics	Everyday forms of resistance (e.g., desertion, evasion, foot-dragging)	Gossip, rumor; rituals of aggression; creation of social space for assertion of dignity	Development of dissident subcultures

Adapted with permission from James C. Scott, 1990, *Domination and the Arts of Resistance: Hidden Transcripts* (New Haven, CT: Yale University Press), 198.

springboards for such actions, and that pattern remains alive today. For example, over the past three decades, rock 'n' roll has recruited and educated citizens for political action. Sting, Peter Gabriel, John Mellencamp, The Blasters, Los Lobos, Bruce Springsteen, and others have made human rights, environmental degradation, and the maldistribution of wealth and incomes household topics among their young followers.[6]

Resistance and Acts of Agency in American Sport

Sporting practices, like other cultural activities, have largely been instruments of reproduction, but they have also been domains for the expression of various forms of resistance and agency. Many athletes and others connected with sport have resisted hegemonic patterns in subtle and not-so-subtle ways. In doing so, they have modified, contradicted, and sometimes transformed definitions and modes of control into opportunities for advancing their own informal norms and values in sport.

I cannot adequately examine here the many resistance and transformational movements that have occurred in American sports. But by describing selected examples, I hope to illustrate several areas of sporting practices in which struggles have taken place in the sports culture.

Class Resistance

Sport has been the site of struggles involving the monopolistic ability to impose the legitimate definition and meaning of sport, as well as the legitimate forms of sporting activities. As part of a larger system of social control, socially elite groups have historically attempted to define appropriate sporting practices. One strategy has been to outlaw certain sports, invariably sports popular with the working class. Just as inevitably, working-class groups opposed and resisted such dominant class sanctions. For example, pit sports such as cockfighting and dogfighting, traditionally popular with the working class, have been illegal in America since colonial times. They have been labeled as violent, inhumane, and cruel to animals and as sports that promote drinking and gambling. Despite the overwhelming sanctions against them, these sports have thrived among a rural subculture of farmers, ranchers, and migrant workers, but they also have an urban working-class following. Contests are held in such diverse spots as barnyards, abandoned sawmills, forest clearings, and abandoned buildings—wherever a pit can be constructed.

Cockfighting culture is grounded in traditional patriarchal masculine definitions of personal honor, competitiveness, combativeness, and individual acts of bravery. One researcher of cockfighting observed, "Cockfighting is part of a formerly legitimate, but presently archaic, cultural pattern which emphasizes certain values epitomized by the characteristic behavior of the ideal gamecock in combat, i.e., gameness, a quality of unquestioning, instinctual bravery of will to fight when fighting is obviously unproductive, or indeed, counterproductive. The romantic valuation of the trait among members of the cocking fraternity is in stark contrast to the rationalistic institutionalizing spirit of the age."[7]

It is impossible to accurately estimate the extent of cockfighting and dogfighting in the United States, but for cockfighting alone there are several nationally distributed monthly publications. Both sports continue to be popular, in resistance to dominant definitions and models of sport practices.

The capitalist workplace has always been a contested terrain; indeed, worker struggles against the power of those who own the means of production are endemic to capitalist production. In chapter 9, I described the long history of professional athletes' struggles against team owners to protect their basic rights as well as their material interests. All professional team sports have eventually established players' unions, always against the wishes of the owners and league commissioners. The growing strength and militancy of the players' unions have enabled them to wrest many concessions from the owners, with perhaps the most significant breakthrough being their successful challenge to the reserve clause.

From the time the Olympic Games were revived in 1896 through most of the 20th century, athletes participating in the Olympic Games were required to be amateurs, meaning they were forbidden to accept money for their athletic performances and achievements. But as the Olympics become more and more commercialized during the past 40 years, and athletes had to train longer and harder to even qualify for the Games, athletes literally became an athletic labor force without a wage. As it became obvious that Olympic Games were generating large sums of money for the International Olympic Committee (IOC), international sport federations, and national Olympic committees, Olympic-level athletes began to protest about the injustices of the amateur model. They did so because it was a model that kept them from materially benefiting from their labor, while everyone else associated with the Olympics was reaping large sums of money.

It was only after years of struggle, led largely by American athletes, that the IOC dropped the amateur model and began allowing Olympic athletes to be paid for their performances.

In chapter 10, I described how an amateur ideology employed by the NCAA allows that organization and its member institutions to exploit intercollegiate athletes by not paying them a wage for their athletic labor. Meanwhile, major universities operate with multimillion dollar budgets, and everyone working in the intercollegiate athletic business—athletic trainers, assistant coaches, strength coaches, athletic directors, etc.—is paid a livable income; indeed, some major college coaches receive salaries and benefits in excess of a million dollars. The exploitation is blatant, but the NCAA and universities have shown little interest in reforming the unjust system.

Intercollegiate athletes, who have no voice in the decision making of college sport policy, have opposed and resisted the amateur system in a variety of ways. In violation of NCAA rules, they have forged an underground economy, accepting under-the-table payments and improper benefits from coaches, boosters, and sports agents. One study of this underground economy found that under-the-table payments were fairly common in football; more than 30 percent of former big-time college football players reported taking illegal payments while they were playing. Furthermore, they saw nothing wrong with violating NCAA rules because they viewed them as exploitative and unjust.[8]

Although these examples of agency among Olympic and intercollegiate athletes do not effectively challenge the commodified, bureaucratic, and rationalized nature of the Olympic Games and big-time intercollegiate athletics, resistance behaviors are not always aimed at wide-scale social change. The Olympic and college athletes do not intend that their actions will have widespread structural ramifications on these forms of sport. Instead, they are struggling for social justice in the distribution of wealth that is being generated from their labor. This type of resistance is an example of James C. Scott's low-profile resistance and infra-politics (see table 12.1).

Olympic athletes' actions did transform dominant social relations into more equitable social relations. For college sports, the underground economy enables athletes to reap some material rewards, and because it will undoubtedly continue as long as the amateur model is retained by the college sport leadership, it will continue to be a destabilizing force. It may ultimately lead colleges to abolish the amateur ideology—and thus bring about some social change. In any case, these examples of human agency illustrate that resistance to powerful groups can be successful, even against overwhelming odds.

Political Resistance

In recent years, sport-related political protests have been waged on behalf of various causes. For example, despite U.S. government and corporate support for South Africa, its apartheid policies led various sport groups to successfully protest the participation of South African athletes in sporting events in the United States. From 1970 until the overthrow of the white government in South Africa in the early 1990s, almost every sporting event in the United States that included South African competitors was met with protests and boycotts to disrupt and stop the sporting event.[9] In fact, sport was one of the most prominent American sites for condemning the South African apartheid government.

Individual athletes and activist groups have used the sporting venue to demonstrate against hegemonic political policies and practices. Students at various colleges have used sport events to stage protests against war, racism, sexism, nuclear proliferation, and environmental pollution. Literature distribution, speeches, and placard displays typically are done outside the playing facility, but demonstrations have also occurred inside during pregame activities or during halftime.

Resistance to Race and Gender Inequities

Although much resistance to sport has revolved around social class relations and political policies, issues of race and gender have also given rise to resistance and opposition. Many African American athletes have been outspoken about racism in American society, and they have challenged the powerful sport establishment over racism in sport in a variety of ways. In 1968, American black athletes threatened to boycott the Mexico Olympic Games to protest racism in the United States. African American athletes Tommie Smith and John Carlos raised gloved, clenched fists during the awards ceremony as a symbol of protest. Heavyweight boxing champion Muhammad Ali refused to serve in the military and participate in the Vietnam War, saying that he did not have anything against the North Vietnamese.

During the past 20 years, black and white athletes and coaches have boycotted several sport events because of racist policies or practices of the sponsors. African Americans have expressed pride in their race through hairstyles and handshakes and other rituals carried out in connection with sport events. Most recently, black and white athletes and coaches have stepped up the pressure on the sport establishment for greater African American representation in coaching and managing. Although black resistance has been episodic and transient, organized sport has become a medium for demonstrating black pride and dignity, affirming black capabilities, and challenging the subordination imposed by politically and socially powerful groups within American society.

Many feminists contend that societal structures and values are defined in male relevant terms, subjecting women to live in a world that celebrates and rewards male values. They argue that dominant sport images are defined and shaped by men's values and men's understandings of the world, tending to alienate women from their sport experiences. For these women, the male-dominated sport world results in little self-fulfillment for females. As a result, initiatives have emerged among women in sport aimed at transforming it from a male-dominated domain to one in which women can express themselves on their own terms and satisfy their own needs.[10]

Certain feminists believe that true liberation for women requires constructing countercultural practices and institutions, and there is a movement in sport aimed at reshaping the emphasis from achieving equality with men to exploring ways and means of establishing female autonomy. Two feminist sport sociologists assert that the male sport model, imbued with patriarchal ideology emphasizing winning, elitism, and rigid hierarchy of authority, is an alienating model for women.

They describe how "women who define themselves as feminists actively construct and maintain alternatives to the male preserve of sport." They report that this alternative form of sport "is process oriented, collective, inclusive, supportive, and infused with an ethic of care."[11] The result is that sport is transformed from a vehicle for bearing male values to a celebration of alternatives for women. Such an alternative sport model displays resistance to masculine hegemony and dominant, male definitions of sport and illustrates that deliberate transformations—collective constructions of different ways of playing sports—are possible.

Nonmainstream Sports as a Form of Resistance

Other forms of resistance and evasion of the dominant, highly competitive organized sport forms can be found in such diverse activities as the martial arts and outdoor and wilderness sports. Several Eastern martial arts have witnessed an enormous growth in popularity. In some, competition is not important for mastery of the skills; indeed, in aikido, competition is forbidden. Outdoor activities such as hiking, orienteering, rock climbing, rafting, hang gliding, skydiving, skateboarding, and scuba diving, where the process (i.e., participation) has priority, have boomed among a clientele who have turned away from the organized, commercial, and corporate forms of American sport. Participation, rather than spectating, is the focal point.

In a study of adolescent skateboarders, the investigator found that skateboarding constituted resistance "to the corporate bureaucratic forms of sport (and as a consequence, corporate bureaucratic social relations)" for the participants. It did this "by creating alternative norms and relations that emphasized participant control of the physical activity and open participation rather than elite competition."[12]

A rapidly growing sport among youth is called "extreme sport." Participants in extreme sports use bicycles, skateboards, in-line skates, skis, and so forth in a unique and high-risk way. They claim they like that there is no Big Brother (coach or parent) to give them orders on how, when, and where to perform their sports. Extreme sport offers individuality and the freedom to go at your own pace. One extreme sport participant asserted, "It's not like another sport where you have a coach telling you what to do. It's like you're in control. It's all freelance."[13]

Sport and Social Transformation

Resistance to hegemonic forms represents an important platform for social transformation. In several cases, sport has demonstrated a transformative potential. This has occurred when people have used sport to confront certain social attitudes, practices, and even laws in an effort to raise public consciousness and effect legal change. As I noted in previous chapters, historically there has been a great deal of intolerance toward homosexuality in America. Despite substantially improved attitudes during the past decade, gays and lesbians still suffer various forms of structured social stigma and inequality.

In an effort to call public attention to discrimination against homosexuals and to improve public attitudes about them, national leaders of the homosexual community planned to hold a Gay Olympic Games in 1982. The event was quickly crushed by a lawsuit from the United States Olympic Committee (USOC), which claimed that the use of the word "Olympics" violated a trademark the USOC was granted under the Amateur Sports Act of 1978. The USOC's suit was upheld by the Supreme Court in 1987 in *San Francisco Arts & Athletics v. United States Olympic Committee*.[14]

The "victory" by the USOC was far from complete. Resistance quickly emerged within the gay and lesbian community, and a

© Richard B. Levine

Gay and lesbian athletes compete at all levels of sport. Leaders of the homosexual community have organzed the Gay Games, five of which have been held. More than 10 thousand athletes from over 40 countries have competed in over 30 events in recent Gay Games.

decision was made that a sporting event for gays and lesbians must go on. The name of the event was changed to the Gay Games, and the first two Gay Games were held in 1982 and 1986 in San Francisco. Both were the largest sporting events in North America in those years. In 1990 the Gay Games were held in Vancouver, British Columbia; in 1994 they were held in New York City, they are scheduled for Amsterdam in 1998. The role they are playing in changing attitudes and advancing social justice for homosexuals was described by the mayor of New York City, when he said he hoped "the Games will be a lesson in tolerance and equality." He even helped secure Yankee Stadium for the closing ceremony.[15]

The Gay Games have helped to transform the attitudes of many "straight" people toward homosexuals. It has also played a transformative role for many members of the gay community, giving them a sense of empowerment and enhanced self-esteem about themselves as human beings as well as capable, competitive athletes.

Alternative Models and Transformation in Sport

During the past two decades, there has been a growing disillusionment with the extreme competitiveness that characterizes organized sport programs and that cultivates the ethos of winning as supreme. Initiatives to transform the dominant sport culture have arisen in various "counterculture" groups. Those struggling to create alternatives to the dominant model have challenged the view of human nature as necessarily competitive and violent. They assert a different nature of humanity, a different structure of self, and they support alternative forms of sport that are not oriented to the combative, violent forms of action found in boxing, football, hockey, and so forth.

Individuals and groups active in trying to reconstruct the social order of sport have devised play activities and games in which competition is muted or entirely removed and in which cooperative, creative forms of play, games, and sport are promoted. Fun and the expressive character of these activities are emphasized precisely because the dominant sport forms lack these qualities and seem "overly rationalized, technological, and bureaucratized."[16]

The best-known of these approaches, "New Games," is fostered and communicated by those whose goal is to change the way people play by replacing competitive games with cooperative, no-win pastimes. By avoiding activities that require unusual physical prowess or specific sport skills, New Games leaders attempt to create an atmosphere of fun and relaxed voluntary participation. Practitioners of this approach emphasize that among its many advantages, cooperative play makes it easier for participants to ad-lib the rules, restructure traditional games, and generally communicate more with one another. Flexibility, creativity, and enhanced human relations are the key ingredients in this form of play.

In addition to New Games, there is growing support from others for games that emphasize cooperation rather than competition, games that promote intrinsic rather than extrinsic rewards, and activities that move people away from the role of spectators and toward active sport involvement. Books like *Changing Kids' Games, New Games for the Whole Family, Everyone Wins!,* and *Playing Smart* describe many physical activities that focus on cooperation and sociability rather than on competition.[17]

The pervasive message in all these approaches is that if American society really values cooperation, then what people learn in sport activities should be less competitive and aggressive. Americans are urged to develop a more critical consciousness of the effects of competition and the need to embrace a spirit of cooperation in all human affairs, including sport.

Obstacles to Change in Sport

Resistance and transformative actions of the type just described are a continuing part of American sport. But I must emphasize that they are not usually coordinated into social expressions of direct challenge to the structure of the larger political economy and cultural hegemony of American society, nor even to the dominant sport culture. It is difficult in any area to coordinate resistance into alternatives to dominant social structures and practices.

The very existence of hegemony greatly restricts the ability of subordinate social groups to create and sustain counterhegemonic initiatives because dominant groups often regulate dissent by structuring social arrangements so that subordinate groups must choose the better of only a few options, none of which are actually in their best interests. Thus, although oppositional efforts often win a hearing among society for a group or movement, the impact on the existing social structure is often disappointingly small. Furthermore, "whatever oppositional content might be found in popular 'alternative' practices can be quickly lost through incorporation."[18]

Some physical activities that began as true alternatives to institutionalized sport in the past 25 years have gradually become incorporated into the commodified sports system. Jogging, Frisbee sports, aerobic exercise, freestyle skiing, surfing, climbing, and in-line skating are examples; others, such as 3-on-3 playground basketball and beach volleyball—once the epitome of informal, player-controlled sports—have recently become commodified with corporate sponsorship, national and international tournaments, and prize money for winning teams. There is even pressure to make the Gay Games more commercialized by organizing them similarly to the Olympic Games and other mainstream sport events. The comments of a professor of labor studies incisively captures the essence of these trends: "No human social activity is beyond the scope of corporate competence . . . in principle no domain or sector under the sun cannot be made to turn a handsome profit."[19]

Although dynamic forces within the sport culture ensure that some social change will always be occurring, the difficulty in successfully achieving meaningful progressive structural change in sport—-or any other sector of American society—is that those who control the means of production and the state apparatus have power over those without such control. History provides few examples of a dominant group voluntarily relinquishing its social privileges to better conditions for the downtrodden, but history is replete with examples of how subordinate groups have successfully struggled to win space for themselves and make conditions more democratic, equitable, and socially just.

Effecting structural change of any kind, then, requires overcoming enormous resources vested in powerful social groups. Struggles against the dominant models and meanings of contemporary sport are met by a variety of tactics. One of the most common, as well as effective, involves working to make oppositional groups appear disruptive and counterproductive to the desired social order of sport. When this is achieved, their efforts are diffused.

Initiatives for resistance and transformation in sport are not always aggressively denounced or rejected by dominant forces. Various forms of institutional accommodation and compromise are sometimes enacted to restore quiescence without conceding major changes. For example, during the past 20 years, numerous concessions and compromises have been made to minorities and women without changing the basic power and ideological structure of American sport.

But despite the overwhelming odds, we can expect everyday forms of resistance to continue. At the individual, personal level is the impulse to play, to enjoy, to experience the rich exhilaration and sheer pleasure that come with the sporting experience. Sport can also be empowering and resistive while the pleasures of the physical activity are being enjoyed. The researcher who studied skateboarders eloquently described what skateboarding meant to them: "Even though the social impact of skateboarding is not transformative for most people, the significance lies in the fact that these participants were empowered to act in their best interests; they created and experienced alternative types of relations that met their needs. The ability of skaters to use a physical activity in this manner suggests that other activities can be created to reclaim power. The knowledge of creating alternatives can serve as a blueprint for future interaction or social actions and cultural products, and it can also inspire and give credence to the idea that there are social choices and that groups of people have the ability to create alternatives."[20]

Those involved in sport who continue to strive to win cultural and societal space represent a major obstacle to the vision and program that hegemony imposes on us all. Even if they have not seriously challenged the overall power structure, little victories, little spaces, and minitransformations have the potential to break out into something larger and more significant. But real alternatives to the present sport culture will have to be linked to the forces and movements that are attempting to overcome the entrenched hegemony of the larger society. This will require a range of small, local initiatives that are coupled to broader, more diverse efforts.

A Vision for the Future of Sport

As I indicated in chapter 1, the intent of a critical perspective is not just to describe and interpret the dynamics of a society, but to consider the ways in which the process of social formation can be modified, improved, or made more democratic and socially just. Esteemed sociologist Anthony Giddens has eloquently described why we might look forward optimistically to a more humane and egalitarian sport system: "As critical theory, sociology does not take the social world as a given, but poses the questions: what types of social change are feasible and desirable, and how should we strive to achieve them?"[21] Although I have no detailed agenda for transforming contemporary sport practices, like many people I have a vision of the kind of sport system I would like to see. I imagine it something like this:

A good society guarantees conditions in which all citizens can develop their potential and control their lives. So efforts toward the reconstruction of American society must proceed along lines that reduce the social inequalities and the other injustices endemic in capitalist societies. The values of a decent, progressive sport system will be centered on developing and advancing the democratic imperative that is fundamental to American society. Equality rather than hierarchy in social relations will be a cornerstone, and power and control will be both democratized and humanized. This does not mean that all positions of authority in sport will be forsaken, but that coaches and other sport leaders will abandon authoritarian roles that deny athletes subjectivity and control to create and explore their own meanings and visions. Sport leaders will carry out their tasks in the context of shared trust and respect. Athletes' needs as autonomous human beings—not merely instruments of production—will be taken into consideration. They will be empowered to think and act critically.

My sport system will provide adequate facilities and equipment for everyone, regardless of means. A truly caring society takes seriously the health of its citizens because it knows good health is the most precious human resource. Because sport and physical recreation promote health, a public commitment will exist to provide all citizens the wherewithal to stay healthy through sport and to enjoy the deep satisfactions of physical efforts.

Cities will give priority in spending public funds to sport and recreation equipment and facilities that benefit a broad spectrum of the community—rich and poor, male and female, young and old, able and disabled, and so forth—rather than subsidizing privately owned sport organizations to build arenas and stadiums that only a few affluent citizens can afford to attend and that promote spectator behavior rather than active participation. Although gifted athletes will be provided reasonable resources to allow them to test their skills against other top athletes, public-resource allocation will emphasize the cultivation of widespread sport experiences.

Maximizing participation will be a major goal for sport. Arbitrary distinctions of sex, race, age, and ableness will cease to function as forms of oppression or criteria for limiting sport opportunities. Doing and enjoying will take precedence over acquiring and achieving. The current commodified sport forms are extrinsically driven rather than being intrinsically oriented. The extrinsic focus in sport is on achieving, winning, profit—the product. An intrinsic orientation is centered on doing, self-expression, personal development, sociability—the process. The current canon of privileging performance, outcome, and profit in sport over other processes and outcomes will be drastically revised to make room for a distinct mode of personally grounded initiatives and values for sport.

In a society committed to egalitarian principles, in which active participation is encouraged and adequate resources are universally available, the vicarious stimulation provided by commodified sport will lose much of its appeal. Sporting practices will be linked to a larger effort to make performers out of spectators. Meeting social needs, rather than maximizing private profits, will be the overarching societal theme.

Sport sociologist Michael Messner has eloquently captured the essence of an overarching notion I have for sport. He argues that sport needs to become "more democratic, equal, peaceful, and humane, but also . . . contribute toward the transformation of other nonsport institutions such as schools, families, and the economy."[22] Only out of such a moral stance will a humane as well as a sensible sporting culture be achieved.

Is such a sport system possible? Of course. Because all social organizations and patterns are socially constructed, social change of almost any kind is possible. However, progressive social change comes only through struggle; it is not granted from above, it is won from below. Antonio Gramsci, the social theorist who popularized hegemony theory, said that those who struggle on behalf of a more progressive society should "have a pessimism of the mind—understand how bad things are, it's a way of arming oneself—and an optimism of the will; keep fighting back."

Renowned anthropologist Margaret Mead noted, "They say a small group of people can't change the world. Indeed, it's the only thing that ever has." Finally social analyst Noam Chomsky said, "If you assume that there's no hope, you guarantee that there will be no hope. If you assume that there . . . are opportunities to change things, there's a chance you may contribute to making a better world. That's your choice. . . . [But] if we relinquish the belief that we can make a difference, then the forces of [oppression and] greed will have won."

Summary

I began this chapter with a summary of the preceding ones. Although the hegemony of capitalist life is pervasive and powerful, people are the creators of their destiny; hegemony does not preclude changes in social structure nor does it totally dominate social relations. Space for resistance, even transformation, is available. Although the odds are overwhelmingly against those who strive for social change in the pursuit of greater freedom and social justice, change can and does occur. As for sporting practices, the presence of hegemony cannot completely stifle the human urge to play nor prevent the immediate, pleasurable satisfaction that many obtain from their sport experiences.

Suggested Readings

Beal, Becky. "Disqualifying the Official: An Exploration of Social Resistance Through the Subculture of Skateboarding." *Sociology of Sport Journal* 12, no. 3 (1995): 252-67.

Donnelly, Peter. "Subcultures in Sport: Resilience and Transformation." In *Sport in Social Development: Traditions, Transitions, and Transformations,* edited by Alan G. Ingham and John W. Loy, 119-45. Champaign, IL: Human Kinetics, 1993.

Gallagher, J. "Fun and Games: The Gay Games 1994." *The Advocate,* 26 July 1994, 20-26.

LeFevre, Dale N. *New Games for the Whole Family.* New York: Putnam, 1988.

Lopiano, Donna A. "Political Analysis: Gender Equity Strategies for the Future." In *Women in Sport: Issues and Controversies,* edited by Greta L. Cohen, 104-16. Newbury Park, CA: Sage, 1993.

Luvmour, Sambhava, and Josette Luvmour. *Everyone Wins!: Cooperative Games and Activities.* Philadelphia: New Society, 1990.

Morgan, William J. *Leftist Theories of Sport: A Critique and Reconstruction.* Urbana: University of Illinois Press, 1994. (See especially chapter 5, "A Reconstructed Critical Theory of Sport: Social Criticism With a Liberal Twist," and "Postscript: Sport in the Larger Scheme of Things.")

Morris, G.D., and James Stiehl. *Changing Kids' Games.* Champaign, IL: Human Kinetics, 1989.

Sack, Allen L. "The Underground Economy of College Football." *Sociology of Sport Journal* 8, no. 1 (1991): 1-15.

Scott, James C. *Weapons of the Weak: Everyday Forms of Peasant Resistance.* New Haven, CT: Yale University Press, 1985.

———. *Domination and the Arts of Resistance: Hidden Transcripts.* New Haven, CT: Yale University Press, 1990.

Waddell, Tom, and Dick Schaap. *Gay Olympian: The Life and Death of Dr. Tom Waddell.* New York: Knopf, 1996.

Zinn, Howard. *A People's History of the United States.* Rev. and updated ed. New York: Harper Perennial, 1995.

Notes

Chapter 1: A Sociological Perspective of Sport

1. Michael Parenti, *Democracy for the Few,* 6th ed. (New York: St. Martin's Press, 1995), 5.

2. C. Wright Mills, *The Sociological Imagination* (New York: Oxford University Press, 1959).

3. Ibid., 9.

4. Ibid., 146; Irving Zeitlin, *Rethinking Sociology: A Critique of Contemporary Theory* (Englewood Cliffs, NJ: Prentice Hall, 1973), 14.

5. E.G. Boring, *History, Psychology, and Science* (New York: Wiley, 1963).

6. Anthony Giddens, *Sociology: A Brief but Critical Introduction,* 2nd ed. (New York: Harcourt Brace Jovanovich, 1987), pp. 24-25.

7. Quoted in P. Holt, "Today's Patriotism Borders on Chauvinism," *Rocky Mountain News,* 25 September 1984, 33.

8. Parenti, *Democracy for the Few,* 6.

9. William J. Morgan, *Leftist Theories of Sport: A Critique and Reconstruction* (Urbana: University of Illinois Press, 1994), 2.

10. Daryl Siedentop, "The Theory and Practice of Sport Education," in *Myths, Models, and Methods in Sport Pedagogy,* edited by Ronald S. Feingold and C. Roger Rees (Champaign, IL: Human Kinetics, 1987), 79.

Chapter 2: Social Images and Sport

1. Jonathan H. Turner, *The Structure of Sociological Theory,* 5th ed. (Belmont, CA: Wadsworth, 1990).

2. Richard Bellamy, ed., *Antonio Gramsci: Pre-Prison Writings* (Cambridge: Cambridge University Press, 1994); see also Benedetto Fontana, *Hegemony and Power* (Minneapolis: University of Minnesota Press, 1993); Roger Simon, *Gramsci's Political Thought: An Introduction* (London: Lawrence & Wishart, 1991).

3. Ibid., p. xxxvii.

4. Antonio Gramsci, *Selections From the Prison Notebooks,* edited by Q. Hoare and G.N. Smith (New York: International Publishers, 1971), 12; see also Dante Germino, *Antonio Gramsci: Architect of a New Politics* (Baton Rouge: Louisiana State University Press, 1990).

5. Gramsci, *Selections From the Prison Notebooks*, 161.

6. Ibid., 57.

7. Ibid., 263.

8. Fontana, *Hegemony and Power*.

9. John Hoffman, *The Gramscian Challenge: Coercion and Consent in Marxist Political Theory* (Oxford: Basil Blackwell, 1984).

10. Raymond Williams, *Marxism and Literature* (Oxford: University of Oxford Press, 1977), 112.

11. Jim McKay, Jennifer Gore, and David Kirk, "Beyond the Limits of Technocratic Physical Education," *Quest* 42 (December 1990): 53.

12. Todd Gitlin, "Television's Screens: Hegemony in Transition," in *American Media and Mass Culture: Left Perspectives*, edited by Donald Lazere (Berkeley: University of California Press, 1987), 241.

13. Charles Lewis and the Center for Public Integrity, *The Buying of the President* (New York: Avon Books, 1996), 222.

14. John McDermott, *Corporate Society: Class, Property, and Contemporary Capitalism* (Boulder, CO: Westview Press, 1991); G. William Domhoff, *The Power Elite and the State: How Policy Is Made in America* (New York: Aldine de Gruyter, 1990); Michael P. Allen, *The Founding Fortunes: A New Anatomy of the Super-Rich Families* (New York: Dutton, 1987).

15. Domhoff, *The Power Elite and the State: How Policy Is Made in America*; Thomas R. Dye, *Who's Running America?* 4th ed. (Englewood Cliffs, NJ: Prentice Hall, 1986); Lewis and the Center for Public Integrity, *The Buying of the President*; Alan Neustadtl and Dan Clawson, "Corporate Political Groupings: Does Ideology Unify Business Political Behavior?" *American Sociological Review* 53 (1988): 172-90.

16. Richard Gruneau, "Sport and the Debate of the State," in *Sport, Culture and the Modern State*, edited by Hart Cantelon and Richard Gruneau (Toronto: University of Toronto Press, 1982), 24; see also William J. Morgan, *Leftist Theories of Sport: A*

Critique and Reconstruction (Urbana, IL: University of Illinois Press, 1994); John Gibson, *Performance v. Results: A Critique of Values in Contemporary Sports* (Albany, NY: SUNY Press, 1993).

Chapter 3: Structures of Social Inequality: Social Class and Sport

1. Esther Ngan-Ling Chow, Doris Wilkinson, and Maxine Baca Zinn, eds., *Race, Class, and Gender: Common Bonds, Different Voices* (Thousand Oaks, CA: Sage, 1996).

2. Martin J. Burke, *The Conundrum of Class: Public Discourse on the Social Order in America* (Chicago: University of Chicago Press, 1995); Michael D. Grimes, *Class in Twentieth-Century American Sociology* (New York: Praeger, 1991).

3. G. William Domhoff, *The Power Elite and the State: How Policy Is Made in America* (New York: Aldine de Gruyter, 1990); Michael P. Allen, *The Founding Fortunes: A New Anatomy of the Super-Rich Families* (New York: Dutton, 1987).

4. Robert Erikson and John H. Goldthorpe, *The Constant Flux: Class Mobility in Industrial Society* (Oxford: Oxford University Press, 1992); Scott McNall, Rhonda F. Levine, and Rick Fantasiz, eds., *Bringing Class Back In: Contemporary and Historical Perspectives* (Boulder, CO: Westview, 1991); Thomas R. Swartz and Kathleen M. Weigert, eds., *America's Working Poor* (South Bend, IN: University of Notre Dame Press, 1997); Sheila Collins, *Let Them Eat Ketchup!: The Politics of Poverty and Inequality* (New York: Monthly Review Press, 1996).

5. Reeve Vanneman and Lynn W. Cannon, *The American Perception of Class* (Philadelphia: Temple University Press, 1987), 55.

6. David Barsamian, "Interviewing Michael Parenti," *Zeta Magazine* 2 (January 1989): 101.

7. Paul Kalra, *The American Class System: Divide and Rule* (Pleasant Hill, CA: Antenna Publishing, 1995), 2.

8. Paul Fussell, *Class* (New York: Ballantine, 1983), 1.

9. Barbara Ehrenreich, *Fear of Falling: The Inner Life of the Middle Class* (New York: Pantheon, 1989), 25; see also Kalra, *The American Class System: Divide and Rule.*

10. Benjamin DeMott, *The Imperial Middle: Why Americans Can't Think Straight About Class* (New York: Morrow, 1990); Mary R. Jackman and R.W. Jackman, *Class Awareness in the United States* (Berkeley: University of California Press, 1982).

11. Reeve Vanneman and Lynn W. Cannon, *The American Perception of Class*; see also Sheldon Danziger and Peter Gottschalk, *America Unequal* (Cambridge: Harvard University Press, 1996).

12. Cyrus Bina, Laurie M. Clements, and Chuck Davis, eds., *Beyond Survival: Wage Labor in the Late Twentieth Century* (Armonk, NY: M.E. Sharpe, 1996); Frank James, "Anger Simmers as Worker Frustration Increases," *The Denver Post*, 1 August 1996, 18A.

13. Loic Wacquant and W.J. Wilson, "Poverty, Joblessness and the Social Transformation of the Inner City," in *Reforming Welfare Policy*, edited by D. Ellwood and P. Cottingham (Cambridge: Harvard University Press, 1989); see also Charles Krauthammer, "Class Warfare Plays Poorly With Middle Class," *Rocky Mountain News*, 26 December 1994, 75A; Danziger and Gottschalk, *America Unequal*; Jacqueline Jones, *The Dispossessed: America's Underclass From the Civil War to the Present* (New York: Basic Books, 1992).

14. H. Seymour, *Baseball: The Early Years* (New York: Oxford University Press, 1960), 15.

15. Thorstein Veblen, *Theory of the Leisure Class* (New York: Macmillan, 1899).

16. Juliet B. Schor, *The Overworked American: The Unexpected Decline of Leisure* (New York: Basic Books, 1991).

17. Jane A. Cauley, Sharyne M. Donfield, Ronald E. LaPorte, and Nancy E. Warhaftig, "Physical Activity by Socioeconomic Status in Two Population Based Cohorts," *Medicine and Science in Sports and Exercise* 23 (March 1991): 343-52.

18. Donald J. Mrozek, *Sport and American Mentality, 1880-1910* (Knoxville: University of Tennessee Press, 1983), 109.

19. Joseph B. Verrengia, "Power Players," *Rocky Mountain News*, 28 July 1991, 10M.

20. Joan Ryan, *Little Girls in Pretty Boxes: The Making and Breaking of Elite Gymnasts and Figure Skaters* (New York: Doubleday, 1995).

21. Naomi Fejgin, "Participation in High School Competitive Sports: A Subversion of School Mission or Contributor to Academic Goals?" *Sociology of Sport Journal* 11, no. 3 (1994): 211-30.

22. D. Jones, "Game Ticket: Companies' Super Perk," *USA Today*, 28 January 1994, 1B; see also "Super Bowl by the Numbers," *USA Today*, 31 January 1994, 5B.

23. Robert H. Frank and Philip J. Cook, *The Winner-Take-All Society* (New York: Free Press, 1995); Joel I. Nelson, *Post-Industrial*

Capitalism: Exploring Economic Inequality in America (Thousand Oaks, CA: Sage, 1995); Edward Wolff, *Top Heavy: A Study of Increasing Inequality of Wealth in America* (New York: The Twentieth Century Fund, 1995).

24. Wilbert M. Leonard II, "The Odds of Transiting From One Level of Sports Participation to Another," *Sociology of Sport Journal* 13, no. 3 (1996): 288-99.

25. Scott Stocker, "Don't Bank on Earning a Division I-A Football Scholarship," *Rocky Mountain News*, 7 February 1995, 16B.

Chapter 4: Structures of Social Inequality: Gender Inequality in Sport

1. Alison M. Dewar, "Incorporation or Resistance?: Towards an Analysis of Women's Responses to Sexual Oppression in Sport," *International Review for the Sociology of Sport* 26, no. 1 (1991): 15-23.

2. Aristotle, *The Politics*, edited by Stephen Everson (Cambridge: Cambridge University Press, 1988), 7; St. Thomas Aquinas, *Summa Theologica,* translated by Fathers of the English Dominican Province (London: Burns, Oates, & Washbourne, 1914), 42; see also Gerda Lerner, *The Creation of Patriarchy* (New York, Oxford University Press, 1986).

3. Reported in "Women's Role in Society," *The Arizona Republic*, 27 March 1996, E1; see also Susan Golombok and Robyn Fivush, *Gender Development* (Cambridge: Cambridge University Press, 1994).

4. Teresa Amott and Julie Matthaei, *Race, Gender, and Work: A Multicultural Economic History of Women in the United States,* rev. ed. (Boston: South End Press, 1996); *191 Facts About U.S. Women* (New York: Women for Racial and Economic Equality, 1995).

5. Randy Albelda and Chris Tilly, *Glass Ceilings and Bottomless Pits* (Boston: South End Press, 1997); J.A. Lopez, "Survey: 3 Factors Keeping Women From Boardrooms," *The Arizona Republic*, 28 February 1996, E1-E2; *Good for Business: Making Full Use of the Nation's Human Capital*, Report 9 (Washington, DC: Federal Glass Ceiling Commission, 1995).

6. "News Watch," *Labor Notes*, November 1997, 4; Jennifer Rothacker, "Gender Wages Uneven," *The Denver Post*, 12 April 1997, 1D; Karen Schwartz, "Women's Pay Still Lagging," *The Arizona Republic,* 16 January 1996, D1; Jerry Jacobs, *Gender Inequality at Work* (Thousand Oaks, CA: Sage, 1995).

7. Associated Press Release, "Lawmaking Is Still a Man's World," *The Arizona Republic*, 14 February 1997, A14; Karen Foerstel and Herbert N. Foerstel, *Climbing the Hill: Gender Conflict in Congress* (Westport, CT: Greenwood, 1996).

8. National Center for Educational Statistics, *Digest of Educational Statistics, 1995* (Washington, DC: U.S. Government Printing Office, 1995).

9. American Association of University Women, *How Schools Shortchange Girls* (Washington, DC: AAUW Education Foundation, 1992).

10. Harriet B. Presser, "Employment Schedules Among Dual-Earner Spouses and the Division of Household Labor by Gender," *American Sociological Review* 59 (June 1994): 348-64; Juliet B. Schor, *The Overworked American: The Unexpected Decline of Leisure* (New York: Basic Books, 1991); Diane Dujon and Ann Withorn, eds., *For Crying Out Loud: Women's Poverty in the United States* (Boston: South End Press, 1996); Teresa Amott and Julie Matthaei, *Race, Gender, and Work: A Multicultural Economic History of Women in the United States.*

11. Mary P. Koss, Lisa A. Goodman, Angela Browne, Louise F. Fitzgerald, Gwendolyn P. Keita, and Nancy F. Russo, *No Safe Haven: Male Violence Against Women at Home, at Work, and in the Community* (Washington, DC: American Psychological Association, 1994); Martha A. Fineman and Roxanne Mykitiuk, eds., *The Public Nature of Private Violence: The Discovery of Domestic Abuse* (New York: Routledge, 1994).

12. Ronald B. Flowers, *The Victimization and Exploitation of Women and Children: A Study of Physical, Mental and Sexual Maltreatment in the United States* (Jefferson, NC: McFarland, 1994).

13. "Violence Against Women on Rise Around the World, U.N. Report Says," *The Arizona Republic*, 1 March 1996, A17.

14. J.A. Mangan and James Walvin, eds., *Manliness and Morality: Middle-Class Masculinity in Britain and America 1800-1940* (New York: St. Martin's Press, 1987), 2-3.

15. Bruce Kidd, "Sports and Masculinity," in *Beyond Patriarchy: Essays by Men on Pleasure, Power, and Change*, edited by M. Kaufman (New York: Oxford University Press, 1987), 255.

16. J. Carroll, "Sport, Virtue and Grace," *Theory, Culture & Society* 3, no. 1 (1986): 98.

17. Michael A. Messner, *Power at Play: Sports and the Problem of Masculinity* (Boston: Beacon Press, 1992), 24.

18. Jane Gaskell and John Willinsky, eds., *Gender In/forms Curriculum* (New York: Teachers College Press, 1995).

19. Susan Birrell and Cheryl L. Cole, eds., *Women, Sport, and Culture* (Champaign, IL: Human Kinetics, 1994); D. Margaret Costa and Sharon R. Guthrie, eds., *Women and Sport: Interdisciplinary Perspectives* (Champaign, IL: Human Kinetics, 1994).

20. Mary Leigh, "Pierre de Coubertin: A Man of His Time," *Quest* 22 (June 1974): 19-24; Sheila Mitchell, "Women's Participation in the Olympic Games, 1900-1926," *Journal of Sport History* 4 (Summer 1977): 213.

21. Linda J. Borish, "Women at the Modern Olympic Games: An Interdisciplinary Look at American Culture," *Quest* 48 (February 1996): 43-56; Wayne Wilson, "The IOC and the Status of Women in the Olympic Movement: 1972-1996," *Research Quarterly for Exercise and Sport* 67 (June 1996): 183-92.

22. Debbie Becker, "Title IX Has Lost Its Clout on Campuses," *USA Today*, 16 September 1986, 2C.

23. Patty Viverito, quoted in Erik Brady, "Title IX Improves Women's Participation," *USA Today*, 3 March 1997, 4C; see also Debbie Becker, "Crew, Soccer Help Schools Close Gender Gap," *USA Today*, 4 March 1997, 6C; Steve Wieberg, "Study: NCAA Women Far From Equity," *USA Today*, 29 April 1997, 1C-2C.

24. Tony Mauro, "Sex Equity in Sports Backed," *USA Today*, 22 April 1997, 1A; Peter L. Shaw, "Achieving Title IX Gender Equity in College Athletics in an Era of Fiscal Austerity," *Journal of Sport and Social Issues* 19 (February 1995): 6-27.

25. Todd W. Crosset, *Outsiders in the Clubhouse: The World of Women's Professional Golf* (Albany, NY: SUNY Press, 1996).

26. Dean F. Anderson and K.S. Gill, "Occupational Socialization Patterns of Men's and Women's Interscholastic Basketball Coaches," *Journal of Sport Behavior* 6, no. 3 (1983): 105-16; Cynthia Hasbrook, Barbara A. Hart, Sharon A. Mathes, and Susan True, "Sex Bias and the Validity of Believed Differences Between Male and Female Interscholastic Coaches," *Research Quarterly for Exercise and Sport* 61 (September 1990): 259-67; Martha Wilkerson, "Explaining the Presence of Men Coaches in Women's Sports: The Uncertainty Hypothesis," *Journal of Sport and Social Issues* 20 (November 1996): 411-26.

27. R. Vivian Acosta and Linda J. Carpenter, *Women in Intercollegiate Sport: A Longitudinal Study—Nineteen Year Update* (Brooklyn, NY: Brooklyn College, Department of Physical Education, 1996).

28. Ibid.; see also Ellen J. Staurowsky, "Examining the Roots of a Gendered Division of Labor in Intercollegiate Athletics: Insights Into the Gender Equity Debate," *Journal of Sport and Social Issues* 19 (February 1995): 28-44; Ellen J. Staurowsky, "Blaming the Victim: Resistance in the Battle Over Gender Equity in Intercollegiate Athletics," *Journal of Sport and Social Issues* 20 (May 1996):194-210.

29. Paul Willis, "Women in Sport in Ideology," in *Women, Sport, and Culture*, edited by Birrell and Cole, 31-45.

30. Quoted in Mariah Nelson, "Label Inhibits Some Women," *USA Today*, 18 September 1991, 10C; see also "Intolerable," *Women's Sports + Fitness* (May/June 1996): 23-24; Alexander Wolff and Christian Stone, "She Said, He Said," *Sports Illustrated*, 22 May 1995, 16.

31. Susan Birrell and Nancy Theberge, "Ideological Control of Women in Sport," in *Women and Sport: Interdisciplinary Perspectives*, edited by D.M. Costa and S.R. Guthrie (Champaign, IL: Human Kinetics, 1994), 353; Helen Linskyj, "Sexuality and Femininity in Sport Contexts: Issues and Alternatives," *Journal of Sport and Social Issues* 18 (November 1994): 356-67; Helen Lenskyj, "Power and Play: Gender and Sexuality Issues in Sport and Physical Activity," *International Review for the Sociology of Sport* 25, no. 3 (1990): 235-43; Pat Griffith, *Strong Women, Deep Closets: Lesbians and Homophobia in Sport* (Champaign, IL: Human Kinetics, 1998).

32. Martina Navratilova, *Martina* (New York: Knopf, 1985); Marcia Chambers, *The Unplayable Lie: The Untold Story of Women and Discrimination in American Golf* (New York: Pocket Books, 1995); John Garrity and Amy Nutt, "No More Disguises," *Sports Illustrated*, 18 March 1996, 71-77.

33. Messner, *Power at Play: Sports and the Problem of Masculinity*, 34.

34. Elaine Blinde, "Unequal Exchange and Exploitation in College Sport: The Case of the Female Athlete," *Arena Review* 13, no. 2 (1989), 110-23; Merrell Noden, "Dying to Win," *Sports Illustrated*, 8 August 1994, 52-60; Herbert A. Haupt, "Substance Abuse by the Athletic Female," in *The Athletic Female*, edited by Arthur J. Pearl (Champaign, IL: Human Kinetics, 1993), 124-40; Jack McCallum and Kastya Kennedy, "Small Steps for a Big Problem," *Sports Illustrated*, 22 January 1996, 21-22; Lauren Kessler, *Full Court Press: A Season in the Life of a Winning Basketball Team and the Women Who Made It Happen* (New York: Dutton, 1997).

Chapter 5: Structures of Social Inequality: Racial Inequality in Sport

1. Kofi B. Hadjor, *Another America: The Politics of Race and Blame* (Boston: South End Press, 1995); Jennifer L. Hochschild, *Facing Up to the American Dream: Race, Class and the Soul of the Nation* (Princeton, NJ: Princeton University Press, 1995).

2. I will use the terms black and African American interchangeably because, although there is some controversy on this issue, I agree with Stephen Burman who says, "It is because both terms remain in current usage that the advantage of employing both as a contribution to elegant variation in the text remains legitimate"; see Stephen Burman, *The Black Progress Question* (Thousand Oaks, CA: Sage, 1995), 23-24.

3. Mary F. Berry, *Black Resistance White Law*, rev. ed. (New York: Penguin, 1994); Carter A. Wilson, *Racism: From Slavery to Advanced Capitalism* (Thousand Oaks, CA: Sage, 1996).

4. Derrick Bell, *Faces at the Bottom of the Well: The Permanence of Racism* (New York: Basic Books, 1992); Wilson, *Racism: From Slavery to Advanced Capitalism.*

5. Donald Tomaskovic-Davey, *Gender and Racial Inequality at Work* (Ithaca, NY: ILR Press, 1993), 3.

6. John M. Jeffries and Richard L. Schaffer, "Changes in the Economy and Labor Market Status of Black Americans," in *The State of Black America 1996,* edited by A. Rowe and J. M. Jeffries (New York: National Urban League, 1990), 12-70; see also Hadjor, *Another America: The Politics of Race and Blame*, 13; William J. Wilson, *When Work Disappears: The World of the New Urban Poor* (New York: Knopf, 1996); Carl T. Rowan, *The Coming Race War* (Boston: Little, Brown, 1996).

7. Salim Muwakkil, "Holding Pattern," *In These Times*, 9 December 1996, 18-20; Huey L. Perry and Wayne Parent, eds., *Blacks and the American Political System* (Gainesville, FL: University Press of Florida, 1995); Ralph C. Gomes and Linda F. Williams, eds., *From Exclusion to Inclusion: The Long Struggle for African American Political Power* (Westport, CT: Greenwood, 1992).

8. William F. Brundage, *Lynching in the New South: Georgia and Virginia, 1880-1930* (Urbana: University of Illinois Press, 1993); Andrew Hacker, *Two Nations: Black and White, Separate, Hostile, Unequal* (New York: Scribners, 1992).

9. *False Patriots: The Threat of Antigovernment Extremists* (Montgomery, AL: Southern Poverty Law Center, 1996); Rowan, *The Coming Race War.*

10. Louis Harris and Associates, *Racism and Violence in American High Schools* (Baltimore: Project TEAMWORK Responds, 1993); Karen B. McLean Donaldson, *Through Students' Eyes: Combating Racism in United States Schools* (New York: Praeger, 1996).

11. Stephen Steinberg, *Turning Back: The Retreat From Racial Justice in American Thought and Policy* (Boston: Beacon, 1995); Burman, *The Black Progress Question;* Wilson, *When Work Disappears: The World of the New Urban Poor.*

12. Robert Peterson, *Only the Ball Was White: History of Legendary Black Players and All-Black Professional Teams* (New York: Oxford University Press, 1992); Robert Gardner and Dennis Shortelle, *The Forgotten Players: The Story of Black Baseball in America* (New York: Walker, 1993); Art Rust Jr., *Get That Nigger Off the Field: The Oral History of the Negro Leagues* (Brooklyn: Book Mail Services, 1992).

13. Ibid.; see also David K. Wiggins, *Glory Bound: Black Athletes in a White America* (Syracuse, NY: Syracuse University Press, 1997).

14. Quoted in John R. Betts, *America's Sporting Heritage* (Reading, MA: Addison-Wesley, 1974), 337; "Dempsey Will Meet Only White Boxers," The *New York Times,* 6 July 1919, 17; see also Arthur Ashe, *A Hard Road to Glory—Boxing: A History of the African American Athlete* (New York: Amistad, 1993).

15. David K. Wiggins, "Prized Performers, but Frequently Overlooked Students: The Involvement of Black Athletes in Intercollegiate Sports on Predominately White University Campuses, 1890-1972," *Research Quarterly for Exercise and Sport* 62 (June 1991): 164-77; Cindy Himes Gissendanner, "African-American Women and Competitive Sport, 1920-60," in *Women, Sport, and Culture*, edited by Susan Birrell and Cheryl L. Cole (Champaign, IL: Human Kinetics, 1994), 81-92.

16. Kenneth L. Shropshire, *In Black and White: Race and Sport in America* (New York: New York University Press, 1996); see also Othello Harris, "African-American Predominance in Collegiate Sport," in *Racism in College Athletics: The African-American Athlete's Experience*, edited by Dana D. Brooks and Ronald C. Althouse (Morgantown, WV: Fitness Information Technology, 1993), 51-74.

17. Timothy Davis, "The Myth of the Superspade: The Persistence of Racism in College Athletics," *Fordham Urban Law Journal* 22, no. 3 (1995), 615-98; Phoebe W. Williams, "Performing in a Racially Hostile Environment," *Marquette Sports Law Journal* 6 (Spring 1996), 287-314; Shropshire, *In Black and White: Race and Sport in America*; John Hoberman, *Darwin's Athletes: How Sport Has Damaged Black America and Preserved the Myth of Race* (Boston: Houghton Mifflin, 1997).

18. Kenneth L. Shropshire, "Merit, Ol' Boy Networks, and the Black-Bottomed Pyramid," *Hastings Law Journal* 47 (January 1996): 455-72; see also Bret L. Billet and Lance J. Formwalt, *America's National Pastime: A Study of Race and Merit in Professional Baseball* (Westport, CT: Praeger, 1995).

19. Kenneth L. Shropshire, "Jackie Robinson's Legacy," *Emerge*, April 1997, 60-63; S.L. Price, "About Time," *Sports Illustrated*, 10 June 1996, 69-75; Jarrett Bell, "Tagliabue, Black Assistant Coaches in 'Constructive' Meeting on Hiring," *USA Today*, 25 March 1997, 2C.

20. Steve Wieberg, "Black Coaches Make Mark at Major Schools," *USA Today*, 22 August 1996, 10C; Richard E. Lapchick, *1996 Racial Report Card* (Boston: Northeastern University, Center for the Study of Sport in Society, 1995); Richard E. Lapchick, ed., *Sport in Society: Equal Opportunity or Business as Usual?* (Thousand Oaks, CA: Sage, 1996).

21. Dana Brooks and Ronald Althouse, "Racial Imbalance in Coaching and Managerial Positions," in *Racism in College Athletics: The African-American Athlete's Experience*, 101-42.

22. Henry Louis Gates Jr., "Delusions of Grandeur," *Sports Illustrated*, 19 August 1991, 78.

23. Richard E. Lapchick, "Athletes Learn the Lesson: The Lou Harris Survey," in *Sport in Society: Equal Opportunity or Business as Usual?* edited by Richard E. Lapchick, 174-75.

24. Audwin Anderson and Donald South, "Racial Differences in Collegiate Recruiting, Retention, and Graduation Rates," in *Racism in College Athletics: The African-American Athlete's Experience*, 79-100.

Chapter 6: Sport and the State: The Political Economy of American Sport

1. Ralph Miliband, *The State in Capitalist Society* (New York: Basic Books, 1969), 1.

2. David Vogel, *Fluctuating Fortunes: The Political Power of Business in America* (New York: Basic Books, 1989).

3. Michael Parenti, *Democracy for the Few*, 6th ed. (New York: St. Martin's Press, 1995).

4. Mark Zepezauer and Arthur Naiman, *Take the Rich Off Welfare* (Tucson, AZ: Odonian Press, 1996); Janet L. Fix, "Group Targets $100 Billion in Tax Breaks," *USA Today*, 25 April 1995, 2B.

5. M. Green, "Stamping Out Corruption," The *New York Times*, 28 October 1986, A35; see also Jean Stefancic and Richard Delgado, *No Mercy: How Conservative Think Tanks and Foundations Changed America's Social Agenda* (Philadelphia: Temple University Press, 1996).

6. Charles Lewis and the Center for Public Integrity, *The Buying of the President* (New York: Avon Books, 1996), 6-7.

7. Vicki Kemper and Deborah Lutterbeck, "The Country Club," *Common Cause Magazine* (Spring/Summer 1996): 16-35.

8. Thomas Ferguson, *The Golden Rule: The Investment Theory of Party Competition and the Logic of Money-Driven Political Systems* (Chicago: University of Chicago Press, 1995); John McDermott, *Corporate Society: Class, Property, and Contemporary Capitalism* (Boulder, CO: Westview, 1991).

9. "The Forbes Four Hundred," *Forbes*, 13 October 1997, 147-352.

10. Lee Lowenfish, *The Imperfect Diamond: A History of Baseball's Labor Wars,* rev. ed. (New York: Da Capo Press, 1991).

11. David A. Klatell and Norman Marcus, *Sports for Sale: Television, Money, and the Fans* (New York: Oxford University Press, 1988).

12. Lowenfish, *The Imperfect Diamond: A History of Baseball's Labor Wars.*

13. Ibid.; see also John Wilson, *Playing by the Rules: Sport, Society, and the State* (Detroit: Wayne State University Press, 1994); Martin B. Vinokur, *More Than a Game: Sports and Politics* (New York: Praeger, 1988).

14. Warren Freedman, *Professional Sports and Antitrust* (New York: Quorum Books, 1987).

15. Lowenfish, *The Imperfect Diamond: A History of Baseball's Labor Wars.*

16. Noam Chomsky, *On Power and Ideology* (Boston: South End Press, 1987), 106.

17. James Fallows, *Looking at the Sun: The Rise of the New East Asian Economic and Political System* (New York: Pantheon, 1994), 58.

18. Ralph Estes, *Tyranny of the Bottom Line: Why Corporations Make Good People Do Bad Things* (San Francisco: Berrett-Koehler, 1996), 172.

19. James Seelmeyer, "Market Competition Is Pocketbook Issue," *The Greeley Tribune*, 22 September 1988, 3A.

20. Ann Imse, "The Game: Pay for Play," *Rocky Mountain News*, 14A-15A; see also Charles C. Euchner, *Playing the Field: Why Sports Teams Move and Cities Fight to Keep Them* (Baltimore: Johns Hopkins University Press, 1993); Mark S. Rosenstraub, *Major League Losers: The Real Cost of Sports and Who's Paying for It* (New York: Basic Books, 1997).

21. George H. Sage, "Stealing Home: Political, Economic, and Media Power and a Publicly-Funded Baseball Stadium in Denver," *Journal of Sport and Social Issues* 17 (August 1993): 110-24; see also Dan McGraw, "Playing the Stadium Game," *U.S. News & World Report*, 3 June 1996, 46-51; Dean Baim, *The Sports Stadium as a Municipal Investment* (Westport, CT: Greenwood Press, 1994); Kenneth L. Shropshire, *The Sports Franchise Game: Cities in Pursuit of Sports Franchises, Events, Stadiums, and Arenas* (Philadelphia: University of Pennsylvania Press, 1995).

22. Ibid.

23. R.A. Baade and R.F. Dye, "Sports Stadiums and Area Development: A Critical View," *Economic Development Quarterly* 2 (1988): 270, 272.

24. Rosentraub, *Major League Losers: The Real Cost of Sports and Who's Paying for It*, 477-78; see also Jon Morgan, *Glory for Sale: Fans, Dollars and the New NFL* (New York: Bancroft Press, 1997).

25. Nicos Poulantzas, *State, Power, and Socialism*, trans. P. Camiller (London: NLB, 1978), 28.

26. J. Berkow, "Once Again, It's the Star-Spangled Super Bowl," The *New York Times*, 27 January 1991, S6; see also Jack McCallum, "Oh, Say Should We Sing?" *Sports Illustrated*, 25 March 1996, 50-54.

27. Wilson, *Playing by the Rules: Sport, Society, and the State.*

28. Joel I. Nelson, *Post-Industrial Capitalism: Exploring Economic Inequality in America* (Thousand Oaks, CA: Sage, 1995); John Cavanagh, *Global Dreams: Imperial Corporations and the New World Order* (New York: Simon & Schuster, 1994).

29. Berch Berberoglu, *The Political Economy of Development: Development Theory and the Prospect for Change in the Third World* (Albany, NY: SUNY Press, 1992).

30. David C. Koren, *When Corporations Rule the World* (San Francisco: Berrett-Koehler, 1995).

31. Donald MacIntosh, Tom Bedicki, and C.E.S. Franks, *Sport and Politics in Canada: Federal Government Involvement Since 1961* (Montreal: McGill-Queen's University Press, 1988), 4; see also Bruce Kidd, *The Struggle for Canadian Sport* (Toronto: University of Toronto Press, 1996).

32. Howard G. Knuttgen, MA Qiwei, and WU Zhongyuan, eds., *Sport in China* (Champaign, IL: Human Kinetics, 1990).

33. L. Jolidon, "Canadians in Seoul Are Angry," *USA Today*, 27 September 1988, 7E.

34. Allen Guttmann, *The Olympics: A History of the Modern Games* (Urbana: University of Illinois Press, 1992).

35. Derick Hulme, *The Political Olympics: Moscow, Afghanistan, and the 1980 US Boycott* (New York: Praeger, 1990); see also Bill Shalkin, *Sport and Politics: The Olympics and the Los Angeles Games* (New York: Praeger, 1988); Wilson, *Playing by the Rules: Sport, Society, and the State*, 380-86.

36. Richard D. Mandell, *The Nazi Olympics* (New York: Macmillan, 1971), frontispiece.

37. James Riordan, *Sport in Soviet Society* (New York: Cambridge University Press, 1977), 364.

38. S. Woodward, "Our Athletes Are Woefully Funded," *USA Today*, 22 August 1988, 2C.

Chapter 7: Commercialization of Sport: From Informal to Corporate Organization

1. John Lucas and Ronald Smith, *Saga of American Sport* (Philadelphia: Lea & Febiger, 1978); Benjamin G. Rader, *American Sports: From the Age of Folk Games to the Age of Televised Sports*, 3rd ed. (Englewood Cliffs, NJ: Prentice Hall, 1996); Betty Spears and Richard A. Swanson, *History of Sport and Physical Education in the United States,* 3rd ed. (Dubuque, IA: Brown, 1988); Ted Vincent, *The Rise and Fall of American Sport: Mudville's Revenge* (Lincoln, NE: University of Nebraska Press, 1994); David K. Wiggins, ed., *Sport in America* (Champaign, IL: Human Kinetics, 1995); Randy Roberts and James Olson, *Winning Is the Only Thing: Sport in America Since 1945* (Baltimore: Johns Hopkins University Press, 1989).

2. Wiggins, *Sport in America*.

3. Ira Berlin, "Class Composition and the Development of the

American Working Class, 1840-1890," in *Power and Culture: Essays on the American Working Class*, edited by Ira Berlin (New York: Pantheon, 1987), 380-94.

4. Michel Beaud, *A History of Capitalism, 1500-1980* (New York: Monthly Review Press, 1983), 83; see also D.M. Gordan, R. Edwards, and M. Reich, *Segmented Work, Divided Workers* (Cambridge: Cambridge University Press, 1982); Judith Stepan-Norris and Maurice Zeitlin, *Talking Union* (Urbana: University of Illinois Press, 1996).

5. Rader, *American Sports: From the Age of Folk Games to the Age of Televised Sports.*

6. Ronald A. Smith, *Sport & Freedom* (New York: Oxford University Press, 1988).

7. Melvin L. Adelman, *A Sporting Time* (Urbana: University of Illinois Press, 1986), 283; see also Michael Kimmel, *Manhood in America: A Cultural History* (New York: Free Press, 1995).

8. Ibid., 286.

9. Spears and Swanson, *History of Sport and Physical Education in the United States.*

10. Richard J. Barnet and John Cavanagh, *Global Dreams: Imperial Corporations and the New World Order* (New York: Simon & Schuster, 1994); David M. Gordon, *Fat and Mean: The Corporate Squeeze of Working Americans and the Myth of Managerial "Downsizing"* (New York: Free Press, 1996).

11. Joel I. Nelson, *Post-Industrial Capitalism: Exploring Economic Inequality in America* (Thousand Oaks, CA: Sage, 1995).

12. Bennett Harrison, *Lean and Mean: The Changing Landscape of Corporate Power in the Age of Flexibility* (New York: Basic Books, 1994); Robert H. Frank and Philip J. Cook, *The Winner-Take-All Society* (New York: Free Press, 1995).

13. Nelson, *Post-Industrial Capitalism: Exploring Economic Inequality in America.*

14. Kimberly S. Schimmel, Alan G. Ingham, and Jeremy W. Howell, "Professional Team Sport and the American City: Urban Politics and Franchise Relocations," in *Sport in Social Development: Traditions, Transitions, and Transformations*, edited by Alan G. Ingham and John W. Loy (Champaign: Human Kinetics, 1993), 211-44.

15. T.R. Young, "The Sociology of Sport: Structural Marxist and Cultural Marxist Approaches," *Sociological Perspectives* 29 (January 1986): 12.

16. Martin Carnoy and Derek Shearer, *Economic Democracy* (Armonk, NY: M.E. Sharpe, 1980), 12; Lawrence Mishel and Jared Bernstein, *The State of Working America, 1994-95* (Armonk, NY: M.E. Sharpe, 1994).

17. Ronald Edsforth, *Class Conflict and Cultural Consensus* (New Brunswick, NJ: Rutgers University Press, 1987).

18. Max Weber, *Economy and Society*, vol. 2 (Berkeley: University of California Press, 1978 [original work published in 1922]).

19. Bruno Rigauer, *Sport and Work* (New York: Columbia University Press, 1981).

20. Jean-Marie Brohm, *Sport: A Prison of Measured Time*, translated by I. Fraser (London: Ink Links, 1978).

21. Rigauer, *Sport and Work*.

22. Rigauer, *Sport and Work*, 48.

23. John Hoberman, *Mortal Engines: The Science of Performance and the Dehumanization of Sport* (New York: Free Press, 1992).

24. John Wilson, *Playing by the Rules: Sport, Society, and the State* (Detroit: Wayne State University Press, 1994).

25. Richard Kraus, "Changing Views of Tomorrow's Leisure," *Journal of Physical Education, Recreation, and Dance* 59 (August 1988): 86.

26. Harry Braverman, *Labor and Monopoly Capital* (New York: Monthly Review Press, 1974), 278-79.

27. Kraus, "Changing Views of Tomorrow's Leisure," 86.

28. Quoted in Vichi Michaelis, "Olympic Day Worth Forgetting," *The Denver Post*, 21 July 1996, 1BB, 8BB.

29. Lonnie D. Kliever, "God and Games in Modern Culture," *The World and I* 3 (October 1988): 567.

30. I am indebted to John Hoberman for a number of the ideas in this section. Hoberman, *Mortal Engines: The Science of Performance and the Dehumanization of Sport*.

31. John J. MacAloon, "An Observer's View of Sport Sociology," *Sociology of Sport Journal* 4 (June 1987): 114.

Chapter 8: Mass Media and Sport: Managing Images, Impressions, and Ideology

1. Herbert I. Schiller, *Culture Inc.: The Corporate Takeover of Public Expression* (New York: Oxford University Press, 1989).

2. Ben H. Bagdikian, *The Media Monopoly*, 4th ed. (Boston: Beacon, 1992).

3. Andrew Collier, "Westinghouse Buys Broadcaster," *The Denver Post*, 21 June 1996, 1C; Joanne Ostrow, "Media Monsters Keep Getting Bigger, More Powerful," *The Denver Post*, 26 June 1996, 1G.

4. Noam Chomsky, *Power and Ideology* (Boston: South End Press, 1987), 125.

5. Edward S. Herman, "The Media Mega-Mergers," *Dollars and Sense* (May/June 1996): 8-13.

6. "Facts and Figures," *Rocky Mountain News*, 13 May 1995, 41D.

7. Hal Himmelstein, *Television Myth and the American Mind*, 2nd ed. (Westport, CT: Praeger, 1994), 5.

8. Quoted in E.V. Sullivan, "Critical Pedagogy and Television," in *Critical Pedagogy and Cultural Power*, edited by D.W. Livingston (South Hadley, MA: Bergin & Garvey, 1987), 60-61.

9. Ben H. Bagdikian, *Double Vision: Reflections on My Heritage, Life, and Profession* (Boston: Beacon, 1995), 48.

10. Matthew P. McAllister, *The Commercialization of American Culture: New Advertising, Control and Democracy* (Thousand Oaks, CA: Sage, 1996); Norman Solomon, "Radio Monopolies Squelch Alternative Voices," *The Arizona Republic*, 22 March 1996, B5; Edward Herman, *Beyond Hypocrisy: Decoding the News in an Age of Propaganda* (Boston: Beacon, 1992); James Fallows, *Breaking the News: How the Media Undermine American Democracy* (New York: Pantheon, 1996).

11. D.L. Moore, "The Perfect Sporting Event," *USA Today*, 31 March 1989, 2A.

12. Carl Jensen, *CENSORED: The News That Didn't Make the News—and Why* (New York: Seven Stories Press, 1996).

13. Joel Bleifuss, "Think Tank Thunk," *In These Times*, 22 July 1996, 6; see also Shanto Iyengar, *Is Anyone Responsible? How Television Frames Political Issues* (Chicago: University of Chicago Press, 1991).

14. Himmelstein, *Television Myth and the American Mind*; Jensen, *CENSORED: The News That Didn't Make the News—and Why*; Ralph Engelman, *Public Radio and Television in America: A Political History* (Thousand Oaks, CA: Sage, 1996).

15. Robert W. McChesney and Edward S. Herman, *The Global Media: The New Missionaries of Corporate Capitalism* (New York: Cassell, 1997); see also J. Meyrowitz, *No Sense of Place: The Impact of Electronic Media on Social Behavior* (New York: Oxford University Press, 1985); Fallows, *Breaking the News: How the Media Undermine American Democracy*.

16. Todd Gitlin, "Television Screens: Hegemony in Transition," in *American Media and Mass Culture: Left Perspectives*, edited by D. Lazere (Berkeley: University of California Press, 1987), 240; see also Mary Cross, ed., *Advertising and Culture: Theoretical Perspectives* (Westport, CT: Praeger, 1996).

17. Bagdikian, *The Media Monopoly*; Michael Parenti, *Inventing Reality: The Politics of News Media,* 2nd ed. (New York: St. Martin's Press, 1993); Martin A. Lee and Norman Soloman, *Unreliable Sources* (New York: Carol Publishing Group, 1990).

18. Staff, "Pact Makes News an Exclusive Sponsor," *Rocky Mountain News*, 18 July 1992, 55, 58.

19. John Wilson, "Sport in the Wired City," chap. 9 in *Playing by the Rules: Sport, Society and the State* (Detroit: Wayne State University, 1994).

20. Mark C. Miller and Janine J. Biden, "The National Entertainment State," *The Nation*, 3 June 1996, 23-27; Michael Hiestand, "Trail of the Dinosaur," *USA Today*, 14 January 1997, 1C.

21. Alan Clarke and John Clarke, "Highlights and Action Replays—Ideology, Sport and the Media," in *Sport, Culture, and Ideology*, edited by John Hargreaves (Boston: Routledge & Kegan Paul, 1982), 69-71.

22. Woody Paige, "What You See Is What Already Has Occurred," *The Denver Post*, 25 July 1996, 1D, 4DD.

23. John Hargreaves, *Sport, Power and Culture* (New York: St. Martin's Press, 1986), p. 145.

24. Himmelstein, *Television Myth and the American Mind*, 295.

25. John Hargreaves, "Sport and Hegemony: Some Theoretical Problems," in *Sport, Culture, and the Modern State*, edited by Hart Cantelon and Rick Gruneau (Toronto: University of Toronto Press, 1982), 127,145; see also Engelman, *Public Radio and Television in America: A Political History*.

26. Ian Bailey and George H. Sage, "Values Communicated by a Sports Event: The Case of the Super Bowl," *Journal of Sport Behavior* 11, no. 3 (1988): 126-43; see also Sullivan, "Critical Pedagogy and Television"; George H. Sage, "Patriotic Images and Capitalist Profit: Contradictions of Professional Team Sports Licensed Merchandise," *Sociology of Sport Journal* 13, no. 1 (1996): 1-11.

27. John Riordan, "Soviet Muscular Socialism: A Durkheimian Analysis," *Sociology of Sport Journal* 4 (December 1987): 376-93.

28. Donald F. Sabo and Joe Panepinto, "Football Ritual and the Social Reproduction of Masculinity," in *Sport, Men, and the Gender*

Order: Critical Feminist Perspectives, edited by Michael A. Messner and Donald F. Sabo (Champaign, IL: Human Kinetics, 1990), 115.

29. Nick Trujillo, "Machines, Missiles, and Men: Images of the Male Body on ABC's *Monday Night Football," Sociology of Sport Journal* 12, no. 4 (1995): 419.

30. Mary Jo Kane and Janet B. Parks, "The Social Construction of Gender Difference and Hierarchy in Sport Journalism—Few New Twists on Very Old Themes," *Women in Sport and Physical Activity Journal* 1 (Fall 1992): 49-83.

31. Nancy Theberge and Alan Cronk, "Work Routines in Newspaper Sports Departments and the Coverage of Women's Sports," *Sociology of Sport Journal* 3, no. 3 (1986): 201.

32. Greta L. Cohen, "Media Portrayals of the Female Athlete," in *Women in Sport: Issues and Controversies,* edited by Greta L. Cohen (Newbury Park, CA: Sage, 1993), 171-84; see also Laurel Davis, *The Swimsuit Issue and Sport: Hegemonic Masculinity in "Sports Illustrated"* (Albany, NY: SUNY Press, 1997); Kathleen M. Kinkema and Janet Harris, "Sport and the Mass Media," in *Exercise and Sport Sciences Reviews,* vol. 20, edited by John D. Holloszy (Baltimore: Williams & Wilkins, 1992), 127-59.

33. "Olympic Games: An Analysis of Television Coverage," *Journal of Sport and Social Issues* 18 (August 1994): 234-46; Gina Dadario, "Chilly Scenes of the 1992 Winter Games: The Mass Media and the Marginalization of Female Athletes," *Sociology of Sport Journal* 11 (September 1994): 275-88; Margaret C. Duncan, Michael Messner, Linda Williams, and Kerry Jensen, "Gender Stereotyping in Sports," in *Women, Sport, and Culture,* edited by Susan Birrell and Cheryl L. Cole (Champaign, IL: Human Kinetics, 1994), 249-72; Bethany Shifflett and Rhonda Revelle, "Gender Equity in Sport Media Coverage: A Review of the *NCAA News," Journal of Sport and Social Issues* 18 (May 1994): 144-50; Christy Halbert and Milissa Latimer, "'Battling' Gendered Language: An Analysis of the Language Used by Sports Commentators in a Televised Coed Tennis Competition," *Sociology of Sport Journal* 11 (September 1994): 298-308.

34. Michael A. Messner, "Sports and Male Domination: The Female Athlete as Contested Ideological Terrain," in *Women, Sport, and Culture,* edited by Birrell and Cole, 75.

35. Mary Jo Kane and Lisa J. Disch, "Sexual Violence and the Reproduction of Male Power in the Locker Room: The 'Lisa Olson Incident,'" *Sociology of Sport Journal* 10 (December 1993): 331-52; see also Susan Fornoff, *Lady in the Locker Room* (Champaign, IL: Sagamore Publishing, 1993).

36. Judith A. Cramer, "Conversations With Women Sports Journalists," in *Women, Media and Sport*, edited by Pamela J. Creedon (Thousand Oaks, CA: Sage, 1994), 159-80; see also Pamela J. Creedon, "Women in Toyland: A Look at Women in American Newspaper Journalism," in *Women, Media and Sport*, edited by Creedon, 67-107.

37. Timothy Davis, "The Myth of the Superspade: The Persistence of Racism in College Athletics," *Fordham Urban Law Journal* 22, no. 3 (1995): 649; see also Jannette L. Dates and William Barlow, eds., *Split Image: African Americans in the Mass Media,* 2nd ed. (Washington DC: Howard University Press, 1993).

38. Ron Thomas, "Black Faces Still Rare in the Press Box," in *Sport in Society: Equal Opportunity or Business as Usual?* edited by Richard E. Lapchick (Thousand Oaks, CA: Sage, 1996), 212-33.

Chapter 9: The Professional Team Sports Industry

1. Benedict Anderson, *Imagined Communities: Reflections on the Origin and Spread of Nationalism*, rev. ed. (New York: Verso, 1991).

2. S. Caulk, "The Villain," *Rocky Mountain News*, 18 June 1989, 17S.

3. Mark S. Rosentraub, *Major League Losers: The Real Cost of Sports and Who's Paying for It* (New York: Basic Books, 1997); Michael N. Danielson, *Home Team: Professional Sports and the American Metropolis* (Princeton, NJ: Princeton University Press, 1997).

4. Ted Vincent, *The Rise & Fall of American Sport: Mudville's Revenge* (Lincoln: University of Nebraska Press, 1994); Eric M. Leifer, *Making the Majors: The Transformation of Team Sports in America* (Cambridge: Harvard University Press, 1995).

5. David Harris, *The League: The Rise and Decline of the NFL* (New York: Bantam Books, 1986).

6. Kurt Badenhausen and Christopher Nikolov, "More Than a Game," *Financial World*, 17 June 1997, pp. 40-50; see also Leifer, *Making the Majors: The Transformation of Team Sports in America.*

7. Richard Gruneau and David Whitson, *Hockey Night in Canada: Sport, Identities and Cultural Politics* (Toronto: Garamond Press, 1993).

8. Charles Cuttone, "Everything Ready for Launch of League," *USA Today*, 3 April 1996, 8C; Jerry Langdon, "League Launches New Look," *USA Today*, 21 March 1997, 3C.

9. Associated Press, "ABL Growing Strong in Its Infancy," *The*

Denver Post, 22 November 1996, 6C; Tom Pedulla, "WNBA," *USA Today*, 31 October 1996, 3C.

10. Warren Freedman, *Professional Sports and Antitrust* (New York: Quorum Books, 1987), 31.

11. James Quirk and Rodney D. Fort, *Pay Dirt: The Business of Professional Team Sports* (Princeton, NJ: Princeton University Press, 1992); Jerry Gorman and Kirk Calhoun, *The Name of the Game: The Business of Sport* (New York: Wiley, 1994); John Wilson, *Playing by the Rules: Sport, Society, and the State* (Detroit: Wayne State University Press, 1994).

12. Stephen R. Lowe, *The Kid on the Sandlot: Congress and Professional Sports, 1910-1992* (Bowling Green, OH: Bowling Green State University Popular Press, 1995).

13. Tracy Ringolsby, "Antitrust Exemption Endures Despite Attempts to End It," *Rocky Mountain News*, 11 August 1994, 13B; Stephan Fatsis, "Baseball's Antitrust Exemption Under Fire," *Rocky Mountain News*, 25 July 1993, 102A-3A.

14. Pete Rozelle, "Antitrust Law and Professional Sports," *Virginia Law Weekly* 4 (June 1964): 94.

15. Lee Lowenfish, *The Imperfect Diamond: A History of Baseball's Labor Wars*, rev. ed. (New York: Da Capo Press, 1991); Andrew Zimbalist, *Baseball and Billions* (New York: Basic Books, 1992).

16. Quoted in Associated Press, "Supreme Court Hands Professional Baseball Several Wins," *Rocky Mountain News*, 25 July 1993, 102A.

17. Kimberly S. Schimmel, Alan G. Ingham, and Jeremy W. Howell, "Professional Team Sports and the American City: Urban Politics and Franchise Relocations," in *Sport in Social Development: Traditions, Transitions, and Transformations*, edited by Alan G. Ingham and John W. Loy (Champaign, IL: Human Kinetics, 1993), 214.

18. Kenneth L. Shropshire, *The Sports Franchise Game: Cities in Pursuit of Sports Franchises, Events, Stadiums, and Arenas* (Philadelphia: University of Pennsylvania Press, 1995); see also Quirk and Fort, *Pay Dirt: The Business of Professional Team Sports*.

19. Freedman, *Professional Sports and Antitrust*, 78-79.

20. Charles C. Euchner, *Playing the Field: Why Sports Teams Move and Cities Fight to Keep Them* (Baltimore: Johns Hopkins University Press, 1993); Tim Crothers, "The Shakedown," *Sports Illustrated*, 19 June 1995, 78-81.

21. Shropshire, *The Sports Franchise Game: Cities in Pursuit of Sports Franchises, Events, Stadiums, and Arenas.*

22. Jon Morgan, *Glory For Sale: Fans, Dollars and the New NFL* (Baltimore: Bancroft Press, 1997); see also Dean Baim, *The Sport Stadium as a Municipal Investment* (Westport, CT: Greenwood Press, 1994); Joanna Cagan and Neil deMause, "The Great Stadium Swindle," *In These Times*, 19 August 1996, 14-17; Dan McGraw, "Playing the Stadium Game," *U.S. News & World Report*, 3 June 1996, 46-51.

23. Alan Snel, "'A Matter of Pride' or 'Extortion'?" *The Denver Post*, 24 November 1996, 1A, 13A; see also Roger Noll and Andrew Zimbalist, eds., *Sports Jobs and Tax: Economic Impact of Sports Teams and Facilities* (Washington, DC: Brookings Institute, 1997); Rosentraub, *Major League Losers: The Real Cost of Sports and Who's Paying for It*; John Fizel, Elizabeth Gustafson, and Lawrence Hadley, eds., *Baseball Economics: Current Research* (Westport, CT: Praeger, 1996).

24. John Helyar, *Lords of the Realm: The Real History of Baseball* (New York: Villard, 1994).

25. Mark Janis, quoted in Michael Hiestand, "Trail of the Dinosaur," *USA Today*, 14 January 1997, 2C; see also Bill Meyers, "Networking a Team Game," *USA Today*, 12 June 1997, 3C.

26. Kenneth L. Shropshire, "Diversity, Racism, and Professional Sports Franchise Ownership: Change Must Come From Within," *University of Colorado Law Review* 67 (Winter 1996): 52.

27. Ibid., 92.

28. B. Brown, "New Order of Business in the NFL?" *USA Today*, 24 October 1988, 2C.

29. Kevin Maney, "Celtics Could Make Foes Green With Envy," *USA Today*, 23 March 1987, 11C.

30. Jeffrey Leib, "Rockies May Hit Financial Homer," *The Denver Post*, 4 August 1991, 1G, 11G.

31. Quirk and Fort, *Pay Dirt: The Business of Professional Team Sports*, 62; see also Fizel et al., ed., *Baseball Economics: Current Research.*

32. Matthew Goodman, "The Home Team," *Zeta Magazine,* vol. 1 (January 1988): Sports Today section, 65; see also Joanna Cagan and Neil deMause, "Buy the Bums Out," *In These Times*, 9 December 1996, 15-17.

33. Euchner, *Playing the Field: Why Sports Teams Move and Cities Fight to Keep Them*; Cagan and deMause, "Buy the Bums Out," *In These Times.*

34. Matthew Goodman, "Why Not Nonprofit Sports?" *Z Magazine*, vol. 3 (November 1990): 88.

35. Associated Press, "Deion Puzzled, Hurt by Rice's Criticism," *Rocky Mountain News*, 21 September 1995, p. 5B; "Reinsdorf's Rules," *USA Today*, 14 August 1997, 3C.

36. Gerald W. Scully, *The Market Structure of Sports* (Chicago: University of Chicago Press, 1995); Rodney J. Morrison, "Sports Fans, Athletes' Salaries, and Economic Rent," *International Review for the Sociology of Sport* 31, no. 3 (1996): 257-69.

37. "Player Poll," *USA Today*, 27 June 1988, 1C.

38. Michael Hiestand, "Algebraic Equations Factor Out for Players," *USA Today*, 8 July 1994, International Edition, 2B.

39. "Collusion: Arbitrator Calls a Third Strike on Owners," *USA Today*, 19 July 1990, 9C; Hal Bodley, "Players Union's New Math: Collusion Payments," *USA Today*, 25 June 1992, 3C.

40. Reeve Vanneman and Lynn W. Cannon, *The American Perception of Class* (Philadelphia: Temple University Press, 1987), 7, 167.

41. Lowenfish, *The Imperfect Diamond: A History of Baseball's Labor Wars*.

42. Anthony Giddens, *Sociology: A Brief but Critical Introduction*, 2nd ed. (New York: Harcourt Brace Jovanovich, 1987), 37; Paul D. Staudohar, *Playing for Dollars: Labor Relations and the Sports Business* (Ithaca, NY: ILR Press, 1996).

Chapter 10: Power and Ideology in Intercollegiate Sport

1. Douglas S. Looney, "Pure and Simple," *Sports Illustrated*, 31 October 1994, 68-80; Geoffrey Norman, "Smart Ball," *Sports Illustrated*, 3 September 1990, 114-25; Debra E. Blum, "Forsaking the Big Time," *The Chronicle of Higher Education*, 9 November 1994, A35-A36.

2. John R. Thelin, *Games Colleges Play: Scandal and Reform in Intercollegiate Athletics* (Baltimore: Johns Hopkins University Press, 1994).

3. Rick Telander, *The Hundred Yard Lie* (New York: Simon & Schuster, 1989); Arthur Padilla, "Big-Time College Sports: Management and Economic Issues," *Journal of Sport and Social Issues* 18 (May 1994): 123-43; Murray Sperber, *College Sports Inc.: The Athletic Department Vs the University* (New York: Henry Holt, 1990); "Measure Seeks Tax on Revenue From Athletics," *The NCAA News*, 13 March 1991, 2.

4. Richard Sheehan, *Keeping Score: The Economics of Big-Time Sports* (South Bend, IN: Diamond Communications, 1996).

5. Paul R. Lawrence, *Unsportsmanlike Conduct: The National Collegiate Athletic Association and the Business of College Football* (New York: Praeger, 1987); William J. Morgan, *Leftist Theories of Sport: A Critique and Reconstruction* (Chicago: University of Illinois Press, 1994), 140-41.

6. Don Yaeger, *Undue Process: The NCAA's Injustice for All* (Champaign, IL: Sagamore, 1991); Arthur A. Fleisher III, Brian L. Goff, and Robert D. Tollison, *The National Collegiate Athletic Association: A Study in Cartel Behavior* (Chicago: The University of Chicago Press, 1992).

7. Tom McMillen, *Out of Bounds* (New York: Simon & Schuster, 1992); Donald Chu, *The Character of American Higher Education and Intercollegiate Sport* (Albany, NY: SUNY Press, 1989); Thelin, *Games Colleges Play: Scandal and Reform in Intercollegiate Athletics*.

8. Ronald A. Smith, "Preludes to the NCAA: Early Failures of Faculty Intercollegiate Athletic Control," *Research Quarterly of Exercise and Sport* 54 (1983): 373.

9. J.A. Mangan, *Athleticism in the Victorian and Edwardian Public School* (London: Cambridge University Press, 1981).

10. Ronald A. Smith, *Sport & Freedom* (New York: Oxford University Press, 1988).

11. Ibid.

12. Ibid.

13. Richard Swanson and Betty Spears, *History of Sport and Physical Education in the United States*, 4th ed. (Madison, WI: Brown & Benchmark, 1995); Paula Welch, "The First Half Century," in *Women in Sport: Issues and Controversies*, edited by Greta L. Cohen (Newbury Park, CA: Sage, 1993), 69-77.

14. Nand Hart-Nibbrig and Clement Cottingham, *The Political Economy of College Sports* (Lexington, MA: Lexington Books, 1986), 22.

15. National Collegiate Athletic Association, *1996-97 NCAA Manual* (Overland Park, KS: National Collegiate Athletic Association, 1996), 5.

16. Bertrand Russell, *Power: A New Social Analysis* (London: Allen and Unwin, 1938), 10.

17. Reggie Rivers, "Athlete's Education Is Not 'Free,'" *Rocky Mountain News*, 27 March 1994, 4B; "Success Pays Off for College Football Coaches," *USA Today*, 21 November 1997, p. 4C.

18. Tom Fasano, "Injury Sidelines St. Aubyn," *The Greeley Tribune*, 23 August 1997, 1B; Timothy Davis says that "courts are sharply divided over the question of whether a student-athlete on scholarship falls within the scope of worker's compensation statutes." See Timothy Davis, "Intercollegiate Athletics: Competing Models and Conflicting Realities," *Rutgers Law Journal* 25 (Winter 1994): 289.

19. Ibid., 273-78.

20. Casper Whitney, *A Sporting Pilgrimage* (New York: Harper, 1895), 163.

21. Walter Camp, *Walter Camp's Book of College Sports* (New York: Century, 1893), 1-2.

22. J. Falla, *NCAA: The Voice of College Sports* (Mission, KS: National Collegiate Athletic Association, 1981), 33.

23. Whitney, *A Sporting Pilgrimage*, 166.

24. William O. Johnson: *The Olympics: A History of the Games* (Birmingham, AL: Oxmoor House, 1992); John Lucas, *The Modern Olympic Games* (South Brunswick, NJ: Barnes, 1980); John J. MacAloon, *This Great Symbol: Pierre de Coubertin and the Origins of the Modern Olympic Games* (Chicago: University of Chicago Press, 1981).

25. David Young, *The Olympic Myth of Greek Amateur Athletes* (Chicago: Ares, 1984), 7, 163.

26. Walter Byers, *Unsportsmanlike Conduct: Exploiting College Athletes* (Ann Arbor: University of Michigan Press, 1995), 376.

27. Yaeger, *Undue Process: The NCAA's Injustice for All*, 105; Fleisher III, Goff, and Tollison, *The National Collegiate Athletic Association: A Study in Cartel Behavior*.

28. B.J. Brooks, "Neuheisel Asks 'Market Value,'" *Rocky Mountain News*, 7 June 1996, 1C, 4C; Bryan Burwell, "For Everyone but Athletes, Tournament Spells Profit," *USA Today*, 17 March 1995, 5C.

29. McMillen, *Out of Bounds*, 103; Dick DeVenzio, "Athletes' Bill of Rights," *Friends of College Athletes*, Fall 1996, 3; quoted in Doug Tucker, "Former NCAA Chief in Favor of Paying Athletes," *The Tuscaloosa (Alabama) News*, 5 January 1995, 1C; see also Steve Rushin, "Inside the Moat," *Sports Illustrated*, 3 March 1997, 68-83.

30. Rick Telander, "Something Must Be Done," *Sports Illustrated*, 2 October 1989, 92-113.

31. Joe Gilmartin, "Everybody Gets a Slice of the Pie Except Players," *The Phoenix Gazette*, 23 April 1993, 1D; Jack McCallum and

Kostya Kennedy, "Dear Diary: The NCAA Is Stupid," *Sports Illustrated,* 27 November 1995, 25; Alexander Wolff, "Abandoned in Cyberspace," *Sports Illustrated,* 4 March 1996, 92; Jack McCallum and Kostya Kennedy, "NCAA's Theater of the Absurd," *Sports Illustrated,* 15 April 1996, 17.

32. B.G. Brooks, "Swoosh the Mark of Success in '90s," *Rocky Mountain News,* 13 October 1995, 12B.

33. Thomas Sowell, "Colleges Don't Play Fair With Their Athletes," *Rocky Mountain News,* 9 January 1989, 31.

34. Sonja Steptoe and E.M. Swift, "Anatomy of Scandal," *Sports Illustrated,* 16 May 1994, 18-28; Douglas S. Looney and John Walters, "Seminole Shame," *Sports Illustrated,* 6 June 1994, 34-37; Alexander Wolff, "Broken Beyond Repair," *Sports Illustrated,* 12 June 1995, 20-26; Jack McCallum, "Paper Trail," *Sports Illustrated,* 28 November 1994, 45-48; Alexander Wolff and Dostya Kennedy, "Winning Ugly," *Sports Illustrated,* 11 September 1995, 14; S.L. Price, "Hard Time?" *Sports Illustrated,* 11 December 1995, 32-33; "Athletic Notes," *The Chronicle of Higher Education,* 23 November 1994, A36; James H. Frey, "Deviance of Organizational Subunits: The Case of the College Athletic Departments," *Journal of Sport and Social Issues* 18 (May 1994): 110-22.

35. K. Allen and S. Wieberg, "Academic, Financial Pressures Dictate Minor Changes," *USA Today,* 30 November 1988, 8C.

36. John S. and James L. Knight Foundation, *Reports of the Knight Foundation: Commission on Intercollegiate Athletics* (One Biscayne Tower, Ste. 3800, 2 S. Biscayne Blvd., Miami; 1993).

37. Byers, *Unsportsmanlike Conduct: Exploiting College Athletes,* 337; quoted in Yaeger, *Undue Process: The NCAA's Injustice for All,* 124; see also Murray Sperber, "Why the NCAA Can't Reform College Athletics," *Academe* 77 (January/February 1991): 13-20.

38. Murray Sperber, *College Sports Inc.: The Athletic Department Vs the University* (New York: Henry Holt, 1990); Allen L. Sack and R. Thiel, "College Football and Social Mobility: A Case Study of Notre Dame Football Players," *Sociology of Education,* 52 (1979): 60-66.

39. William Ryan, *Blaming the Victim,* rev. ed. (New York: Vintage Books, 1976), 6.

40. Timothy Davis, "African-American Student-Athletes: Marginalizing the NCAA Regulatory Structure?" *Marquette Sports Law Journal* 6 (Spring 1996): 199-227.

41. Quoted in *Friends of College Athletes* (Fall 1995): 9.

42. Byers, *Unsportsmanlike Conduct: Exploiting College Athletes*; see also Steve Wulf, "Tote That Ball, Lift That Revenue," *Time*, 21 October 1996, 94.

43. Timothy Davis, "A Model of Institutional Governance for Inter-collegiate Athletics," *Wisconsin Law Review* no. 3 (1995): 599-645; Wilford S. Bailey and Taylor D. Littleton, *Athletics and Academe: An Anatomy of Abuses and a Prescription for Reform* (New York: American Council on Education/Macmillan, 1991); McMillen, *Out of Bounds*.

Chapter 11: Building Character Through Youth and School Sport

1. Roger Daniels, *Coming to America: A History of Immigration and Ethnicity in America* (New York: Harper-Collins, 1990).

2. David B. Tyack, *Tinkering Toward Utopia: A Century of Public School Reform* (Cambridge: Harvard University Press, 1995).

3. Joel H. Spring, *The American School, 1642-1993*, 3rd ed. (New York: McGraw-Hill, 1994); Joel Spring, *Conflicts of Interests: The Politics of American Education*, 2nd ed. (New York: Longman, 1993).

4. Michael W. Apple, *Education and Power* (New York: Routledge, 1995); see also Michael W. Apple, *Cultural Politics and Education* (New York: Teachers College Press, 1996); Henry A. Giroux, *Border Crossings: Cultural Workers and the Politics of Education* (New York: Routledge, 1992); Thomas S. Popkewitz, *A Political Sociology of Educational Reform* (New York: Teachers College Press, 1991).

5. Stephen Hardy, *How Boston Played* (Boston: Northeastern University Press, 1982), 112, 115.

6. G.S. Lowman, "The Regulation and Control of Sports in Secondary Schools of the United States," *American Physical Education Review* 12 (1907): 307-23; J.H. McCurdy, "Study of the Characteristics of Physical Training in Public Schools of the U.S.," *American Physical Education Review* 10 (1905): 202-13.

7. Hardy, *How Boston Played*, 121, 123.

8. Ibid., 104; see also Dominick Cavallo, *Muscles and Morals: Organized Playgrounds and Urban Reform, 1880-1920* (Philadelphia: University of Pennsylvania Press, 1981).

9. Jacob Riis, *Children of the Tenements* (New York: Macmillan, 1903), 1.

10. Jack W. Berryman, "The Rise of Highly Organized Sports for Preadolescent Boys," in *Children in Sport*, edited by Frank L. Smoll, Richard A. Magill, and Michael J. Ash, 3rd ed. (Champaign, IL: Human Kinetics, 1988), 6.

11. Ibid., 10.

12. Joan Ryan, *Little Girls in Pretty Boxes: The Making and Breaking of Elite Gymnasts and Figure Skaters* (New York: Doubleday, 1995); Christine Brennan, *Inside Edge: A Revealing Journey Into the Secret World of Figure Skating* (New York: Scribners, 1996); Julie Cart, "Ugly Horror Story," *The Arizona Republic*, 29 January 1996, C8.

13. Andrew W. Miracle Jr. and C. Roger Rees, *Lessons of the Locker Room: The Myth of School Sports* (Amherst, NY: Prometheus Books, 1994); T. O'Hanlon, "Interscholastic Athletics, 1900-1940: Shaping Citizens for Unequal Roles in the Modern Industrial State," *Educational Theory* 30 (1980): 89-103.

14. O'Hanlon, "Interscholastic Athletics, 1900-1940: Shaping Citizens for Unequal Roles in the Modern Industrial State," 89.

15. Miracle Jr. and Rees, *Lessons of the Locker Room: The Myth of School Sports*; David Lyle Light Shields and Brenda Jo Light Bredemeier, *Character Development and Physical Activity* (Champaign, IL: Human Kinetics, 1995).

16. Donald J. Mrozek, *Sport and American Mentality, 1880-1910* (Knoxville: University of Tennessee Press, 1983), xiii.

17. J.A. Mangan, *Athleticism in the Victorian and Edwardian Public School* (London: Cambridge University Press, 1981); J.A. Mangan, *The Games Ethic and Imperialism* (New York: Viking Penguin, 1986).

18. Christopher F. Armstrong, "The Lessons of Sports: Class Socialization in British and American Boarding Schools," *Sociology of Sport Journal* 1 (December 1984): 315.

19. Peter C. McIntosh, "Games and Gymnastics for Two Nations in One," in *Landmarks in the History of Physical Education*," edited by J.G. Dixon, P.C. McIntosh, A.D. Munrow, and R.F. Willetts (London: Routledge & Kegan Paul, 1957), 178.

20. Mangan, *The Games Ethic and Imperialism*, 18.

21. Elizabeth Longford, *Wellington—The Years of the Sword* (New York: Harper & Row, 1969), 15-17.

22. David Whitson, "Structure, Agency and the Sociology of Sport Debates," *Theory, Culture, and Society* 3 (1986): 101.

23. Gary Fine, *With the Boys: Little League Baseball and Preadolescent Culture* (Chicago: University of Chicago Press, 1987), 51.

24. Miracle Jr. and Rees, *Lessons of the Locker Room: The Myth of School Sports*; and Apple, *Education and Power*.

25. NASPE Position Statement, "Exploitation of the Interscholastic Athlete," *Update*, NASPE Supplement (September 1993): 1.

26. Ryan, *Little Girls in Pretty Boxes: The Making and Breaking of Elite Gymnasts and Figure Skaters*, 4-5; see also Brennan, *Inside Edge: A Revealing Journey Into the Secret World of Figure Skating*; Peter D. Donnelly, "Problems Associated With Youth Involvement in High-Performance Sport," in *Intensive Participation in Children's Sports*, edited by Bernard D. Cahill and Arthur J. Pearl (Champaign, IL: Human Kinetics, 1993), 95-126.

27. Miracle Jr. and Rees, *Lessons of the Locker Room: The Myth of School Sports*; Shields and Bredemeier, *Character Development and Physical Activity*; Angela Lumpkin, Sharon K. Stoll, and Jennifer M. Beller, *Sport Ethics: Applications for Fair Play* (St. Louis: Mosby, 1994); George H. Sage, "Sports Participation as a Builder of Character?" *The World & I* 3 (October 1988): 628-41.

28. Shields and Bredemeier, *Character Development and Physical Activity*, 178.

29. Miracle Jr. and Rees, *Lessons of the Locker Room: The Myth of School Sports*, 96.

30. Jennifer M. Beller and Sharon K. Stoll, "Sport Participation and its Effect on Moral Reasoning of High School Student Athletes and General Students," *Research Quarterly for Exercise and Sport* 65 (Supplement) (March 1994): A94; see also David Decker and Kevin Lasley, "Participation in Youth Sports, Gender, and the Moral Point of View," *The Physical Educator* 53 (Winter 1995): 14-21.

31. Tim Green, "Cheating to Win Is Rule of Thumb for Teams' Survival," *USA Today*, 6 November 1997, p. 4C; see also John Gibson, *Performance v. Results: A Critique of Values in Contemporary Sport* (Albany, NY: SUNY Press, 1993).

32. T.R. Young, "The Sociology of Sport: Structural Marxist and Cultural Marxist Approaches," *Sociological Perspectives* 29 (1986): 7.

33. Richard Gruneau, "Considerations on the Politics of Play and Youth Sport," in *Career Patterns and Career Contingencies in Sport,* edited by A.G. Ingham and E.F. Broom (Vancouver: University of British Columbia, Department of Physical Education, 1982), 50; see also Frank Smoll and Ronald E. Smith, eds., *Children and Youth in Sport: A Biopsychosocial Perspective* (Madison, WI: Brown & Benchmark, 1996).

34. See, for example, Craig Clifford and Randolph M. Feezell, *Coaching for Character* (Champaign, IL: Human Kinetics, 1997); Martin Lee, *Children in Sport* (New York: E & FN Spon, 1993); Jim Thompson, *Positive Coaching: Building Character and Self-Esteem Through Sports* (Dubuque, IA: Brown & Benchmark, 1993); Eric A. Margenau, *Sports Without Pressure* (New York: Gardner Press, 1990).

Chapter 12: Sport as a Site for Agency: Resistance and Transformation

1. Peter Donnelly, "Prolympism: Sport Monoculture as Crisis and Opportunity," *Quest* 48 (February 1996): 25-42.

2. Richard Gruneau, "Power and Play in Canadian Social Development," in *Working Papers in the Sociological Study of Sports and Leisure* (published as part of the Sports Studies Research Group, Queens University, Kingston, Ontario, 1979), 2.

3. Robin Williams, *Marxism and Literature* (Oxford: University of Oxford Press, 1977), 112.

4. James C. Scott, *Domination and the Arts of Resistance: Hidden Transcripts* (New Haven, CT: Yale University Press, 1990), 136; see also James C. Scott, *Weapons of the Weak: Everyday Forms of Peasant Resistance* (New Haven, CT: Yale University Press, 1985); Harry C. Boyte, *Commonwealth: A Return to Citizen Politics* (New York: Free Press, 1989).

5. Howard Zinn, *A People's History of the United States*, rev. and updated ed. (New York: Harper Perennial, 1995).

6. Reebee Garofalo, ed., *Rockin' the Boat: Mass Music and Mass Movements* (Boston: South End Press, 1992); Sandy Carter, "Slippin' & Slidin,'" *Z Magazine* 5 (October 1992): 69-72.

7. Fred Hawley, "Cockfighting in the Piney Woods: Gameness in the New South," *Sport Place: An International Journal of Sports Geography* 1 (Fall 1987): 25; see also Bruce Frankel, "ASPCA Sees No Sport, Cracks Down on Cockfights," *USA Today*, 28 March 1995, 3A.

8. Allen L. Sack, "The Underground Economy of College Football," *Sociology of Sport Journal* 8, no. 1 (March 1991): 1-15.

9. Richard E. Lapchick, "Under African Skies," in *Sport in Society: Equal Opportunity or Business As Usual?* edited by Richard E. Lapchick (Thousand Oaks, CA: Sage, 1996).

10. Donna A. Lopiano, "Political Analysis: Gender Equity Strategies for the Future," in *Women in Sport: Issues and Controversies,*

edited by Greta L. Cohen (Newbury Park, CA: Sage, 1993), 104-16.

11. Susan Birrell and D.M. Richter, "Is a Diamond Forever? Feminist Transformations of Sport," *Women's Studies International Forum* 10 (1987): 395.

12. Becky Beal, "Disqualifying the Official: An Exploration of Social Resistance Through the Subculture of Skateboarding," *Sociology of Sport Journal* 12, no. 3 (1995): 254.

13. Karen Thomas, "Going to the Extreme," *USA Today*, 13 August 1997, 2A.

14. Tom Waddell and Dick Schaap, *Gay Olympian: The Life and Death of Dr. Tom Waddell* (New York: Knopf, 1996).

15. "Gay Games Huge Athletic Event," *Greeley* (CO) *Tribune*, 18 June 1994, 8A; see also J. Gallagher, "Fun and Games: The Gay Games 1994," *The Advocate*, 26 July 1994, 20-26.

16. Peter Donnelly, "Sport as a Site for 'Popular' Resistance," in *Popular Cultures and Political Practice*, edited by Richard Gruneau (Toronto: Garamond Press, 1988), 74.

17. G.D. Morris and James Stiehl, *Changing Kids' Games* (Champaign, IL: Human Kinetics, 1989); Dale N. LeFevre, *New Games for the Whole Family* (New York: Putnam, 1988); Sambhava Luvmour and Josette Luvmour, *Everyone Wins!: Cooperative Games and Activities* (Philadelphia: New Society, 1990); Susan Perry, *Playing Smart* (Minneapolis: Free Spirit, 1990).

18. Donnelly, "Sport as a Site for 'Popular' Resistance," 74.

19. John McDermott, *The Corporate Society: Class, Property, and Contemporary Capitalism* (Boulder, CO: Westview Press, 1991), 120; see also Peter Donnelly, "Subcultures in Sport: Resilience and Transformation," in *Sport in Social Development: Traditions, Transitions, and Transformations*, edited by Alan G. Ingham and John W. Loy (Champaign, IL: Human Kinetics, 1993), 119-45; Peter Donnelly, "Prolympism: Sport Monoculture as Crisis and Opportunity," 25-42.

20. Beal, "Disqualifying the Official: An Exploration of Social Resistance Through the Subculture of Skateboarding," 266.

21. Anthony Giddens, *Sociology: A Brief but Critical Introduction*, 2nd (New York: Harcourt Brace Jovanovich, 1987), 157.

22. Michael A. Messner, "Studying Up on Sex," *Sociology of Sport Journal* 13, no. 3 (1996): 229-30; for a thoughtful vision of a reconstructed critical theory of sport, see chapter 5, "A Recon-

structed Critical Theory of Sport: Social Criticism With a Liberal Twist," and "Postscript: Sport in the Larger Scheme of Things," in William J. Morgan, *Leftist Theories of Sport: A Critique and Reconstruction* (Urbana: University of Illinois Press, 1994).

Index

About the Author

George H. Sage, EdD, was a professor for many years at the University of Northern Colorado in Greeley, Colorado. He has received numerous awards for his work, including selection as the 1985-86 Alliance Scholar for the American Alliance for Health, Physical Education, Recreation and Dance (AAHPERD) and the 1991 Distinguished Scholar by the National Association for Physical Education in Higher Education (NAPEHE).

Dr. Sage is the coauthor of *Sociology of North American Sport*. He is the author of more than forty articles in research publications.

Dr. Sage is a member of the North American Society for the Sociology of Sport and the American Alliance for Health, Physical Education, Recreation and Dance.

He and his wife Elizabeth live in Greeley. His favorite leisure activities include golf, reading, and world travel.

More Socio-Cultural Issues Books From Human Kinetics

The 11 critical essays in *Sport in Social Development* challenge the common assumptions about sport in modern society. Internationally recognized sport sociologists Alan G. Ingham and John W. Loy use a cultural studies approach to examine how class and gender cultures affect sport *and* how sport affects culture—especially subcultures.

By drawing from such diverse fields as sociology, history, anthropology, and politics, this cultural studies approach provides a cross-disciplinary orientation to looking at sport in society. Sport sociologists, cultural studies scholars, anthropologists, and historians will find it an exciting challenge to conventional paradigms.

1993 • Cloth • 296 pp • Item BING0467
ISBN 0-87322-467-1 • $45.00 ($67.50 Canadian)

The Sports Process uses a historical/developmental approach to explore the development of sport, its international diffusion, and ongoing changes in sport around the world.

Beginning with sport in the ancient world and progressing through the end of the cold war, 13 international leaders in the sociology of sport field examine how sport development is affected by politics, gender roles, nationalism, capitalism, class, race conflict, and economics.

1993 • Paper • 336 pp • Item BDUN0624
ISBN 0-88011-624-2 • $24.00 ($35.95 Canadian)

To place your order, U.S. customers call TOLL FREE 1-800-747-4457. Customers outside the U.S. place your order using the appropriate telephone number/address shown in the front of this book.

HUMAN KINETICS
The Information Leader in Physical Activity
http://www.humankinetics.com